Introduction to Decision Theory

**Irwin Series in
Quantitative Analysis for Business**

Consulting Editor   ROBERT B. FETTER   *Yale University*

Introduction to Decision Theory

J. MORGAN JONES
Associate Professor of Operations Research
Graduate School of Management
University of California, Los Angeles

1977

RICHARD D. IRWIN, INC. Homewood, Illinois 60430
Irwin-Dorsey Limited Georgetown, Ontario L7G 4B3

519.54
J 77

© RICHARD D. IRWIN, INC., 1977

First Printing February 1977

ISBN 0-256-01950-9
Library of Congress Catalog Card No. 76–47765
Printed in the United States of America

To Judy—
Who gives me immeasurable support, inspiration,
hope, and drive

Preface

THIS TEXT results from many years of teaching an introductory decision theory course at UCLA. It is designed to give the mathematically naïve student an introduction to decision theory. It was written especially to include three aspects of decision theory. First, a thorough discussion of the development and use of sampling strategies in deci-Second, an attempt to bring the concepts of decision theory into practice. This is the content of Chaper 13. Third, an attempt to re-sion theory problems. This material is contained in Chapters 5 and 6. lieve students of the computational burden associated with solving many decision theory problems. This is accomplished through a series of interactive computer programs, written in both APL and BASIC, which are carefully designed to remove the computational burden while not removing the conceptual learning task from the student. The instructor's manual describes these programs and how to obtain and use them.

This book is designed to be used as an introductory textbook for an upper division or graduate course in decision theory. The mathematical prerequisite for most of the book is algebra. The exceptions are in Chapter 10 and other starred (asterisked) sections throughout the book, where a knowledge of integral calculus is assumed. Probability and statistical concepts are introduced as needed, beginning with Chapter 2, which introduces the notions of probability and expected value. This chapter can be used as an introduction for a class that has no experience with probability, and for review in those classes whose background includes probability.

Of the remainder of the book, Chapters 3, 4, and 5 introduce the expected value concept of decision theory, the use of utility theory, and the use of sampling. Chapters 6 through 12 then apply these concepts to binomial and normal sampling distribution problems. Finally, Chapter 13 proposes methods for putting these concepts into practice, and Chapter 14 provides a summary and prognosis.

A book is never written without much interaction between the author and many others. I want to thank the many people who have contributed to this book in all its stages. My UCLA colleague, Steven A. Lippman, and a UCLA student, Robert Amos, worked with the manuscript and made many valuable suggestions. Part of the revision was done while I was on sabbatic leave at MIT. I especially want to thank John D. C. Little for providing support for me while I was there, and Brenda L. Ferriero for providing computer time to develop the BASIC version of the interactive programs. The majority of the instructor's manual was prepared by a UCLA student, Mr. S. Sitaraman. My interactions with him made this long and demanding experience a truly rewarding one.

Finally, special thanks go to the various secretaries with whom I worked throughout this project. The major burden of typing the original manuscript fell to Dolores Warrick at UCLA. This Promethian task she handled capably and pleasantly. The revised manuscript was typed by Ms. Warrick and Barbara Tennison at UCLA, and Dottie Moreau at MIT. Thanks go to them all for their patience and ability.

December 1976   J. MORGAN JONES

Contents

xi

1

Introduction

THIS TEXTBOOK is designed to provide an introduction to the science known as decision theory. Decision theory is a study of how to make decisions under conditions of uncertainty. For example, a company might need to make a decision about how big a new plant should be. The best size for this new plant depends upon the future demand for the product of this plant, and is uncertain. This is the prototypical problem which is addressed in decision theory. One action must be chosen in the face of uncertainty about some events (occurrences not subject to control by the decision maker). Decision theory gives specific techniques for addressing such problems.

In this chapter we shall first ask why decision theory should be studied, and then provide a more thorough description of what decision theory is. The chapter will then conclude with an overview of the book, so that a student will have a feeling for where he is going.

1.1 WHY STUDY DECISION THEORY?

Every student who opens this book should, at some point, ask himself this question. And, in fact, the question may be asked in two quite different circumstances. The first is by the student who feels that all of his experiences in life to this point have taught him to be a pretty good decision maker. Why then should he bother taking the time to study the material in this book? The second context is the methodologically based one, asked by the student who knows that the material in this book is heavily based on mathematics and its related disciplines, probability and statistics. In this case the student's question is probably phrased something like, I don't want to learn all that math for a subject which doesn't seem to be that useful to me! Why should I bother? The investment in time and effort will not produce a reasonable return!

We will answer the conceptual question first. It is true that there are no important conceptual breakthroughs in the pages to come. The heuristic method any decision maker uses to make decisions is the method used in this book to make decisions. We will discuss in the next section more precisely what that is, but we can outline the method here. The basic underlying concept of decision theory is to take the consequences associated with an action, determine the chances of the various uncertain events, and combine these two sets of quantities to arrive at a best decision. This is exactly the same conceptual framework used by any rational decision maker. The basic difference between the science of decision theory and the decision theory practiced by all of us is that the former is precise. This precision is terribly important, because it can be shown that human beings are very imprecise information processors. This occurs in decision theory in two ways, which can only be described heuristically here, since we do not yet have the mathematical foundation to make them precise.

The first imprecision from which human beings suffer is the imprecision of a true concept of large or small numbers. Although practically everyone could tell (within certain reasonable bounds of estimation) when a minute has past, their ability to determine how long 1,000 minutes is—without the mathematical conversion to days, hours, etc.—is extremely poor, and their ability to determine the length of 1,000,000 minutes is even worse. This is because, relative to 1, most people have a poor concept of how big 1,000 is, and a much poorer concept of how big 1,000,000 is. Therefore, any time any of the consequences or chances in a decision problem gets outside a very limited range of values, human beings become very imprecise about processing them.

The second kind of imprecision in human decision processing comes from improperly accounting for sample information. A subject that will occupy several chapters in this text is that of obtaining additional information on the uncertain event. We assume throughout, however, that the information does not give a precise answer as to which event will occur, but only (hopefully) a better indication. Human beings have very poor capabilities to account adequately for this kind of information. An anecdote described by Raiffa[1] beautifully illustrates this point.

> Professor Ward Edwards, a psychologist at the University of Michigan, has investigated the intuitive reactions of many subjects to ex-

---

[1] Howard Raiffa, *Decision Analysis: Introductory Lectures on Choices under Uncertainty* (Addison-Wesley, 1968), pp. 20–21.

perimental, probabilistic evidence. In one of his experiments he poses the following problem.

I have two canvas book bags filled with poker chips. The first bag contains 70 green chips and 30 white chips, and I shall refer to this as the *predominantly green* bag. The second bag contains 70 white chips and 30 green chips, and I shall refer to this as the *predominantly white* bag. The chips are all identical except for color. I now mix up the two bags so that you don't know which is which, and put one of them aside. I shall be concerned with your judgments about whether the remaining bag is predominantly green or not. Now suppose that you choose 12 chips at random with replacement from this remaining bag and it turns out that you draw eight green chips and four white chips, in some particular order. What do you think the odds are that the bag you have sampled from is predominantly green?

At a cocktail party a few years ago I asked a group of lawyers, who were discussing the interpretation of probabilistic evidence, what they would answer as subjects in Edwards' experiment. First of all, they wanted to know whether there was any malice aforethought in the actions of the experimenter. I assured them of the neutrality of the experimenter, and told them that it would be appropriate to assign a .5 chance to "predominantly green" before any sampling took place.

"In this case," one lawyer exclaimed after thinking awhile, "I would bet the unknown bag is predominantly *white*."

"No, you don't understand," one of his colleagues retorted, "you have drawn eight greens and four whites from this bag. Not the other way around."

"Yes, I understand, but in my experience at the bar, *life is just plain perverse, and I would still bet on predominantly white!* But I really am not a betting man."

The other lawyers all agreed that this was not a very rational thing to do—that the evidence was in favor of the bag's being predominantly green.

"But by how much?" I persisted. After a while a consensus emerged: The evidence is meager; the odds might go up from 50–50 to 55–45; but ". . . as lawyers we are trained to be skeptical, so we would slant our best judgments downward and act as if the odds were still roughly 50–50."

The answer to the question "By how much?" can be computed in a straightforward fashion, . . . and there is no controversy about the answer. The probability that the bag is predominantly green, given a sample of eight green and four white chips, is .964. Yes, .964. This bag is predominantly green "beyond a reasonable doubt." This story points out the fact that most subjects vastly underestimate the power of a small sample. The lawyers described above had an extreme reaction, but even my statistics students clustered their guesses around .70.

As a result of the imprecision in human decision processing, the techniques that will be learned in this text are valuable in arriving at the *best* answer. Therefore, to the student who feels that he knows enough about decision making already, we say that *conceptually* he is correct, but mechanically he would have a hard time doing as well as the application of the techniques contained within this text will allow him to do.

To the student who is worried about investing time in learning mathematics, the answer is really a variation of what we discussed above. The very essence of decision theory lies in its ability to be precise and to know how to determine the quantities (probabilities and payoffs) it needs. Therefore, the mathematics is an absolute necessity. Decision theory without mathematics would be like a building without a supporting framework. Both would be meaningless piles of rubble.

It should also be mentioned to the student who is worried about learning all the mathematics that this book is designed to give as little mathematics as is possible, consistent with the overriding goal of establishing a working understanding of decision theory, and to provide it at a palatable pace. Therefore, the book should be enjoyable to all except the mathematically sophisticated reader, who will find it ponderous and boring. But, after all, the objective of this book is to bring decision theory to the mathematically naive reader. The mathematically sophisticated reader can select from many other excellent texts in this field.

1.2 WHAT IS DECISION THEORY?

Decision theory can best be explained in the context of an example. Suppose that when you awake tomorrow morning, you look out the window and find it is overcast. Since that might mean it will rain before the end of the day, you should consider taking along some means of protection, let's say an umbrella. This problem is prototypical of decision theory problems. In each we are faced with a choice among a number of possible *actions*. In this example there are two actions:

1. Carry an umbrella today
2. Do not carry an umbrella today

Only one action can be chosen. Furthermore, one of several occurrences outside the control of the decision maker will happen. These occurrences are called *events*. In the umbrella problem the events are:

1. It will rain today
2. It will not rain today

However, it is uncertain which of the events will occur. Unfortunately, the consequences of taking various actions depend upon which event occurs, and different actions are best for different events. In the umbrella choice problem, for instance, the consequences of not carrying an umbrella when it rains is that you will get wet. On the other hand, if you carry an umbrella and it doesn't rain, then you are left with the nuisance of handling an umbrella all day.

The crux of a decision theory problem is that we must choose only one action, and the choice of an action must be made *before* it is known which event will occur. We have all personally developed a procedure for dealing with these kinds of problems, which is to take the *consequences of the various actions* (which presumably vary depending upon which of the events occurs) and the *chances of the various events* into account in reaching a final decision. That same technique provides the conceptual foundation of decision theory. However, even given all of the framework we have introduced here, much is still unknown. This text will deal with these unknowns, which can be divided into three distinct questions which must be answered.

1. *How* (i.e., by what conceptual process) do we combine the chances and consequences to arrive at a decision?
2. Decision theory is based on quantifying these chances and consequences. Therefore, *how* do we, and even more importantly, *can* we determine numerical values for the chances and consequences?
3. If we have the option to seek more information on which event will occur, how should this information be integrated into the structure of the problem?

1.3 A LOOK AT WHAT'S AHEAD

Chapters 3 through 14 of this text are devoted to answering these three central questions. Before that material can be read, however, the student must have a rudimentary understanding of the concepts of probability and random variables. This material is contained in Chapter 2. It is very important for the student to understand the material contained in Chapter 2, because it forms the basis of the material in the rest of the text.

Once the material in Chapter 2 is mastered the student can move on to the more exciting subject matter in Chapters 3 through 14. Decision theory is an interesting subject in that it is conceptually easy but mechanically difficult. Therefore, by the end of Chapter 4 the student will have learned the basic answers to the first two questions posed above. Chapter 5 then moves on to give *two distinct ways* to answer the question of how to deal with additional information. Therefore, by the end of Chapter 5 the student will have learned all the conceptual aspects of decision theory.

Unfortunately, while the concepts in decision theory are straightforward, the mechanics are not. Once the concepts contained in Chapters 3 through 5 are learned, the mechanics of applying these concepts to the two most frequently occuring practical situations occupy Chapters 6 through 12. Chapters 6 through 10 are concerned with the situation in which the numerical value of a probability is the uncertain event. Chapters 11 and 12 discuss the methodology surrounding the case when the numerical value of a mean is the unknown event.

Chapter 13 contains a veritable potpourri of topics and techniques ranging from numerical analysis to statistics. It is designed for the student who wants to make practical use of the concepts and methodology he has learned in this book. As a result, it is a compendium of facts and techniques the author has found useful in moving from theory and mechanics to practice.

Chapter 14 closes the text a discussion of what has been covered, and, more importantly, an indication of what has not been covered, and a prognosis for the future developments and applications of decision theory.

2

Some Probability Tools

THIS CHAPTER is devoted to a study of the elementary concepts of probability. It is necessary to know these concepts in order to understand even the most elementary aspects of decision theory. Therefore, the probability concepts are presented in this chapter and the introductory decision theory material is delayed to Chapter 3.

2.1 WHY STUDY PROBABILITY?

As discussed in Chapter 1, decision theory is the study of how to make good decisions in the face of uncertainty. The uncertainty comes from not knowing which event will occur. In order to use the methods of decision theory, however, more than the mere existance of uncertainty must be known. Decision theory requires that we must also know (or be willing to make educated guesses at) the *relative likelihood* of the various events. For example, suppose when you wake up in the morning you must decide whether or not to carry an umbrella to work. You must make this decision because there is some *uncertainty* about what today's weather will be. To use decision theory methods to solve this problem, you would need to know (among other things) the *relative chances* of rain today. Your decision would probably be quite different if the chances for rain were 3 in 4 rather than 1 in 20, and that is why it is important not only to *acknowledge* the uncertainty but actually to quantify it.

This chapter will begin by defining one of the two types of probability we will use in this book, and then spend a great deal of time showing how to manipulate probabilities in various ways to get other probabilities. The chapter then concludes with a special type of probabilistic phenomenon called random variables, which use we will find very important in decision theory.

2.2 PROBABILITIES OF EVENTS

2.2.1 Making Lists of Events

In order to quantify the *relative* chances of uncertain events, a list of all events is required. If we do not even know the various things that might occur, how can we possibly assign relative chances to these? Making such a list is often a difficult task. One method which can be used as an aid is the technique of successive dichotomizations. For example, in the umbrella decision problem given above, the first division of weather might be "Rain or No Rain." Then the rain category could be further divided into "Light Mist or Heavier Rain," and the No Rain category into "Wet Snow or All Else." Thus, by a series of successive dichotomizations, the list of four (relevant) events for this problem is:

Light Mist
Heavier Rain
Wet Snow
All Else

This breakdown is probably sufficient to analyze the umbrella problem.

Two important points need to be made about this dichotomization technique. First, it is not necessary to have the same number of divisions in each category. For example, it might have been sufficient not to dichotomize the "No Rain" event further. (Especially in geographical areas where there is no snow!) This would have resulted in a list of *three* final events rather than four. The important point about selecting events is that *all relevant and differentiable* (with respect to the outcome) states should be included.

The second aspect of the dichotomization procedure is that there is always at least one event in the final list that is a collective "All Else" event. Decision theory does not require an exhaustive list of all possible events to be given. Only those events that are differentiable in outcome need to be listed separately. For example, in the umbrella problem the "All Else" category contains the widely different weather conditions "Nice Day" and "Hurricane." While their difference is obvious, the conclusion that one would not use an umbrella in either circumstance allows them to be collected in the same category *as far as this problem is concerned.* Therefore, decision problems do not require a complete list of all possible events. Instead, only those events relevant to the outcomes of various actions need to be specifically acknowledged. All other outcomes can be collected in an "All Else" category.

However the list of relevant events is developed, this collection of events must obey two properties. First, it must be *mutually exclusive.* This means that if one of the events on the list happens, then no other one will occur *at the same time.* The second property is that the list is *collectively exhaustive.* This means that one of the events has to occur each time. Another way to explain this property is to say that no event has been left out. Therefore, nothing can occur that is not given on our list. Both of these properties are naturally satisfied if the list of events is developed using the dichotomization procedure. If other methods are used to develop the list of events, then the reader is urged to be careful that the list satisfies these properties.

Some simple examples will help demonstrate complete lists of events. The reader is urged to study these carefully, as they will be referred to in subsequent sections. Some of these examples will be of common random devices with which everyone is familiar. Some will describe more complex (and hence less obvious) situations.

1. The most common example of a probabilistic mechanism is flipping a coin. At each flip the outcome is uncertain. The list of outcomes (events) is:

    H = A "head" will occur when the coin is tossed
    T = A "tail" will occur when the coin is tossed.

    Thus, if we ignore the possibility that the coin will land on its edge (which seems like a highly improbable event), the above is a complete list of occurrences. As such the list is collectively exhaustive. Furthermore, the list is mutually exclusive. If a head occurs, then, *on the same flip of the coin,* a tail cannot; and vice versa.

2. The next most common examples come from rolling dice. If a single die is rolled, then the outcomes (events) are:

    1—A single spot occurred
    2—Two spots occurred
    3—Three spots occurred
    4—Four spots occurred
    5—Five spots occurred
    6—Six spots occurred.

    This list is also mutually exclusive and collectively exhaustive.

3. If two dice are rolled *and* the outcome is defined as the sum of the spots on the two dice, then the events list is:

2—The sum of the spots on the two dice was 2
3—The sum of the spots on the two dice was 3
.
.
.

12—The sum of the spots on the two dice was 12.

This list is also mutually exclusive and collectively exhaustive.

4. When two dice are rolled, other outcomes can be defined. For instance, the outcome could be the *maximum* of the values on the two dice. In this case, the events list would be:

1—The maximum number of spots showing on either die was 1
2—The maximum number of spots showing on either die was 2
.
.
.

6—The maximum number of spots showing on either die was 6.

5. Other, less familiar situations can be used. For instance, one could flip a thumbtack. The outcomes here are:

U = The thumbtack lands "points up"
L = The thumbtack is lying on its side.

These mutually exclusive and collectively exhaustive outcomes are illustrated in Figure 2.1.

FIGURE 2.1
The Two Possible Outcomes of
Flipping a Thumbtack

Points Up   Lying on Its Side

6. A certain locale has three types of weather: fair, raining, and snowing. The outcome list is, obviously:

F = The day is fair
R = The day has rainy weather
S = It is snowing today.

7. Demand for a certain product will be either 0, 1, or 4 units per day. The outcome list then is:

0 = 0 units demanded today
1 = 1 unit demanded today
4 = 4 units demanded today.

The above discussion and list of examples serves to illustrate the events with which we will be dealing in this book. The remainder of this section will discuss the concepts, properties, and mechanisms for calculation of the probabilities for these events.

2.2.2 Probabilities: Concepts and Properties

What is a probability? A probability is a number that expresses the *relative* chance that some event will occur. Since a probability is used in a relative context, it is convenient to give its value as a number lying between 0 and 1. A probability of 0 indicates an event will never occur, and a probability of 1 indicates a "sure thing"—an event that is certain to occur. Events that might occur but about which we are not certain receive fractional values for their probabilities. As an example, consider tossing a coin once. We can say with almost total certainty that the coin will not land on its edge. Therefore, we state that the probability of the coin landing on its edge, in a single toss of the coin, is zero. Furthermore, there are two events, "Heads" and "Tails," that make up the list of credible events, and for a normal coin neither of these is a sure thing. The probabilities of these two events then, lie somewhere between zero and one. Usually we assume that each outcome is equally likely, and we will show later that this implies the probability of each is ½.

It becomes very clumsy to discuss probabilities without some shorthand notation. In the future we shall adopt

$$P(E)$$

to denote the probability (P) that event E will occur. For example, for the single toss of a fair coin:

$$P(\text{Heads}) = \tfrac{1}{2}; P(\text{Tails}) = \tfrac{1}{2},$$

or, making the shorthand even more cryptic by adopting the abbreviations for the events given in Example 1, we have:

$$P(H) = \tfrac{1}{2}; P(T) = \tfrac{1}{2}.$$

The general property of probabilities—that they lie between 0 and 1—can be expressed in this notation as:

$$0 \leq P(E) \leq 1,$$

and this is a general rule that applies to *any* event E.

Many times in calculating probabilities we will be interested in determining the probabilities of certain *combinations* of events. We will find there are two ways to combine events. These are denoted by the English words "or" and "and." The "and" method of combination will be described later. A combination of two events using "or" implies the occurrence of one or the other or both. For instance,

$$H \text{ or } T$$

denotes an event which is the occurrence of *either* a head *or* a tail on the single toss of a coin. Furthermore, the probability of this event is denoted

$$P(H \text{ or } T).$$

It is clear in the case of flipping a coin that H and T are the only two events that can occur. Therefore, on a single toss one or the other is certain to occur. In terms of probability this means

$$P(H \text{ or } T) = 1.$$

This statement not only holds true for a single toss of a coin, but for any *collectively exhaustive* list of events. Thus, we can say, for instance, that if A, B, C, and D represent a collectively exhaustive set of events for some problem, then

$$P(A \text{ or } B \text{ or } C \text{ or } D) = 1.$$

In addition to the two properties we discussed above, there is one more basic property of the probabilities of events. If A and B are two *mutually exclusive* events, then

$$P(A \text{ or } B) = P(A) + P(B).$$

This is a very useful rule, for it allows us to calculate the probabilities of composite events if the probabilities of elementary events are known.

As an illustration of the use of this rule, consider the example of tossing a fair coin. On a single toss of the coin, H and T are mutually exclusive outcomes, so

$$P(H \text{ or } T) = P(H) + P(T).$$

Furthermore, except for the simplicity of this particular example, the above formula would prove helpful in calculating the value of $P(H \text{ or } T)$.

In summary, a list of events has the following properties.

1. For each event, E, the probability lies between 0 and 1; that is, $0 \leq P(E) \leq 1$.
2. The probability of the certain event, C, is 1; that is, $P(C) = 1$.
3. The probability of one or the other of two mutually exclusive events occurring is the sum of the individual probabilities of the events. Thus, if A and B are mutually exclusive:

$$P(A \text{ or } B) = P(A) + P(B),$$

and the obvious extension holds for any number of events.

We now know some numerical conventions for probabilities, but what do they mean? What, for instance, does it mean to say that for a fair coin $P(H) = \frac{1}{2}$? It certainly does not mean that on each toss we will get half a head! Nor does it mean that we can be guaranteed that on two tosses we will get exactly one head. (We could just as likely get two heads or two tails). What exactly then does $P(H) = \frac{1}{2}$ mean?

There are two concepts of the value of a probability we shall treat in this book. The one that follows is based upon a relative frequency interpretation of probability. The other, which will be discussed in Section 3.2.4, is based on a subjective concept of probability. Before we discuss the relative frequency concept of probability, it is important to point out that while the philosophical bases of these two concepts of probability are widely divergent, the mechanics of use, such as the above three laws, hold for both. Therefore, except for the brief explanations below and in Section 3.2.4, no distinction is made in this text between the two interpretations of what probability values mean.

While we cannot be guaranteed half a head on each flip of a coin, or one head in two flips, or even 20 heads in 40 flips, the relative frequency interpretation of $P(H) = \frac{1}{2}$ defines the value of the probability as the relative proportion of times heads occurs after many flips of the coin. Figure 2.2 illustrates how a relative frequency might be derived. It shows how the relative proportion of heads gets closer and closer to $\frac{1}{2}$ as the total number of flips increases. In the beginning of the experi-

FIGURE 2.2
The Relative Proportion of Heads after Many Tosses of the Same Fair Coin

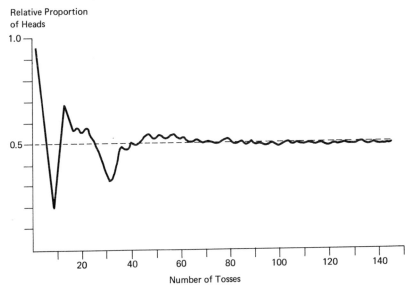

ment the relative frequency of heads is quite far away from ½, but as the number of tosses grows the relative frequency settles down more and more to the long run value of ½.

There is an important assumption implicit in this method. *It assumes that the experiment is repeatable under the same conditions,* so that the probability can be empirically obtained. Furthermore, if this repeatability condition does not hold, then any notion of a probability existing is disallowed by those who believe in relative frequency. This is the crux of the philosophical difference between those who avow the relative frequency approach, and those who believe in the subjective approach. The subjectivists would say there are many situations in life that are not repeatable under the same conditions, and yet for which it is reasonable to assign probabilities to various outcomes. For example, a man asking the woman of his dreams to marry him is an experiment that is not repeatable under the same conditions. Having asked the big question changes these people's relationship in an essential way. In spite of this it seems reasonable to assign probabilities to the various outcomes. We will show how to do this in Chapter 3.

2.2.3   Calculation of Probabilities for Elementary Events

While the relative frequency concept is appealing, its application is extremely time consuming. A method that will often be used in this text to obtain the probabilities of the events in a problem is a comparison of the relative likelihoods for the events. The simplest of these situations occurs when all the outcomes in a problem are equally likely. For example, we will often speak of a "fair" coin or a "fair" die. This fairness label really means that each outcome is equally likely.

If each outcome in a problem is equally likely, then it is an easy matter to obtain values for the probabilities of each event. In this case the total probability for all events must be evenly divided among the various outcomes. Thus, a fair coin has two outcomes, and

$$P(H) = P(T) = \tfrac{1}{2}.$$

Similarly, as in Example 2, a fair die has six possible outcomes, and

$$P(1) = P(2) = P(3) = P(4) = P(5) = P(6) = \tfrac{1}{6}.$$

One thing the reader must be careful of is the overuse of this equally likely events rule. It makes sense, when one considers the physical structure of a coin or a die, that all outcomes should be equally likely. On the other hand, when one considers flipping a thumbtack the equally likely outcomes assumption is no longer appealing. The physical structure of the thumbtack is more complicated than that of a coin, and this makes us uncertain about the relative chances of the outcomes. Thus, even in situations such as the thumbtack, where the total number of outcomes is known, the reader is warned against a willy-nilly application of the equally likely events rule.

Relative likelihoods can also be used to derive unequally probability values. Suppose for the weather example we know that fair weather occurs twice as frequently as rain, and rain occurs three times as frequently as snow. In order to determine the probabilities of these three events we will use algebra, these relative likelihoods, and the mutually exclusive and collectively exhaustive properties of probabilities. These latter in combination imply

$$P(F) + P(R) + P(S) = 1.$$

Furthermore, the relative likelihoods are

$$P(F) = 2P(R); \text{ and } P(R) = 3P(S),$$

where F = Fair weather, R = Rain, and S = Snow.

In order to obtain the probabilities we will cast everything in terms of $P(S)$. Thus we are given

$$P(R) = 3P(S).$$

Furthermore, since $P(F) = 2P(R)$, we have

$$P(F) = 2[3P(S)] = 6P(S).$$

These can be substituted into

$$P(F) + P(R) + P(S) = 1$$

and we get

$$6P(S) + 3P(S) + P(S) = 1,$$

which, when solved for $P(S)$ yields

$$P(S) = \tfrac{1}{10}.$$

The other two probabilities can be determined by their relationship to $P(S)$; in particular,

$$P(F) = \tfrac{6}{10}; \text{ and } P(R) = \tfrac{3}{10}.$$

2.2.4 Composite Events and Their Probabilities

Many times it is convenient to define events in other ways than by using the most simple categorization. For instance, when a die is rolled, we might define an event A as

A = The occurrence of either a 2 or a 4 on the single roll of a die.

Such an event will be called a "composite" event. To distinguish between such an event and its components, we will label the components "elementary" events. Thus, the elementary events 2 and 4 make up the composite event A.

Let's take another example. In the weather example, define the composite event BW (for bad weather) as the occurrence of either of the elementary events R or S. Thus,

BW = The occurrence of either R or S on a single day.

In addition to defining such events, we need to know how to determine their probabilities. The process is easy using the rule for calculating the probabilities of mutually exclusive events. As an example, for the event A defined above,

$$P(A) = P(2 \text{ or } 4) = P(2) + P(4).$$

Therefore, the probability of event A can be obtained once the probabilities of its component elementary events are known. Thus, if the die is fair:

$$P(A) = P(2) + P(4) = \tfrac{1}{6} + \tfrac{1}{6} = \tfrac{1}{3}.$$

A similar calculation can be made to obtain the probability of bad weather, $P(BW)$. In this case

$$\begin{aligned} P(BW) &= P(R \text{ or } S) \\ &= P(R) + P(S) \\ &= \tfrac{3}{10} + \tfrac{1}{10} \\ &= \tfrac{4}{10}. \end{aligned}$$

There is another method that can be used to obtain $P(BW)$. By defining BW we have divided the possible states of weather into two categories, F and BW. These are mutually exclusive and collectively exhaustive, so

$$P(F \text{ or } BW) = P(F) + P(BW) = 1.$$

When two events are mutually exclusive and collectively exhaustive, as these two are, one is called the *complement* of the other. Once two events are defined and are found to be complements of each other, a simple rearrangement of the above equation,

$$P(BW) = 1 - P(F)$$

can be used to determine the probability of BW. In this case, since $P(F) = \tfrac{6}{10}$,

$$\begin{aligned} P(BW) &= 1 - \tfrac{6}{10} \\ &= \tfrac{4}{10}. \end{aligned}$$

2.3 PROBABILITY RULES AND THEIR USE

The previous section was devoted to a study of what probabilities are, and how they can be calculated for the simplest types of events. Unfortunately, most events for which we want to calculate probabilities are not as simple as those discussed in the previous section. This section will discuss more probability rules—ones that can be used to calculate more of the probabilities for the types of events encountered in real life situations.

2.3.1 Two Rules for Generating Compound Events

Several of the probability rules discussed in this section are based upon a composite event. It is helpful first to discuss rules by which events can be combined, so that the probability rules can be based upon these.

There are two ways in which a pair of events can be combined. One, the "or" rule, was discussed in Section 2.2.2 for mutually exclusive events. However, the principle holds for any pair of events. If F and G represent any two events, then the "or" combination of these is defined to be:

> F or G is all outcomes (elementary events) common to *either F or G or both.*

This rule, and many of those that follow in this chapter, can be illustrated by the simple toss of a die. In this case the elementary events are:

1—A single spot occurs on one roll of the die
2—Two spots occur on one roll of the die
.
.
.
6—Six spots occur on one roll of the die.

In addition to these it is helpful to define some composite events as well:

A = Either a 2 or a 4 occurs on a single roll of the die
B = Either a 1 or a 3 occurs on a single roll of the die
C = Either a 1 or a 2 occurs on a single roll of the die.

Given these various events, the "or" rule can be illustrated in a number of ways. In particular, the composite events can be defined using the elementary events and the "or" rule:

A = 2 or 4
B = 1 or 3
C = 1 or 2,

and we can speak of various combinations of the composite events.

A or *B* = The outcome of either a 1 or a 2 or a 3 or a 4 on a single roll of the die
= 1 or 2 or 3 or 4,

B or *C* = The outcome of either a 1 or a 2 or a 3 on a single roll of the die
= 1 or 2 or 3.

The second rule for combining events is the "and" rule. It is defined as:

F and *G* is all outcomes (elementary events) common to *both F and G*.

This rule can also be illustrated using the above events defined for the die. For instance:

B and *C* = The outcome of a 1 on a single roll of the die
= 1.

Most other pairs of events for the die-rolling example are mutually exclusive. Thus, for example, since the event *A* and the event *B* are mutually exclusive:

A and *B* contains no elementary events.

2.3.2 Probability Rules for Combining Events Using "And" and "Or"

Once we know the rules for combining events, the probabilities can be calculated in one of two ways. The first, and many times the easier, is by determining the probabilities of the resulting elementary events. For instance, in the example of rolling a single die, since *B* and *C* = 1 we have:

$$P(B \text{ and } C) = P(1) = \tfrac{1}{6}.$$

Similarly, since *B* or *C* = 1 or 2 or 3, we have

$$P(B \text{ or } C) = P(1 \text{ or } 2 \text{ or } 3) = \tfrac{1}{2}.$$

In this context we need to mention the probability of joining two mutually exclusive events using the "and" rule. We previously found, for instance, that

A and *B* contains no elementary events.

Knowing this, how can we calculate $P(A \text{ and } B$ ' The result is very easy if we just use a little common sense. *A* and *i*   means the event of *both A and B* occurring on the single roll of a di :. Since these events are mutually exclusive, it is not possible for both A and B to occur on a single roll of the die. Another way to state this is to say that the chances of this joint event happening are zero. Thus,

$$P(A \text{ and } B) = 0,$$

and this rule holds whenever two events are mutually exclusive.

In addition to the common sense way of calculating probabilities of events combined using "and" or "or," there are also some formal rules for accomplishing the same thing. In some instances these rules are easier to use than the method given above, and in some instances they are more difficult. It will be up to the reader to decide (in each situation) which approach is best.

For the "or" combination of events the rule is

$$P(F \text{ or } G) = P(F) + P(G) - P(F \text{ and } G).$$

As an example of the use of this rule, consider event A and event C in rolling the die. For these events we have

$$P(A) = P(2 \text{ or } 4) = \tfrac{1}{3}$$
$$P(C) = P(1 \text{ or } 2) = \tfrac{1}{3}$$
$$P(A \text{ and } C) = P(2) = \tfrac{1}{6}.$$

Therefore,

$$P(A \text{ or } C) = P(A) + P(C) - P(A \text{ and } C)$$
$$= \tfrac{1}{3} + \tfrac{1}{3} - \tfrac{1}{6}$$
$$= \tfrac{1}{2}.$$

2.3.3 Conditional Probabilities

Before we discuss a formal rule for calculating the probability of an event created by the "and" rule, it is helpful to discuss conditional probabilities. The events we have been expressing up to this point assume that all possible elementary events might occur. Many times, however, we know *partial* information about which event occurred, and we would like to refine our original (unconditional) probabilities to account for this. The result of making this revision is called a *conditional* probability. A conditional probability is defined as the probability of some event, say F, given (knowing) that some other event, say G, has occurred. It is denoted $P(F|G)$, where the vertical line is read as "given."

The calculation of $P(F|G)$ is quite straightforward:

$$P(F|G) = \frac{P(F \text{ and } G)}{P(G)}.$$

The rationale for this formula is quite simple. Since G is known to have occurred, only those elements of F which are also elements of G, F and G, can occur. The probability of F given G is the likelihood of F and G relative to the likelihood of G in total.

As an example, consider the weather problem. We had calculated

$$P(F) = \tfrac{6}{10}, \ P(R) = \tfrac{3}{10}, \ P(S) = \tfrac{1}{10}, \ P(BW) = \tfrac{4}{10}.$$

Suppose we ask a friend in the locale what the weather is, and he says it is bad weather. What then are the chances it is raining? The probability expression is:

$$P(R|BW) = \frac{P(R \text{ and } BW)}{P(BW)}$$

and $P(R \text{ and } BW) = P(R) = \tfrac{3}{10}$. Therefore

$$P(R|BW) = \frac{\tfrac{3}{10}}{\tfrac{4}{10}} = \tfrac{3}{4}.$$

As another example, in the die rolling problem suppose we want to find the probability that event A will occur, given that event C has occurred. In this case

$$P(A \text{ and } C) = P(2) = \tfrac{1}{6}$$

and

$$P(A|C) = \frac{P(A \text{ and } C)}{P(C)}$$

$$= \frac{\tfrac{1}{6}}{\tfrac{1}{3}}$$

$$= \tfrac{1}{2}.$$

2.3.4 A Formal Rule for Calculating "And" Probabilities

In addition to their intrinsic usefulness, conditional probabilities are sometimes helpful in calculating the probability of F and G. The formula for calculating a conditional probability

$$P(F|G) = \frac{P(F \text{ and } G)}{P(G)}$$

can be rearranged to isolate $P(F \text{ and } G)$:

$$P(F \text{ and } G) = P(F|G)P(G).$$

The following example will illustrate the use of this rule.

At a certain new car dealership 80% of all purchases are made by men. Of those cars purchased by men, 30% are small cars, whereas

50% of cars purchased by women are small cars. For this example, if we define the events as

M = A man purchased the car
W = A woman purchased the car
L = The car purchased was a large car
S = The car purchased was a small car

then the probabilities given are

$$P(M) = 0.8; P(S|M) = 0.3; P(S|W) = 0.5.$$

The complementarity rule can be used to obtain the other probabilities needed for this problem. In particular, since all buyers must be men or women,

$$P(W) = 1 - P(M)$$
$$= 1 - 0.8$$
$$= 0.2.$$

A similar rule applies to conditional probabilities. Since a car purchased is (presumably) either small or large, it is true that $P(L|M)$ is the complement of $P(S|M)$. Thus,

$$P(L|M) = 1 - P(S|M)$$
$$= 1 - 0.3$$
$$= 0.7,$$

and, similarly,

$$P(L|W) = 1 - P(S|W)$$
$$= 1 - 0.5$$
$$= 0.5.$$

Using these stated and implied probabilities, many other quantities can be calculated. As an example of the rule for calculating an "and" probability using a conditional probability, we have:

$$P(L \text{ and } W) = P(L|W)P(W)$$
$$= 0.5 \times 0.2$$
$$= 0.1.$$

One thing the reader should notice at this point is that there are two ways to calculate the probability of two events joined by the "and" rule using conditional probabilities. In particular, both

$$P(F|G) = \frac{P(F \text{ and } G)}{P(G)}$$

and

$$P(G|F) = \frac{P(G \text{ and } F)}{P(F)}$$

can be rearranged to calculate $P(F \text{ and } G)$.

If there are two alternatives, which one should be used? The answer to this question is determined by the form of the data. For instance, in the new car example, $P(L$ and $W)$ can be calculated as either

$$P(L \text{ and } W) = P(L|W)P(W)$$

or

$$P(L \text{ and } W) = P(W|L)P(L)$$

The former form was used in this case because the values for $P(L|W)$ and $P(W)$ were easily available from the statement of the problem. While the second of the above expressions could have been used, we find below (in Sections 2.3.6 and 2.3.7) that it is much more time consuming to obtain the values for $P(L|W)$ and $P(L)$.

2.3.5 Independence

One of the notions frequently used in probability is that of independence. By definition:

Two events are *independent* if knowing that one has occurred does not change the probability that the other will occur.

This definition can be expressed symbolically by

$$P(F|G) = P(F),$$

that is, F and G are independent if the unconditional probability of F occurring has the same value as the conditional probability of F given G.

As an example of independence, consider the following two events for the die rolling example:

A = The outcome is a 2 or a 4
D = The outcome is a 1 or a 2 or a 3

The probability of A occurring on a single roll of the die is $\frac{1}{3}$. In order to calculate the conditional probability of A given D, we use the formula

$$P(A|D) = \frac{P(A \text{ and } D)}{P(D)},$$

and

$$P(A \text{ and } D) = P(2) = \frac{1}{6},$$
$$P(D) = \frac{1}{2},$$

so

$$P(A|D) = \frac{\frac{1}{6}}{\frac{1}{2}} = \frac{1}{3}.$$

Therefore, since $P(A|D) = P(A)$, A and D are independent events.

Note carefully what independence means in this context. It is a property that is calculated from the characteristics of the problem. Many novices in probability interpret independence as synonymous with the mutually exclusive property, yet these properties are, in reality, far different. In this example the events are *not* mutually exclusive, yet they are independent. Furthermore, except for very special events whose probabilities are zero, mutually exclusive events are never independent.

If it is known that two events are independent, a simplification of the "and" probability rule can be obtained. We have previously derived the rule

$$P(F \text{ and } G) = P(F|G)P(G).$$

However, if F and G are independent this rule reduces to

$$P(F \text{ and } G) = P(F)P(G).$$

This rule is frequently used to calculate probabilities. As with any rule in frequent use, it is frequently misused as well. The reader is cautioned to verify (either through calculation or reasoning) that the events being considered are independent *before* this rule is applied! We have demonstrated the method for calculating independence above. We will next show how independence can be verified through the *structure* of the problem.

Many times probability problems deal with two (or more) similar occurrences taking place jointly or sequentially. Usually the outcomes of these events are assumed independent. For example, if one rolls the same die twice, a sufficiently vigorous roll will insure that the second outcome is independent of the first. Similarly, if two dice are rolled at the same time there is no reason why the outcome of one should affect the outcome of the other. Therefore, we can assume that these two outcomes are *independent* of one another.

As an example of how this assumption can be used, suppose we are rolling two dice, and want to find the probability that the sum of their outcomes will be four. There are several ways in which the sum of the outcomes can be four. In particular, both dice can display two spots, or one die can have one spot showing and one die have three spots showing. Let's assume, for simplicity, that one die is green and one is red, and adopt the notation

1 and 3

to denote that the green die had one spot showing and the red die had three spots showing. The three events that can lead to a sum of four, then, are

1 and 3,
2 and 2,
3 and 1.

The probabilities of each of these events can be determined using independence. In particular

$$P(1 \text{ and } 3) = P(1)P(3).$$

If we assume that both dice are "fair," we have

$$P(1) = \tfrac{1}{6} \text{ (for the green die)}$$
$$P(3) = \tfrac{1}{6} \text{ (for the red die)},$$

and

$$P(1 \text{ and } 3) = \tfrac{1}{6} \times \tfrac{1}{6} = \tfrac{1}{36}.$$

The other joint probabilities can be obtained in an analogous manner and we find:

$$P(2 \text{ and } 2) = \tfrac{1}{36}$$
$$P(3 \text{ and } 1) = \tfrac{1}{36}.$$

These three probabilities can then be combined to calculate the overall probability of the sum being four. Since the joint events are mutually exclusive (why?), we have

$$P(\text{Sum} = 4) = P(1 \text{ and } 3) + P(2 \text{ and } 2) + P(3 \text{ and } 1)$$
$$= \tfrac{1}{36} + \tfrac{1}{36} + \tfrac{1}{36}$$
$$= \tfrac{3}{36}.$$

Independence cannot be assumed in *all* sequential situations. As an example of this, suppose we have a bowl containing four marbles, one red and three green. If a marble is randomly withdrawn from the bowl, and then a second marble is randomly withdrawn *without replacing the first,* the outcomes of the two draws are not independent. The probability of drawing a green marble on the second draw depends upon which color marble was selected the first time. Therefore, the two draws are not independent. This example again shows that independence must be assumed with caution, if it is assumed at all.

2.3.6 Partitioning

Partitioning is a process through which probabilities can be calculated by dividing the set of all elementary events into a number of mutually exclusive events. The overall probability of an event is then obtained by determining the probability of the event in each of the partitions (mutually exclusive events). For example, suppose in the new car dealership problem we want to know what proportion of new cars sold are small cars. That is, we want to find the value of $P(S)$. This value is not given in the statement of the problem, nor can it be easily calculated using complementarity.

In order to calculate $P(S)$ we first partition all events into a number of mutually exclusive parts. In this case, as we shall see from the numbers given below, a convenient partition is the M, W pair. Since M is mutually exclusive of W, it follows that the event S and M is mutually exclusive of the event S and W. Furthermore, S can only occur by occurring jointly with M or with W. Therefore

$$P(S) = P(S \text{ and } M) + P(S \text{ and } W).$$

The above formula represents the essence of partitioning. The partition is the M, W pair of events. As with any partition, these are mutually exclusive and collectively exhaustive. Therefore, the probability of any event (S in this case) can be obtained by adding the probabilities that S will occur with each of the parts of the partition.

The reason the M, W partition is especially valuable in this problem is because of the values which are given in the statement of the problem. Each of the joint probabilities,

$$P(S \text{ and } M) \quad \text{and} \quad P(S \text{ and } W),$$

can be calculated using conditional probabilities

$$P(S \text{ and } M) = P(S|M)P(M)$$

and

$$P(S \text{ and } W) = P(S|W)P(W),$$

and the values for the above right-hand side elements are easily available from the statement of the problem.

Using the products of probabilities given above, the partitioning formula becomes

$$P(S) = P(S|M) \ P(M) + P(S|W) \ P(W).$$

Inserting numbers, we have

$$P(S) = 0.3 \times 0.8 + 0.5 \times 0.2 = 0.34.$$

This last form, using conditional probabilities, is the most useful way to obtain probabilities using the concept of partitioning. As a general rule, it can be written:

$$P(F) = P(F|H_1)P(H_1) + P(F|H_2)P(H_2) + \cdots + P(F|H_n)P(H_n),$$

where

F is any event, and
$H_1, H_2, \ldots, H_n$ form a *partition* (a mutually exclusive, collectively exhaustive division) of all pertinent events in a problem.

2.3.7   Bayes' Rule

As we shall discover in Chapter 5, Bayes' rule[1] is the most important probability calculation rule in decision theory. It is a method that can be used to calculate certain conditional probabilities not given in the original statement of a problem. The rule can best be presented through the development of an example. Suppose in the new car dealership problem we want to know the probability that a man purchased the car, given that a small car was purchased; that is, we want $P(M|S)$. The conditional probability formula for this quantity is:

$$P(M|S) = \frac{P(S \text{ and } M)}{P(S)}.$$

Neither of the quantities in the quotient on the right-hand side is immediately known from the statement of the problem. However, they can be calculated from the quantities given in the problem statement. The numerator is

$$P(S \text{ and } M) = P(S|M)P(M)$$
$$= 0.3 \times 0.8$$
$$= 0.24.$$

The denominator can be calculated using the partitioning rule. This was demonstrated above.

$$P(S) = P(S|M)P(M) + P(S|W)P(W)$$
$$= 0.3 \times 0.8 + 0.5 \times 0.2$$
$$= 0.34.$$

Then, once these values are calculated,

$$P(M|S) = \frac{P(S \text{ and } M)}{P(S)} = \frac{0.24}{0.34} = 0.706.$$

Bayes' rule allows $P(M|S)$ to be calculated directly rather than in stages. It is nothing more than a restatement of the original conditional probability formula

$$P(M|S) = \frac{P(S \text{ and } M)}{P(S)},$$

in terms of the quantities given in the problem

$$P(M|S) = \frac{P(S|M)\,P(M)}{P(S|M)P(M) + P(S|W)P(W)}.$$

---

[1] Named for the English philosopher and theologian Rev. Thomas Bayes.

Although it may be useful to remember this formula, it is the author's experience that students are able to use the rule more correctly if they understand the derivation rather than the final formula.

Another example will illustrate Bayes' rule further. News magazines have available for advertisers certain statistics that describe their readership. Suppose for three of these, *Time, Newsweek* and *U.S. News,* the statistics are:

Income level	Percent of Readers		
(in 000)	Time	Newsweek	U.S. News
Less than 5	1	1	—
5–10	5	7	5
10–20	36	53	25
20–50	48	26	46
More than 50	10	13	24

Furthermore, a survey by a market research group has shown that among readers who regularly read one of the three news magazines the distribution of readership is

Magazine	Proportion of Readership
Time	42
Newsweek	38
U.S. News	20

Knowing these statistics, a potential advertiser would like to know what proportion of all news magazine readers in the $20,000 to $50,000 income bracket he will reach with an ad in *Time.*

If we let A through E represent the income categories "less than 5" through "more than 50," respectively, and T, N, and U represent the readership options *Time, Newsweek,* and *U.S. News,* then the advertiser would like to know the value of $P(T|D)$. This can be obtained using Bayes' rule, whose derivation is as follows:

$$P(T|D) = \frac{P(T \text{ and } D)}{P(D)}$$

$$= \frac{P(D|T)P(T)}{P(D|T)P(T) + P(D|N)P(N) + P(D|U)P(U)}$$

$$= \frac{0.48 \times 0.42}{0.48 \times 0.42 + 0.26 \times 0.38 + 0.46 \times 0.20}$$

$$= 0.514.$$

Note: In calculating numerical expressions involving both multiplication and either addition or subtraction, the convention of this text shall be that, unless otherwise indicated by parentheses, all multiplications shall be performed *first,* and then all additions or subtractions. For example,

$$0.3 \times 0.4 + 0.8 \times 0.2 - 0.1 \times 0.6$$

is correctly calculated by first performing all multiplications:

$$0.12 + 0.16 - 0.06$$

and then the addition and subtraction:

$$0.22.$$

2.4   RANDOM VARIABLES AND EXPECTATION

Random variables are special probabilistic situations in which the outcomes have only numerical values. For instance, in Section 2.2.1, the dice rolling and demand for a certain product examples generate random variables because each outcome has a numerical value. The other examples, tossing a coin, flipping a thumbtack, and the weather conditions in a certain locale do not generate random variables.

Random variables are usually denoted by capital letters, which represent the *outcomes* of the probabilistic process. In the roll of a fair die, for instance, let D be the random variable. Then D can take on any value between 1 and 6, and the probability of each of these outcomes is $\frac{1}{6}$. To denote these probabilities we will change our notation slightly and write:

$$P(D = 1) = \tfrac{1}{6}, \, P(D = 2) = \tfrac{1}{6}, \text{ etc.}$$

Another random variable is obtained from the example in which two dice are rolled. There the outcome is the sum of the outcomes of each of the dice. Let S (or sum) represent this random variable. We derived (in Section 2.3.5) the probability that S will have a value of four. There we found

$$P(S = 4) = \tfrac{3}{36}.$$

Similar calculations can be made for the other values of S. The results are given in Table 2.1.

TABLE 2.1
The Probabilities of the Values of S, the Sum of the Outcomes on the Roll of Two Dice

Value of S	2	3	4	5	6	7	8	9	10	11	12
Probability	$\frac{1}{36}$	$\frac{2}{36}$	$\frac{3}{36}$	$\frac{4}{36}$	$\frac{5}{36}$	$\frac{6}{36}$	$\frac{5}{36}$	$\frac{4}{36}$	$\frac{3}{36}$	$\frac{2}{36}$	$\frac{1}{36}$

Two final examples can be obtained from the manufacturing example. There the demand for a certain product was either 0, 1, or 4 units per day. Let us assume that the probabilities for these demand levels are, respectively, $\frac{1}{3}$, $\frac{1}{2}$, and $\frac{1}{6}$. This number of units demanded per day, which we shall denote by N, is a random variable. Its probability values are

$$P(N = 0) = \frac{1}{3}; P(N = 1) = \frac{1}{2}; P(N = 4) = \frac{1}{6}.$$

Other random variables for more than one day's demand can be derived from these values if we assume that demand from one day to the next is independent. Consider, for instance, the total demand that occurs in two days. This is a random variable, which we shall call T. The values T can take on are the combinations of sums of N values, or

$$0, 1, 2, 4, 5, 8.$$

Probabilities can be obtained for each of these values of T using methods similar to the methods used to obtain the probabilities for the S values. The results of doing these calculations are given in Table 2.2

TABLE 2.2
The Probabilities of the Values of T, the Total Demand for the Product for Two Days

Values of T	0	1	2	4	5	8
Probability	$\frac{1}{9}$	$\frac{1}{3}$	$\frac{1}{4}$	$\frac{1}{9}$	$\frac{1}{6}$	$\frac{1}{36}$

2.4.1 Characterizations of Random Variables

One of the reasons random variables are studied separately from other probabilistic phenomena is that additional characterizations can be made of them—characterizations that aid our understanding. Because the values of a random variable can be ordered, certain additional manipulations can be made of it. For instance, we can not only give the probability of a random variable having a specific value, say

$$P(D = 3) \text{ or } P(T = 5)$$

but we can also give the probability of a random variable taking on a *range* of values. For instance, for the random variable D defined above,

$$P(2 \leq D \leq 4) = P(D = 2) + P(D = 3) + P(D = 4)$$
$$= \frac{1}{6} + \frac{1}{6} + \frac{1}{6}$$
$$= \frac{1}{2}.$$

Similarly, for the random variable T,

$$P(T \leq 4) = P(T = 0) + P(T = 1) + P(T = 2) + P(T = 4)$$
$$= \frac{1}{9} + \frac{1}{3} + \frac{1}{4} + \frac{1}{9}$$
$$= {}^{29}\!\!/_{36}.$$

Such probabilities can even be defined where the endpoints are not outcome values of the random variable. For instance, for the outcome of rolling two dice, S,

$$P(3.5 \leq S \leq 6.897) = P(S = 4) + P(S = 5) + P(S = 6)$$
$$= \frac{3}{36} + \frac{4}{36} + \frac{5}{36}$$
$$= \frac{1}{3},$$

and

$$P(S \geq 14) = 0,$$

and

$$P(S \leq 103.659) = P(S = 2) + P(S = 3) + \cdots + P(S = 12)$$
$$= 1.0.$$

Although expressing probabilities for intervals of values will not be especially important to us now, it will be very important when we encounter continuous random variables in Chapters 9 through 14.

Another useful characterization of random variables that can be obtained because the values can be ordered is a "picture" (graph) of the *probability distribution*. This graph is obtained by plotting the values of the random variable along the horizontal axis, and the values of the probabilities along the vertical axis. Each probability is then represented by a point at the intersection of the outcome value and the probability value.

As an example of this, suppose we graph the probability distribution for D, the outcome of the roll of a single die. The horizontal axis must contain the values of the random variable, 1 through 6, and the vertical axis must contain the range of probability values. In this case there is only one probability value, $\frac{1}{6}$. Such a system of coordinates is illustrated in Figure 2.3. Once these are given, the probability values can be plotted.

FIGURE 2.3
The Coordinate Axes for Graphing the
Probability Distribution of D

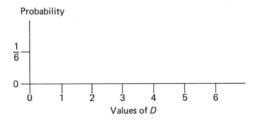

As an example, suppose we wish to plot $P(D = 1) = \frac{1}{6}$. This is illustrated in Figure 2.4. The fact that $P(D = 1)$ has a value of $\frac{1}{6}$ is illustrated by the heavy dot at the intersection $D = 1$ and probability $= \frac{1}{6}$ values. Then, for clarity, this dot is connected by a vertical dashed

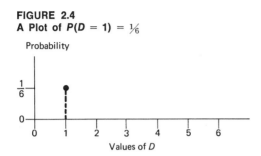

FIGURE 2.4
A Plot of $P(D = 1) = \frac{1}{6}$

line to the value of D to which it corresponds. We shall adopt this plotting convention throughout the book.

A similar procedure is followed for the other values of D. The result is *a graph of the probability distribution* of D, and is illustrated in Figure 2.5. Once this graph is obtained, it gives a good visual description

FIGURE 2.5
A Graph of the Probability Distribution of D

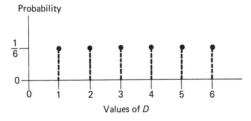

of the probability distribution. Students familiar with different types of probability distributions use these graphs for comparative purposes. In this case we see that the values of D are evenly distributed along the number line from 1 to 6, and that each value is equally likely.

Figure 2.6 shows the graph of the probability distribution of the random variable S, the sum of the outcomes of the roll of two dice. In this case you see that the distribution is "triangular" in shape and is symmetrical. The most probable outcomes are in the "middle" of the set of values and the least probable outcomes are at the extremes.

FIGURE 2.6
The Probability Distribution of S

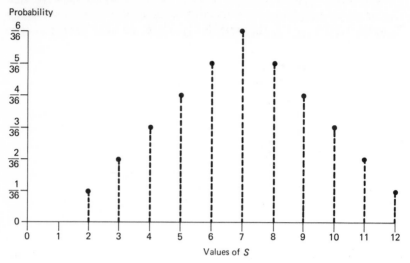

2.4.2 Expected Value

Once a probability distribution is developed for a random variable, it is often useful to "describe" it with a few numbers rather than by listing all the values and their probabilities. Two descriptive measures of the distribution are widely used—a measure of the *location* of the distribution and a measure of the *degree of dispersion*. Appropriate measures for these quantities are presented in this section.

In describing the *location* of a probability distribution, several alternative measures are currently being used. We shall use a quantity called the *expected value*. It is a number that is calculated by taking each value of the random variable, multiplying it by its probability, and adding the results together. For example, the expected value of the random variable D, which is denoted $E(D)$, is

$$E(D) = \text{Sum of (values of } D \times \text{ probabilities of these values)}$$
$$= 1 \times \tfrac{1}{6} + 2 \times \tfrac{1}{6} + 3 \times \tfrac{1}{6} + 4 \times \tfrac{1}{6} + 5 \times \tfrac{1}{6} + 6 \times \tfrac{1}{6}$$
$$= 3\tfrac{1}{2}.$$

Similarly, for the random variable N,

$$E(N) = 0 \times \tfrac{1}{3} + 1 \times \tfrac{1}{2} + 4 \times \tfrac{1}{6} = \tfrac{7}{6},$$

and for the random variable S,

$$E(S) = 2 \times \tfrac{1}{36} + 3 \times \tfrac{2}{36} + 4 \times \tfrac{3}{36} + \cdots + 12 \times \tfrac{1}{36}$$
$$= 7.$$

The expected value summarizes the entire probability distribution into a single number. The fact that $E(D) = 3\frac{1}{2}$ tells us that the values of D are scattered around $3\frac{1}{2}$ rather than around some other number, say 15. However, a much more important property of the expected value constitutes the major reason for using it. Expected value has a long-run interpretation similar to the relative frequency interpretation of a probability. That is, if we repeatedly obtain values of the random variable, these values will be, on the average, very close to the expected value. For instance, if a die was rolled 200 times, and each outcome recorded, then the average outcome (the sum of all outcomes divided by the number of trials, 200) would be a number very close to $3\frac{1}{2}$. Figure 2.7 is a plot of the successive averages obtained by rolling a single die. Notice how the value of the average gets closer and closer to $3\frac{1}{2}$ as the number of trials goes up, and at 200 trials, the value of the average is 3.51, a number extremely close to $3\frac{1}{2}$.

2.4.3 Variance and Standard Deviation

Once the expected value of a probability distribution is calculated, a measure of dispersion, the *variance*, can be obtained. Like the expected value, the variance is the sum of some values times some probabilities. In this case the values are the squared deviations of the random variable values from the expected value. For example, for the random variable D we found $E(D) = 3\frac{1}{2}$. Therefore, when $D = 1$ the squared deviation between this value of D (1) and the expected value of D ($3\frac{1}{2}$) is

$$(1 - 3\frac{1}{2})^2 = (-2\frac{1}{2})^2 = {}^{25}\!/_4.$$

Similarly, the squared deviation between the D value of 5 and the expected value is

$$(5 - 3\frac{1}{2})^2 = (1\frac{1}{2})^2 = {}^9\!/_4.$$

These squared deviations are then multiplied by the appropriate probabilities, summed, and the result is the variance of D, which is denoted Var(D). Thus

Var(D) = Sum of (squared deviations of D values times the probabilities of these D values)
$$= (1 - 3\frac{1}{2})^2 \times \frac{1}{6} + (2 - 3\frac{1}{2})^2 \times \frac{1}{6} + (3 - 3\frac{1}{2})^2 \times \frac{1}{6}$$
$$+ (4 - 3\frac{1}{2})^2 \times \frac{1}{6} + (5 - 3\frac{1}{2})^2 \times \frac{1}{6} + (6 - 3\frac{1}{2})^2 \times \frac{1}{6}$$
$$= {}^{70}\!/_{24}$$
$$= 2.917.$$

A similar calculation can be used to find the variance of the random variable N. In this case we found $E(N) = \frac{7}{6}$, so

Var(N) $= (0 - \frac{7}{6})^2 \times \frac{1}{3} + (1 - \frac{7}{6})^2 \times \frac{1}{2} + (4 - \frac{7}{6})^2 \times \frac{1}{6}$
$$= {}^{390}\!/_{216}$$
$$= 1.806.$$

FIGURE 2.7
Average Outcome for Various Numbers of Die Rolls

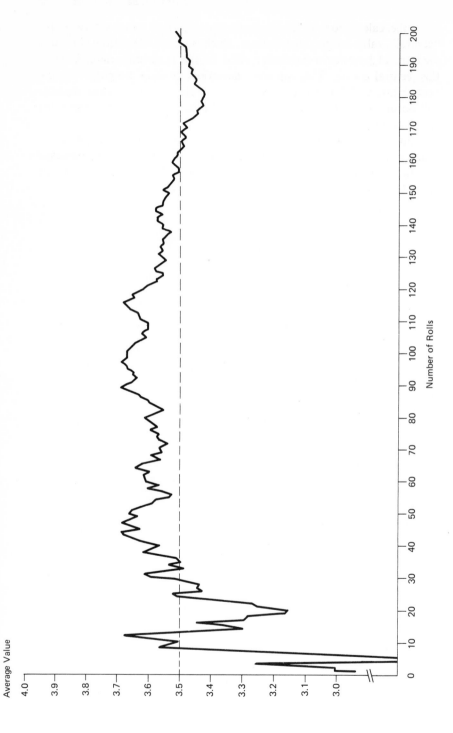

Average Value

Number of Rolls

In the calculation of the variance the expected value serves as the "central" value of the distribution. Each squared deviation is then a measure of how far a particular value of the random variable is from this central value. This squared deviation is then weighted by the probability, which is the chance that this value of the random variable will occur. Thus, the variance is a (weighted) measure of dispersion for the distribution.

Another measure of the dispersion of a probability distribution we shall encounter in later chapters is the *standard deviation*. The standard deviation is the square root of the variance. Thus, for the random variable D,

$$\text{Var}(D) = 2.917$$

$$\text{Standard Deviation of } D = \sqrt{2.917} = 1.708,$$

and for the random variable N

$$\text{Var}(N) = 1.806$$

$$\text{Standard Deviation of } N = \sqrt{1.806} = 1.344.$$

Neither the variance nor the standard deviation is used extensively in this text, but the reader should bear in mind the close relationship between the two, and know that if the value of one is given the value of the other can be quickly obtained.

2.4.4 Derived Random Variables

In addition to probabilistic mechanisms in which the outcomes naturally generate random variables, random variables can also be *derived* from any probabilistic mechanism. For example, consider the following game a friend is offering to play with you.

A fair coin is flipped. If heads occurs, your friend pays you $5, while if tails occurs, you pay your friend $6.

Although the outcomes of the toss of a coin, heads and tails, do not generate a random variable, the outcome of the game is numerical, and a random variable describing the outcome of the game can be *derived* from the coin flip mechanism. In this case, if we let P be a random variable, which gives the amount your friend pays you, then the probability distribution of P is

Value of P	-6	$+5$
Probability	$\frac{1}{2}$	$\frac{1}{2}$

where a negative number indicates that you pay your friend.

Once the derived probability distribution is established, all the characterizations we discussed for random variables can be applied to P. In particular, you should be interested in the expected value of P:

$$E(P) = -6 \times \tfrac{1}{2} + 5 \times \tfrac{1}{2} = -\tfrac{1}{2}.$$

Since $E(P)$ is not zero, you know that this is an unfair game. (You probably already realized that!). Futhermore, the value of $-\tfrac{1}{2}$ tells you that if you were to play this game many times with your friend, you would lose, on the average, 50¢ *per game*.

Derived random variables are obtained from many probabilistic mechanisms, including those that are inherently random variables. As an example of how such a situation might arise, consider the following transformation of the random variable N, the demand for a certain item, which was discussed above.

Suppose N (whose possible values are 0, 1, and 4) represents the demand (in bunches) for flowers, which cannot be sold the following day. The cost of purchasing these flowers from the supplier is $5 per bunch, and the selling price is $8 per bunch. The decision as to how many bunches to order from the supplier must be made at the beginning of the day, before any demand occurs. The demand for bunches that are not available for sale is lost, and unsold bunches at the end of the day are worthless.

Suppose you are faced with this situation and decide to order one bunch for the day. Then the net profits for various levels of demand are:

Demand of 0: Net Profit = $0 Revenue − $5 cost
    = −5
Demand of 1: Net Profit = $8 Revenue − $5 cost
    = +3
Demand of 4: Net Profit = $8 Revenue − $5 cost
    = +3

If we denote net profit by R, then R is a derived random variable with the following probability distribution:

Value of R −5   +3
Probability   ⅓   ⅔

The probability of +3 is ⅔ because a net profit of 3 occurs whenever either 1 or 4 bunches is demanded.

In order to evaluate the policy of buying one bunch from your supplier, we will calculate the expected value of R. In this case:

$$E(R) = -5 \times \tfrac{1}{3} + 3 \times \tfrac{2}{3} = \tfrac{1}{3},$$

and this value says the policy of buying one is better than the policy of not even ordering (and hence always incurring zero net profits), and the average profit per day is $\$\frac{1}{3}$. This result does *not* tell us, of course, whether the policy of ordering only one bunch from the supplier is better than the policy of ordering four bunches from the supplier.

We can also obtain a measure of dispersion for the random variable R. In this case

$$\begin{aligned} \text{Var}(R) &= (-5 - \tfrac{1}{3})^2 \times \tfrac{1}{3} + (3 - \tfrac{1}{3})^2 \times \tfrac{2}{3} \\ &= {}^{384}\!\!/\!_{27} \\ &= 14.22, \end{aligned}$$

and

$$\text{Standard Deviation of } R = \sqrt{14.22} = 3.771.$$

Unfortunately, these measures do not have easy long-run interpretations like the expected value. The most one can get from these is that, relative to the expected profit per day, the dispersion of actual profit values will be large.

2.4.5 Conditional Probability Distributions and Expected Values

A probability distribution we will often encounter in this text is the conditional probability distribution. The basic concept underlying this is quite simple, although the mechanics of calculation can sometimes be excessive. As an example, consider the case in which we roll two dice, and the outcome is S, the sum of the values. A conditional probability distribution can be obtained by taking a value of S as given, and determining the outcome of the green die. For instance, suppose we know that the value of S is 4. Then the only values the green die can have are 1, 2, or 3. We want to find the probabilities of these outcomes. Since they are numerically valued, they can be represented by a random variable. Let X be the value of the green die. Then the conditional probability of X being 2, given S is 4 is written $P(X = 2 | S = 4)$ and is calculated in the same manner as any other conditional probability:

$$P(X = 2 | S = 4) = \frac{P(X = 2 \text{ and } S = 4)}{P(S = 4)}.$$

Now the numerator of the right-hand side of this expression is the same as the probability that both dice have an outcome of 2:

$$\begin{aligned} P(X = 2 \text{ and } S = 4) &= P(\text{the green die} = 2 \text{ and the red die} = 2) \\ &= P(\text{green die} = 2)\, P(\text{red die} = 2) \\ &= \tfrac{1}{6} \times \tfrac{1}{6} \\ &= \tfrac{1}{36}. \end{aligned}$$

Furthermore, Table 2.1 gives $P(S = 4) = \frac{3}{36}$, and so

$$P(X = 2|S = 4) = \frac{\frac{1}{36}}{\frac{3}{36}} = \frac{1}{3}.$$

The probabilities for $X = 1$ and $X = 3$ given $S = 4$ can be calculated in a similar manner. The result is

$$P(X = 1|S = 4) = \frac{1}{3}; \; P(X = 2|S = 4) = \frac{1}{3}; \; P(X = 3|S = 4) = \frac{1}{3},$$

and these values form a *conditional* probability distribution.

Conditional probability distributions can be characterized in the same ways that unconditional probability distributions can. The conditional probability distribution can be graphed, probabilities of X lying within an interval can be obtained, and an expected value, a variance and a standard deviation can be calculated for it. We are mainly interested in the expected value. For the random variable X, the outcome of the green die, the *conditional* expected value is

$$E(X|S = 4) = 1 \times \frac{1}{3} + 2 \times \frac{1}{3} + 3 \times \frac{1}{3} = 2.$$

Here the expected value notation mimics the conditional probability notation to denote that we are finding the expected value of a *conditional* probability distribution.

Let's take one more example. Consider the product whose demand is 0, 1, or 4. For this example we defined the random variable T to be the total demand for two days. We will illustrate the calculation of conditional probability distributions of N, the second day's demand, given various values of T, the total demand for two days.

Let's start with $T = 0$. For this value N can only have the value 0, so we have

$$P(N = 0|T = 0) = 1.$$

For $T = 1$ there are two possible values for N, 0 and 1. We have

$$P(N = 0|T = 1) = \frac{P(N = 0 \text{ and } T = 1)}{P(T = 1)}$$

$$= \frac{P(\text{first day had 1 and second day had none})}{P(T = 1)}$$

$$= \frac{P(\text{first day had 1}) \, P(\text{second day had none})}{P(T = 1)}$$

$$= \frac{\frac{1}{2} \times \frac{1}{3}}{\frac{1}{3}}$$

$$= \frac{1}{2},$$

and a similar calculation or an appeal to complementarity will show that

$$P(N = 1 | T = 1) = \tfrac{1}{2}.$$

When similar calculations are made conditional on all values of T the results are those given in Table 2.3. This table contains six conditional

TABLE 2.3
The Conditional Probability Distributions, $P(N|T)$

	\multicolumn{6}{c}{Value of T}
Value of N	0	1	2	4	5	8
0	1	½	0	½	0	0
1	0	½	1	0	½	0
4	0	0	0	½	½	1

probability distributions. If we wish to calculate the expected value of one of these, say the conditional distribution when $T = 4$, the calculation is quite straightforward.

$$E(N|T = 4) = 0 \times \tfrac{1}{2} + 1 \times 0 + 4 \times \tfrac{1}{2} = 2.$$

2.4.6 A Special Property of Conditional Expectations

Table 2.3 contains six conditional probability distributions, and similar to the calculation just above, an expected value can be obtained for each. Table 2.4 contains these expected values.

TABLE 2.4
The Values of $E(N|T)$ for all T

Value of T	0	1	2	4	5	8
$E(N|T)$	0	$^1/_2$	1	2	$^5/_2$	4

They will be used to demonstrate the following important principle:

> An unconditional expected value can be obtained by weighting conditional expected values by the probability of the outcome being conditioned on and summing.

The usefulness of this property to decision theory will be shown in Chapter 5. Our goal here is to demonstrate that the property holds for the example we are studying. The above statement says that we should be able to obtain the unconditional expected value—$E(N)$ in this case —by taking the conditional expected values, weighting by the probabilities of the outcome being conditioned on (the T values in this case) and summing. Thus, it should be true that

$$
\begin{aligned}
E(N) &= E(N|T = 0)P(T = 0) + E(N|T = 1)P(T = 1) \\
&\quad + E(N|T = 2)P(T = 2) + E(N|T = 4)P(T = 4) \\
&\quad + E(N|T = 5)P(T = 5) + E(N|T = 8)P(T = 8) \\
&= 0 \times \tfrac{1}{9} + \tfrac{1}{2} \times \tfrac{1}{3} + 1 \times \tfrac{1}{4} + 2 \times \tfrac{1}{9} + \tfrac{5}{2} \times \tfrac{1}{6} + 4 \times \tfrac{1}{36} \\
&= \tfrac{42}{36} \\
&= \tfrac{7}{6}.
\end{aligned}
$$

This value, $\tfrac{7}{6}$, is the same as the value for $E(N)$ which was calculated in Section 2.4.2. Thus, the property stated above is verified for this example. While this method seems extremely clumsy, and not one that would ever be used in practice, we will find in Chapter 5 that it will prove to be very useful.

2.5 SUMMARY

This chapter concentrated on the techniques used to obtain probabilities in certain situations, and the definition and characterization of random variables. These ideas will be used extensively in the following chapters.

PROBLEMS

1. The income distribution of Anytown, U.S.A., is

	Income Range			
	Less than $5,000	$5,000–10,000	$10,000–20,000	Above $20,000
Proportion of population......	40%	30%	20%	10%

What is the probability that a person selected at random from Anytown will have an income of $10,000 or more? $5,000 or more?

2. A tetrahedron is a four sided pyramid whose faces are equilateral triangles. Suppose we have a "fair" tetrahedron whose faces are numbered 1, 2, 3, and 4. If we consider the outcome as the face that is down, what is the probability that the outcome resulting from rolling this tetrahedron will be:
   a. A 1?
   b. Either a 1 or a 4?

3. Show that, for a situation with n mutually exclusive elementary events, $E_1, E_2, \ldots, E_n$, and for which the outcome is "fair" (each event is

equally likely) that

$$P(E_i) = \frac{1}{n}$$

for all events E_i.

4. Three parts are vital to the maintenance of a paper machine at Pen And, Inc. The company is trying to determine the probability that each part will be needed at each maintenance check. It has been found that only one of the three is needed (if any) at each maintenance check. A survey of the previous orders of these parts shows

	Part		
	A	X	CD
Number of times ordered	48	24	78

   a. Given that one of these three parts is needed, what is the probability that it will be part A? Part CD?
   b. The maintenance supervisor has found that 20% of the time none of these parts is needed. Find the probability that, at the next maintenance check, the condition will be (1) No part needed; (2) Part A needed; (3) Part X needed; (4) Part CD needed.

5. In Section 2.3.1 we defined three events, A, B, and C, which describe various outcomes of rolling a single die. It is true that $P(A)$, $P(B)$, and $P(C)$ all have a value of $\frac{1}{3}$. Could the notion of "fairness," first introduced in Section 2.2.3, be used to obtain these probabilities? Why or why not?

6. State why the three events of rolling two dice considered in Section 2.3.5,

   1 and 3
   2 and 2
   3 and 1

   are mutually exclusive.

7. In the new cars example, what event is complementary to the event M or S? What is the probability of this complementary event? Using the complementarity rule, find $P(M \text{ or } S)$.

8. Consider a fair die that is rolled three times. What is the probability that one or more "fours" will occur in these three rolls? (Hint: Complementarity is a great help in solving this problem. What event is complementary to one or more "fours" in three rolls?)

9. In the news magazine example of Section 2.3.7, what event is the complement of T or N or A or B or C or D? What event is the complement of U or C or D or E?

10. Using the results of Problem 9, find

    $$P(T \text{ or } N \text{ or } A \text{ or } B \text{ or } C \text{ or } D).$$

11. In the new car example of Section 2.3.4, what is the probability of choosing a buyer who is a man or who purchased a small car? Use the probability rule for "or."

12. Consider the jar containing one red and three green marbles described in Section 2.3.5. What is the probability of drawing a green marble on the first draw? What is the probability of drawing a green marble on the second draw, *given that the first draw yielded a green marble that was not replaced before the second draw?* What is this probability if the red marble had been drawn the first time instead of one of the green ones?

13. In the news magazine example of Section 2.3.7, what is the probability of obtaining the *Time* reader whose income is between $10,000 and $20,000 on a single random draw from the population of news magazine readers?

14. For the news magazine problem of Section 2.3.7, find
    a. $P(T \text{ and } D)$
    b. $P(N \text{ and } A)$
    c. $P(B|U)$
    d. $P(U \text{ and } B)$

15. In the news magazine example of Section 2.3.7, what is the probability of selecting a newsmagazine reader whose income is $10,000 or more and who reads *Time* or *Newsweek?*

16. In Section 2.3.5 we showed that events A and D (in rolling a die) are independent by showing that

    $$P(A|D) = P(A).$$

    Independence also works "the other way around"; that is, since A and D are independent events,

    $$P(D|A) = P(D)$$

    is also true.
    a. Verify that $P(D|A) = P(D)$ for this problem.
    b. Consider any two independent events, F and G. Show that both

    $$P(F|G) = P(F)$$

    and

    $$P(G|F) = P(G)$$

    are true.

17. Suppose two fair dice are rolled, and the outcome is the value of the *maximum* of the outcomes of the individual dice. Find
    a. The probability that the maximum outcome will be 3;
    b. The probabilities of the other possible values of the maximum outcome.

18. Your friend has four special dice, *A, B, C,* and *D,* whose outcomes are displayed below. You are playing a game with him in which you first pick a die, then he picks a die, and then the two dice you have picked are rolled. The winner of the game is the person with the highest outcome for his die. A tie in outcomes results in no winner. Which die should you choose if you want to maximize your chances of winning the game?

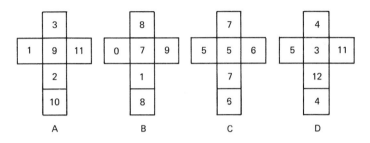

19. For the news magazine problem of Section 2.3.7, find
   a. $P(N)$
   b. $P(C)$
   c. $P(N|C)$
   d. $P(A)$
   e. $P(U|E)$
   f. $P(T|E)$

20. Color blindness is a sex-linked characteristic. It has been found that

   $P(\text{person is color blind}|\text{person is male}) = 0.05$
   $P(\text{person is color blind}|\text{person is female}) = 0.0025$.

   A person is drawn at random from the population, and found to be color blind. Assuming an equal number of male and female persons in the population, what is the chance of the color blind person being male? female?

21. Suppose there were a very reliable method for predicting major earthquakes, with the properties that:

   $P(\text{Test predicts earthquake in coming month}|\text{Earthquake is coming within a month}) = 0.92$
   $P(\text{Test predicts no quake in coming month}|\text{No quake is coming within a month}) = 0.87$.

   a. If the frequency of major earthquakes is such that one occurs (on the average) every 50 years (i.e., the probability of an earthquake in any month is $\dfrac{1}{50 \times 12} = 0.00167$) what is the probability that an earthquake really will occur, *given* that the test predicts it will?

    b. Suppose the test is absolutely reliable; that is, the above probabilities are 1. Now what is the probability that an earthquake will occur, given that the test predicts it will?

22. A garment company, Wear'm Scare'm, Inc., has a machine that knits ladies' panty hose. A certain number of pairs of hose from each run are defective, but many more are defective if the operator has set up the machine incorrectly. The company has three classifications of defects:

    Class A: Small knots, no holes or tears
    Class B: Larger knots and/or holes, no tears
    Class C: Large knots and/or holes, and/or tears.

The probabilities of each of these defects occurring in any particular pair in a run is given below for the two types of machine setups:

	Class		
	A	B	C
Machine setup correct	0.05	0.01	0.002
Machine setup incorrect	0.12	0.07	0.02

that is,

    $P(\text{Class A defect}|\text{Machine setup correct}) = 0.05$, etc.

The operator sets up the machine correctly 90% of the time. What is the probability the machine is set up correctly if
a. A pair of hose drawn at random from the run has a Class A defect?
b. A pair of hose drawn at random from the run has a Class C defect?
c. A pair of hose drawn at random from the run has no defect?

23. Suppose two dice are rolled. What is the probability that the sum of their outcomes is 4, if you know that the sum is *not* a 7?

24. Suppose you roll two fair dice, one blue and one white. What is the probability that the *minimum* of the two outcomes will be two or less? Calculate the probability that the blue die has an outcome of 4, given that the minimum is 2.

25. Develop the probability that S, the sum of the outcomes of two dice, will have a value of 6. (Verify your answer with the answer in Table 2.1).

26. Verify (by calculation) the probabilities given in Table 2.1.

27. Verify (by calculation) the probabilities given in Table 2.2.

28. For problem 2, where a tetrahedron is being rolled, let X be the sum of the values on three rolls. What is the probability that X is greater than or equal to 11?

29. Consider flipping a fair coin three times. Define a random variable, X, as the number of heads that appear in these three tosses of the coin.
    a. What values can X have?
    b. What is $P(X = 1)$?
    c. What is the probability distribution of X?
    d. Graph this probability distribution
    e. Find $P(X \leq 2)$
    f. Find $E(X)$, $\text{Var}(X)$, and the standard deviation of X.

30. Answer the above questions if, instead of a fair coin, you are flipping a thumbtack with $P(U) = \frac{1}{3}$, $P(L) = \frac{2}{3}$. Let X be the number of points up, U, which occur in the three tosses.

31. Let M denote the maximum outcome of the roll of two dice. Using the probabilities obtained in Problem 17,
    a. Graph the probability distribution
    b. Find $P(M \geq 3)$ and $P(1.368 \leq M \leq 4)$
    c. Find $E(M)$, $\text{Var}(M)$, and the standard deviation of M.

32. For Problem 2, in which a tetrahedron is rolled, what is the expected value, variance, and standard deviation of the outcome of one roll of the tetrahedron?

33. For the random variable P of Section 2.4.4, calculate the variance and standard deviation.

34. Suppose you are playing a game with a friend. In this game you roll two dice. If the maximum outcome of the two is 2, 3, or 5, you win $1. If the maximum outcome is 4 or 6, you lose $1. If the maximum outcome is 1, no money changes hands.
    a. Using the probabilities derived in Problem 17, give the probability distribution of your *net* earnings for one play of this game.
    b. What is the expected value of your net earnings? Who is better off, you or your friend?
    c. What is the variance of your net earnings?

35. For the flower vendor's problem of Section 2.4.4, what is the expected value and variance of profit if he stocks four bunches? Which is better, to stock one bunch or four bunches?

36. Joe Abalone, the manager of the local gasoline station, is trying to determine how many automobile batteries to order. Each battery costs Joe $20, and he sells them for $40. Batteries wear out and cannot be sold more than a year past their purchase date. The probability distribution for the number of batteries requested from Joe's station each year is

				Demand				
	0	1	2	3	4	5	6	7
Probability	0.1	0.2	0.3	0.1	0.1	0.1	0.05	0.05

Suppose Joe decides to order four batteries for this coming year.

a. What is the probability distribution of profit resulting from this decision?

b. Find the expected value and variance of this profit distribution.

c. Answer the questions in parts (*a*) and (*b*) if Joe orders two batteries instead of four. Which order policy is better? Why?

37. You have two jars with the following contents.

> Jar I: 3 red marbles, 5 black marbles
> Jar II: 10 red marbles, 2 black marbles.

A jar is randomly selected, and a marble is randomly chosen from that jar. You are playing a game with a friend in which you pay him $1 if the marble drawn is red, while he pays you $2 if the marble drawn is black.

a. Find the conditional probability distribution of your payoff given Jar I is selected, and its expected value.

b. Find the conditional probability distribution of your payoff given Jar II is selected, and its expected value.

c. What is the expected overall payoff of this game?

3

Analyzing Problems without Sampling

THE PURPOSE of this book is to analyze problems that involve uncertainty. In this chapter we will discuss the most simple of these problems, making a decision when there is no opportunity for sampling. While situations of this type are less frequently met in practice, it is important to read this chapter carefully, because the problems and techniques discussed here provide the foundations for all the future topics we will discuss.

3.1 CHARACTERISTICS OF DECISION THEORY PROBLEMS

As with all formal problem solving techniques, decision theory can be applied only to problems that possess certain characteristics. We begin by presenting a problem that can be solved using decision theory; we then go on to analyze the characteristics of this problem—i.e., what properties does it possess that make it amenable to decision theory analysis.

Recreation: It is Friday afternoon and John is trying to decide how to spend his limited funds for Saturday's recreation. He can either go to the movies, go on a picnic, or go sailing. (In the latter two cases his funds are spent on picnic materials.) Each activity would cost the same, and would use all his funds, so multiple activities are not possible. He realizes, however, that the amount of enjoyment he will receive from these activities depends upon Saturday's weather. If the weather is bad he will get no enjoyment out of either the picnic or the sailing.

47

If the weather is sunny and calm (no wind), he will enjoy the picnic most, and if the weather is sunny and breezy, he will enjoy sailing the most. John feels that his enjoyment can be measured by the number of hours he will spend with the activity. The movie lasts for four hours; the picnic for six hours if it is sunny and calm, and four hours if it is sunny and breezy; and sailing for five hours if it is sunny and calm, and 13 hours if it is sunny and breezy. Unfortunately, if he chooses sailing he will have to devote three hours to cleaning his boat on Friday night, and this will subtract that number of hours from Saturday's enjoyment. Finally, John has no access to weather reports for Saturday, and must make his decision immediately, in order to obtain a date for the activity he decides upon.

Which activity should John select?

The above problem can be analyzed by decision theory (as well as by other methods), and we will later discuss these solution techniques. For the moment, however, let us analyze the characteristics of the problem.

In John's problem (and decision theory in general), we assume that *each possible activity is known to the decision maker, and that only one of these can be selected.* In the language of decision theory the decision maker's potential activities are called *actions.*

In John's case, the amount of enjoyment he will receive depends not only upon the action he chooses but upon Saturday's weather as well. The various states of the weather we call *events.* Notice that the whole decision problem hinges upon John's uncertainty as to which event will occur. Notice further that we assume exactly one of these events will occur. That is, a weather condition that is both sunny and breezy and bad weather cannot occur; neither can some weather condition *other than* sunny and breezy, sunny and calm, or bad weather occur. Thus we are assuming that the listed events are *mutually exclusive* and *collectively exhaustive.* However, we are *not* assuming that every possible weather condition is listed as a separate event. The event bad weather is a composite category containing such (separate and potentially distinguishable) events as rain, hail, snow, hurricane, etc.

The information given in John's problem allows us to establish a table that will give the *net* hours of enjoyment for each action, given each event.

Events \ Actions	S	P	M
SB	10	4	4
SC	2	6	4
BW	−3	0	4

where

$$S = \text{Sailing}$$
$$P = \text{Picnic}$$
$$M = \text{Movies}$$
$$SB = \text{Sunny and Breezy}$$
$$SC = \text{Sunny and Calm}$$
$$BW = \text{Bad Weather}$$

The values in the table are obtained from the statement of the problem. For example, the movie gives John four hours of enjoyment, no matter what the weather is. On the other hand, if John chooses sailing and bad weather occurs, he will have gained no hours of enjoyment, and have lost three hours in cleaning his boat, so the *net gain* is —3.

Being able to construct such a table is very important to decision theory problems. It implies that we can attach a *single numerical value* to represent our gain for each event-action pair. In the future, we shall call this table of consequences the *payoff table,* even when the consequences have a negative utility.

This requirement of adopting a single numerical value for each event-action pair is not as restrictive as it might seem. A technique called utility theory, which is discussed in the next chapter, allows us to take many seemingly nonnumerical or multinumerical situations and develop for each event-action pair a single numerical quantity that represents the utility of that pair to the decision maker. For example, if the best evaluations that John can give for sailing are Good, Fair, and Terrible, then utility theory can provide a method for quantifying these evaluations. On the other hand, John may want to consider several criteria in making his choice, rather than just the number of hours of enjoyment he receives. Utility theory can also be used to convert multiple criteria into a single numerical criterion. Therefore, using decision theory with utility theory provides a powerful set of tools for analyzing many types of problems.

To summarize, John's problem and decision theory problems in general require:

1. The decision maker has all potential actions known to him, and he must choose exactly one of them.
2. A list of the events (states of uncertainty) that are mutually exclusive and collectively exhaustive can be compiled.
3. To each event-action pair the decision maker must be able to assign a single numerical value to represent the consequence of choosing that action and having that event occur. (Utility theory can be used to aid this process.)

We shall restrict all future discussions to problems which have these properties.

3.2   METHODS FOR SELECTING A BEST ACTION

Now that we have discussed the characteristics of the problem we will be dealing with, we want to investigate two methods for choosing the best decision. Each method provides a different perspective (philosophical set) toward the problem, and we discuss each here to give the student perspective, although only one will be used in all subsequent analysis.

3.2.1   The Maximin Approach

This selection criterion is quite easily stated:

Choose the action whose worst possible consequence is best.

When we apply this approach to John's payoff table, we find that the best decision is achieved if John attends the movies. The worst possible consequence for each action is the *minimum* of the values within a column. Thus, sailing has a worst possible consequence of -3, etc. Once these minima are found, the best or the one with the maximum payoff is obtained. The action corresponding to the maximum of the minima is the one that should be chosen. These numbers for John's problem are illustrated in the following table:

Events \ Actions	S	P	M
SB	10	4	4
SC	2	6	4
BW	−3	0	4
Column Minimums	−3	0	4*

*The asterisk denotes the maximin value and the corresponding maximin decision is Movies.

The use of the maximin approach has some interesting implications on how the decision maker views his world. By choosing this approach, he must feel that the mechanism that chooses events is a malevolent adversary. So no matter what action John takes, he has the attitude, in accepting this approach, that the weather will be such that he will achieve the *least* enjoyment from that action. While certain situations might dictate such a strategy,[1] we will take the view in this book that the device that selects which event will occur is neutral—neither male-

---

[1] Such an approach seems perfectly logical when the "event" that will occur is chosen by a competitor. The study of such situations is called game theory. An excellent introduction to this topic can be found in J. D. Williams' *The Compleat Strategyst* (New York: McGraw-Hill, 1954).

volent nor benevolent. With this in mind we turn toward the approach used to solve the problems we discuss in this book.

3.2.2 The Expected Value Approach

This criterion is as simple as the previous one:

Assign probabilities to event outcomes, and choose the decision whose expected payoff is highest.

In John's case, if we assume $P(SB) = \frac{1}{2}$, $P(SC) = \frac{3}{8}$, and $P(BW) = \frac{1}{8}$, then we have

The expected payoff from sailing,

$$E(S) = 10 \times \frac{1}{2} + 2 \times \frac{3}{8} + (-3) \times \frac{1}{8} = 5\frac{3}{8}$$

The expected payoff from the picnic,

$$E(P) = 4 \times \frac{1}{2} + 6 \times \frac{3}{8} + 0 \times \frac{1}{8} = 4\frac{1}{4}$$

The expected payoff from the movies,

$$E(M) = 4 \times \frac{1}{2} + 4 \times \frac{3}{8} + 4 \times \frac{1}{8} = 4$$

and the best decision is to choose sailing, since this action gives the maximum expected payoff.

There are two very fundamental questions concerning the expected value approach. First, we must ask whether it is legitimate to assign probabilities to event outcomes and, if it is, where we obtain the values of the probabilities. Second, given that probabilities can be assigned and values obtained, is the expected value criterion the appropriate one to use, or should other measures of the distribution of payoffs (the variance, for instance) be used as an additional criterion? The answer to the first question is contained in section 3.2.4. The answer to the second question is deferred to Chapter 4.

We saw previously that the maximin approach to solving decision problems assumes that the event choice mechanism is malevolent—that is, dedicated to giving the decision maker as little as possible. On the other hand, when we use the expected value approach, we are assuming that the event choice mechanism is *neutral*—that is, it chooses events neither in our favor nor against it.

3.2.3 Comparing the Maximin Approach with the Expected Value Approach

It is always tempting to ask which one is better when one is given two methods to solve a problem. We will deliberately skirt that issue here, because the argument becomes not one of which approach is better but one of which philosophical set is correct. If we accept the premise that the event-choice mechanism is malevolent, it is easy to show that the maximin approach is better than the expected value approach. On the other hand, if we accept the premise of a neutral event-choice mechanism, it is almost as easy to show that the expected value approach is better than the maximin approach, *in the long run.* So the argument of which approach is better really becomes an argument as to whether the event-choice mechanism is malevolent or neutral. Certainly this aspect will vary from problem to problem, and we leave the determination of the appropriate condition of the event-choice mechanism, and the corresponding choice of solution technique, to the decision maker. This book will only treat problems that have a *neutral* event-choice mechanism, and the objective of the book is to present methods to solve such problems.

3.2.4 Assigning Probabilities to Events

When we were discussing the expected value approach to solving decision problems, we noted the need to verify that we could attach probabilities to event occurrences and to obtain values for these probabilities. We shall take these questions in reverse order, first presenting a method for obtaining the probabilities, then discussing what these probabilities imply.

When a decision maker has a number of events, such as the three *SB, SC,* and *BW* from John's problem, he obtains probabilities by first attaching numerical weights to these events in proportion to the likelihood that *he* (the decision maker) thinks they will occur. For the person who feels comfortable with probabilities, these weights can be actual probabilities, and no further transformation is necessary to use these in solving the problem. For others who do not feel comfortable with using probabilities, the following procedure is usually helpful.

Start by assigning a relatively large number (say 100) to the *most* likely event. For example, suppose in his problem John has determined that *SB* is the most likely event, and he assigns a weight of 100 to that event. The next step is to assign weights to the other events. *These weights must express the likelihood of this event occurring relative to the weight attached to the most likely event and its liklihood.* Thus, if John feels that *SC* is about 75 percent as likely as *SB,* then he should attach a weight of 75 to *SB.* Similarly, if he feels *SB* is four times as likely as *BW,* then he should assign a weight of 25 to *BW.*

Once the weights have been attached to the events, it is a simple matter to normalize them to obtain probabilities. Simply add up all the weights, and divide each weight by this sum to obtain the corresponding probabilities. Thus in John's problem, the sum of the weights is $25 + 75 + 100 = 200$ and the corresponding probabilities are:

$$^{25}/_{200}(= \frac{1}{8}) \text{ for } BW$$
$$^{100}/_{200}(= \frac{1}{2}) \text{ for } SB$$
$$^{75}/_{200}(= \frac{3}{8}) \text{ for } SC.$$

It is important to reiterate at this point that the events must be *mutually exclusive* and *collectively exhaustive*. Otherwise, the above weighting scheme won't work.

Some readers may balk at this point, saying that while some people can make intelligent estimates to attach weights to events, they cannot. This is nonsense! Any adult who has been making decisions has implicitly been making such assignments for years. The only additional requirement imposed upon you by decision theory is that you make these assignments explicit. In doing so you gain the tremendous advantages of being able to scrutinize closely the comparative values of your weights, and in being able to apply the techniques of decision theory toward solving your problem.

Now that we have discussed the mechanics for obtaining probabilities, let us discuss the nature of these probabilities. We have seen that they are subjective probabilities. Someone does not *tell* John that the probability of *SB* will have a value of $\frac{1}{2}$, it is *his best guess* as to the value for the probability of that event. Certainly the mechanics of solving the problem would not be changed if someone (probably the weatherman) had told John that $P(SB) = \frac{1}{2}$. The point is that for many decision problems the probabilities of the events are *not* available, except through a subjective process by the decision maker himself. While decision theorists accept subjective probabilities as being the best that can be obtained, there are schools of statisticians and probabilists who completely reject decision theory—mainly on the basis that it condones the use of subjective probabilities. While this is not the appropriate place to discuss these arguments, the student of decision theory should be aware that he may someday meet a "disbeliever," and he should be aware of the foundation for their disbelief.

3.3 THE CONCEPT OF OPPORTUNITY LOSS

There is another viewpoint from which to look at the types of decision problems discussed in this chapter. It involves using similar techniques for solving a problem, but having a payoff matrix developed from "hindsight." Some interesting and useful conclusions come out of such an analysis. Further analysis of John's problem will set the stage for our discussion.

Suppose John is relaxing on the Sunday *following* his Saturday sailing date, and reflecting that the day had been, unfortunately, sunny and calm. He realizes that *knowing* which event occurred, he can evaluate the three actions relative to the best of these. Thus for a sunny and calm day, the best action would have been *P*, and by choosing *S* instead, he sacrificed four $(6 - 2)$ hours of enjoyment over the best decision *given that event*. If instead he had chosen *M*, he would have sacrificed two $(6 - 4)$ hours of enjoyment. If he chose *P*, of course, he would have sacrificed zero $(6 - 6)$ hours relative to the best decision.

While he feels a little silly wasting his time on such a project (after all, the decision is past), John realizes that he can apply the same technique to the other rows of the payoff matrix. For instance, if *SB* had occurred, the best action would be *S*, and if he had chosen either *P* or *M* he would have sacrificed six $(10 - 4)$ hours of enjoyment relative to the best decision. A similar argument applies to the bottom row of the payoff matrix, and the "hours sacrificed" can be written in a matrix form as:

Events ＼ Actions	S	P	M
SB	0	6	6
SC	4	0	2
BW	7	4	0

It is important to note the entry in the *BW-S* position. For *BW* the best action is *M*, and if *S* had been chosen the loss would be the *sum* of the four hours of movie entertainment foregone, plus the three hours needed to clean out the boat. Fortunately, the same process can be obtained if we are careful in using algebra to subtract the payoff for *BW-S* from the payoff for *BW-M*: $4 - (-3) = 7$.

The numbers that result from comparing any payoff with the best payoff for that event are called *opportunity losses,* and the matrix of all such values is called the *opportunity loss matrix*. While the technique of calculating opportunity losses seems very straightforward, the reader must beware situations where the entries in the payoff matrix represent *costs,* or other outcomes that have negative utility, and where consequently, the objective is to *minimize* rather than maximize, as it was in John's problem. We will find it helpful in future applications always to have opportunity losses be nonnegative numbers (zero or positive numbers), and in order to satisfy this requirement, the calculation of opportunity losses in cost situations must be changed to subtracting the *best* (minimum) cost from every other cost in the same row. An example will serve to illustrate this procedure.

Car: Mike needs a car, and he is trying to decide whether to buy a new car or a used car. He feels the crux of the decision is the number of useful years he will get out of the used car. After careful consideration he has developed the following table of *costs* for each action and event.

Events Used Car Will Last	Buy a New Car	Buy a Used Car
Less than 1 year	$4,000	$5,000
Between 1 and 4 years	$4,000	$3,000
More than 4 years	$4,000	$2,000

For this example the best action is the one with the lowest cost. Thus if we choose the first event (less than one year), the best action is to buy a new car, and the opportunity loss for buying a used car is $1,000. This value is obtained by subtracting the *cost* for the best decision from the cost for the other decision, and is consistant with the concept that opportunity loss expresses something that the decision maker has "lost." (In this case, an additional $1,000.) The same reasoning applies for the rest of the matrix, and the resulting opportunity loss matrix is:

Events Used Car Lasts	Buy a New Car	Buy a Used Car
Less than 1 year	0	$1,000
Between 1 and 4 years	$1,000	0
More than 4 years	$2,000	0

3.4 ANALYZING THE PROBLEM USING THE OPPORTUNITY LOSS MATRIX

Once John has developed the opportunity loss matrix for his problem, he realizes that he has another, different matrix of numbers, and that he can analyze his problem by applying approaches similar to the maximin and expected value approaches he used with the payoff matrix. John is also quite perceptive, however, and realizes that the opportunity loss matrix contains values with negative utilities, and that he may have to appropriately adapt the approaches he used in analyzing the payoff matrix when he analyzes the opportunity loss matrix.

3.4.1 Minimax Loss

John first considers the application of an approach where the event choice mechanism is malevolent. He realizes, however, that such a mechanism would attempt to give him the *highest possible* opportunity loss. (Rather than the lowest possible value, which was the case when John was working with the payoff matrix.) After careful consideration, John realizes that an appropriate approach for this situation is:

Choose the action whose worst possible outcome is least bad.

This approach is called *minimax loss,*[2] because it chooses the minimum of a set of maximum opportunity losses. For John's opportunity loss matrix, both *P* and *M* have maximum opportunity losses of 6, and this value is less than the maximum opportunity loss for *S*. Thus, if John

Events \ Actions	S	P	M
SB	0	6	6
SC	4	0	2
BW	7	4	0
Column Maximums	7	6	6

chose a minimax loss approach for solving his problem, he would be indifferent between *P* and *M* as the best action.

3.4.2 The Expected Loss Approach

Just as he found the expected payoffs for each action when he was analyzing the payoff matrix, John can quickly find the expected losses for each action. Recall that $P(SB) = \frac{1}{2}$; $P(SC) = \frac{3}{8}$; $P(BW) = \frac{1}{8}$. Then, John has:

Expected Opportunity Loss for sailing[3]

$$= \mathcal{E}(S) = 0 \times \frac{1}{2} + 4 \times \frac{3}{8} + 7 \times \frac{1}{8} = 2\frac{3}{8}$$

Expected Opportunity Loss for Picnic

$$= \mathcal{E}(P) = 6 \times \frac{1}{2} + 0 \times \frac{3}{8} + 4 \times \frac{1}{8} = 3\frac{4}{8}$$

Expected Opportunity Loss for Movies

$$= \mathcal{E}(M) = 6 \times \frac{1}{2} + 2 \times \frac{3}{8} + 0 \times \frac{1}{8} = 3\frac{6}{8}$$

Finally, John realizes that opportunity losses have negative utility, and the best action is thus to choose sailing, the action with the *minimum* expected loss.

---

[2] Some authors call opportunity loss "regret," and this approach is then called minimax regret.

[3] In order to differentiate between expected payoffs and expected opportunity losses in this text, we shall consistently use $E(A)$ for the former, and $\mathcal{E}(A)$ for the latter.

3.4.3 Comparing the Payoff and Loss Approaches for Solving a Decision Problem

Recall that John's best action using the maximin approach was M, and using the expected payoff approach was S. Essentially the same outcomes were obtained when corresponding techniques were used on the opportunity loss matrix. Is this pure coincidence, or are the payoff and opportunity loss analyses closely related? It is coincidence in the case of comparing the maximin payoff and minimax loss approaches, but it is *not* coincidence when the expected payoff and expected opportunity loss approaches are compared. It is true that:

The expected payoff and expected opportunity loss approaches always yield the same best action as a solution to *any* decision problem.[4]

3.4.4 The Cost of Uncertainty

The reader may wonder why we bother discussing opportunity losses, since the expected value approach yields the same action whether we use a payoff matrix or a loss matrix. There are two reasons why we analyze a problem using opportunity losses. The first involves a technical consideration. When we use opportunity losses we create zero values. This will be surprisingly helpful to us in later work, when the arithmetic becomes very messy, and a nice multiplication by zero is always welcomed. The second and much more important reason for using opportunity loss is that it yields the cost of uncertainty, or expected value of perfect information. We will illustrate this for John's problem.

Suppose John faced a similar decision situation every weekend for a number of weekends, and that while the weather varied from weekend to weekend, John knew *exactly* which kind of weather was going to occur *before* he had to make his decision. In such a situation John would of course choose S when he knew the weather was going to be SB, choose P when he knew the weather was going to be SC, and choose M when he knew the weather was going to be BW. On the average, how many hours of enjoyment would John realize in a weekend? If SB occurred half the time, SC three eights of the time, and BW one eighth of the time, John's average enjoyment per week would be $10 \times \frac{1}{2} + 6 \times \frac{3}{8} + 4 \times \frac{1}{8} = 7\frac{6}{8}$ hours.

How much does John sacrifice by not having this information? When he is uncertain about the weather he always chooses sailing, and his ex-

---

[4] Proving this statement may be beyond the ability or interest of some readers. It is left as an exercise (Problem 10) at the end of the chapter for those who wish to tackle it.

pected payoff is $5\frac{3}{8}$. Thus, by not having perfect information about Saturday's weather on Friday, John sacrifices $7\frac{6}{8} - 5\frac{3}{8} = 2\frac{3}{8}$ hours, exactly the expected opportunity loss for sailing! Thus if one analyzes a decision problem using the expected loss approach, the minimum expected loss not only indicates the best action, but its value is also the amount that is sacrificed by not having perfect information as to which event will occur. The value of the minimum expected opportunity loss is called the *cost of uncertainty* or the *expected value of perfect information* (abbreviated EVPI). While this quantity does us no good at this point, most succeeding chapters of this book are concerned with decision problems in which the decision is postponed while more information is obtained (sampling occurs). Unfortunately, sampling usually costs money, and the basic question becomes whether or not the sampling information is worth its cost. When we encounter such situations, the EVPI gives an upper bound on the amount we would be willing to pay for sampling.

3.5 THE TECHNIQUES SUMMARIZED—AN ANALYSIS OF MIKE'S CAR PURCHASING PROBLEM

In this section we want to review the techniques of solving a decision problem by applying them to Mike's problem. For this problem the *cost* and opportunity loss matrices were:

Cost Matrix		
	N	U
<1	$4,000	$5,000
1–4	$4,000	$3,000
>4	$4,000	$2,000

Opportunity Loss Matrix		
	N	U
<1	0	$1,000
1–4	$1,000	0
>4	$2,000	0

where

N = Buy a New Car
U = Buy a Used Car
<1 = Used car lasts less than one year
1–4 = Used car lasts between one and four years
>4 = Used car lasts more than four years

This problem is a good problem for illustration, since the "payoff" matrix is really a matrix of costs, and the approaches taken are slightly different from those used on John's problem. For instance, while a maximin approach is appropriate to use on a payoff matrix, a minimax approach is the appropriate technique for a cost matrix. (We saw the same thing happening with the opportunity loss matrix.) Thus, for

Mike's cost matrix the minimax solution is N (Buy a New Car) since this action's maximum value is smaller than U's maximum value. On the other hand, when we apply the minimax solution to the opportunity loss matrix, the best action is U.

In order to determine the best action using the expected value criterion, we need to develop probabilities of the various events.[5] Suppose Mike selects the most likely event to be 1–4, and assigns a weight of 100 to this event. He further feels that relative to this number, the weights for <1 and >4 should be 40 and 60, respectively. Then the sum of the weights is 200, and we have $P(<1) = 40/200 = 0.2$; $P(1-4) = 100/200 = 0.5; P(>4) = 60/200 = 0.3$.

Once these probabilities have been determined, they can be applied to either the cost matrix or the opportunity loss matrix to determine the best action. We shall apply them to both here, but it must be emphasized that this is for illustrative purposes only. Only one of the two is required to solve any problem.

Using the cost matrix, we have

$$E(N) = 4,000 \times 0.2 + 4,000 \times 0.5 + 4,000 \times 0.3 = 4,000,$$
$$E(U) = 5,000 \times 0.2 + 3,000 \times 0.5 + 2,000 \times 0.3 = 3,100,$$

and the best action is U. Notice that we chose the action with the *minimum* expected value, since we are dealing with a cost matrix rather than a payoff matrix. Similarly, the expected values for the opportunity loss matrix are:

$$\mathcal{E}(N) = 0 \times 0.2 + 1,000 \times 0.5 + 2,000 \times 0.3 = 1,100,$$
$$\mathcal{E}(U) = 1,000 \times 0.2 + 0 \times 0.5 + 0 \times 0.3 = 200,$$

and again we verify that the best action is U. We also notice that the cost of uncertainty is 200, which seems fairly high, and might indicate that Mike should seek some information. (He might be able to find a great deal of information for a lot less than $200!)

3.6 DECISION TREES—A DIAGRAMMATIC METHOD FOR REPRESENTING AND ANALYZING DECISION PROBLEMS

One of the useful tools in decision theory is the decision tree. A decision tree is merely a diagram of the problem facing the decision maker. The major features of the tree are branching points, and each branching point designates either a choice of actions, one of which must be taken by the decision maker, or a group of chance outcomes, one of which will occur. The former type of branching point is called

---

[5] It would be helpful to the reader to go through this excercise himself, estimating his own probabilities.

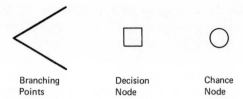

| Branching | Decision | Chance |
| Points | Node | Node |

a *decision node,* and is pictured as a square, and the latter type of branching point is called a *chance node,* and is pictured as a circle. The tree is developed from left to right, with the (left to right) order of nodes representing the chronological order in which the decision maker "encounters" the nodal situations.

An example will help to illustrate the development of a decision tree. Consider John's recreation problem discussed earlier in this chapter. Chronologically, John will encounter two things. First, he must make a decision as to which activity to engage in: sailing, picnic, or movies. Then, after one of these actions is chosen, he will observe what Saturday's weather is. Thus, his first branching point starts from a decision node, and there are three branches, one representing each action.

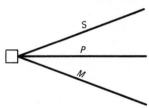

If John chooses the lowest branch of the tree (chooses the action *M*), he will encounter no more decision or chance situations. His payoff is fixed at four hours of enjoyment. If he chooses *S* or *P*, however, he will encounter a chance situation (the weather), which will affect his payoff. Therefore, John's complete tree is:

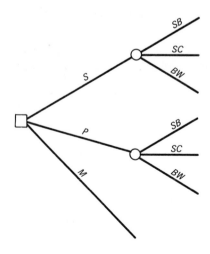

This tree completely describes John's encounters. First, at the left of the tree, he must choose from among his three potential actions, and then, moving to the right on the tree, if he chooses *S* or *P*, his payoff will be affected by which of the chance events (types of weather) occurs.

In addition to providing a useful diagram of a decision problem, a decision tree can be used to analyze a problem. In particular, the rules are:

1. Assign payoffs (or costs or opportunity losses) to the rightmost tips of the tree.
2. Assign probabilities to the chance outcomes.
3. Work from right to left through the tree, calculating expected values at each chance node, and choosing the best value at each decision node.

We will demonstrate the application of these rules to John's tree. With Steps 1 and 2 completed, and using the hours of enjoyment as payoffs, John's tree is:

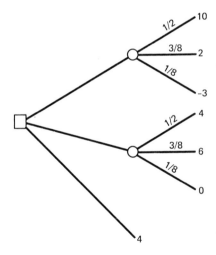

Given this, the expected values at the chance nodes must be determined. For the top chance node we have an expected value of

$$10 \times \tfrac{1}{2} + 2 \times \tfrac{3}{8} + (-3) \times \tfrac{1}{8} = 5\tfrac{3}{8}$$

and for the other chance node the expected value is

$$4 \times \tfrac{1}{2} + 6 \times \tfrac{3}{8} + 0 \times \tfrac{1}{8} = 4\tfrac{1}{4}.$$

These are, of course, the same expected values we obtained in section 3.2.2. Given these results the tree becomes:

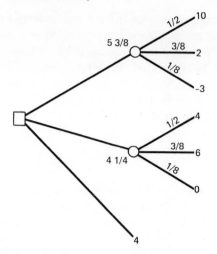

and the best choice at the decision node is to choose that decision branch with the highest value. In this case that value is 5⅜, and the fully analyzed tree is:[6]

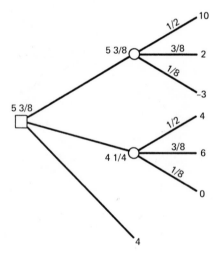

This analysis tells us that the best action will have an expected value of 5⅜ (the value on the leftmost node of the tree). Furthermore, the best action can be determined by determining the origin of the optimal value. In this case the 5⅜ obviously came from the *S* branch of the tree, so sailing is John's best action. Although extracting "what to do" was patently simple in this problem, it will become more complex for the problems encountered in Chapter 5 and beyond. It will not ever be, however, a strenuous mental exercise!

---

[6] In the future we shall jump directly from the tree describing the problem to the fully analyzed tree. The two intermediate trees were used this once to help the student understand the steps in the analysis.

As a final example we will draw and analyze the decision tree for Mike's car problem. Furthermore, we will illustrate how the technique can be used with opportunity losses in this problem. In this case Mike first encounters a choice between two actions, followed by a chance outcome depending on how long the used car would have lasted. Thus, the decision tree is

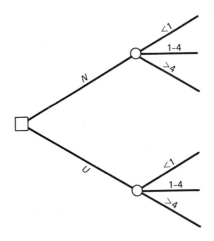

where

N = Buy a New Car
U = Buy a Used Car
<1 = Used car lasts less than one year
$1-4$ = Used car lasts between one and four years
>4 = Used car lasts more than four years

Using the opportunity losses and probabilities given earlier, the tree becomes

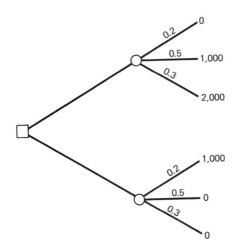

and the fully analyzed tree is

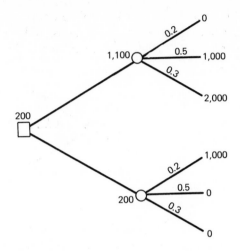

Therefore, the expected opportunity loss for the best action is 200, and the action which yields that value is *U*. Hence, Mike should buy a used car, and his cost of uncertainty is 200. This agrees (as it should) with the answers obtained in section 3.5.

3.7 SUMMARY AND PROSPECTS

This chapter presented several variations for solving decision problems, but all are based on the single theme of using expected value. This approach will continue to be used in all subsequent chapters. Decision theory is truly doing nothing more than formalizing a procedure most of us take as a natural course in making decisions. Whether we are choosing a recreational activity, buying a car, choosing a spouse, choosing a stock to buy or sell, or any of a myriad of other decisions, the important theme is to consider for each action the values of the various consequences and the chances that these consequences will occur. This is exactly what decision theory formalizes into the expected value approach.

Decision theory is one of the few fields in which the basic concept is discussed immediately. Future chapters in this book do nothing more than broaden the student's perspective on how to apply the expected value approach to various problem situations. The danger in future chapters is that the reader will become so involved in the mechanics of solving a particular class of problems that he loses sight of the overriding principle. Care should always be taken by the reader that he *not* lose sight of the principle of expected value.

PROBLEMS

1. Discuss why S is a bad solution to John's problem if the event choice mechanism is malevolent, and why M is a bad solution to John's problem if the event choice mechanism is neutral.

2. Explain what is meant by a minimax approach, and why it (rather than maximin) is used when we are dealing with a cost or opportunity loss matrix.

3. If the number of hours of enjoyment John receives from a picnic on a sunny, breezy day is five instead of four, show that the best action for the maximin payoff approach is different from the best action for the minimax loss approach.

4. A manufacturer has the option to buy a machine that is subject to technological obsolescence. The machine will initially cost $10,000. If the machine does not become obsolete during a year, the profit which the manufacturer will receive is $11,000. If the machine becomes obsolete during the year, the manufacturer will receive nothing. If he buys the machine, the manufacturer can scrap it at the end of the first year and receive $5,000, or repair it for another year at the cost of $1,000. At the end of the second year he can scrap it and receive $2,000, or repair it for another year at a cost of $3,000. At the end of the third year the machine will no longer be useful. If a decision to buy the machine is made, a contract for the repairs must be signed at the time the machine is purchased. The contractor agrees to make repairs (and be paid for these repairs) only if the machine is not technologically obsolete. Furthermore, the machine only has scrap value if it is not technologically obsolete.

    a. State very clearly and precisely what the actions are in this problem.
    b. If the events are the following:
        1. Technological obsolescence occurs in the first year
        2. Technological obsolescence occurs in the second year
        3. Technological obsolescence occurs in the third year
        4. Technological obsolescence occurs in four or more years.
        Construct a payoff table for this problem.

5. Planning Development Queries (PDQ), a management consulting firm, is considering three UCLA graduates as future employees. The major field of each of the prospective employees, and the salaries required to hire them are:

Man	Major	Yearly Salary
1	Marketing	$10,000
2	Quantitative Methods	$12,000
3	Quantitative Methods	$15,000

Each man is expected to bring the company a certain amount of extra contracts. The gross yearly profit (income minus all expenses *except* salary) for each man depends upon the state of the economy, and is:

State of Economy	Man 1	Gross Profit Man 2	Man 3
Good	$15,000	$15,000	$28,000
Mediocre	$ 9,000	$12,000	$20,000
Poor	$ 6,000	$ 8,000	$12,000

However, there are some complications. Man 1 and Man 2 are good friends, and work well together. To compensate for this, PDQ management has decided that the gross profit for each will be 1½ times that given above if both are hired. Also, since Man 2 and Man 3 are in the same field, their talents overlap. It has been decided, therefore, that each would only bring in ¾ of the above gross yearly profit if both are hired. (Note: Since PDQ is located in beautiful downtown Burbank, they know any employment offer they give will be accepted.)

a.   State very clearly the actions open to PDQ.

b.   Using the states of the economy as possible events, construct a *net* profit payoff table for the problem. (To avoid confusion, consider the payoffs for *one* year only.)

6.   The newsboy on Westwood Avenue must decide each day how many *Herald Examiners* to stock for the afternoon. In the past he has observed the following frequency of requests to the closest 100 papers:

Number of Papers Requested	Proportion of Days
100	0.1
200	0.2
300	0.4
400	0.3

Each paper costs the newsboy 6¢ and he sells them for 10¢. Unsold newspapers may be sold to scrap paper dealers for ¼¢ a piece. If he can assume that he does not lose business as a result of not being able to fill a customer's request:

a.   Construct a payoff table for the actions "stock 100 to 400 papers," and the events "sale of 100 to 400 papers."

b.   Draw up a *loss* table for the same decision.

c.   Find the best action and the cost of uncertainty.

7.   Suppose the newsboy in the problem above is faced with the same costs and profits, but in addition he feels that for every request he cannot fill he loses k¢ in future profits. Find which action maximizes profit for each value of $k = 0, 1, 2, 3, \cdots$.

8.   A manufacturing company needs a machine lathe for various jobs. There are four kinds available. The profit potential of each depends upon the number of jobs on which the lathe can be used. If the set of actions is:

$A_1 = $ Buy lathe #1
$A_2 = $ Buy lathe #2
$A_3 = $ Buy lathe #3
$A_4 = $ Buy lathe #4

and the set of events is

E_1 = The lathe will be used on 50 jobs
E_2 = The lathe will be used on 30 jobs
E_3 = The lathe will be used on 10 jobs
E_4 = The lathe won't be used

then management has calculated the payoff matrix to be:

Events \ Actions	A_1	A_2	A_3	A_4
E_1	3	6	13	12
E_2	5	−4	5	−2
E_3	3	1	6	6
E_4	−3	−7	−25	−22

    a. Construct the opportunity loss matrix for this problem if the objective is to maximize expected payoff.

    b. If management estimates the probabilities as: $P(E_1) = 0.1$; $P(E_2) = 0.4$; $P(E_3) = 0.45$; and $P(E_4) = 0.05$, which lathe should be chosen? What is the cost of uncertainty?

9. Given any loss matrix of the form

Events \ Actions	A_1	A_2
E_1	a	0
E_2	0	b

with probability p of occurrence of E_1, and probability $1 - p$ of occurrence of E_2, show that the probability p that minimizes the cost of uncertainty is either $p = 0$ or $p = 1$.

10. *a.* Verify that when you are maximizing expected payoff, the sum of expected payoff and expected opportunity loss is a constant for any decision.

    b. Using the result from (*a*), verify that the decision that maximizes expected payoff also minimizes expected opportunity loss.

    c. In terms of what you have developed above, explain why the minimum expected opportunity loss is the cost of uncertainty. (Hint: Look closely at the constant to which the two values sum.)

    d. What statement similar to the statement in (*a*) can you make (about the relationship between expected payoff and expected opportunity loss for any decision) when you are minimizing expected payoff? Use this new relation to verify the statement in (*b*) in this case.

Problems 11, 12, 13, and 14 are concerned with the concept of dominance. Dominance occurs when the payoffs for one action are larger than the payoffs for each of the other actions, *no matter which event occurs.* Thus, in the payoff matrix below, A_3 is the dominant action.

Events \ Actions	A_1	A_2	A_3
E_1	4	2	5
E_2	−1	16	17

11. One should clearly choose a dominant action if there is one. Show that if a problem has a dominant action, it will be the action chosen when we maximize expected value.

12. Show that if a problem has a dominant action, that action will be chosen if we use the maximin approach to solve the problem.

13. Show that if we use expected opportunity loss to analyze a problem with a dominant action, the dominant action will be chosen as the best action. What is the cost of uncertainty in this case? Explain why it has this value.

14. For decision problems with many possible actions, it is sometimes useful to be able to "reduce" the problem as much as possible. Toward that end we recognize that one action can dominate another without there being a dominant action for the entire problem. For instance, in the table below, A_5 dominates A_4, yet A_5 is *not* a dominant action.

    a. Show that decision problems can be reduced in size by eliminating dominated actions (i.e., show that a dominated action can never be optimal.)

    b. Using the above idea, reduce the decision problem whose payoff matrix is given below, if the objective is to *maximize* payoff.

Events \ Actions	A_1	A_2	A_3	A_4	A_5	A_6	A_7	A_8	A_9	A_{10}
E_1	0	5	−3	15	16	6	6	1	−1	−4
E_2	0	3	5	3	4	6	8	7	−3	1
E_3	0	−2	−6	1	2	−10	−1	13	−2	−18

An Extended Analysis of the Expected Value Criterion

IN THE PREVIOUS CHAPTER we established the framework for decision theory problems and presented the basic technique—that of using expected values—for determining the best action. In this chapter we will explore that expected value criterion, and show when it is valid and when it is not. Furthermore, for problems for which the expected value criterion is not acceptable we will develop a new technique—called utility theory—for solving them.

4.1 AN EXPLORATION OF THE EXPECTED VALUE CRITERION

The best way to explore the expected value criterion is to explore reasons why people do not like it. In the author's experience there are four criticisms usually raised against it:

1. The true outcome is uncertain. The expected value criterion tells us *nothing* about what really might happen!
2. There is more involved in a chance outcome than the expected value! What about the variance?
3. Some of the payoffs in this problem would seriously affect me (perhaps destroy my business) if they occurred. Expected value does not adequately take these into account.
4. I have a choice between two multimillion dollar actions. Using an expected value criterion shows one to be about $100,000 better than the other, and you expect me to make a choice based on that

small difference? I won't do it. I think there is more to the problem than what is expressed by the expected values.

Each of these criticisms will be explored in turn. We will find that the first cannot be solved by decision theory at all, that the second and third can both be solved by the technique to be presented in this chapter and that the last criticism can partially be solved by utility theory and partially only by common sense.

4.1.1 The Uncertainty of Expected Value

Some students of decision theory dislike the expected value criterion because of its inherent risk. A person who feels this way will commonly argue that the expected value is meaningless compared to the actual payoffs associated with an action. For instance, in John's recreation problem the expected value for sailing is 5⅜, while the actual hours of enjoyment will be either 10, 2, or −3. When pressed to explain *why* he doesn't like expected value in this case, the person will probably state that, although the expected value makes sailing look attractive, you could lose as much as three hours by choosing that activity!

This person is not looking at the value of sailing *on the average,* but only at the *worst possible* value associated with sailing. The fact that the event that would create this value has a small probability of occurring is irrelevant to him. All he can see is the negative aspects of the consequences if it should occur. In a sense, then, this student would like to base the decision only on the *payoffs* of the decision problem, and ignore the chances of these payoffs occurring. As a consequence, the expected value criterion is not appropriate for this person. The student would be well advised to ignore the concepts presented in this book, and use a maximin strategy instead. There is no modification of the expected value criterion that can make it appealing.

4.1.2 A Paradox—Two Choices with the Same Expected Value and Different Desirabilities

The second reason why some people dislike expected value can best be explored by an example. Suppose a student, let's call him Paul, is approached by an oddsmaker in Las Vegas, and offered either one of the following two bets:

Bet I: A fair coin is flipped. If heads appears the student is paid $2, while if tails appears the student pays the oddsmaker $1;

Bet II: A fair coin is flipped. If heads appears the student is paid $105, while if tails appears the student pays the oddsmaker $104.

To make life simple at this point we will assume that Paul can engage in either of these bets as often as he likes. Furthermore, Paul also has the option of refusing to engage in either bet.

We can analyze Paul's options using the expected value criterion presented in the Chapter 3. The decision tree for doing this is shown in Figure 4.1, and the analyzed tree in Figure 4.2. Given the expected values displayed in this figure, Paul should be indifferent to the two bets, and prefer either of them to the "Do Nothing" alternative.

FIGURE 4.1
The Decision Tree for Paul's Problem

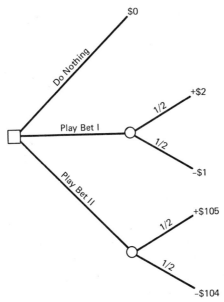

In spite of the fact that the expected value analysis of this problem reveals that the bets are of the same value, each reader probably has a preference for one of the two bets. For instance, in surveys of his classes the author has found that the great majority of students prefer Bet I to Bet II. Bet I represents a little recreational gambling, while a Bet II loss might prevent a student from being able to eat this month. Other people, of course, prefer Bet II to Bet I, because they feel that such a small gamble as the one represented by Bet I would not present sufficient challenge to them. The major point is not which bet anyone would choose, but that one bet would be chosen by most people in preference to the other.

The fact that most people have a preference for either Bet I or Bet II

FIGURE 4.2
The Analysis of Paul's Decision Tree

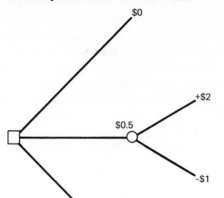

means that the expected value criterion is not rich enough to capture all of the essence of realistic decision problems. Hence the paradox described in the title of this section—two actions with equal expected values yet unequal desirabilities. The next section of this chapter will be devoted to describing utility theory, and how it can be used to capture the true richness of a decision problem.

Before utility theory is discussed, however, we should consider another approach to solving the paradox presented above. One that captures some of the richness of the true problem, yet not as much as the utility theory approach we will discuss later, is to consider *both* the expected value and the variance of the payoffs in making a choice between actions. For example, in Paul's problem we find that the variances of payoffs for the two bets are:

$$\text{Var (Bet I)} = \tfrac{1}{2}(2 - 0.5)^2 + \tfrac{1}{2}(-1 - 0.5)^2 = 2.25;$$
$$\text{Var (Bet II)} = \tfrac{1}{2}(105 - 0.5)^2 + \tfrac{1}{2}(-104 - 0.5)^2 = 10{,}920.25.$$

In this case, therefore, even though the expected values of the two bets are equal, the variances are significantly different, and can be used to choose between the alternatives.

Thus, one alternative to only using expected value as a decision criterion is to use a combination of expected value and variance. For the majority who prefer Bet I to Bet II, the lower variance of Bet I would signal that it is a better choice. Furthermore, if these people were considering two actions with different expected values but equal variances, they would prefer the action with the best expected value.

This idea of using both expected values and variances in decision problems has been used in several applications. Notable among these is the theory of portfolio choice in finance,[1] where this concept has been used extensively. It has also been proposed as a method for deciding whether to launch a new product.[2] The drawback of this approach is that there is no distinct way of choosing between certain pairs of actions. For instance, suppose the decision maker is faced with a choice between two actions whose characteristics are:

Action	Expected Value	Variance
A	50	10
B	75	20

Which action should he choose? Action A has the preferred variance, but action B has the preferred expected value. This is the problem of using a joint criterion such as expected value-variance. While schemes have been proposed to allow a decision maker to resolve such conflicts, it can be shown[3] that using only two measures to describe the uncertainty of the payoffs is not as good as using the utility theory, which is discussed next.

4.2   UTILITY THEORY

Utility theory is designed to take into account the (relative) *magnitude* of payoffs in decision problems, as well as their expected value. This section will describe how to establish and use utilities. As with many other parts of this book, we use an example to illustrate the technique.[4]

Hilbert (Hil) Crouse, the brilliant young scientist, manager of Airless Packs, Inc., is trying to make a major policy decision for his company. Several years ago, Hil developed a way of keeping food fresher by packaging it in pure nitrogen, rather than in air, which is a mixture

---

[1] W. F. Sharp, *Portfolio Theory and Capital Market Theory* (McGraw Hill, 1970), and Keith V. Smith, *Portfolio Management* (Holt, Rinehart & Winston, 1970).

[2] L. S. Simon, and M. Freimer, *Analytical Marketing* (Harcourt, Brace, and World, 1970), pp. 80–90.

[3] Karl H. Borch, *The Economics of Uncertainty* (Princeton University Press, 1968).

[4] Apologies and thanks to my good friend, D.C., for this example.

of nitrogen and oxygen. The reactive agent in air, as far as food is concerned, is the oxygen, so by packaging the food in pure nitrogen, the preservation period is much longer. Over the years since his original development in this area, Hil's company has been growing slowly because his method represents a radical innovation in the food packaging business, and there have been very few companies that have been willing to take the initial risk of using Hil's packaging method. The idea is just starting to catch on, and Hil feels that the future of his company is very bright. In the past Hil has been involved in the development of appropriate containers for the food products packaged in pure nitrogen, and in providing technical expertise to the companies that have been using his idea. He feels now, however, that he should expand the company. There are two basic ways in which he can do this. In the past he has been relying upon other companies to produce his nitrogen for him. The nitrogen he has been buying is actually purer than it need be, and he is considering hiring a group into his company that will be concerned with designing on site nitrogen development plants wherever they are needed. This will provide adequately pure nitrogen at about $\frac{2}{3}$ the cost of the current supplies. As a result of doing this Hil feels his ability to meet the needs of the very large food companies will be much greater. The other option open to Hil is to engage in another form of vertical integration, which is designing the packaging machines for Airless Packs. In the past Hil has had to go into each particular company who wanted his services, and modify the company's current packaging machine to do the additional task of inserting nitrogen into the package. Hil feels that if he had a packaging machine development group within his company, the company would be able to grow much faster. The actions open to Hil are thus:

A_1: Do nothing, i.e., continue the current method of doing business,
A_2: Hire a nitrogen development group only;
A_3: Hire a packaging machine development group only;
A_4: Hire both a packaging and a nitrogen development group.

The payoffs that will accrue from each of these actions depend upon the state of the economy within the next five years, and also upon the rate of growth of Hil's idea within the food industry. In addition, of course, there is considerable downside risk in any of the last three actions. If Hil invests in the development of any of these groups, and the company's growth does not materialize, Hil's company could be in serious financial difficulties. After considerable deliberation Hil feels that the combination of economic and company growth conditions can be categorized in three different states, which Hil (quite arbitrarily) describes as "Good," "Indifferent," and "Bad." Furthermore, the resultant payoffs to the company from the various event-action combinations are given in the following table,

Events \ Actions	A_1	A_2	A_3	A_4
Good	+30	+100	+150	+450
Indifferent	+2	+20	0	+50
Bad	−10	−50	−80	−150

where all figures are in thousands of dollars. Hil feels that the probabilities of the events, Good, Indifferent, and Bad, are 0.3, 0.5, and 0.2, respectively. Hil also knows that the payoffs in the above table represent significant amounts of money to his company, and he has decided that an expected value approach is *not* an appropriate way to solve this problem.

Hil's problem can be solved within the framework of the utility theory technique. Presumably, one of the reasons Hil is unwilling to use the expected value criterion is that he knows that some of the payoffs (e.g., the loss of $150,000 under the Bad-$A_4$ pair), would jeopardize the future of his company. Therefore, Hil cannot make this decision divorced from the other, broader aspects of survival for his business. However, if Hil were to add all of the other aspects of his business decision making to this problem, the total problem would become horrendously complicated, and undoubtedly beyond the realm of solution. As an alternative we propose the theory of utility. It will serve to separate this decision problem from the rest of Hil's business decisions, while still accounting for the seriousness of a loss of $150,000.

4.2.1 The Concept of an Equivalent Lottery Ticket

In order to analyze Hil's problem we need to replace each payoff with a lottery ticket. The lottery ticket for each payoff will be selected so that its value (to Hil) will be *exactly* the same as the value of the payoff. Each lottery ticket will have two payoffs—one with good consequences (called W) and one with bad consequences (called L)—and a stated probability, π, of winning the "good" payoff. Figure 4.3 depicts such a lottery ticket. Each lottery ticket will have a specified value of π, and, for any single problem, the values of W and L will be assumed to be the same for all tickets.

For Hil's problem we will choose W to be a gain of $450,000, and L to represent the payment (loss) of $150,000. For most of the problems in this book the quantities W and L will be payments, but there is absolutely no requirement that they be payments, or even be numerical

FIGURE 4.3
The Two Faces of a Lottery Ticket

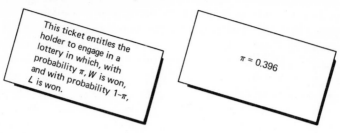

in value. For instance, W might be a pair of season's tickets to the Los
Angeles Rams games, and L might be a year's worth of washing dishes
at your house.

The only requirement of the values of W and L is that they encompass the values of all the payoffs in the problem. Since we will be asking
Hil to select a lottery ticket equivalent to every payoff he faces, we
need to be able to provide reasonable alternatives to all payoffs. As an
example of a set of lottery tickets that would *not* satisfy this property,
suppose we approached Hil with tickets for which $W = \$100,000$ and
$L = -\$150,000$. He would not be willing to trade his potential
$\$450,000$ for *any* lottery ticket, even one in which the probability of
winning W was 1.0 ($\pi = 1.0$), because it would be like trading
$\$450,000$ for $\$100,000$.

4.2.2   Use of Equivalent Lottery Tickets

Suppose, then, we are offering Hil a complete range of lottery tickets
(all values of π from 0.0 to 1.0) each of whose W value is $\$450,000$,
and whose L value is $-\$150,000$. In order to use utility theory Hil
must be willing to pick a lottery ticket exactly equivalent to each payoff.
Clearly he will pick the lottery ticket with $\pi = 1.0$ as equivalent to the
payoff of $\$450,000$, and the lottery ticket with $\pi = 0.0$ as equivalent
to the payoff of $-\$150,000$. But what about the other payoffs for the
problem? What lottery ticket (value of π) will Hil choose as being
equal to $\$50,000$?

There is no theory that will tell us what choices Hil will make.
Utility theory is subjective and temporal. For example, the reader would
probably choose a different lottery ticket from the one Hil would
choose for this $\$50,000$ payoff. Furthermore, if Hil is faced with a
similar decision problem five years hence he could easily choose a
different lottery ticket for the $\$50,000$ at that time than the one he
chooses today. This difference would not be due to any inherent difference in the problem, but simply that Hil has a different attitude (about

the $50,000) at that time from the attitude he has now. Therefore, utility curves (which are discussed below) will have to be individually developed at the time of their use by the appropriate decision maker.[5]

Assuming that Hil must make his decision now, we will develop his utility curve. In order to do that we must exchange each distinct payoff in Hil's payoff table for an equivalent lottery ticket. As an example, Hil needs to select a lottery ticket he feels is equivalent to the $50,000 payoff we have been discussing. Suppose, after careful consideration, he chooses a lottery ticket with $\pi = 0.494$ as being equivalent to $50,000. Similarly, we will suppose he chooses (a lottery ticket with) $\pi = 0.29$ as being equivalent to $-$50,000, and $\pi = 0.657$ as being equivalent to $150,000. Using these, and the endpoints discussed above, we now have the partial list of equivalent lottery ticket values given in Table 4.1.

TABLE 4.1
Some of Hil's Payoffs and their Equivalent Basic Lottery Tickets (payoffs expressed in thousands of dollars)

Payoff	−150	−50	50	150	450
π of an equivalent Lottery Ticket........	0	0.29	0.494	0.657	1.0

There are two ways to obtain the π values equivalent to the other payoffs in Hil's table. One is the obvious method of simply asking Hil to select seven more lottery tickets. The second method, however, is easier, and provides us with a visual representation of utility, which will be useful in subsequent discussions. The essence of this second method is to develop a curve from which the π value equivalent to any payoff in the range between $-$150,000 and $450,000 can be obtained.

In order to draw Hil's utility curve, the values of π equivalent to two more payoffs in the range from $-$150,000 to $450,000 will be helpful. To provide an even spacing of points from which the curve can be drawn, we will determine equivalent π values for payoffs of $250,000 and $350,000. Suppose Hil chooses π values of 0.795 and 0.91 for these payoffs.

Once the π values for these evenly spaced payoffs are determined, a utility curve can be drawn. The payoff-π pairs developed above were used to draw the curve shown in Figure 4.4. This curve is called a utility curve. Once we have this curve, we can use it to obtain the π-value equivalent to any payoff within the appropriate range.

---

[5] Special problems regarding utility are encountered when the outcome affects a group of people (e.g., the public or the stockholders of a company) rather than a single individual. Although methods exist for treating these situations, we will not discuss them in this text.

FIGURE 4.4
The Graph of Payoffs Versus Equivalent Lottery Probilities for Hil's Problem

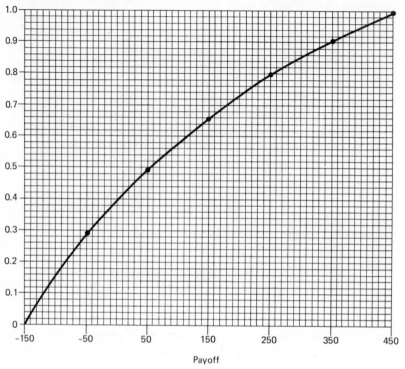

Equivalent Probability
of Basic Reference Lottery Ticket

Payoff

Given this utility curve, the π values for lottery tickets equivalent to the other payoffs in Hil's problem can be obtained. For instance, the π value corresponding to a payoff of $-\$80,000$ is 0.215. Using this same technique for the other payoffs results in the numbers in Table 4.2.

TABLE 4.2
Equivalent Probabilities for the Remaining Payoffs in Hil's Problem

Payoffs	−80	−10	0	2	20	30	100
Equivalent Probabilities, π	0.215	0.380	0.4	0.404	0.440	0.460	0.580

How can Hil use these equivalent lottery tickets? This question is best answered by considering Hil's decision tree, depicted in Figure

4.5. Since each lottery ticket was selected as exactly equivalent to some payoff in Hil's problem, *Hil should be indifferent between his original problem, whose tree is shown in Figure 4.5, and a similar problem with equivalent lottery tickets replacing the payoffs.* Furthermore, any lottery

FIGURE 4.5
The Original Decision Tree for Hil's Problem (in thousands of dollars)

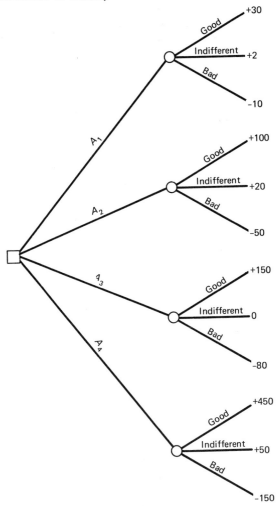

ticket can be expressed in decision tree notation as a chance node. For example, Hil's lottery ticket with $\pi = 0.46$ (equivalent to a payoff of $30,000) can be depicted as the following chance node:

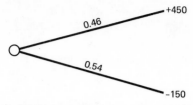

where, as in Figure 4.5, the payoffs are expressed in thousands of dollars.

Using these two notions, we can depict a new decision tree for Hil *which is equivalent to his original tree of Figure 4.5.* This is shown in Figure 4.6. This tree can be analyzed by reducing the sequential chance node structure. This is demonstrated below. We should point out, however, that the seemingly obvious way to reduce the tree—using expected values—has been ruled out by Hil as being inappropriate. Therefore, another method must be used to effect a decision.

Consider the set of chance nodes associated with Hil's first action, A_1. These, along with their payoffs and probabilities, are depicted below. Our goal in this analysis is to develop a single two-forked chance

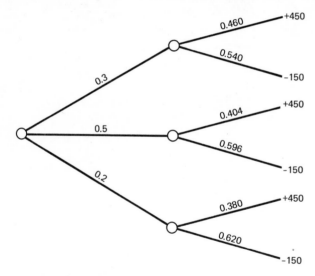

node whose payoffs are $450,000 and −$150,000, and whose probabilities represent the overall probabilities of achieving each of these outcomes.

What is the composite probability that Hil will receive $450,000 given the above branch of the tree? It is probably easiest to answer this question by finding the answer to an equivalent problem:

There are three jars, exactly alike in appearance, each with 1,000 marbles in it. The marbles in the jars are black and white and each

FIGURE 4.6
Hil's Expanded Decision Tree—Replacing Payoffs with
Equivalent Lotteries

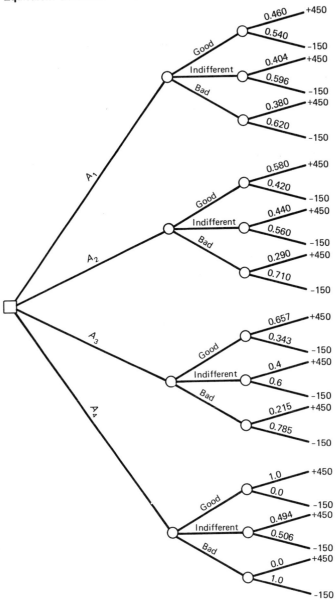

jar varies from the others in its relative composition of black and white marbles. White marbles correspond to winning $450,000, and black marbles correspond to losing $150,000. The composition of the jars is:

Jar I: 460 white marbles, 540 black marbles;
Jar II: 404 white marbles, 596 black marbles;
Jar III: 380 white marbles, 620 black marbles.

The following scheme is used in picking a marble. First, a random mechanism that selects Jar I 30 percent of the time, Jar II 50 percent of the time, and Jar III 20 percent of the time is utilized. Then a single marble is randomly selected from the jar that is picked.

If we can determine the overall probability of selecting a white marble using this scheme, we will also have determined the probability of Hil's receiving $450,000 in the dual chance fork shown above.

In Chapter 2 the technique called partitioning was developed. It can be used to advantage here to determine the probability of obtaining a white marble. A white marble can come from any of the three jars, and drawing a white marble from Jar I specifically excludes drawing it from Jars II and III. Therefore, we can write

$$P(\text{White}) = P(\text{White and Jar I}) + P(\text{White and Jar II}) + P(\text{White and Jar III}).$$

Furthermore, the joint probabilities on the right-hand side of the above equation can be rewritten as the product of a conditional probability times an unconditional probability. For example:

$$P(\text{White and Jar I}) = P(\text{White}|\text{Jar I})P(\text{Jar I}).$$

Using this technique for all three joint probabilities we have

$$P(\text{White}) = P(\text{White}|\text{Jar I})P(\text{Jar I}) + P(\text{White}|\text{Jar II})P(\text{Jar II}) + P(\text{White}|\text{Jar III})P(\text{Jar III}).$$

This expression can be used to calculate the overall probability of drawing a white marble, since we have numbers for all the quantities on the right-hand side of the expression. In particular, since there are 460 white marbles in Jar I,

$$P(\text{White}|\text{Jar I}) = \frac{460}{1,000} = 0.460,$$

and, since Jar I is selected 30 percent of the time,

$$P(\text{Jar I}) = 0.30.$$

The values for the other probabilities can be derived in a similar fashion. The net result is that

$$P(\text{White}) = 0.460 \times 0.3 + 0.404 \times 0.5 + 0.380 \times 0.2$$
$$= 0.416.$$

Thus, the overall probability of drawing a white marble (and the overall probability of winning $450,000) is 0.416. Since the only other event that can occur in the jars example is drawing a black marble, we know that

$$P(\text{Black}) = 1 - P(\text{White})$$
$$= 1 - 0.416$$
$$= 0.584.$$

(This result could also have been obtained by using a partitioning formula.)

Since the jars example is equivalent to the portion of the decision tree we were originally working with, the net effect of this effort has been to reduce the A_1 chance nodes

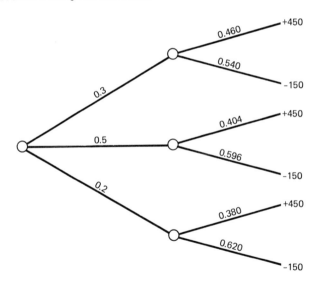

to the much simpler chance process

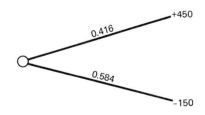

It is important that the reader thoroughly understand how this has happened. Its development is crucial to the development of utility theory, and the reader is urged to reread this section if the process by which the decision tree is simplified is not clear.

The simplified chance node that was developed above has no meaning when compared to the other alternatives open to Hil. In order to exploit this property the remaining sequential chance nodes must be reduced in the same way. The reduction technique will be demonstrated in a more straightforward way for the branch associated with A_2 below. Given these two examples it will then be assumed the reader is capable of performing the remaining reductions on his own.

For action A_2 the sequential chance nodes are:

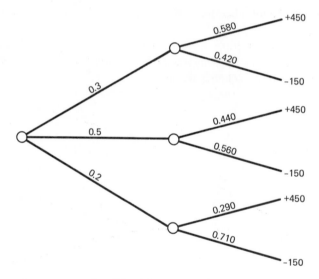

and we again want to simplify this part of the tree to a single chance fork, two outcome situation. This can be accomplished by developing the composite probability of winning $450,000.

If we let W represent the event of winning $450,000 and L represent losing $150,000, then the partitioning formula is

$$P(W) = P(W|G)P(G) + P(W|I)P(I) + P(W|B)P(B)$$

where G, I, and B are the three events Hil faces—good, indifferent, and bad. Given this formula the probability of winning $450,000 is

$$P(W) = 0.580 \times 0.3 + 0.440 \times 0.5 + 0.290 \times 0.2$$
$$= 0.452.$$

Then, using complementarity:

$$P(L) = 1 - P(W) = 1 - 0.452 = 0.548.$$

With these numbers we can write out the reduction of the above portion of Hil's tree. It is

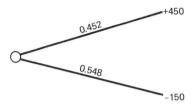

Calculations for the two branches associated with actions A_3 and A_4 can be reduced in a similar manner. The resulting complete tree is shown in Figure 4.7. This reduced tree can be used by Hil to make a

FIGURE 4.7
The Reduced Decision Tree for Hil's Problem

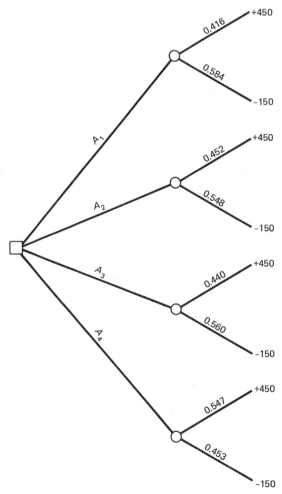

decision. However, it is important to note that expected value cannot be used to analyze the tree at this stage. Hil has rejected the principle of using expected value in this case, so some other procedure must be used instead.

The procedure we shall use to choose an action for this problem is deceptively simple. Notice that each chance fork has the same set of payoffs. Therefore, the best action is the one that has the highest probability of the good payoff (winning $450,000 in this case). Of the four actions available to Hil, A_4 (hire both a packaging and a nitrogen development group) is the best. The potentially positive payoffs resulting from this option outweigh (using Hil's utility curve) the negative payoffs.

4.2.3   A Summary of the Utility Theory (Lottery Ticket) Approach

Many pages have been spent developing the utility theory approach. It is important to summarize at this point so that the reader will have an idea of the scope and requirements of utility theory.

We began by assuming that the consequences of the actions being considered were serious enough so that the decision maker could not use expected value as a criterion for making his decision. In order to circumvent this problem a set of lottery tickets were proposed. These lottery tickets have payoffs that encompass the range of payoffs for the problem being considered and are available with all different probabilities for the payoffs. The key aspect of utility theory then comes in. A lottery ticket the decision maker feels is equivalent is chosen to replace *each* payoff in the problem. These equivalent lotteries can either be each selected individually, or by first establishing a utility curve. Thus, the decision maker has "traded in" his original problem on a new one he feels is equivalent in every aspect. The decision tree corresponding to this new problem is then reduced, so that the decision maker is left with a choice between several chance outcomes. Each of these chance outcomes has the same set of (two) payoffs, however, so the choice becomes the simple one of selecting the action with the highest probability of winning.

Therefore, ignoring the expected value criterion completely, we have still been able to develop a method for solving a decision problem. The only assumption throughout is that the decision maker is willing to accept risk. A person who is not willing to accept risk would not trade the "sure" outcomes of a decision problem for the risky lotteries. Given that a person is willing to make such trade offs, however, a method is available to solve his decision problem without any appeal to or use of the expected value criterion.

The interesting bridge from utility theory back to expected value is contained in the next section. There we will find that the expected value criterion can be used even in problems such as Hil's. This concept is very important because, as we stated in Chapter 3, the expected value criterion forms the basis of the decision making framework in the remainder of this book. What we will find in the next section is that it applies to a wide range of problems that, because of some of the objections raised at the beginning of this chapter, could not otherwise be handled by decision theory.

4.3 BACK TO EXPECTED VALUE AGAIN

In this section we will obtain closure on the concept of utility, both from a conceptual point of view, and from a mechanical point of view with regard to solving decision theory problems. We will find that the utility curve developed in the previous section, or a special variant of that curve, will provide a method for again using expected values to analyze decision problems, *while at the same time taking into account the fact that decision makers react differently to large versus small gains or losses.* Quite simply, this is achieved by first making the transformation from payoffs to equivalent bets, as we did before, and then conducting an expected value analysis on the resulting decision tree. The important result we obtain, of course, is that the analysis we have discussed previously and this new combination technique will always produce an identical ordering of the actions.

There are several different mechanical means of accomplishing what we have outlined above. We shall start by discussing the technique that seems most straightforward, and then get into the (seemingly) more esoteric techniques. We will find, however, when we discuss the relationship between utility and money, that all the ideas we have been using are really variants of the same thing.

The most straightforward way to consider solving a problem in which utilities must be taken into account is to start with a tree in which the normal payoffs have been replaced by equivalent basic lotteries, such as the diagram of Hil's problem in Figure 4.6, and analyze it using the decision theory techniques we learned in Chapter 3; that is, we calculate the expected value at each chance node, and take the best value at each decision node. For instance, for Figure 4.6 we find that the expected value of the topmost lottery is:

$$0.46 \times 450 + 0.54 \times (-150) = 126,$$

etc., and the tree that results from calculating all the rightmost expected values is given in Figure 4.8. Proceeding in the same manner, we then take the expected values of the next chance nodes, and the result of these calculations is illustrated in Figure 4.9.

FIGURE 4.8
The First Expected Value Reduction of the Decision
Tree Given in Figure 4.6

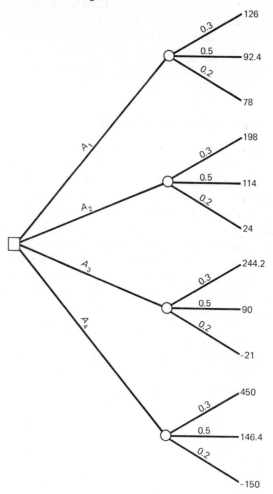

Now that we have performed this strange combination of equivalent lottery and expected value analysis, it is useful to compare Figure 4.9 and 4.7. (Figure 4.7 was obtained by applying the equivalent lottery analysis only.) The important thing you should notice when you compare these two diagrams is that the best action is the same for both trees. Furthermore, even the ordering of the actions is the same. That is, in both trees A_4 is the best action, A_2 is the next best action, A_3 is the third best action, and A_1 is the worst action. That this is true is not a coincidence, nor is it a result specific to this problem. The two seem-

FIGURE 4.9
A Final Reduction of the Decision Tree in
Figure 4.6

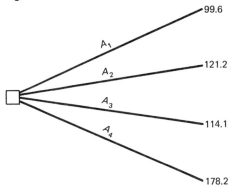

ingly different methods of analysis are really variants of the same process, and will yield the same best action (and ranking of actions) for all problems.

The fact that the two techniques we have discussed are equivalent to one another is important from a mechanical point of view. Instead of imposing a whole new structure of analysis on decision theory problems, we now have a method for analyzing these problems using essentially the same format as was used in Chapter 3, and which will be used throughout the remainder of this book. The only additional step that must be taken is that the original payoffs must be replaced with equivalent lotteries, and the first step becomes that of calculating the expected value of the lottery.

We are not quite finished, however. There is one additional shortcut that can be taken in this analysis, and which will again yield the same ordering of actions. In this case we replace the original payoffs with *the probabilities of winning the lottery*. Thus, if we were using this method we would take Hil's original decision tree, given in Figure 4.5, and replace the payoffs with their corresponding *probabilities* of winning the lottery. The resulting decision tree is illustrated in Figure 4.10. This seems like a very strange idea, but we will find it works quite well.

Now, just as in the previous method, we will take the expected values of the various chance nodes. These expected values have absolutely no physical or economic relationship to the original payoff values, but we will again find that the relative values are important. The reduced tree that contains these expected values is shown in Figure 4.11. Notice that, just as in the other two types of analysis that were applied to Hil's problem, A_4 is the best action, and the other three actions are ranked in the order: A_2, A_3, and A_1.

FIGURE 4.10
Hil's Decision Tree with the Probabilities of Winning the Lottery Replacing the Payoffs

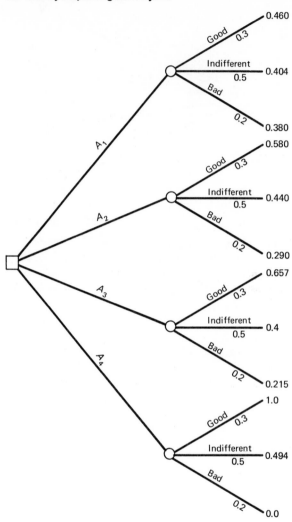

There are three important points that can be drawn from this analysis. First, we can state that this technique will always give the same best action and the same rank ordering of the actions as the more complicated technique we studied first in Section 4.2.2. Second, there are important mechanical implications of using this simpler technique. Instead of replacing the payoffs of any problem with some *lottery,* we can merely replace them with a single value. Therefore, the expected value criterion can be applied to problems in which utility must be included! Except for needing to originally establish the utility function,

FIGURE 4.11
The Reduction (by Taking Expected
Values) of the Decision Tree of Figure 4.10

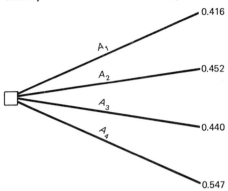

and transform the payoffs into equivalent probabilities, the rest of the analysis which we learned in Chapter 3 proceeds as before, because we are replacing one number (the payoff) with another number (the equivalent probability).

The third point is illustrated by comparing the values obtained from reducing the original decision problem using lotteries and this manufactured problem in which the payoffs are replaced with the probabilities of winning the lotteries. The results of these two analyses are contained in Figures 4.7 and 4.11. Notice that the expected values at the action branches of Figure 4.11 are the same as the probabilities of winning the lotteries in Figure 4.7. How can this happen? The Figure 4.7 probabilities were calculated using the joint and conditional probability formulas, while the expected values in Figure 4.11 were obtained using the expected value formula. While this is true, a close comparison will reveal that the calculations are in fact identical. Therefore, the more complicated procedure which we used in the reduction of the original decision tree was nothing more than a different way to obtain expected values. Furthermore, notice that the complicated lottery analysis of section 4.2.2 does not have to be used in order to invoke the concepts of utility. All that must be done is to replace the original payoffs of any problem with their equivalent probabilities of winning a lottery.

4.4 THE UTILITY OF MONEY CURVE

We want to discuss next why the intermediate method for solving utility problems (that of replacing payoffs with a lottery and then using expected values) is equivalent to the other two methods discussed in this chapter. The reason, which is demonstrated below, is because the utility curve of Figure 4.4 can be replaced with any similar curve, and one such replacement is the one used in this intermediate method. We shall also see that another such transformation will result in a curve we call the "utility of money" curve, and it is this curve that is often used to replace payoffs in any decision theory problem.

The new curves equivalent to the utility curve of Figure 4.4 are all derived by taking some *positive linear transformation* of that curve. In order to understand the concept of a linear transformation, consider the relationship between the probability of winning a lottery and the expected payoff of that lottery. The expected value of Hil's lottery is

$$E(\text{lottery}) = 450 \times P(\text{Win}) + (-150) \times P(\text{Loss}).$$

However, since the probabilities must add to one, we have:

$$P(\text{Loss}) = 1 - P(\text{Win}),$$

and when this is substituted into the expected value expression the result is

$$E(\text{lottery}) = 450 \times P(\text{Win}) + (-150) \times [1 - P(\text{Win})]$$
$$= 600 \times P(\text{Win}) - 150.$$

The above expression gives $E(\text{lottery})$ as a positive linear transformation of $P(\text{Win})$. A positive linear transformation of some quantity —in this case $P(\text{Win})$—is obtained by multiplying that quantity by a positive number—600 in this case—and then adding or subtracting some other number from the resulting product. (In this case 150 is being subtracted.)

We saw in Section 4.3 that when either $P(\text{Win})$ or $E(\text{lottery})$ was used in place of payoffs, and the resulting tree analyzed in the usual (expected value) manner, the result (that is, the relative ordering of the actions) was the same. The reason that $E(\text{lottery})$ works as well as $P(\text{Win})$ is that $E(\text{lottery})$ can be expressed as a positive linear function of $P(\text{Win})$. Although we will not prove it here, it can be shown that *any* positive linear transformation of $P(\text{Win})$ will work as well in giving the same ordering to the actions.

Let's take an example of this concept. Suppose we let some new variable, say u, be a positive linear transformation of $P(\text{Win})$. Specifically, let

$$u = 500 \, P(\text{Win}) - 200.$$

Now we will analyze the decision tree using u values in place of payoffs. There are two ways we can accomplish this. We can either first determine the values of $P(\text{Win})$ corresponding to each of the problem's payoffs and then use the above equation to translate these $P(\text{Win})$ values into u values, or we can use the above equation in concert with a graph like Figure 4.4 to develop a new graph that relates the payoff values directly to the u values. We will choose the latter approach, but demonstrate the former while achieving the latter.

To generate the graph given in Figure 4.4, Hil started with a number of equivalent probabilities and payoffs. These quantities are given in Table 4.3. In order to draw a graph relating the values of u to the pay-

TABLE 4.3
Hil's Payoffs and Equivalent Basic Reference Lottery Ticket Probabilities

Payoff..........	−150	−50	50	150	250	350	450
Probability	0	0.29	0.494	0.657	0.795	0.91	1

off values, we must have a set of specific points that relate payoffs to u values. These can be obtained from Table 4.3 by finding the u value that corresponds to each of the payoffs. The way to find these u values is to use the $P(\text{Win})$ value corresponding to each payoff and the function that relates the u values to the $P(\text{Win})$ values. Thus, for a payoff of −150, the $P(\text{Win})$ value is 0.0, and the corresponding u value is:

$$u = 500 \times 0.0 - 200 = -200.$$

Similarly, for a payoff of −50, the $P(\text{Win})$ value is 0.29 and the corresponding u value is:

$$u = \$500 \times 0.29 - 200 = -55.$$

These calculations can be continued in the same manner, and the result is a set of corresponding values between payoff and u. These values are given in Table 4.4. Once these points are obtained they may be used to draw a graph. The graph relating the u values directly to the payoffs is given in Figure 4.12.

Once this graph is obtained, it can be used in place of any of the other quantities—$P(\text{Win})$ or $E(\text{lottery})$—to directly determine the best action. Following the analysis through for Hil's problem, we find that the u values we need in addition to those given in Table 4.4 are listed in Table 4.5, and using these values in combination with the values in

TABLE 4.4
Hil's Payoffs and Equivalent u Values

Payoff	−150	−50	50	150	250	350	450
u Value	−200	−55	47	128.5	197.5	255	300

FIGURE 4.12
Payoffs and Equivalent *u* Values for Hil's Problem

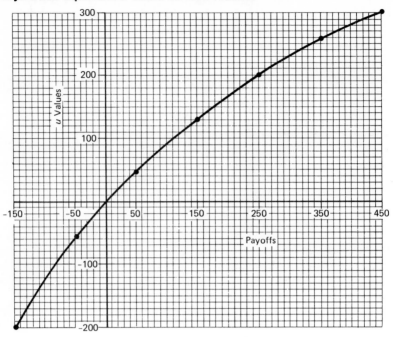

TABLE 4.5
Some of the Payoffs in Hil's Problem and Their Corresponding *u* Values

Payoffs...........	−80	−10	0	2	20	30	100
u Values	−92.5	−10	0	2	20	30	90

Table 4.4 yields the decision tree with *u* values replacing payoffs depicted in Figure 4.13.

Once we have gone through all the work needed to obtain these *u* values, the analysis of the tree proceeds just as when we were using $P(\text{Win})$ or $E(\text{lottery})$ values. That is, we take the expected values at the chance nodes, and the best value at the decision nodes. This analysis for the tree in Figure 4.13 is depicted in Figure 4.14, and you can see that the relative ordering of the actions is the same as when we were using any of the methods previously discussed. As with the other methods, this is not a coincidence of this problem, but a general principle that using *u* values instead of payoffs will yield an ordering of the actions the same as the ordering achieved by replacing the payoffs with the

FIGURE 4.13
Hil's Decision Tree with *u* Values Replacing Payoffs

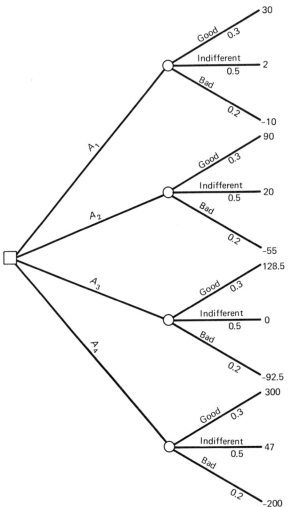

equivalent lottery tickets and performing the analysis without using expected values.

Now that we have performed all the mechanics, let's go back and
pick up all the loose methodological ends. The transformation that was
selected to represent the *u* values was carefully chosen so that the
resulting relationship between the *u* values and the payoffs (Figure
4.12) could represent the utility of money curve. The *u* values represent
the *utility* of various amounts of money (the payoffs) to the decision
maker. That, of course, is why they were named *u* values! Thus, the

FIGURE 4.14
The Result of an Expected Value Analysis
of Hil's Decision Tree When *u* Values Replace Payoffs

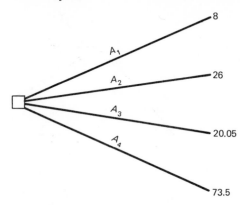

payoffs for any decision problem Hil is facing can, by using the curve, be translated into their corresponding utilities, and the utilities used in any decision problem calculation.

Why bother creating the utility of money curve? It seems one could do just as well by using the equivalent lottery probabilities, and save the additional complication of constructing the utility of money curve. However, there are some inherent advantages to the utility of money curve. The first of these has to do with the fact that usually lurking in the background of any decision theory problem is the option to do nothing and thereby realize neither a gain nor a loss. Because of the way the utility of money curve is constructed, all negative payoffs have negative utilities, and all positive payoffs have positive utilities. (Another way of saying this is to say that the utility of zero dollars is zero.) As a consequence, using the utility of money curve allows the potential option of doing nothing to remain implicit, rather than becoming explicit as it would in other calculations; that is, if analysis is performed on a certain problem and all actions have negative expected utilities, then it is better, if possible, to do nothing and realize a *zero* utility instead! On the other hand, if a decision maker is facing a problem such as Hil's, in which all the actions have a positive expected utility, he knows that any of them are better than not doing anything. Therefore, the coincidence of the zeros on the dollar and utility scales results in our being able to easily classify any action as being worthy or not worthy.

Another aspect of the utility of money function worth mentioning is that for small payoffs (between roughly $50,000 and −$50,000 for Hil's problem) the utility values are the same as the payoff values. It makes sense that this should be the case, since it was on the grounds of the seriousness of the consequences of the payoffs that we developed the concept of utility in the first place. Therefore, for payoffs whose consequences are not serious, it is reasonable that the utilities should be the same as the payoffs.

The one thing we cannot discuss in this book is the method for obtaining the utility function, since the technique requires a knowledge of the rudiments of calculus. We have, of course, discussed how to generate the curve relating the payoffs to the probabilities for the equivalent lotteries. However, the reader cannot generate his own utility of money curve because we have not discussed how to determine the coefficients of the linear transformation from $P(\text{Win})$ to the u values. We can only give the principle of that here, since the mechanics requires an understanding of mathematics beyond the assumed level of this text. For those students who have more mathematics background, Problem 4.12 demonstrates the method. All we can say at this point is that the two concepts used in the generation of the coefficients of the linear transformation associated with u is that the utility of money curve will pass through the origin (zero dollars = zero utility) and that the slope of the function at this point is unity.

4.5 EXPECTED UTILITY VERSUS EXPECTED PAYOFF

The method presented above calculates an expected utility for each action, and then chooses the action with the best expected utility. This method, rather than a similar method using expected payoffs, which is discussed in Chapter 3, is used because the consequences associated with some of the payoffs in a decision problem are too extreme. Since we have two competing methods for analyzing problems, it is important to discuss the conditions under which each is used.

The question really becomes one, then, of determining when the consequences of some of the payoffs are extreme enough to warrant using utility theory. Since using utility theory is more time consuming than merely using expected monetary value, up to what point can expected monetary value be used as a criterion? Unfortunately, there is no good answer to this question. Expected monetary value analysis is as good as (will give the same answers as) expected utility analysis in the range around $0 where utility and monetary amounts are approximately the same. For Hil's problem we have already noted that this occurs in the range of payoffs between —50 and 50. From Table 4.4, the utility of these amounts are —55 and 47, respectively. Furthermore, dollar amounts even closer to zero than these have even more similar utility values, as evidenced by some of the numbers in Table 4.5.

The net result of the monetary and utility values being essentially equal is that the expectations of these two quantities will also be equal.

As an example of this, the expected monetary value of Hil's A_1 is

$$E(A_1) = 30 \times 0.3 + 2 \times 0.5 + (-10) \times 0.2$$
$$= 8,$$

which is *exactly* the expected utility (from Figure 4.14) for that same action! Therefore, actions whose payoffs are in the range in which utility values are approximately the same as monetary values will have the same ordering of desirability for the decision maker. Within this range it makes sense to ignore the utility curve and use expected monetary value as a decision criterion, since it is mechanically easier to use.

However, there is a logical flaw in the preceding development. *The utility curve must be developed to determine in what range it can be ignored!* To avoid this pitfall, expected monetary value is often used *except* when the decision maker refuses to accept the action proposed. Only then is the utility curve developed. As a consequence of this, and because of the relative ease of use of the expected monetary value approach, the remainder of this book deals exclusively with expected monetary value. This practice is not meant to imply, however, that utility theory is not worth using. On the contrary, utility theory allows us to extend decision theory analysis to problems that could not otherwise be solved using this approach. More of this will be discussed below.

In a comparative analysis of expected monetary value with expected utility it is helpful to turn the question around to ask what is implied about the utility curve of a decision maker who is *always* content with expected monetary value. The answer can be quite easily obtained. Let us suppose, for instance, that another decision maker, Dale, is facing Hil's problem. However, Dale feels that the expected monetary value criterion is always acceptable to him. This implies that Dale is indifferent between a sure payoff of some amount (say $5) and a lottery ticket whose expected value is the same amount. Given this, a utility curve can easily be developed for Dale. Suppose he is faced with lottery tickets whose payoffs are $-$150,000 and $450,000, just as Hil was. If he must choose a lottery ticket whose value is equivalent to $50,000, say, then he will choose a lottery ticket whose expected value is $50,000. We previously derived the formula for the expected value of this lottery:

$$E(\text{lottery}) = 600 \, P(\text{Win}) - 150.$$

Since this expected value must be equal to $50,000 in this case, we have (in thousands of dollars)

$$600 \, P(\text{Win}) - 150 = 50,$$

or,

$$P(\text{Win}) = {}^{200}\!/_{600} = \tfrac{1}{3}.$$

Therefore, Dale would choose a lottery ticket with $\pi = \frac{1}{3}$ as equivalent to the \$50,000.

The same analysis applied to other monetary values between -150 and 450 yields the equivalent probabilities given in Table 4.6.

TABLE 4.6
Probabilities for Equivalent Lottery Tickets for Dale

Payoff	-150	-50	50	150	250	350	450
Equivalent Probability	0	$\frac{1}{6}$	$\frac{1}{3}$	$\frac{1}{2}$	$\frac{2}{3}$	$\frac{5}{6}$	1

When these points are plotted, Dale's utility curve (as shown in Figure 4.15) is a straight line. Therefore, *the utility curve of a decision maker who always accepts expected monetary value is a straight line.*

This fact is helpful in two ways. First, it gives an idea of what we are doing when we take a utility curve for a decision maker like Hil and use it in a range where expected monetary value is a good approxi-

FIGURE 4.15
Dale's Utility Curve

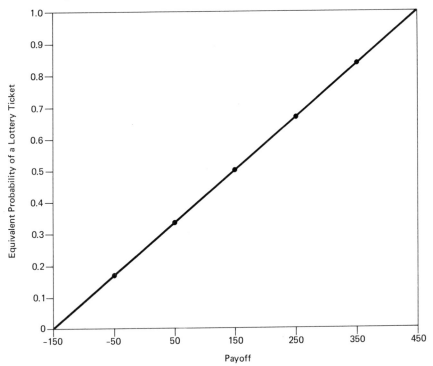

mation to expected utility. In essence, we are saying that the curvilinear utility function for Hil *can be approximated near $0* with a straight line. If this is so, and to the extent that this is so, expected monetary value can be used in place of expected utility.

The second use of the straight line utility function comes in comparing various individuals with regard to their willingness to take risk. As we have already seen, Hil would worry about the big money payoffs $450,000 and —$150,000, while Dale would be willing to accept an expected monetary value criterion throughout this problem. In decision theory we classify all decision makers relative to a person like Dale. Relative to him, since Hil worries about the consequences of the big payoffs, we call him *risk averse*. On the other side, a person who would prefer a lottery ticket to a payoff with the same value as the expected value of the lottery ticket is called *risk prone*.

These three positions (plus one additional one) are indicated in Figure 4.16. The utility curve of the risk averse individual (Hil) lies above the utility curve for Dale, while the utility curve for the risk prone individual lies below Dale's. Furthermore, a graph like this is helpful to

FIGURE 4.16
Utility Curves for a Number of Individuals

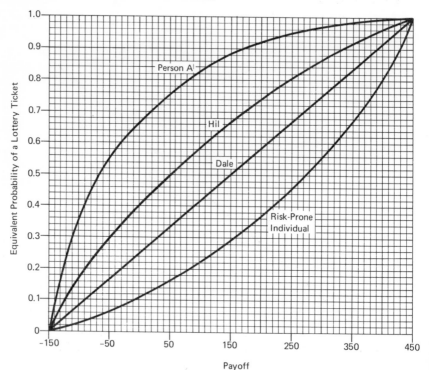

determine the *degree* of risk averseness or risk proneness. The fourth curve in the figure shows a person (Person *A*) who is even more risk averse than Hil.

4.6 OTHER ASPECTS OF UTILITY

4.6.1 Ordinal and Cardinal Utility

The utility theory discussed in this chapter is not, in the field of economics, the only concept of utility that has been proposed. The type of utility discussed in this chapter is known in the parlance of economists as *cardinal utility*. Economists also describe utility in a purely relational way, which is called *ordinal utility*. Ordinal utility determines which of two quantities, or bundles of goods, is preferred to the other. Thus, ordinal utility only considers pairwise relationships between bundles of goods. On the other hand, cardinal utility expresses not only that bundle *A* is preferred to bundle *B*, but by how much. For instance, if the (cardinal) utility of bundle A is 150, while the utility of bundle B is 15, then bundle A has 135 more units of utility than bundle B. Thus, cardinal utilities are expressed in numbers, and these numbers are expected to mean something in relation to one another.

4.6.2 Utility for Other Goods and Multiple Outcomes

Although we have only discussed developing utility curves for monetary amounts, it should be clear to the reader that the same technique can be applied to any other physical or metaphysical good. For instance, utility functions for oranges, for ideas, for religious experiences, etc., could also be developed. Furthermore, in theory, and to some extent in practice, it is possible to develop utility functions for groups of goods rather than a single good. Decision makers frequently face problems in which each event-action pair results in several different outcomes (such as profit, labor utilization, pollution potential, etc.) and the resulting decision problem becomes extremely complicated. If, however, the decision maker could know how to generate a utility function that combined these several attributes into a single utility value, then all the techniques we have been discussing thus far could be applied to this more complicated problem. Significant progress is being made in the development of multiple outcome utility functions, and probably within five years these developments will be widely available to managers. Such development makes decision theory appropriate to solve an even larger class of problems, and makes what you are studying in this book even more relevant.

4.7 SUMMARY AND PROGNOSIS

In this chapter the concept of utility theory has been developed. The basic concept involves replacing payoffs of significant consequence with lotteries the decision maker feels are equivalent. Furthermore, through an appropriate linear transformation, a curve can be developed for the utility of dollar amounts. These developments are important from both a mechanical and a conceptual standpoint. Mechanically, the *u* versus $ curve allows one to continue to use expected values for all decision making, with the important caveat that if the dollar amounts are significant enough they must be replaced with utilities.

The examples discussed in subsequent chapters of this book deal with dollar amounts only. However, it is important for the reader to keep in mind that this is only for convenience. Problems with larger payoffs, and thus to which utility theory must be applied, could just as well be discussed. However, the development of a utility curve for each problem is cumbersome, so the subsequent discussion will be limited to dollar amounts.

Finally, in addition to significant problems with single outcomes, we saw in Section 4.6.2 that decision theory will soon be able to be applied to significant multiple outcome problems. This makes the scope of decision theory problem solving very large, and would include many complex problems. For example, in economics there is an empirical relationship called the Phillips curve, which relates the observed level of unemployment to the inflation rate.[6] A public policy maker, in determining economic policy, must take into account the multiple effects on the economy of trying to manipulate one or the other of these two factors. Another example from the public policy area is the manifold outcomes involved in bringing a major city's expenditures in line with its revenues. The recent financial crisis in New York City is a good example of this kind of problem.

In short, the prognosis for decision theory is excellent. Its ability to solve more complex problems is being extended every day. It would be well for the student to keep this in mind as he reads the remainder of this text. The examples and problems are constructed to allow the student to become familiar with the techniques and concepts of decision theory. In order to do this the complexity and magnitude of the outcomes in the problems are kept to a minimum.

PROBLEMS

1. If Hil had been willing to accept an expected monetary value criterion, show that his choice ranking of actions would be the same as that de-

---

[6] Although recent observations (1973, 1974, 1975) tend to fall off the curve.

rived using utility theory. Since this is the case, why did he bother using utility theory?

2. Determine the relative ranking of the four actions of Hil's problem for
    a. The risk prone individual whose utility curve is given in Figure 4.16.
    b. Person A, whose utility curve is given in Figure 4.16.

3. Calculate the variance of the (monetary) payoffs for each action in Hil's problem. Using these and the expected monetary values calculated in Problem 1, which actions can be eliminated because they are decidedly inferior? Why? Which actions cannot be eliminated from further consideration? Why?

4. Any actions that were eliminated as a result of calculating the variances in Problem 3 imply an ordering of desirability of actions. Is the implicit ordering consistent with the orderings of actions obtained for the risk prone individual and for person A in Problem 2? Why or why not?

5. Choose any positive linear transformation, apply it to Hil's utility curve, and show that the result is the same ordering of actions, A_4, A_2, A_3, A_1.

6. Using the linear transformation,

    $$\ell = -50 \, P(\text{Win}) + 10,$$

    calculate the expected ℓ values for each of Hil's actions. Based on your results, describe why only *positive* linear transformations of $P(\text{Win})$ were considered in Section 4.4.

7. What would the utility of money curve be for Dale? What are the values of a and b for Dale in the positive linear transformation of $P(\text{Win})$ to utility:

    $$u = a \, P(\text{Win}) + b$$

8. I. Emma Switch is the founder and sole owner of INTCIRC, Inc., a company that manufactures integrated circuits on a tiny chip of material for use in hand-held calculators and microcomputers. INTCIRC currently manufactures these chips and markets their products to the various producers of hand-held calculators and microcomputers. However, a new development from INTCIRC's developmental laboratory has made Emma reconsider her company's position in the market.

    In the past certain mathematical operations, such as finding the value of e (a mathematical constant) raised to a power, or the sine of an angle, were available on hand-held calculators and microcomputers only indirectly through numerical approximations. However, INTCIRC has discovered a way to employ the wave properties of electricity to do these types of calculations directly. Therefore, these calculations can be introduced into a machine by adding just one chip instead of the complicated calculation and memory circuit currently being used.

As a result of this development Emma is considering expanding her company into the calculator sales business. She feels that this new chip is revolutionary enough to give INTCIRC's hand-held calculators (if they are produced) a distinct marketing advantage. On the other hand, of course, such an expansion of INTCIRC is very costly, and if the market for hand-held calculators should drop precipitously, Emma's company could lose a lot of money.

There is also an intermediate strategy available to INTCIRC. The company can develop a prototype calculator using its new circuit. This prototype could then be used as a sales-generating device when the chip is being marketed to calculator and microcomputer manufacturers. Thus, the actions available to Emma are:

A_1: Do nothing (i.e., do not market the newly developed chip).

A_2: Market the newly developed chip in the same manner as INTCIRC's other chips.

A_3: Develop a prototype calculator as a marketing device and market the new chip in the same manner as the other chips.

A_4: Expand INTCIRC into the hand-held calculator business.

The costs for these four actions vary. In discussions with her executive committee Emma has determined that the best guesses of these are:

Actions	A_1	A_2	A_3	A_4
Cost of Implementation	0	$65,000	$100,000	$285,000

The profits also vary, and they vary with the future market for hand-held calculators and microcomputers. After much analysis, INTCIRC's marketing department has proposed the following incomes for three potential rates of growth in the integrated chip market:

Rate of Growth	Actions			
	A_1	A_2	A_3	A_4
+10%	0	$140,000	$225,000	$710,000
+2%	0	$ 90,000	$175,000	$210,000
−3%	0	0	0	$145,000

Furthermore, the marketing department has estimated that the chances of +10%, +2%, and −3% growth rates are 0.15, 0.6, and 0.25 respectively. The decision now facing Emma is which action to choose.

a. Which action should Emma choose if she is willing to maximize expected monetary value?

b. If Emma has a utility curve like person A in Figure 4.16, which action will she prefer?

   c. If Emma has the same utility curve as Hil Crouse, which action will she prefer?

9. U. Betyur Liif, a foreign student at UCLA, wants to develop a utility function for money in the range of −$200 to +$300. In order to do so, he has developed the following table:

Payoff....	−200	−150	−100	0	100	200	300
π	0	0.46	0.67	0.85	0.93	0.975	1

   a. Using these values, graph the utility curve for Mr. Liif.

   b. While he is in the United States, Mr. Liif feels he needs to purchase an inexpensive car. After consulting a Los Angeles paper, he has found five cars within his budget limitation. He knows, however, that any car he buys may turn out to require a lot of repairs. (His American friends call such a car a "lemon.") To help him make his decision he has classified the possible mechanical condition of the cars he has investigated as "Good," "Bad," and "Lemon." The cars and their payoffs are:

Mechanical Condition	Car				
	A	*B*	*C*	*D*	*E*
Good	+100	+300	+25	+150	+50
Bad	+25	−50	−25	0	+5
Lemon	−75	−200	0	−150	−50

Using the utility curve developed in part (*a*), and the probabilities of 0.4, 0.4, 0.2 for Good, Bad, and Lemon respectively, which car should Mr. Liif choose?

   c. In order to improve his expected outcome, Betyur is considering "risk-sharing." That is, he is considering buying a car jointly with some friends. The only car they (that is, Betyur and four friends) can all agree on has the following payoffs:

Car F	
Good	+$120
Lemon	−$120

with $P(\text{Good}) = 0.6$ and $P(\text{Lemon}) = 0.4$. If Betyur has the option of buying this car himself or sharing it (and thus the payoffs) with any number of up to four friends, which would he most prefer? Can he be guaranteed all his friends will feel the same? Why or why not?

10. In the text a graph of monetary value (call it M) in dollars versus utility (u) was derived. Sometimes this graph is expressed as a mathematical function such as:

$$u = 20,000 \sqrt[3]{\frac{M + 10,000}{20,000}} - 15,880$$

Suppose the owner of a pet store, Lovable Cuddles, Inc., has a utility curve expressed by this function. He is trying to decide which of three actions to engage in. The payoffs for these actions are:

Events \ Actions	A_1	A_2	A_3
E_1	2,000	2,500	5,000
E_2	−2,000	−2,500	−5,000

where all payoffs are expressed in dollar amounts. If $P(E_1) = 0.6$ and $P(E_2) = 0.4$, which action should the pet store owner choose?

11. *a.* Using the five points −$100, −$50, 0, +$50, +$100, sketch a utility curve for yourself on the interval −$100 to +$100. Be honest in your evaluation!

   b. Using this curve, rank the following bets available to you.

	Payoff	Probability
A.	+$50	0.2
	0	0.8
B.	+$25	0.9
	−$25	0.1
C.	Do nothing	

12.[7] Develop a utility of money curve for Person A, whose utility curve is shown in Figure 4.16. Throughout this problem assume the positive linear transformation from $P(\text{Win})$ to utility is expressed as

$$u = a\, P(\text{Win}) + b$$

and a mathematical representation of Person A's utility curve in Figure 4.16 is

$$P(\text{Win}) = f(\$).$$

   a. Derive the utility of money curve by

   1. Showing that $a = 1 \Big/ \dfrac{df}{d\$}$, if the slope of the utility of money curve must be unity at zero dollars.

   2. Determining (by numerical approximation) the slope of $f(\$)$ at zero dollars, and then the value of a.

---

[7] Problems 12 and 13 require a knowledge of differential calculus to solve.

      3.   Calculating the value of b, knowing that $u = 0$ at zero dollars.

      4.   Writing out the final mathematical expression for u in terms of a, b, and $f(\$)$.

      5.   Graphing the utility of money curve.

   b. Over what range of dollar values is this curve roughly linear?

13. Using the utility of money curve derived in Problem 12, reanalyze Problem 8*b*. Explain the advantage using this curve has over using the original curve of Figure 4.16.

5

The Analysis of Simple
Sampling Situations

IN CHAPTER 3 we introduced the expected value technique for solving decision problems, and applied it to certain "simple" kinds of problems. The purpose of this chapter is to extend the technique to situations in which the decision maker can seek further information (about which event will occur) *before* an action must be chosen. Seeking and obtaining information usually costs something, and one of the first questions we must consider is whether the value of the information is higher than its cost. Once it has been determined that the information is worthwhile, the best action must be determined. This chapter will be devoted to answering these two questions. First we will develop one technique— called *the enumeration of strategies approach*—for answering these questions. Then we will show how the *decision tree approach* can also be used to answer these questions.

5.1 THE CONCEPT OF SAMPLING

The objective of this chapter is to analyze information sources. Just exactly what is an information source? The information sources we deal with in this book are situations whose outcomes can be known *before* an action must be chosen, and whose outcomes should change the (subjective) probabilities of the events occurring. For example, for John's recreational decision problem in Chapter 3, he might seek various information sources—he can telephone the weatherman and get his prediction, he can read the prediction in the newspaper, or he can simply look out the window and make his own prediction. Each of these information sources has some measure of uncertainty in it (a cloudy sky tonight does not *assure* bad weather tomorrow), so we adopt the language of the statistician and call the process *sampling.* The sample outcome (cloudy sky, weatherman predicts a sunny day, etc.) can be observed *before* an action is chosen, and helps to predict which event will occur. An example will help illustrate sampling.

Legislator: Phillip A. Buster is currently a member of the House of Representatives. It is September and he has a decision to make for the coming November election. He can either run for his same Congressional seat, which he is virtually assured of winning, or he can run for the Senate. The President has strongly urged that he do the latter. If Phil runs for the Senate, of course, he has a chance of losing. In fact, he estimates the probability of winning the Senatorial race to be 0.4. Over the six year term of a Senator, Phil feels his House of Representatives post would be worth \$200,000, and being a Senator would be worth \$300,000. If he lost the race, Phil could resume his old law practice, and this he feels would be worth \$100,000. Because he feels his chances of winning are not high, Phil is very reluctant to run for the Senate. To convince him, the central committee of his party has agreed to pay for a poll taken on Phil's behalf in his home state. The poll would ask people whether they would vote for Phil or the incumbent Senator, *if the election were held now.*

Phil is facing a sampling problem. The outcome of the poll will be known before Phil must make a decision, and the electorate's attitude toward Phil *now* should give him a better feeling about what their attitude will be in November. On the other hand, there is uncertainty in the sample (poll) outcome. For example, Phil could lose the election in November, even if he is preferred by a majority of the electorate now.

This example is typical of problems involving sampling. The sample outcome gives you *partial* information on which event will occur. To evaluate and use a sampling situation, we must know how to employ this partial information to our advantage. This will be discussed in the following section, after we develop the concept of a strategy.

5.2 STRATEGIES AND THEIR USE

In this chapter, and throughout the rest of the book, the concept of a strategy is very important. As used in this book, a strategy is a "master plan" that tells us which action to take for every sample outcome.[1] The decision problem of importance when sampling is present is that of choosing the best strategy. The strategy will then dictate which is the best action for every possible sample outcome.

---

[1] "Contingency plan" is another name for the same concept.

It is best to illustrate the concept of strategies by using an example. To make life simple, let us assume that the only relevant outcomes of the poll for Phil are:

Y = A majority of the voters prefer Phil now;
N = A minority of the voters prefer Phil now;

and let us designate Phil's actions as:

R = Run for the House of Representatives;
S = Run for the Senate.

Then a strategy which Phil might adopt is:

Run for the House of Representatives if a majority of the voters prefer Phil now;
Run for the Senate if a minority of the voters prefer Phil now.

The reader probably feels that Phil would be stupid to adopt such a strategy, but we shall save questions of evaluating strategies for later. The important thing to realize at this point is that the above does constitute a strategy. It provides a specific action for each sample outcome.

Since writing out strategies as above is lengthy and time consuming, we shall adopt the following shorthand notation for a strategy. Each sample outcome-action pair will be denoted by the pair of symbols for these separated by a hyphen, and the entire strategy will be enclosed by braces. Thus, the above strategy would be noted as $\{Y\text{-}R, N\text{-}S\}$.

5.2.1 Enumerating Strategies

In order to pick the best strategy we must be able to list all possible strategies. Sometimes this is an easy problem, and at other times it becomes quite difficult. We shall begin by discussing the list of all strategies for Phil's problem, then expand our knowledge to the general case.

How does one define the complete list of strategies? *The list of strategies will be complete when we have considered all combinations of sample outcome-action pairs.* For Phil's problem Y can be paired with either R or S, and N can also be paired with either R or S, so the total list of strategies is:

$s_1 = \{Y\text{-}R, N\text{-}R\},$
$s_2 = \{Y\text{-}R, N\text{-}S\},$
$s_3 = \{Y\text{-}S, N\text{-}R\},$
$s_4 = \{Y\text{-}S, N\text{-}S\}.$

Note that each strategy is distinct, and that every possible strategy has been listed.[2] Furthermore, we have given each member of the list a distinct label so that we can quickly identify it. In the above list, s_2 is the strategy we discussed above.

What clues do we have to help us develop a list of strategies? It is quite straightforward to develop a formula that tells us the number of strategies in the list. If there are n actions that can be taken for each of k possible sample outcomes, the total number of strategies can be shown[3] to be n^k. Thus, after the list has been developed, the number obtained can be compared to the number predicted from the formula to check for omissions and duplications in the list.

The formula for the number of strategies can also tell us something about the way we approach decision problems. If, as in Phil's case, we have a problem with two actions and two sample outcomes, there are $2^2 = 4$ possible strategies. Similarly, a problem with three actions and two sample outcomes has $3^2 = 9$ strategies, and a problem with ten actions and six sample outcomes has $10^6 = 1,000,000$ strategies. The total number of strategies increases very quickly as the number of actions and/or sample outcomes increases. Thus, except for problems with small numbers of actions and sample outcomes, the mere listing of the strategies, let alone their evaluation, would be onerous. In such cases we must find rules that eliminate many strategies from consideration. Such situations will be discussed in Chapters 6 through 12. For the moment we will limit our discussion to problems in which it is feasible to list and evaluate all strategies, since working through such problems will provide insight to the more complex problems we will discuss later.

5.2.2 Evaluating Strategies

We cannot evaluate strategies without information as to how sample outcomes relate to events. Specifically, we need to know the probability of every sample outcome given every event, or:

$$P(\text{Sample Outcome}|\text{Event}).$$

Many times such probabilities are dictated by the sampling procedure. Other times they may have to be subjectively estimated. Phil's problem is a good example of a situation in which these probabilities can only be obtained subjectively. Let us assume that Phil has estimated the following values for his conditional probabilities:

$$P(Y|W) = 0.6; P(Y|L) = 0.3;$$
$$P(N|W) = 0.4; P(N|L) = 0.7;$$

---

[2] Listing strategies will probably be difficult for the novice, but he will quickly become quite proficient at it.

[3] The student familiar with combinatorial analysis will find this formula easy to verify.

where:

W = The event that Phil would win the Senatorial race (in November);
L = The event that Phil would lose the Senatorial race (in November).

These probabilities can be conveniently displayed in a table in which each row represents an event and each column a sample outcome.

	Y	N
W	0.6	0.4
L	0.3	0.7

Notice that each row of the matrix sums to one, as it should, since the entries in any row form a conditional probability distribution. We call the entire set of distributions the *sampling distributions* for the problem. A problem with sampling cannot be solved unless a set of sampling distributions is provided.

Let us now discuss a method for evaluating Phil's strategies. It is helpful to develop the evaluation technique by analogy with the technique we used in the no sampling situation. Therefore, we will first solve Phil's problem as if no sampling were available.

Phil's payoff matrix is

	R	S
W	$200,000	$300,000
L	$200,000	$100,000

and $P(W) = 0.4; P(L) = 0.6$. Then

$$E(R) = 200,000 \times 0.4 + 200,000 \times 0.6 = 200,000$$
$$E(S) = 300,000 \times 0.4 + 100,000 \times 0.6 = 180,000$$

and Phil is better off to run for the House of Representatives.

Let us develop an analogous technique for evaluating strategies. We shall first develop a payoff table, then determine the expected payoff for each strategy. To develop the payoff table we have stated that we must choose among strategies, so our payoff table will replace a set of potential actions with a set of potential strategies. Thus, to evaluate strategies we must develop payoffs to fill the following table:

Events \ Strategies	S_1	S_2	S_3	S_4
W				
L				

where

$$s_1 = \{ Y\text{-}R, N\text{-}R \};$$
$$s_2 = \{ Y\text{-}R, N\text{-}S \};$$
$$s_3 = \{ Y\text{-}S, N\text{-}R \};$$
$$s_4 = \{ Y\text{-}S, N\text{-}S \}.$$

Consider first the payoff of s_1 if W occurs. s_1 is a simple strategy that says that Phil should choose R, whatever the outcome of the poll. Thus, the payoff for s_1 when W occurs (as well as the payoff for s_1 when L occurs) is 200,000.

Determination of the payoff for s_2 if W occurs is not nearly so easy. The amount of the payoff depends upon whether R or S is taken as the action, and the choice between these depends upon which sample outcome occurs. Even if we are *given* that W will occur, the sample outcome is uncertain and hence the payoff is uncertain. Can we determine a value for a payoff in this situation? Fortunately, the answer is yes. It will later be shown that the appropriate value to place in this square is the *expected* payoff for s_2 when W occurs. For s_2, given W, the payoff will be 200,000 if Y occurs (since s_2 dictates R will be chosen if Y occurs, and the payoff for R given W is 200,000) and the payoff will be 300,000 if N occurs. The probabilities for Y and N occuring, given W, are 0.6 and 0.4, respectively. Thus, the expected payoff for s_2 given W is

$$E(s_2|W) = 200,000 \times 0.6 + 300,000 \times 0.4 = 240,000.$$

Thus, we have taken each sample outcome-action pair of the strategy, and multiplied its payoff by its probability. The sum of these products is the expected payoff for the strategy, *given an event*. In symbols, we have:

$$E(s_2|W) = \text{payoff}(Y\text{-}R|W)P(Y\text{-}R|W) + \text{payoff}(N\text{-}S|W)P(N\text{-}S|W)$$

$$= \text{payoff}(R|W)P(Y|W) + \text{payoff}(S|W)P(N|W).$$

The above development recognizes the important fact that the payoff of a sample outcome-action pair is determined by the action, while the probability the pair will occur is determined by the probability of the sample outcome.

The above development has determined only $E(s_2|W)$. We also need $E(s_2|L)$, which is

$$E(s_2|L) = \text{payoff}(Y\text{-}R|L)P(Y\text{-}R|L) + \text{payoff}(N\text{-}S|L)P(N\text{-}S|L)$$

$$= \text{payoff}(R|L)P(Y|L) + \text{payoff}(S|L)P(N|L)$$

$$= 200,000 \times 0.3 + 100,000 \times 0.7 = 130,000.$$

Similarly, the rest of the payoff table can be determined as:

$$E(s_3|W) = 300,000 \times 0.6 + 200,000 \times 0.4 = 260,000$$
$$E(s_3|L) = 100,000 \times 0.3 + 200,000 \times 0.7 = 170,000$$
$$E(s_4|W) = 300,000$$
$$E(s_4|L) = 100,000$$

and the completed table is

	s_1	s_2	s_3	s_4
W	\$200,000	\$240,000	\$260,000	\$300,000
L	\$200,000	\$130,000	\$170,000	\$100,000

Finally, to evaluate the strategies the values in the above payoff table are weighted by the probabilities of the events and summed, just as in the no sampling case. Thus, we have:

$$E(s_1) = 200,000 \times 0.4 + 200,000 \times 0.6 = 200,000$$
$$E(s_2) = 240,000 \times 0.4 + 130,000 \times 0.6 = 174,000$$
$$E(s_3) = 260,000 \times 0.4 + 170,000 \times 0.6 = 206,000$$
$$E(s_4) = 300,000 \times 0.4 + 100,000 \times 0.6 = 180,000.$$

We see that s_3 is the best strategy, and we also confirm our previous belief that s_2 is a poor strategy.

5.2.3 Summary of the Enumeration of Strategies Approach

We have seen through discussion of the above example that a simple sampling scheme can be analyzed by

1. Listing all possible sample outcomes.
2. Listing all possible strategies.
3. Determining the sampling distributions.
4. Calculating conditional expected payoffs (or losses) for each strategy, *given each event.*
5. Multiplying the conditional expected payoffs by the probabilities of events and summing to get the overall expected payoff of the strategy.

There are several loose ends we must take care of at this point. First, for the purist, an appeal to the discussion in Section 2.4.6 will demonstrate that the procedure we used to obtain the overall expected payoff for a strategy is a valid one. Second, there is the question of opportunity loss. If we use opportunity losses instead of payoffs, how is the analysis changed? As one might expect, the analysis is identical except that the best strategy is the strategy with the *minimum* overall expected loss. An example will be discussed below using opportunity loss analysis.

A third problem concerns the question of whether or not a sample should be taken. To a certain extent the answer to this question hinges upon the discussion of sample cost in the next section. However, several important points can be made now. The reader has undoubtedly noticed that two of the four strategies in Phil's list are very simplistic strategies. They each dictate that one of the actions should be taken, no matter which sample outcome occurs. Notice that the expected values of these strategies are the same as the expected values of the actions themselves! That is:

$$E(s_1) = E(R) \text{ and } E(s_4) = E(S),$$

and this makes perfect sense, because R is the only action used in s_1 and S is the only action used in s_4. Every strategy list will contain these simple strategies, and their evaluation will help us answer the question of whether or not the sampling should be used. In Phil's problem, for instance, $E(s_3)$ is better than either $E(s_1)$ or $E(s_4)$, indicating that sampling is better than not sampling. Similar conclusions can be drawn when the sample costs something, but more care must be taken in the calculation. We will now turn to a discussion of problems involving sampling cost.

5.3 INCORPORATING SAMPLING COSTS

In our previous discussion of Phil's problem, we carefully avoided any consideration of the cost of sampling by stating that Phil's political party would pay for the poll. However, a much more likely situation occurs if Phil has to pay for the poll himself. Two related questions to which we will address ourselves are:

1. If the price of the poll is known, should the poll be used? and
2. What is the worth of the poll to Phil?

We shall adopt the following procedure for answering the first question. The cost of the poll *detracts* from the payoff Phil would otherwise realize, so the *net* worth of the sampling scheme can be obtained by taking the best payoff and subtracting the sample cost. For example, if the price of the poll were $5,000, the net worth of the best sampling scheme (s_3) is $206,000 − $5,000 = $201,000.

Once we have determined the net worth of the poll we can determine whether or not the poll should be used by comparing its *net* worth to the expected payoff for the best terminal action.[4] The sampling scheme is used *only* if its net worth is larger than the worth of making an immediate decision.

What happens if the best strategy is a simple strategy—one for which the same action is taken for every sample outcome? In this case the decision maker has the choice between taking the sample, incurring the cost of that sample, then regardless of the outcome of the sample, always taking the same action, or merely taking the action in the first place, without waiting for *and paying for* the sample outcome. Clearly immediate action is best in this case, and the sample should not be taken.

The above can be simply summarized:

1. Determine the best strategy.
2. Is the best strategy a "simple" strategy (only involving one action)? If so, then taking immediate action is better than sampling. If not, go to 3.
3. Subtract the cost of the sample from the expected payoff for the best strategy. Is the result higher than the best payoff for the simple strategies? If so, it is best to sample and adopt the best strategy. If not, it is better to take an immediate action.

The reader should be cautioned that step 3 will change if he is dealing with costs or opportunity losses instead of payoffs. In these cases the cost of the sample will be *added* to the expected value for the best strategy, and the overall best will be chosen by finding the minimum rather than the maximum. This is demonstrated in the example that concludes the chapter.

A word should be said about alternative sampling schemes. Suppose the decision maker has several information sources available to him. If he wants to answer the question: Which *single source* should I use, straightforward extensions of the above reasoning will guide him. However, a much more realistic situation occurs when several sources can potentially be used together, either jointly or sequentially. Although the ideas developed in this chapter could be applied with essentially no modification to these situations, the analysis of the problem becomes extremely messy. Not much advice can be offered to help in solving these problems. The student should be aware that these problems exist, and that their complexity can be immense.

Let us now return to our second question, that of determining the worth of a sampling scheme. In Chapter 3 we discussed the expected value of perfect information, EVPI. A similar quantity can be calculated

---

[4] Henceforth the phrase "terminal action" refers to the final choice made by the decision maker. For instance, in Phil's problem, the terminal actions are *R* & *S*. Nonterminal actions are "sampling" and "not sampling."

for any single sampling scheme. This quantity is called the expected value of sample information, EVSI, and expresses the additional worth of the sample over the best action that could have been taken without sampling. Thus, in Phil's case, we have:

$$\text{EVSI} = E(s_3) - E(R) = \$206,000 - \$200,000 = \$6,000.$$

The EVSI can also be used in making the decision whether to use the sample or not. If the sample cost is less than its value (EVSI), then it is worthwhile to use, whereas if the cost is greater than the value, the sample should not be used.

Can a sample ever be rejected out of hand—without first evaluating it? Sometimes it can. We discussed the concept of EVPI in Chapter 3. It can be shown that EVSI is always less than or equal to EVPI. Thus, if the cost of a sample is greater than EVPI, we know it will never have a value as great as its cost, and it can be rejected out of hand. If a sampling plan has a cost less than EVPI, however, we can only determine its usefulness by evaluating it.

5.4 A FURTHER EXAMPLE

Another example will help set the ideas expressed above. The analysis of the problem will be essentially the same as for Phil's problem, except we shall analyze this problem by using opportunity loss. The student is urged to practice his understanding of the material up to this point by reading the statement of the problem, and trying to solve it by himself before reading the solution presented here.

Publishing: A publisher of college textbooks is considering publishing a manuscript written by a certain Professor Jones. The publisher has two alternatives:

1. Do not publish;
2. Publish a version of the manuscript.

Reviewers have looked at Professor Jones' manuscript, and estimate it has a 50 percent chance of being a big seller, and a 50 percent chance of being a poor seller. The payoffs to the publisher are:

	Don't Publish	Publish
Poor Seller	0	−$180
Good Seller	0	+$300

Sometimes in a situation like this the publisher will ask another professor who could potentially teach out of the book to evaluate the manuscript. From past experience, the publisher has found there are three possible responses to the question: Would you adopt this textbook for use in your classes?

1. No
2. Yes, for all classes
3. Yes, for honor classes,

and the conditional probabilities of each of these outcomes, given either event, is

	No	All Classes	Honor Classes
Poor Seller	0.7	0.1	0.2
Good Seller	0.3	0.5	0.2

Unfortunately, this additional review costs $30. Which decision should the publisher make?

Solution: Let

B = The book will be a poor seller
G = The book will be a good seller
DP = Don't publish the book
PU = Publish the book
N = No, the reviewer would not use the book
A = The reviewer would use the book for all classes
H = The reviewer would use the book for honor classes only.

The opportunity loss matrix for the problem is:

	DP	PU
B	0	180
G	300	0

and there are $2^3 = 8$ strategies. These are

$s_1 = \{N\text{-}DP, A\text{-}DP, H\text{-}DP\};$
$s_2 = \{N\text{-}DP, A\text{-}DP, H\text{-}PU\};$
$s_3 = \{N\text{-}DP, A\text{-}PU, H\text{-}DP\};$
$s_4 = \{N\text{-}PU, A\text{-}DP, H\text{-}DP\};$
$s_5 = \{N\text{-}DP, A\text{-}PU, H\text{-}PU\};$
$s_6 = \{N\text{-}PU, A\text{-}DP, H\text{-}PU\};$
$s_7 = \{N\text{-}PU, A\text{-}PU, H\text{-}DP\};$
$s_8 = \{N\text{-}PU, A\text{-}PU, H\text{-}PU\}.$

Then we have

$$\mathcal{E}(s_1|B) = \text{loss}(N\text{-}DP|B)P(N\text{-}DP|B) + \text{loss}(A\text{-}DP|B)P(A\text{-}DP|B)$$
$$+ \text{loss}(H\text{-}DP|B)P(H\text{-}DP|B)$$
$$= 0 \times 0.7 + 0 \times 0.1 + 0 \times 0.2 = 0$$
$$\mathcal{E}(s_2|B) = 0 \times 0.7 + 0 \times 0.1 + 180 \times 0.2 = 36$$
$$\mathcal{E}(s_3|B) = 0 \times 0.7 + 180 \times 0.1 + 0 \times 0.2 = 18$$

.

.

.

etc., from which we get

	s_1	s_2	s_3	s_4	s_5	s_6	s_7	s_8
B	0	36	18	126	54	162	144	180
G	300	240	150	210	90	150	60	0

and the overall expected values are

$$\mathcal{E}(s_1) = 0 \times 0.5 + \$300 \times 0.5 = \$150$$
$$\mathcal{E}(s_2) = \$36 \times 0.5 + \$240 \times 0.5 = \$138$$
$$\mathcal{E}(s_3) = \$18 \times 0.5 + \$150 \times 0.5 = \$84$$
$$\mathcal{E}(s_4) = \$126 \times 0.5 + \$210 \times 0.5 = \$168$$
$$\mathcal{E}(s_5) = \$54 \times 0.5 + \$90 \times 0.5 = \$72$$
$$\mathcal{E}(s_6) = \$162 \times 0.5 + \$150 \times 0.5 = \$156$$
$$\mathcal{E}(s_7) = \$144 \times 0.5 + \$60 \times 0.5 = \$102$$
$$\mathcal{E}(s_8) = \$180 \times 0.5 + 0 \times 0.5 = \$90.$$

So, without considering sample costs the best strategy is s_5. However, when we add in sample costs the total is *higher* than the best of the simple strategies. (The simple strategies are s_1 and s_8.) Hence, it is best *not* to sample, and the best terminal action is *PU*.

5.5 USING DECISION TREES TO SOLVE SAMPLING PROBLEMS

In the previous sections we analyzed simple sampling situations by enumerating and evaluating strategies. In the remainder of this chapter we will discuss another approach for solving the same kinds of problems. This approach will develop the best strategy by determining which action is best for any particular sample outcome. Although in technique the method is quite different from the enumeration of strategies approach discussed above, the results of the two techniques are always identical. That is, whatever the optimal decision and associated payoff is for the enumeration of strategies approach, the decision tree approach will give the same optimal decision and associated payoff.

Why do we study both methods if they are identical? The two methods are identical in results, but quite different in technique, and it is this difference that makes the knowledge of both very useful. As we move to solving more complex problems in later chapters we will find the knowledge of both techniques a valuable asset in being able to solve many problems.

In Section 5.1 we introduced the concept that the sample outcome should change one's attitude toward which event should occur, and yet we never really seemed to use the idea. However, that idea forms the heart of the decision tree technique, and we shall study it thoroughly throughout the rest of this chapter. The mechanics of changing the probabilities are based upon the use of Bayes' rule.[5]

5.5.1 Developing a Tree for Phil's Entire Problem

In order to analyze Phil's full problem, we must have a decision tree for the problem. The tree will be developed in this section. The development of the tree will follow exactly the same rules as the development of a tree without sampling.

Starting at the left of the tree, Phil first faces the choice of whether or not to sample:

The remainder of the "No Poll" branch will be a tree depicting what Phil's decision would be if no sampling were available:

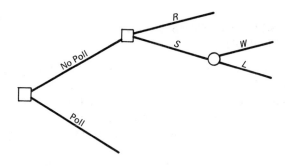

---

[5] The fact that Bayes' rule is such an integral part of this technique has provoked some authors to call the subject we are studying in this book Bayesian decision theory, although its development was not at all affected by Rev. Bayes.

If Phil decides to have the poll taken, the next branch he encounters is
the branch depicting the sample outcomes:

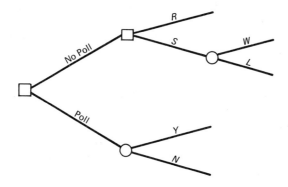

where

    Y = A majority of the people would vote for Phil in a Senatorial race
        held now,
    N = A minority of the people would vote for Phil in a Senatorial race
        held now.

Once the sample outcome is known, Phil must choose one of the two
actions available to him, R and S, and if he chooses S there is a chance
outcome of W or L. Thus, attached to the sample outcome branches
are branches just like Phil's no-sampling problem, and the decision tree
for Phil's entire problem is:

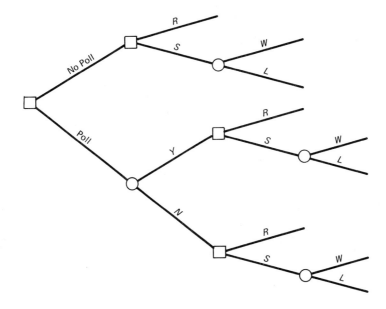

5.5.2   Assigning Probabilities to Complex Trees

If we were studying Phil's no-sampling problem we would find it easy
to assign probabilities to chance branches. Unfortunately, any time we
have sequences of chance outcomes, as we do in the above tree, we
must be very careful about which probabilities we assign to any branch.
The rule is:

1. If there are no chance nodes preceeding (to the left of) this
    chance node, assign *unconditional* probabilities to the outcomes.
2. If chance nodes precede the (chance) node under consideration,
    assign probabilities to the outcomes *conditional* on any previous
    chance outcomes. (Any chance outcomes to the left of the one
    under consideration.)

Thus, Phil's tree, with the notation for the appropriate probabilities
assigned, is:

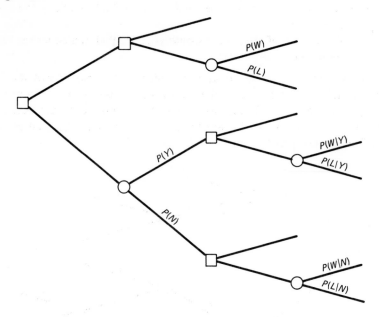

In Phil's problem we have sequences of only two chance nodes. If there
were more, the last (rightmost) chance outcome would have a probability assigned that was *conditional upon every other chance outcome*
preceding it *in its portion of the tree*.

Unfortunately, we see from the above tree that the probabilities
we need for the "poll" portion of the tree are:

$$P(Y); P(N); P(W|Y); P(L|Y); P(W|N); P(L|N)$$

and the numbers we have been given in the statement of the problem are:

$$P(W) = 0.4; \; P(L) = 0.6; \; P(Y|W) = 0.6; \; P(N|W) = 0.4;$$
$$P(Y|L) = 0.3; \; P(N|L) = 0.7.$$

The two sets are related, so we don't need to estimate any more numbers. However, we must go through some rather messy calculations in order to get the probabilities we want.

The two probability relationships we shall use were discussed in Chapter 2. They are illustrated here for Phil's problem:

Partitioning: $P(Y) = P(Y|W)P(W) + P(Y|L)P(L)$; and

Bayes' rule: $P(W|Y) = \dfrac{P(Y|W)P(W)}{P(Y|W)P(W) + P(Y|L)P(L)}.$

Notice that the denominator of the Bayes' rule expression is the quantity calculated in the first expression, so if we are careful we can cut down on the total amount of calculation that must be done. The entire set of calculations for Phil's problem is:

$$P(Y) = P(Y|W)P(W) + P(Y|L)P(L)$$
$$= 0.6 \times 0.4 + 0.3 \times 0.6 = 0.42$$
$$P(N) = P(N|W)P(W) + P(N|L)P(L)$$
$$= 0.4 \times 0.4 + 0.7 \times 0.6 = 0.58$$

(These two sum to one, as they should!)

$$P(W|Y) = \frac{P(Y|W)P(W)}{P(Y|W)P(W) + P(Y|L)P(L)}$$
$$= \frac{0.6 \times 0.4}{0.42} = 0.571$$
$$P(L|Y) = \frac{P(Y|L)P(L)}{P(Y|W)P(W) + P(Y|L)P(L)}$$
$$= \frac{0.3 \times 0.6}{0.42} = 0.429$$

(Again, we have two quantities which sum to one, as they should.)

$$P(W|N) = \frac{P(N|W)P(W)}{P(N|W)P(W) + P(N|L)P(L)}$$
$$= \frac{0.4 \times 0.4}{0.58} = 0.276$$

$$P(L|N) = \frac{P(N|L)P(N)}{P(N|W)P(W) + P(N|L)P(L)}$$

$$= \frac{0.7 \times 0.6}{0.58} = 0.724$$

(And these last two sum to one, as they should.)

5.5.3   Full Analysis of Phil's Problem

After we have completed the above calculations,[6] we are ready to analyze Phil's tree. The tree, complete with payoffs, probabilities, and full analysis, is:

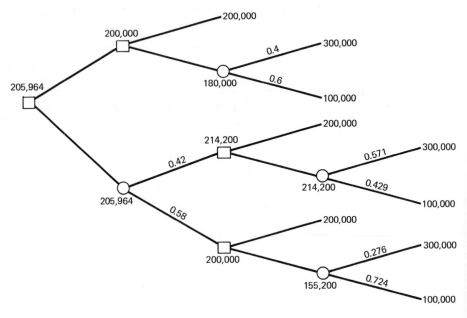

Thus, Phil's maximum expected payoff is approximately $206,000,[7] and we must work back through the tree to obtain his strategy. When we work back through the tree we find that Phil should use the poll, and his action should be S or R respectively, depending upon whether the outcome of the poll is Y or N. Thus, except for rounding error, the best value and strategy obtained by using decision tree analysis is exactly the same as these outcomes obtained from the enumeration of strategies approach. This coincidence between the decision tree ap-

---

[6] Other methods exist for deriving these probabilities. If the student prefers to use another method, it is certainly encouraged.

[7] Comparison with the enumeration of strategies approach says the value should be *exactly* $206,000. The error arises because we have three place approximations for our conditional probabilities.

proach and the enumeration of strategies approach holds for *all* decision problems.

5.5.4 Including Sample Costs

Up to this point we have considered Phil's problem without sample costs. How do we handle the problem if the sample (poll) will cost Phil something? We simply subtract the sample cost from any expected payoff for the sample branch, or add the sample cost to any expected cost or opportunity loss for the sample branch. Thus, the expected payoff for the sample branch in Phil's problem was $205,964. If the poll cost Phil $5,000, the net payoff for sampling would be

$$\$205,964 - \$5,000 = \$200,964.$$

Raiffa[s] provides an interesting device for including sample costs. To any sampling branch he adds a "tollgate" depicted as

and attaches the sample cost to the tollgate. Thus, Phil's tree when the poll costs $5,000 would be:

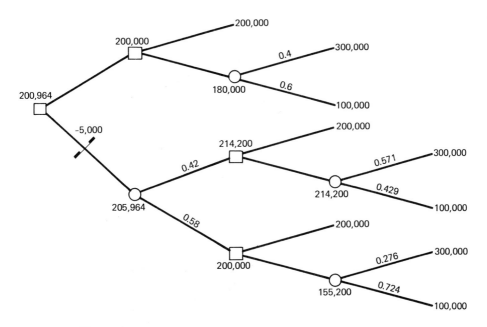

---

[s] Howard Raiffa, *Decision Analysis* (Addison-Wesley, 1968).

We shall adopt Raiffa's method for including sample costs in a decision tree.

5.6 DECISION TREE ANALYSIS OF THE PUBLISHER'S PROBLEM

As a conclusion, let us analyze the publisher's problem, introduced above in Section 5.4, using a decision tree. We shall analyze the tree using opportunity losses, to demonstrate the (few) changes that are involved in using these rather than payoffs.

The publisher's decision tree is quite similar to Phil's. He must first decide whether or not to sample. If he does not sample, he must then make a choice between publishing and not publishing. If he decides to sample, he will observe one of three sample outcomes, and *then* he must decide which action to choose. Thus, the full tree is:

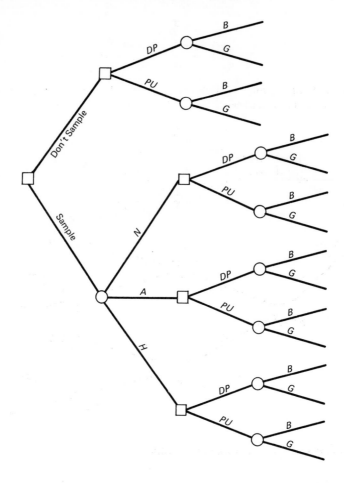

where

DP = Don't publish
PU = Publish
 B = A poor seller
 G = A good seller
 N = Reviewer will use in no classes
 A = Reviewer will use in all classes
 H = Reviewer will use in honor classes.

It is very important to notice in this tree that a two-event chance node is attached to each DP branch. This is because when we use opportunity loss, the DP action does *not* have a single value, but rather an opportunity loss that depends upon which event occurs.

The loss matrix for this problem is

	DP	PU
B	0	$180
G	$300	0

and the probabilities we have are

$$P(B) = 0.5; \quad P(G) = 0.5; P(N|B) = 0.7$$
$$P(A|B) = 0.1; P(H|B) = 0.2; P(N|G) = 0.3$$
$$P(A|G) = 0.5; P(H|G) = 0.2.$$

The probabilities we need to develop are

$$P(N) = P(N|B)P(B) + P(N|G)P(G)$$
$$= 0.7 \times 0.5 + 0.3 \times 0.5 = 0.5$$
$$P(A) = P(A|B)P(B) + P(A|G)P(G)$$
$$= 0.1 \times 0.5 + 0.5 \times 0.5 = 0.3$$
$$P(H) = P(H|B)P(B) + P(H|G)P(G)$$
$$= 0.2 \times 0.5 + 0.2 \times 0.5 = 0.2$$

$$P(B|N) = \frac{P(N|B)P(B)}{P(N)} = \frac{0.7 \times 0.5}{0.5} = 0.7$$

$$P(G|N) = 1 - P(B|N) = 0.3$$

$$P(B|A) = \frac{P(A|B)P(B)}{P(A)} = \frac{0.1 \times 0.5}{0.3} = 0.167$$

$$P(G|A) = 1 - P(B|A) = 0.833$$

$$P(B|H) = \frac{P(H|B)P(B)}{P(H)} = \frac{0.2 \times 0.5}{0.2} = 0.5$$

$$P(G|H) = 1 - P(B|H) = 0.5.$$

With these values we are ready to analyze the tree. Its analysis is:

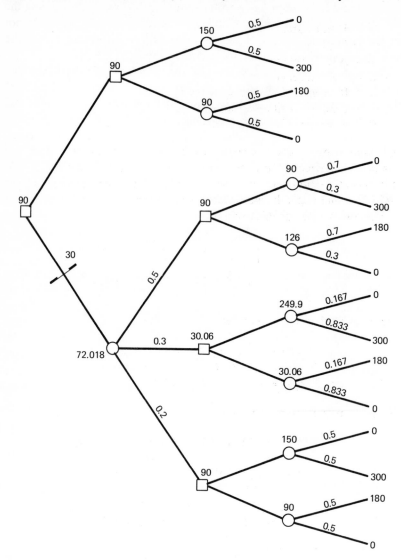

There are two important ways in which this opportunity loss analysis differed from a payoff analysis. First, the best value at each decision node was the *minimum* value rather than the maximum value. Second, the sample cost is *added* to the expected opportunity loss for the sampling branch to get the overall expected loss for the sampling situation.

Once we have analyzed the above tree, we must work back through it to obtain the best decision. In this case, the best decision is to immediately publish without requesting another review. If the cost of the review would have been less so that sampling was worthwhile, then the best strategy would be to not publish if the reviewer said he would not use the book, and publish if the reviewer said he would either use the book in all classes or in his honor classes.

There are two important aspects of this problem that should be discussed. First, the cost of sampling (30) is much less than the EVPI (90).[9] Hence, the sampling plan cannot be rejected out of hand, and yet the analysis demonstrates that it is not worthwhile. Second, if the reviewer were to say that he would adopt the book for his honor classes, that response gives the publisher no information because it does not change his probabilities on the events: $P(B) = 0.5$ and $P(B|H) = 0.5$. Certain sampling situations (or parts of them) are "informationless," as H is. However, most sample outcomes will allow the decision maker to discriminate better between events.

5.7 SUMMARY—COMPARING THE TWO APPROACHES

We have now seen two approaches for analyzing simple sampling problems. Although they are quite different in technique, we have stated, and seen for a couple of sample problems, that they yield the same answer when applied to the same problem. In later work we will find it very useful to have both approaches, since some problems will be easier to solve using an enumeration of strategies approach, and others will best be solved using a decision tree approach. It is very important for the student facing a decision problem to consider both approaches, since one may be easiest to apply, but many times *both* provide valuable insights to the solution of the problem.

To summarize, the enumeration of strategies approach evaluates strategies given events, then takes out the conditioning on events, while the decision tree approach evaluates actions given sample outcomes, then takes out the conditioning on sample outcomes.

PROBLEMS

1. Following a disasterous oil leak in the Santa Barbara Channel, the California State Department of Interior was faced with the following problem: Should they make the legislation for offshore drilling of oil more restrictive or not? The secretary of the department has decided that three actions are available to them:

   A_1: make offshore drilling illegal
   A_2: impose more stringent standards for offshore drilling
   A_3: do not change current laws.

---

[9] The reader should be sure that he knows how the EVPI for this problem was obtained and where (in the analysis) it came from.

Which decision is best depends upon the geological structure off shore. In consultation with a department geologist, they have found three important distinctions for offshore geology:

E_1: low danger of future leaks
E_2: medium danger of future leaks
E_3: high danger of future leaks.

The most difficult part of such a project is determining benefits and costs, and in this case there are many issues, from conservation to oil industry economics. Fortunately, the department was able to determine the following benefit matrix.

	A_1	A_2	A_3
E_1	+8M	+2M	+12M
E_2	−2M	+6M	−2M
E_3	+2M	−2M	−10M

where M represents millions of dollars.

a. Derive the opportunity loss matrix for the above problem, and determine the best decision if $P(E_1) = 0.3$, $P(E_2) = 0.4$, $P(E_3) = 0.3$.

Suppose that a study by a series of world renown geologists can be made. If it is made, the possible reports are:

O_1: the offshore geology is relatively stable
O_2: the offshore geology is relatively unstable.

And the geologists predict that this will lead to the following conditional probabilities:

	O_1	O_2
E_1	0.9	0.1
E_2	0.4	0.6
E_3	0.5	0.5

i.e., $P(O_1|E_1) = 0.8$, $P(O_1|E_2) = 0.4$, etc.

b. List all the strategies available to the department.
c. Using opportunity losses, determine the best strategy for this problem using the enumeration of strategies approach.
d. Determine the best strategy for this problem using a decision tree.
e. Should the experiment be undertaken if it costs $100,000?
f. Suppose the department cannot predict the cost in advance. What is the *maximum* they would be willing to pay for the study?
g. Is expected value an adequate criterion in this case? Why or why not?

2. George has an Outasight motorcycle that is extremely fast but not too
    dependable. At any rate, it very often quits on him. When this happens
    he must determine to which of two mechanics to take it. He knows from
    past experience that one of three things might be wrong with his
    motorcycle:

    E_1: Distributor trouble
    E_2: Carburetor trouble
    E_3: Fuel pump trouble

One of the mechanics specializes in electrical troubles and the other in
fuel system troubles. As a consequence, George knows the repair will
cost him:

	M_1	M_2
E_1	20	10
E_2	20	30
E_3	30	35

a. Construct an opportunity loss matrix for this problem, and deter-
    mine George's best decision if:

$$P(E_1) = 0.6; \ P(E_2) = 0.1; \ P(E_3) = 0.3$$

In addition to taking his cycle directly to a mechanic, George has
the option of having the trouble electronically diagnosed. There are
two possible diagnostic outcomes:

   O_1: Electrical trouble is indicated
   O_2: Fuel system trouble is indicated

The test is not perfect, of course. The conditional probabilities are:

	O_1	O_2
E_1	0.8	0.2
E_2	0.4	0.6
E_3	0.1	0.9

   i.e., $P(O_1|E_1) = 0.9$, etc.
b. If the test costs $1, should George consider having it done?
c. List all possible strategies open to George.
d. Using the enumeration of strategies approach, what is George's
    best strategy? Should the electronic diagnosis be purchased?
e. Solve this problem using a decision tree.

3. Take John's recreational problem from Chapter 3, but now consider
    the possibility of one of two sampling schemes. The first is to just look
    out the window to determine whether or not it is cloudy tonight. The
    sampling distribution for this experiment is:

Events \ Outcomes	Clear	Cloudy
SB	0.7	0.3
SC	0.7	0.3
BW	0.4	0.6

The second scheme involves calling the weatherman. If he does this, John will receive a very technical report. For his purposes he classifies each report as Looks Good or Looks Bad. For this scheme the sample distribution is:

Events \ Outcomes	Looks Good	Looks Bad
SB	0.9	0.1
SC	0.7	0.3
BW	0.2	0.8

Assume in all answers to this problem that John will use *only one of the two experiments.*

a. List all strategies available to John.

b. Determine John's best strategy using an enumeration of strategies approach.

c. Solve John's problem using a decision tree.

4. For the above problem, assume each experiment can be used only once, but that John can consider doing both before finally choosing an action. Multiple sampling schemes such as in this problem make consideration of *joint* and *sequential* sampling possible. A joint sampling scheme would be one in which *both* experiments are conducted, and their outcomes known, before any action is chosen. A sequential scheme, on the other hand, considers using one of the two sampling plans first and then, based on that outcome, taking any of the terminal actions *or* engaging in the other sampling plan before choosing a terminal action.

a. Draw the decision tree for Problem 3 if each sampling plan can be used at most once, but joint and sequential sampling plans are allowed.

b. Assume the outcomes of "looking out the window" are (probabilistically) independent of the outcomes obtained from "calling the weatherman." Analyze John's tree.

c. What does the assumption of independence given in part (*b*) mean? Is that a realistic assumption in this case?

5. Hiram Fye is an electronics nut, and owns a very complicated stereo system. Although it generally produces excellent sound, there are occasions when it doesn't and Hi must figure out what is wrong. The trouble

always lies in one (and only one) of two possible components, the tuner or the amplifier. The probabilities that each of these components is the source of the fault are 0.3 and 0.7 respectively. Hi has yet to find a foolproof diagnostic test. The best available has the following sampling distribution:

	Probability That the Test Result is	
Location of Fault	Positive	Negative
Tuner	0.75	0.25
Amplifier	0.4	0.6

Hi has found it takes him three hours to find and correct a fault in the tuner (or realize that there is no fault) and five hours to find and correct a fault in the amplifier.

a. List the events, actions, and sample outcomes for this problem.
b. If Hi's goal is to minimize the time he spends repairing his stereo, what is his loss matrix? Which action should he take if he doesn't do any testing?
c. List the strategies available to Hi.
d. Determine Hi's best strategy using the enumeration of strategies approach.
e. Draw and analyze a decision tree for Hi's problem.

6. Pacific Union Chemical Company (PU) has a problem with one of their processes. A by-product of the reaction involved is hydrogen sulfide, a gas that smells like rotten eggs. In the past this gas, along with other, nonnoxious gases, has been exhausted through the company's smokestack. However, PU has recently realized its obligation to its employees and the townspeople, and has purchased three devices to eliminate the hydrogen sulfide from the exhaust gases. The question facing PU is—which of the three devices should be used on any particular day? (The hydrogen sulfide content varies from day to day, depending upon the sulfur content of the raw materials used in the reaction.) The economics of the three are:

Device A. All exhaust gases are passed through a chemical solution that absorbs the hydrogen sulfide. There is a fixed cost of $100 for connecting this device, and a variable cost of $500p$, where p = proportion of hydrogen sulfide in the exhaust gases.

Device B. Place a solid chemical absorbant in the smokestack. There is a cost of $350 to do this, and the absorbant has capacity for any concentration of hydrogen sulfide. (But it must be replaced at the end of the day.)

Device C. Burn the exhaust gases, turning the hydrogen sulfide into water and sulfur dioxide. This sulfur dioxide can then be absorbed by water, and this solution sold as weak sulfuric acid. The daily cost of this process is $600, but the weak sulfuric acid yields a return proportional to p, $500p$.

From previous experience PU feels that the proportion of hydrogen sulfide in the exhaust gases will be either 0.1, 0.3, 0.5, 0.7, or 0.9, with corresponding probabilities 0.19, 0.18, 0.23, 0.21, 0.19.

a. List the actions and events for this problem.
b. Construct a loss table for this problem.
c. Which of the actions is best?

The raw material PU uses in its process is classified as either high, medium, or low sulfur content. From past experience PU has found that each of these levels of sulfur content result in the following distributions of p:

Sulfur Content of Raw Material \ Proportion of Hydrogen Sulfide in Stack Gases	0.1	0.3	0.5	0.7	0.9
High	0.1	0.1	0.1	0.4	0.3
Medium	0.1	0.2	0.3	0.2	0.2
Low	0.4	0.2	0.2	0.1	0.1

(Be careful to understand what these numbers are!)

d. Suppose raw material to be used in a day can be restricted to one of the three grades. Which device should PU use for each of the three grades of raw material?
e. PU's current supplier of raw material has material that is 20 percent high sulfur content, 50 percent medium sulfur content, and 30 percent low sulfur content. A new company is trying to secure PU's raw material business, and guarantees 40 percent of their stock has a low sulfur content. However, they also admit that the remaining 60 percent has a high sulfur content. Should PU switch suppliers?

Binomial Sampling Problems—I

THE REST of this text, except for Chapters 13 and 14, deals with applying the techniques we discussed in the previous three chapters to problems in which the sampling distributions are either binomial or normal. Discussing these types of problems serves two purposes. First, these are problems that will commonly be met in practice, because binomial or normal sampling situations are frequently encountered in practice. Second, these problems have far too many strategies to be analyzed in the straightforward manner we discussed previously. Consequently, the study of these problems will give the student some good insights into how to analyze a problem that is *not* amenable to a complete enumeration of strategies.

It must be emphasized that the *same* concepts and techniques developed in the previous chapters will be applied to the problems discussed in this and subsequent chapters. The difference lies in the mechanics of applying these techniques. It is important for the student to realize this, and to be constantly on guard so that he doesn't get so involved in the mechanics of solving a problem that he loses sight of the underlying concepts and techniques.

Because the mechanics of solving these problems are so complicated, we will restrict our discussion to *two-action problems*. Nothing but complexity is to be gained by considering problems with more than two actions; the mechanics are essentially the same. After he has mastered the material on two-action problems, the student who is interested is invited to solve Problem 6.18, which is a three-action problem. This will not only give him an insight into multiaction problems, but will thoroughly test his understanding of the mechanics discussed in this chapter.

6.1   THE PROBABILITY ASPECTS OF BINOMIAL SAMPLING

If we are going to study problems involving binomial sampling, we must first understand the situations in which binomial sampling occurs, and the mechanics of calculating probabilities for the sample outcomes in these instances.

Binomial sampling occurs when we have a probability process consisting of a number of trials, and:

1.   At each trial one of two outcomes can occur.
2.   The probability of each outcome is constant throughout all trials.
3.   The outcome of one trial is independent of the outcome of all other trials.

One can think of many examples where binomial sampling occurs. The classic example is that of flipping coins. At each flip (trial) there are two possible outcomes, heads (H) and tails (T). The probabilities of heads and tails remain the same (they have a value of $\frac{1}{2}$) throughout all flips, and the outcome of one flip does not influence the other outcomes.

How do we determine the probabilities of the various outcomes when binomial sampling occurs? We will give the reader an idea of the development of these probabilities, then a general formula and some instructions on how to read a table. Consider first an example. Suppose we flip a coin three times. Then the list of all possible outcomes is:

$$\{HHH, HHT, HTH, THH, HTT, THT, TTH, TTT\}$$

where, for example, *HHT* represents a head on each of the first two trials and a tail on the third trial.

Although the above is a complete listing of the sample outcomes, we will discover in subsequent sections of this chapter that we will be interested in knowing the probabilities of composite events, rather than the elementary events listed above. We are, in fact, most interested in the probabilities of the following events:

$$\{3 \text{ Heads}, 2 \text{ Heads}, 1 \text{ Head}, 0 \text{ Heads}\}$$

where, for instance, the event "2 Heads" is a composite of *HHT, HTH,* and *THH* from the original list.

The relationship between the composite event "2 Heads" and the elementary events *HHT, HTH,* and *THH* can lead us to a development of the probability of two heads, $P(2 \text{ Heads})$. First notice that if we apply the rule for independence, we have

$$P(HHT) = P(H)\ P(H)\ P(T) = [P(H)]^2\ P(T)$$

for the first of the elementary events. An important property of binomial sampling situations is that this same expression, $[P(H)]^2\ P(T)$, represents the probability of each of the other elementary events, HTH and THH, as well.[1]

The second fact that will be important to us is that, since HHT, HTH, and THH are elementary events, they are mutually exclusive. Thus

$$P(2 \text{ Heads}) = P(HHT \text{ or } HTH \text{ or } THH)$$
$$= P(HHT) + P(HTH) + P(THH).$$

In the preceding paragraph, we found that each of these last expressions is equal to $[P(H)]^2P(T)$. Thus

$$P(2 \text{ Heads}) = [P(H)]^2P(T) + [P(H)]^2P(T) + [P(H)]^2P(T)$$
$$= 3 \times [P(H)]^2P(T).$$

This final expression is analogous to the general binomial sampling probability formula. In both the probability is the product of the number of elementary events making up the particular compound event with the probability of *any one* of the *elementary* events. The formula for the number of elementary events that make up a particular compound event is

$$\frac{n!}{k!(n-k)!}$$

where $n!$ (read n factorial) is the product of the integers from 1 to n:

$$n! = 1 \times 2 \times 3 \times \cdots \times n.$$

Since k or $n - k$ can sometimes be 0, we also must define $0! \equiv 1$.

In the above formula n is the number of trials in the binomial sampling process, and k is the number of outcomes of one kind occurring in the compound event. Thus, the number of different ways that two heads can occur in three tosses of a coin is (using the formula)

$$\frac{3!}{2!(3-2)!} = \frac{1 \times 2 \times 3}{1 \times 2 \times 1} = 3,$$

which, of course, verifies the previous listing of HHT, HTH, and THH.

The expression for the probability of an elementary event, which we will multiply by the counting formula given above, is easily derived. If p is the probability of an outcome of one kind *on any particular trial,*

---

[1] The reader should verify this personally.

then the elementary event consisting of k of these outcomes and $n - k$ outcomes of the other kind must have a probability of

$$p^k (1 - p)^{n-k}$$

since each trial is independent of all others.

Combining the two expressions we have derived above, we get the general expression for binomial sampling probabilities:

$$P(k \text{ outcomes of one kind in } n \text{ trials}) = \frac{n!}{k!(n-k)!} p^k(1-p)^{n-k}.$$

This is a complicated looking formula, and it is difficult to evaluate for all save the simplest p values and small values of n and k. In the next subsection we will discuss using Table I at the back of the text to determine the values for these probabilities. Before we do that, however, we should point out that if we consider a random variable X, which counts the number of occurrences of one kind in n trials, then X has the set of outcomes

$$\{0, 1, 2, \cdots, n\}$$

and

$$P(X = k) = \frac{n!}{k!(n-k)!} p^k(1-p)^{n-k} \quad \text{for} \quad 0 \le k \le n.$$

These probabilities form a distribution, of course, called the *binomial distribution,* and

$$E(X) = np; \ \text{Var}(X) = np(1-p).$$

As an example of the binomial distribution, suppose we know that 60 percent of the voters in a certain precinct favor a new school bond proposal. If we interview a random sample of size 4 (with replacement) from the population, we might find that any number (between 0 and 4) of those interviewed favor the school bond. If we let X be the number (of those interviewed) who favor the school bond, then

$$P(X = 0) = \frac{4!}{0!4!} (0.6)^0(1 - 0.6)^4 = 0.0256$$

$$P(X = 1) = \frac{4!}{1!3!} (0.6)^1(1 - 0.6)^3 = 0.1536$$

$$P(X = 2) = \frac{4!}{2!2!} (0.6)^2(1 - 0.6)^2 = 0.3456$$

$$P(X = 3) = \frac{4!}{3!1!} (0.6)^3(1 - 0.6)^1 = 0.3456$$

$$P(X = 4) = \frac{4!}{4!0!} (0.6)^4(1 - 0.6)^0 = 0.1296$$

and

$$E(X) = 4 \times 0.6 = 2.4; \; \text{Var}(X) = 4 \times 0.6 \times 0.4 = 0.96.$$

6.1.1 Obtaining Binomial Probabilities from Table I

Table I (at the back of the text) contains the values of the *cumulative* binomial distribution

$$P(X \geq r|n,p)$$

for values of p between 0.01 and 0.5 and values of n between 1 and 20 as well as 50 and 100. This Table lists cumulative probabilities because they are more valuable to us in solving binomial sampling problems.

As an example of the Table's use, suppose we want to find the probability of two or more heads in three tosses of a fair coin. In this case $n = 3$, $r = 2$, and $p = \frac{1}{2}$. Note that p must be the probability of a head on any trial in this case, since X measures the number of *heads* in three trials. We have

$$P(X \geq 2|n = 3, \, p = \tfrac{1}{2}) = 0.5000$$

from the second page of Table I. Notice that the table assumes you know that the probability is a fraction, and lists only the significant digits of the fraction, 5000. *You* must add the decimal point and the preceding zero.

Since the table lists cumulative binomial probabilities, we need a method to obtain the probabilities for individual events. Suppose we want to know the probability of *exactly* one head in three tosses of a fair coin. This can be obtained by subtracting one cumulative probability from another. The probability of one or more heads includes the events "1 head," "2 heads," and "3 heads," while the probability of two or more heads includes the events "2 heads" and "3 heads." Thus, the probability of exactly one head is the difference between the two. In symbols:

$$
\begin{aligned}
P(X = 1|n = 3, \, p = \tfrac{1}{2}) \\
&= P(X \geq 1|n = 3, \, p = \tfrac{1}{2}) - P(X \geq 2|n = 3, \, p = \tfrac{1}{2}) \\
&= 0.8750 - 0.5000 \\
&= 0.3750.
\end{aligned}
$$

The table also has no entries for p values greater than 0.5. If such a probability is desired, the probability of the complementary event must be obtained. For example, in the illustration of voters favoring a school bond, we found that $p = 0.6$ when X denotes the number of those interviewed who favor the school bond. This problem can be cast in terms of a p value less than 0.5 by letting X indicate the number of interviewers who *do not favor* the school bond. With this the value of *p* is the probability that a person will *not* favor the bond issue, which is 0.4. Furthermore, suppose we are interested in finding the probability that three of those interviewed favor the bond issue. If three (out of the four interviewed) favor the issue, then one does not. Hence, the probability that three favor the issue is the same as the probability that one person does not favor the issue. This is the concept that is used to determine binomial probabilities when *p* is greater than 0.5. They are equated to the probabilities of the complementary events, and for these the *p* value is less than 0.5. In symbols, for the voter problem we have:

$$P(3 \text{ [out of 4] favor issue}) = P(1 \text{ [out of 4] do not favor issue}).$$

The probability on the left side of the above equation cannot be evaluated from Table I. However, the probability on the right side can, and it is

$$P(1 \text{ [out of 4] do not favor issue}) = P(X = 1 | n = 4, p = 0.4)$$
$$= 0.3456,$$

where the numerical value for the probability is obtained from Table I.

A similar argument can be applied to cumulative probabilities. When that is done, we find that the general formula is

$$P(X \geq r | n, p) = P(X < n - r + 1 | n, 1 - p)$$
$$= 1 - P(X \geq n - r + 1 | n, 1 - p).$$

Thus, in our voting example, if we want the probability that three or more of those interviewed will favor the school bond we have

$$P(X \geq 3 | n = 4, p = 0.6) = 1 - P(X \geq 2 | n = 4, p = 0.4)$$
$$= 1 - 0.5248$$
$$= 0.4752$$

which agrees with our previous values.

6.2 THE SET OF EVENTS IN BINOMIAL SAMPLING

What are we trying to determine when we conduct binomial sampling? Almost always we are trying to determine a value for *p*. If we are flipping a balanced coin, physical considerations dictate that *p* should be approximately ½. However, what if we are flipping a thumbtack? As noted in Chapter 2, there are two positions it can land in,

Points Up

On Its Side

and the probability of points up on any trial is probably quite constant and independent from trial to trial. But what is the *value* of the probability of points up? Is it 0.4 or 0.2, or perhaps 0.67253, or what? The physical considerations that allowed us to establish $p = \frac{1}{2}$ for the coin are, if not absent, much more complex in the case of the thumbtack. So, probably the easiest way to determine the value of p is to flip the thumbtack a number of times.

Just as, for curiosity's sake, we would like to know the value of p for a thumbtack, there are many decision problems whose solution depends upon the determination of an unknown value of p. Thus, we set up the problem with various potential values of p as the event set. The reader might realize that this event set is quite different from the event sets we have previously considered. In previous problems there have always been a *small* number of events. Here, p can potentially take on any value between 0 and 1, so there is a whole continuum of potential values for p.

Handling event sets with a continuum of values will be deferred until Chapter 9. For the moment we will discuss problems in which a small number of potential p values are considered. We first consider these simpler problems to set some ideas. These ideas will be quite valuable when we consider problems involving the entire spectrum of potential p values.

6.3 AN EXAMPLE

An example can illustrate the types of problems we will be discussing in this chapter. It will also conveniently serve as a basis for discussion of the techniques in subsequent sections of the chapter.

Coffee: Valley Sisters Coffee Company has a coffee can-filling machine. From past experience they know that, essentially according to independent trials, the probability of a can being filled improperly is p. Before each new run the machine is cleaned and adjusted, and a new p results. The question facing the production manager is whether to accept the new cleaning without expert inspection, or to take the time to inspect the machine before a new run begins.

The costs involved are as follows. If the machine is inspected, the lost time is worth \$6 to the company. Furthermore, the inspector is good enough so that virtually no defective cans are present in the run following inspection. On the other hand, if the run is allowed to continue, each can that is misfilled must be opened and a new can used for refilling. The cost of the lost can is 6¢. Each production run totals 2,000 cans.

From past experience the production manager knows that the potential values of p are 0.01, 0.02, 0.04, and 0.15, and the frequency with which each of these occur is 0.4, 0.3, 0.2, and 0.1 respectively.

The production manager has the option of sampling a few cans at the start of the run before he makes his decision concerning the inspector. How many cans should he sample, and what should his strategy be?

Before we turn to the sampling considerations, it is helpful to analyze the production manager's problem without sampling. In order to do this we must develop a cost table for the problem. The cost for the inspection is $6, no matter what the value of p is. However, the cost of rejected cans will increase rapidly as p increases. We must evaluate this relationship.

Unfortunately, since the can filling is a random process, we cannot predict *exactly* how many cans will be incorrectly filled, even if we knew the exact value for p. As always, we seek an expected value in place of a certain value, and such a value can be developed in this case. The entire run (2,000 cans) can be considered as a binomial process with $n = 2,000$. Then the expected number of defective cans, by the formula for the expected value of a binomial distribution is $2,000p$ cans. The total cost of these defective cans is $0.06 \times 2,000p = \$120p$. This is the formula we need to establish the cost table:

Events \ Actions	A	N
$p = 0.01$	$6	$ 1.20
$p = 0.02$	$6	$ 2.40
$p = 0.04$	$6	$ 4.80
$p = 0.15$	$6	$18.

where

A = Call in the expert to inspect and adjust the machine
N = No inspection; i.e., continue the run.

In later developments we will find it much more useful to analyze the problem using opportunity losses. The opportunity losses for this problem are:

	A	N
$p = 0.01$	$4.80	0
$p = 0.02$	$3.60	0
$p = 0.04$	$1.20	0
$p = 0.15$	0	$12

and the expected opportunity losses for each action are

$$\mathcal{E}(A) = 4.80 \times 0.4 + 3.60 \times 0.3 + 1.20 \times 0.2 + 0 \times 0.1 = 3.24$$
$$\mathcal{E}(N) = 0 \times 0.4 + 0 \times 0.3 + 0 \times 0.2 + 12 \times 0.1 = 1.20.$$

Hence, it is best to continue the run without inspection.

6.4   STRATEGIES IN BINOMIAL SAMPLING PROBLEMS

Let us now turn to the larger question asked by the production manager. Should he sample; if so, how many cans should he sample, and what strategy is best for the optimum number of cans sampled? If we adopt an enumeration of strategies approach for solving this problem, we must first list all the strategies (for all sample sizes) for this problem. Let us consider doing that.

Consider a particular sample size, say $n = 3$, and all the possible outcomes. If we let G = good (properly filled) can, and B = bad (improperly filled) can, then the set of all outcomes is

$$\{GGG, GGB, GBG, BGG, GBB, BGB, BBG, BBB\}.$$

There are eight outcomes, and our rule for counting strategies tells us there will be $2^8 = 256$ strategies to evaluate. This is a very large number of potential strategies to evaluate, and remember that these are only the strategies for $n = 3$. If we consider a series of n's (as we should, in order to find the best one), the total number of strategies becomes astronomical! For $n = 6$ *alone* the total number of strategies is 18,446,744,073,709,551,616. Clearly some reduction must be made in the number of strategies we evaluate.

The first simplification arises because different outcomes have the same probability of occurrence. In the above set, for instance, $P(GGB) = P(GBG) = P(BGG)$, *no matter what the value of p is.* It can be shown[2] that outcomes with identical sampling distributions lead to identical strategies, no matter what the probabilities of the events are. Thus, outcomes with identical sampling distributions can be grouped into a single category, and the relevant outcomes for $n = 3$ become

$$\{\text{none bad, 1 bad, 2 bad, 3 bad}\}$$

This simplification represents quite a saving. The total number of strategies for $n = 3$ now becomes $2^4 = 16$. However, if we consider evaluating every strategy from $n = 1$ to $n = 20$ we will have to evaluate 4,194,300 strategies, still far too many.

There are two other simplifications that reduce the number of strategies even further. If we adopt the following abbreviation for the sample outcomes for $n = 3$,

$$\{0, 1, 2, 3\}$$

then the 16 strategies we are considering at this point are:

$$s_1 = \{0\text{-}A, 1\text{-}A, 2\text{-}A, 3\text{-}A\};$$
$$s_2 = \{0\text{-}A, 1\text{-}A, 2\text{-}A, 3\text{-}N\};$$

---

[2] The reader can quickly verify this by considering a two branch decision tree with both branches having the same sampling distribution.

$$s_3 = \{0\text{-}A, 1\text{-}A, 2\text{-}N, 3\text{-}A\};$$
$$s_4 = \{0\text{-}A, 1\text{-}N, 2\text{-}A, 3\text{-}A\};$$
$$s_5 = \{0\text{-}N, 1\text{-}A, 2\text{-}A, 3\text{-}A\};$$
$$s_6 = \{0\text{-}A, 1\text{-}A, 2\text{-}N, 3\text{-}N\};$$
$$s_7 = \{0\text{-}A, 1\text{-}N, 2\text{-}A, 3\text{-}N\};$$
$$s_8 = \{0\text{-}A, 1\text{-}N, 2\text{-}N, 3\text{-}A\};$$
$$s_9 = \{0\text{-}N, 1\text{-}A, 2\text{-}A, 3\text{-}N\};$$
$$s_{10} = \{0\text{-}N, 1\text{-}A, 2\text{-}N, 3\text{-}A\};$$
$$s_{11} = \{0\text{-}N, 1\text{-}N, 2\text{-}A, 3\text{-}A\};$$
$$s_{12} = \{0\text{-}A, 1\text{-}N, 2\text{-}N, 3\text{-}N\};$$
$$s_{13} = \{0\text{-}N, 1\text{-}A, 2\text{-}N, 3\text{-}N\};$$
$$s_{14} = \{0\text{-}N, 1\text{-}N, 2\text{-}A, 3\text{-}N\};$$
$$s_{15} = \{0\text{-}N, 1\text{-}N, 2\text{-}N, 3\text{-}A\};$$
$$s_{16} = \{0\text{-}N, 1\text{-}N, 2\text{-}N, 3\text{-}N\}.$$

The first of these simplifications can be expressed as:

A "cross-over" strategy will never be optimal.

An example of a cross-over strategy is s_3. This strategy dictates A should be chosen for 0 and 1 bad cans, N for two bad cans, then back to A for 3 bad cans. The cross-over strategies for $n = 3$ are s_3, s_4, s_7, s_8, s_9, s_{10}, s_{13}, and s_{14}. So, by applying the above rule we have reduced the number of strategies to be considered from 16 to 8.

The second half of our simplification leads to even further reductions. Consider two of the remaining strategies:

$$s_6 = \{0\text{-}A, 1\text{-}A, 2\text{-}N, 3\text{-}N\} \text{ and } s_{11} = \{0\text{-}N, 1\text{-}N, 2\text{-}A, 3\text{-}A\}.$$

s_6 can be expressed in words as

For small numbers of bad cans inspect the machine and for large numbers of bad cans continue the run.

On the other hand, s_{11} is just the opposite strategy

For small numbers of bad cans continue the run and for large numbers of bad cans inspect the machine.

Of these two strategies, s_{11} is much more intuitively appealing, and it can be shown that our intuition is correct. Similar reasoning leads to the elimination of s_2, s_6, and s_{12}.

From the original 256 strategies for $n = 3$ we have reduced the number of strategies that must be considered (through the application of various rules) to five. This is certainly a meaningful reduction in the amount of work that must be done to analyze the problem. This reduction makes the analysis of binomial sampling problems feasible. In considering a range of n values from 1 to 20, there are still many (250) strategies to evaluate, but the number is now reduced to a reasonable level. We later give more shortcuts when we discuss the evaluation of these strategies.

6.4.1 The Concept of a Cutoff Point

Consider the five strategies we must evaluate for $n = 3$.

$$s_1 = \{0\text{-}A, 1\text{-}A, 2\text{-}A, 3\text{-}A\};$$
$$s_5 = \{0\text{-}N, 1\text{-}A, 2\text{-}A, 3\text{-}A\};$$
$$s_{11} = \{0\text{-}N, 1\text{-}N, 2\text{-}A, 3\text{-}A\};$$
$$s_{15} = \{0\text{-}N, 1\text{-}N, 2\text{-}N, 3\text{-}A\};$$
$$s_{16} = \{0\text{-}N, 1\text{-}N, 2\text{-}N, 3\text{-}N\}.$$

This *group* of strategies can be described by the following composite strategy

Take action N if the number of bad cans is less than c, take action A if the number of bad cans is greater than or equal to c

where c, the *cutoff point,* ranges from 0 to 4.

If we let B represent the random variable describing the number of bad cans in the sample, then the composite strategy can be written as:

$$\{\text{If } B < c \text{ then } N, \text{ if } B \geq c \text{ then } A\}.$$

Any binomial sampling problem for which n is fixed has a similar kind of composite strategy. In future discussions of these problems we will immediately adopt the composite strategy as the best strategy, rather than going through a lengthy verification similar to that above.

6.5 FINDING THE BEST STRATEGY FOR n FIXED—FINDING $c*$

The problem of finding the best strategy when n is fixed is merely the problem of finding the best value for c. We denote this best value $c*$. Thus, $c* = 2$ means that the expected opportunity loss for s_{11} is smaller than the expected opportunity losses for s_1, s_5, s_{15}, and s_{16}.

Let us analyze the five strategies to see which is the best. To do this, the sampling distributions are needed. Using Table I

$$P(B = 2|n = 3, p = 0.04)$$
$$= P(B \geq 2|n = 3, p = 0.04) - P(B \geq 3|n = 3, p = 0.04)$$
$$= 0.0047 - 0.0001$$
$$= 0.0046.$$

The other probabilities are derived in a similar fashion, and the sampling distributions are:

	$B = 0$	$B = 1$	$B = 2$	$B = 3$
$p = 0.01$	0.9703	0.0294	0.0003	0
$p = 0.02$	0.9412	0.0576	0.0012	0
$p = 0.04$	0.8847	0.1106	0.0046	0.0001
$p = 0.15$	0.6141	0.3251	0.0574	0.0034

Given these sampling distributions, we must calculate the expected loss for each strategy given that a particular event will occur. As an example:

$$\mathcal{E}(s_{11}|p = 0.01) = \text{loss}(0\text{-}N|p = 0.01)P(0\text{-}N|p = 0.01)$$
$$+ \text{loss}(1\text{-}N|p = 0.01)P(1\text{-}N|p = 0.01)$$
$$+ \text{loss}(2\text{-}A|p = 0.01)P(2\text{-}A|p = 0.01)$$
$$+ \text{loss}(3\text{-}A|p = 0.01)P(3\text{-}A|p = 0.01).$$

Remember that the losses depend only upon the action part of the strategy, and the probabilities depend only upon the sample outcome part of the strategy. The above expression reduces to:

$$\mathcal{E}(s_{11}|p = 0.01) = \text{loss}(N|p = 0.01)P(B = 0|n = 3, p = 0.01)$$
$$+ \text{loss}(N|p = 0.01)P(B = 1|n = 3, p = 0.01)$$
$$+ \text{loss}(A|p = 0.01)P(B = 2|n = 3, p = 0.01)$$
$$+ \text{loss}(A|p = 0.01)P(B = 3|n = 3, p = 0.01)$$
$$= 0 \times 0.9703 + 0 \times 0.0294 + 4.8 \times 0.0003 + 4.8 \times 0$$
$$= 0.00144.$$

Using similar calculations for the other entries, the table of conditional expected losses for $n = 3$ is

Strategies / Events	s_1 $(c = 0)$	s_3 $(c = 1)$	s_{11} $(c = 2)$	s_{15} $(c = 3)$	s_{16} $(c = 4)$
$p = 0.01$	4.8	0.14256	0.00144	0	0
$p = 0.02$	3.6	0.21168	0.00432	0	0
$p = 0.04$	1.2	0.13836	0.00564	0.00012	0
$p = 0.15$	0	7.3692	11.2704	11.9592	12

Finally, to obtain the unconditional expected opportunity loss for a strategy, we take the conditional expected losses, multiply by the probabilities of the events:

$$P(p = 0.01) = 0.4; \; P(p = 0.02) = 0.3; \; P(p = 0.04) = 0.2;$$
$$P(p = 0.15) = 0.1,$$

and sum. Thus

$$\mathcal{E}(s_1) = 4.8 \times 0.4 + 3.6 \times 0.3 + 1.2 \times 0.2 + 0 \times 0.1 = 3.24$$

and similar calculations yield

$$\mathcal{E}(s_5) = 0.885;\ \mathcal{E}(s_{11}) = 1.13;\ \mathcal{E}(s_{15}) = 1.20;\ \mathcal{E}(s_{16}) = 1.20.$$

Hence, $s_5(c = 1)$ is the best strategy, since it has the minimum unconditional expected loss. Notice also that s_1 and s_{16} are "pure" strategies—they select the same action no matter what the sample outcome is—and their unconditional expected losses agree with the values we calculated in Section 6.3.

6.6 COMPUTATIONAL SHORTCUTS

Although the determination of the best strategy for $n = 3$ does not seem extremely taxing, imagine solving the same problem for all values of n between 1 and 20. This would be quite a feat to accomplish, and it is important to explore all the shortcuts that can be made in the calculations.

6.6.1 Shortcuts for Conditional Expected Losses

Consider the expression for the conditional expected loss of s_{11}, given $p = 0.01$:

$$
\begin{aligned}
\mathcal{E}(s_{11}|p = 0.01) = {} & \text{loss}(N|p = 0.01)P(B = 0|n = 3, p = 0.01) \\
& + \text{loss}(N|p = 0.01)P(B = 1|n = 3, p = 0.01) \\
& + \text{loss}(A|p = 0.01)P(B = 2|n = 3, p = 0.01) \\
& + \text{loss}(A|p = 0.01)P(B = 3|n = 3, p = 0.01)
\end{aligned}
$$

The terms loss $(N|p = 0.01)$ and $\text{loss}(A|p = 0.01)$ each appear twice, and the expression can be rearranged as:

$$
\begin{aligned}
\mathcal{E}(s_{11}|p = 0.01) = {} & \text{loss}(N|p = 0.01)[P(B = 0|n = 3, p = 0.01) \\
& + P(B = 1|n = 3, p = 0.01)] \\
& + \text{loss}(A|p = 0.01)[P(B = 2|n = 3, p = 0.01) \\
& + P(B = 3|n = 3, p = 0.01)]
\end{aligned}
$$

and the two probabilities can be added to form a cumulative probability:

$$
\begin{aligned}
\mathcal{E}(s_{11}|p = 0.01) = {} & \text{loss}(N|p = 0.01)P(B \le 1|n = 3, p = 0.01) \\
& + \text{loss}(A|p = 0.01)P(B \ge 2|n = 3, p = 0.01).
\end{aligned}
$$

Now, we have already stated that $c = 2$ for s_{11}. The above expression can be generalized, and we find

The conditional expected opportunity loss for a strategy whose cutoff point is c is

$$\text{loss}(N|p)P(B < c|n,p) + \text{loss}(A|p)P(B \ge c|n,p)$$

and the expression is, in a very real sense, the conditional expected opportunity loss for the composite strategy given in Section 6.4.1.

It should now be obvious to the reader why the binomial table is a cumulative table. It is these cumulative probabilities we will find most useful in our binomial sampling work.

There is an additional computational shortcut that can be employed in calculating the conditional expected opportunity losses. Notice that *for two action problems,* either $\text{loss}(N|p)$ or $\text{loss}(A|p)$ is zero for all values of p. Thus,

$$\mathcal{E}(s_{11}|p = 0.01) = \text{loss}(A|p = 0.01)P(B \geq 2|n = 3, p = 0.01)$$

and

$$\mathcal{E}(s_{11}|p = 0.15) = \text{loss}(N|p = 0.15)P(B < 2|n = 3, p = 0.15)$$

only because $\text{loss}(N|p = 0.01) = 0$ and $\text{loss}(A|p = 0.15) = 0$, not because the expected value calculation only has one term. Hence, the conditional expected losses for this problem are:

$$
\begin{aligned}
\text{Conditional} \\
\text{Expected Loss}
\end{aligned}
=
\begin{cases}
\text{loss}(A|p)P(B \geq c|n, p) \text{ if } p = 0.01 \text{ or } 0.02 \text{ or } 0.04 \\
\text{loss}(N|p)P(B < c|n, p) \text{ if } p = 0.15.
\end{cases}
$$

6.6.2 The Unconditional Expected Loss as a Function of c

Consider a plot of the unconditional expected opportunity losses as a function of c shown in Figure 6.1. The expected opportunity losses as a function of c have a *single* minimum at $c = 1$. This property is true for any fixed value of n, and leads to another shortcut in finding the best strategy for fixed n. Since there is a single minimum in the function, a value of c is optimal if the expected opportunity losses for the strategies $c - 1$ and $c + 1$ are larger. In the case we have been studying, the fact that the expected opportunity loss at $c = 1$ is lower than the expected opportunity losses at either $c = 0$ or $c = 2$ indicates that the optimal value of c is 1 ($c^* = 1$). Thus, the best strategy can be found by evaluating as few as three of the strategies, rather than all five.

6.6.3 One Last Shortcut

Since fewer than all of the strategies have to be evaluated for any n, it helps to calculate the unconditional expected losses (henceforth abbreviated UEL) for each strategy separately, rather than developing the full table of conditional expected losses as was done in Section 6.5. In the process, one more computational shortcut is realized.

FIGURE 6.1
**Graph of Overall Losses Versus c Values for n = 3 in the
Valley Sisters Problem**

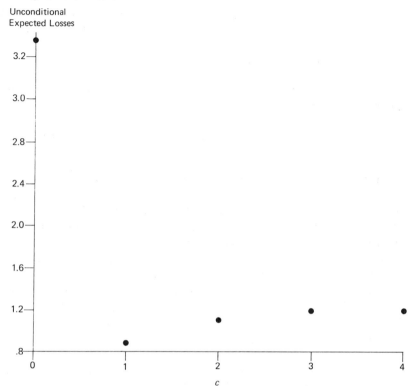

Consider UEL for s_{11},

$$\text{UEL} = \mathcal{E}(s_{11}|p = 0.01)P(p = 0.01) + \mathcal{E}(s_{11}|p = 0.02)P(p = 0.02)$$
$$+ \mathcal{E}(s_{11}|p = 0.04)P(p = 0.04) + \mathcal{E}(s_{11}|p = 0.15)P(p = 0.15).$$

Using the compact expressions for the conditional expected losses developed in Section 6.6.1, the UEL for s_{11} becomes:

$$\text{UEL} = \text{loss}(A|p = 0.01)P(B \geq 2|n, p = 0.01)P(p = 0.01)$$
$$+ \text{loss}(A|p = 0.02)P(B \geq 2|n, p = 0.02)P(p = 0.02)$$
$$+ \text{loss}(A|p = 0.04)P(B \geq 2|n, p = 0.04)P(p = 0.04)$$
$$+ \text{loss}(N|p = 0.15)P(B < 2|n, p = 0.15)P(p = 0.15).$$

Notice that two of the expressions in each of the four terms do not vary with either n or c. The only quantities that change values as the n and c change are the binomial probabilities. Thus, for any problem a preliminary calculation can be made that multiplies the *non-zero* losses in the loss table by the corresponding probabilities of events. For the Valley Sisters problem:

$$\text{loss}(A|p = 0.01)P(p = 0.01) = 4.80 \times 0.4 = 1.92$$
$$\text{loss}(A|p = 0.02)P(p = 0.02) = 3.60 \times 0.3 = 1.08$$
$$\text{loss}(A|p = 0.04)P(p = 0.04) = 1.20 \times 0.2 = 0.24$$
$$\text{loss}(N|p = 0.15)P(p = 0.15) = 12 \times 0.1 = 1.20$$

and the general expression for evaluating a strategy for Valley Sisters *for any value of n or c* is

$$\text{UEL} = 1.92 \times P(B \geq c|n, p = 0.01) + 1.08 \times P(B \geq c|n, p = 0.02)$$
$$+ 0.24 \times P(B \geq c|n, p = 0.04) + 1.2 \times P(B < c|n, p = 0.15).$$

This formula will be used to calculate the best value for c when $n = 6$. In this case c can take on any value from 0 to 7. In Section 6.6.2 we found that, with luck, only three strategies (values of c) need to be evaluated. However, there is no systematic procedure by which the best value of c can be obtained. Only a trial and error search can be used. Thus, there could be as few as three strategies evaluated or as many as all eight, and it is very important to pick a "reasonable" starting point for the search procedure. Techniques for doing this are discussed in Section 6.7.3. For the moment, since we found that $c^* = 1$ for $n = 3$, it seems reasonable that c^* should be "close to" 1 for $n = 6$. Therefore, the strategy $c = 1$ will be evaluated first. For $c = 1$:

$$\text{UEL} = 1.92 \times 0.0585 + 1.08 \times 0.1142 + 0.24 \times 0.2172$$
$$+ 1.2 \times 0.3771 = 0.740.$$

To determine if $c = 1$ is the best strategy, the UEL of the neighboring c values must be calculated. For $c = 2$:

$$\text{UEL} = 1.92 \times 0.0015 + 1.08 \times 0.0057 + 0.24 + 0.0216$$
$$+ 1.2 \times 0.7765 = 0.946,$$

and $c = 1$ is better than $c = 2$ because its UEL is lower.

What about $c = 0$? Fortunately, this strategy does not have to be evaluated. Recall that $c = 0$ was a pure strategy (always choose A) for $n = 3$. The same holds true for any value of n. The UEL for $c = 0$ (calculated in Section 6.3) is 3.24. Using this and the UEL for $c = 2$ we conclude that $c^* = 1$, that is, the optimal strategy is

> Choose N if no bad cans occur in the sample, and choose A if one or more bad cans occur in the sample.

and its UEL is 0.740.

6.7 OVERVIEW AND ANOTHER EXAMPLE

This chapter contains many ideas, and it is important to summarize what we have discussed. This section will contain a summary of what you have learned, what the general method for tackling a binomial sampling problem is, and a final example that illustrates this technique.

6.7.1 An Overview of Binomial Sampling Problems

Binomial sampling problems are characterized by a number, n, of trials, each with two possible outcomes, and a constant probability for each outcome on each trial. The overall problem associated with binomial sampling is to determine the optimal number of trials to sample—balancing the sample costs against the additional information received from that sample. However, learning to do this is a large task, and this chapter concentrated on the smaller problem of finding the best strategy for a fixed sample size. The knowledge gained in this chapter is used in Chapter 7 to solve the overall problem.

In the analysis of strategies in this chapter we found many shortcuts. Many of the original list of strategies were eliminated, and the composite statement of the ones which remained was:

$$\{ \text{If } B < c \text{ then } N; \text{ If } B \geq c \text{ then } A \}$$

where c was an arbitrary "cutoff point." In addition to the shortcuts that were made because of technical considerations, there were several computational shortcuts to determining the best policy. The major one involved an acknowledgement that there was a single minimum when the UELs of the strategies are plotted as a function of c. Thus, with luck, only three strategies need to be evaluated for any n. On the other hand, there is no systematic procedure for determining the best strategy, so the search for the best strategy is a trial and error procedure. Therefore, while the minimum number of strategy evaluations is three, the maximum—if the person conducting the search is not thoughtful—could be very large, especially for large n.

6.7.2 Summary of the Procedure for Finding the Best Strategy (Best Value for c) for Fixed n.

To find the best strategy, one should:

1. Determine the composite strategy for this problem. Basically, this involves deciding which action should be associated with small numbers of the outcome, and which action should be associated with large numbers of the outcome.

2. Write down the corresponding conditional expected loss expression for this strategy (as a function of c). Multiply the loss of any outcome-action pair by the probability that this pair will occur and sum.
3. Simplify the conditional expected loss expressions by eliminating the parts of each expression where the loss is zero.
4. Develop the UEL expression by multiplying conditional expected losses by the probabilities of the events and summing.
5. Simplify the UEL expression by multiplying the loss part of each term by the probability of the event, since neither depend on c.
6. Perform a trial and error search over the values of c to find the strategy with the best (minimum) UEL. Remember that c is optimal if the UEL for c is smaller than the UELs for $c - 1$ and $c + 1$. Also remember that $c = 0$ and $c = n + 1$ correspond to simple strategies whose UEL is easily calculated in other ways.

Each of these steps will be demonstrated in the drug problem which follows.

6.7.3 Another Example of the Application of Binomial Sampling

To give another view of the process we have developed, we shall solve the New Drug problem.

New Drug: A new drug has been found promising by the research staff of an ethical drug manufacturer. If the drug lives up to promise, the probability, p, of it curing a person will be $\frac{3}{4}$. Currently, the probability of a person being cured is $\frac{1}{2}$. The president of the company must make a decision whether to market the drug or not. He faces an opportunity loss table:

	Market	Don't Market
Promising Drug ($p = \frac{3}{4}$)	0	$50,000
Ineffective Drug ($p = \frac{1}{2}$)	$20,000	0

and his staff has told him that the probability that the drug will be effective is 0.2.[3]

_____

[3] This problem is purposely simplistic in design. Clearly, any drug manufacturer about to market his product, or test it on human subjects, has many ethical and legal considerations as well as profit goals. However, these other issues are not treated here so that the student can concentrate on learning binomial sampling techniques. In a more realistic setting the drug manufacturer would use the concepts of utility theory, as discussed in Chapter 4, to combine profit, ethical, and legal considerations in his analysis of the problem.

The first step in the analysis of any problem is to determine the expected payoffs or expected losses for immediate decisions. In this case, if we let

M = Market the drug
D = Don't market the drug

then the expected opportunity losses are

$$\mathcal{E}(M) = 0 \times 0.2 + \$20,000 \times 0.8 = \$16,000$$
$$\mathcal{E}(D) = \$50,000 \times 0.2 + 0 \times 0.8 = \$10,000$$

and the best decision without sampling is D.

To find the best strategy for any sample size we can follow the steps given in Section 6.7.2. The first step is to determine the composite strategy for the problem, and in order to do that the type of sample outcome must be known. In this case, the members of the sample will be people suffering from the disease the drug is designed to cure, and the corresponding sample outcome is the number of people (in the sample) who are cured. Note that an alternative sample outcome is the number of people who are *not* cured, but that outcome is not consistent with the definition of the events. The p's measure the probability of a person being cured. Therefore, the (random) sample outcome will be K, the number of people cured. (K is used instead of C because the latter could be confused with the cutoff point, c).

The only strategies that should be considered are those for which one action is chosen for small values of K and the other action is chosen for large values of K. Therefore, the only problem remaining is to use our intuition to determine which action should be associated with small values of K, and which with large values. It makes sense in this case to not market the drug if the number of cures is small, and to market the drug if the number of cures is large. Therefore, the composite strategy is:

$$s = \{\text{If } K < c \text{ then } D, \text{ if } K \geq c \text{ then } M\}$$

The next step in the process of finding the best strategy is to develop the conditional expected loss expression for the composite strategy. Recall that conditional expected loss is the loss of any outcome-action pair of the strategy times the probability that that pair will occur, summed over all pairs. Thus, for this problem:

$$\mathcal{E}(s|p) = \text{loss}(K < c \text{ and } D|p)P(K < c \text{ and } D|p)$$
$$+ \text{loss}(K \geq c \text{ and } M|p)P(K \geq c \text{ and } M|p),$$

and this expression can be simplified because the losses depend only upon the action and the probabilities depend only upon the sample outcome. Furthermore, the probabilities are binomial probabilities, and depend upon n as well as p. The simplified conditional expected loss expression is

$$\mathcal{E}(s|p) = \text{loss}(D|p)P(K < c|n, p) + \text{loss}(M|p)P(K \geq c|n, p).$$

Step 3 of our best strategy development procedure calls for further simplification of the conditional expected loss expression. In this case $\text{loss}(D|p = \frac{1}{2})$ and $\text{loss}(M|p = \frac{3}{4})$ are both zero, so one of the terms can be eliminated from each conditional loss expression (there are two expressions because there are two values of p), and we get

$$\mathcal{E}(s|p = \frac{3}{4}) = \text{loss}(D|p = \frac{3}{4})P(K < c|n, p = \frac{3}{4})$$
$$\mathcal{E}(s|p = \frac{1}{2}) = \text{loss}(M|p = \frac{1}{2})P(K \geq c|n, p = \frac{1}{2}).$$

When the nonzero lossses are inserted from the opportunity loss table these expressions become

$$\mathcal{E}(s|p = \frac{3}{4}) = 50,000 \times P(K < c|n, p = \frac{3}{4})$$
$$\mathcal{E}(s|p = \frac{1}{2}) = 20,000 \times P(K \geq c|n, p = \frac{3}{4}).$$

Moving on to steps 4 and 5 we have:

$$\begin{aligned}
\text{UEL} &= \mathcal{E}(s|p = \frac{3}{4})P(p = \frac{3}{4}) + \mathcal{E}(s|p = \frac{1}{2})P(p = \frac{1}{2}) \\
&= 50,000 \times P(K < c|n, p = \frac{3}{4}) \times 0.2 + 20,000 \\
&\quad \times P(K \geq c|n, p = \frac{1}{2}) \times 0.8 \\
&= 10,000 \times P(K < c|n, p = \frac{3}{4}) + 16,000 P(K \geq c|n, p = \frac{1}{2}).
\end{aligned}$$

This final expression allows us to evaluate the UEL of any strategy. Note that a strategy is defined by specifying values for c and n, and a numerical value for UEL can be calculated from the above expression as soon as c and n values are given.

The only step remaining in the process for finding the best strategy is to fix a value for n and perform a trial and error search to find the best value for c. This is the step that requires the most common sense (if a lot of work is to be avoided) and we will proceed slowly so that the reader can have a good grasp of the nuances of this problem. The best strategy will be found for both $n = 5$ and $n = 15$.

6.7.3.1 Finding the Best Strategy for $n = 5$.   The first question facing a person solving this problem is What value of c should be chosen first? To answer this question requires a look at the original problem statement. Judging from the p values, if about $\frac{1}{2}$ the sample patients are cured, we would suspect the drug is ineffective ($p = \frac{1}{2}$), whereas if $\frac{3}{4}$ of the sample patients are cured we would suspect the drug is effective ($p = \frac{3}{4}$). Half of 5 is 2.5 and $\frac{3}{4}$ of 5 is 3.75, so try $c = 3$ as the first value. For $c = 3$

$$\begin{aligned}
\text{UEL} &= 10,000 \times P(K < 3|n = 5, p = \frac{3}{4}) \\
&\quad + 16,000 \times P(K \geq 3|n = 5, p = \frac{1}{2}) \\
&= 10,000 \times 0.1035 + 16,000 \times 0.5 = 9,035.
\end{aligned}$$

The only way to determine whether this is a good strategy is to evaluate the neighboring ($c = 2$ and $c = 4$) strategies. For $c = 4$

$$
\begin{aligned}
\text{UEL} &= 10,000 \times P(K < 4 | n = 5, p = \tfrac{3}{4}) \\
&+ 16,000 \times P(K \geq 4 | n = 5, p = \tfrac{1}{2}) \\
&= 10,000 \times 0.3672 + 16,000 \times 0.1875 = 6,672.
\end{aligned}
$$

This is the point where common sense is so important. Before evaluating $c = 4$, the plan was to evaluate *both* $c = 2$ and $c = 4$. However, since $c = 4$ is a better strategy than $c = 3$ there is no longer a need to evaluate $c = 2$. Since the UEL function has a single minimum, and we have found that $c = 4$ is better than $c = 3$, $c = 2$ *cannot* be better than $c = 3$. Another way to state this same principle is to say that as soon as we have the UEL for two neighboring values of c we will know in which region the optimal c lies. In this case, since the UEL for $c = 4$ is smaller than the UEL for $c = 3$, we know that c^* will be either 4, 5, or 6. It cannot be larger than 6, because the sample size is only 5. It cannot be smaller than 4 because the UEL for $c = 3$ is larger than the UEL for $c = 4$.

The UEL for $c = 4$ has already been determined, and the UEL for $c = 6$ is known because $c = 6$ is a simple strategy (always choose D). Therefore, the only strategy whose UEL needs to be evaluated is $c = 5$. For $c = 5$

$$
\begin{aligned}
\text{UEL} &= 10,000 \times P(K < 5 | n = 5, p = \tfrac{3}{4}) \\
&+ 16,000 \times P(K \geq 5 | n = 5, p = \tfrac{1}{2}) \\
&= 10,000 \times 0.7626 + 16,000 \times 0.0313 = 8,127.
\end{aligned}
$$

Since the UEL for $c = 5$ is larger than the UEL for $c = 4$, and we have already found the UEL for $c = 3$ is also larger, the best strategy must be $c = 4$.

6.7.3.2 Finding the Best Strategy for n = 15.   This problem will be approached in the same way the $n = 5$ problem was approached. Half of 15 is 7.5 and $\tfrac{3}{4}$ of 15 is 11.25 so try $c = 10$ to start with. For $c = 10$

$$
\begin{aligned}
\text{UEL} &= 10,000 \times P(K < 10 | n = 15, p = \tfrac{3}{4}) \\
&+ 16,000 \times P(K \geq 10 | n = 15, p = \tfrac{1}{2}) \\
&= 10,000 \times 0.1484 + 16,000 \times 0.1509 = 3,898.
\end{aligned}
$$

To compare it with its neighbors, try $c = 11$. For $c = 11$

$$
\begin{aligned}
\text{UEL} &= 10,000 \times P(K < 11 | n = 15, p = \tfrac{3}{4}) \\
&+ 16,000 \times P(K \geq 11 | n = 15, p = \tfrac{1}{2}) \\
&= 10,000 \times 0.3135 + 16,000 \times 0.0592 = 4,082,
\end{aligned}
$$

which is larger. For $c = 9$

$$\text{UEL} = 10,000 \times P(K < 9 | n = 15, p = \tfrac{3}{4})$$
$$+ 16,000 \times P(K \geq 9 | n = 15, p = \tfrac{1}{2})$$
$$= 10,000 \times 0.0566 + 16,000 \times 0.3036 = 5,424.$$

Hence, $c = 10$ is the best strategy.

6.8   SUMMARY

This chapter started the investigation of binomial sampling problems by determining the best strategy for a fixed sample size. Chapter 7 will continue the investigation by considering the larger question of how big a sample should be taken. The techniques developed in this chapter will be very important in the following two chapters. Therefore, if the reader feels uneasy about his understanding of this chapter, he is urged to re-read it and test his ability on some of the problems before going on to Chapter 7.

PROBLEMS

Problems 1 to 5 deal with the binomial distribution.

1.   Suppose you are flipping a fair coin. What is the probability that *exactly* half the outcomes will be heads if you flip the coin 4 times? 10 times? 50 times?

2.   If it is known that three out of five workers in a large plant favor unionization, what is the probability that a random sample of five workers will have a majority favoring unionization?

3.   Suppose you are flipping the thumbtack described in the beginning of the chapter. If you flip it eight times, what is the probability of five "points-up" if the probability of "points-up" on any trial is 0.3? 0.4? 0.6? 0.9?

4.   Grain ships from Europe arrive at Hudson Bay to get Canadian grain on the average of two ships every five days. If no more than one ship arrives each day, what is the probability that there will be a ship in port every day for the next four days? three out of the next four days? none tomorrow and then one in each of the next three days?
Over the next 30 days, how many ships would you expect to arrive?

5.   You are playing a game with a friend. You roll a fair die and if the outcome is a four or a six, you win $5. On the other hand, if the outcome is anything else you must pay your friend $2. After 5 rolls, what is the probability that your *net* winnings are $25? $11? −$3? What is the expected value of your winnings over five rolls?

6.   What strategy should the New Drug manager select if $n = 10$? $n = 20$?

7. Suppose, in the Valley Sisters problem, the cost for inspection is $4.

    a. What is the new payoff table, and which of the immediate actions, *A* or *N*, is best?

    b. What is the composite strategy for this problem, and what is its UEL expression?

    c. Which strategy should be selected if $n = 15$?

8. The Spark Ling Co. has a soapbox-filling machine for packaging "DozenT." The machine misfills any box in a run with probability p, and it can be assumed that p is a constant from box to box. A production run consists of 5,050 boxes, and the cost of a misfilled box is $0.04. If p is too high, the company has the option of having an expert readjust the machine. The cost for the expert has been found to be a fixed cost of $10 plus a cost proportional to the number of mistakes the machine is likely to make, $2p$. From past experience the company has found the values of p that occur are 0.01, 0.03, 0.05, 0.07, and 0.1, with frequencies 0.1, 0.2, 0.3, 0.3, and 0.1 respectively.

    a. What are the payoff and loss matrices for this problem?

    b. What action should be taken if no sampling takes place?

    c. What is the value of c^* if $n = 10$? $n = 50$?

9. A playful monarch hands one of his subjects a coin and states that either the coin is balanced or the probability of throwing heads is 0.6. The subject may toss the coin n times and then state whether or not the coin is balanced. The reward for a correct statement is to be 100 copper pieces. The penalty for calling the coin unbalanced if in fact it is balanced is to be 300 copper pieces. The penalty for calling the coin balanced if in fact it is unbalanced is 200 copper pieces. (In the case of penalties, the subject pays the king.)

    a. Construct a payoff and loss matrix for this problem.

    b. The subject has observed in the past that the monarch used the unbalanced coin 25% of the time. If $n = 50$, what value of c should be chosen?

    c. Suppose the subject is allowed 10 tosses. He can also purchase an *additional* 10 tosses for one copper piece, but he must decide whether to purchase the extra 10 *before* he samples the first 10. Should the first 10 be used? Should the second 10 be purchased?

10. Count Cash is a young accountant with the firm of Peter Peterson & Co., Certified Public Accountants. Count is auditing the books of Acme Corp., and suspects the company might be juggling the books. To determine whether this is so, Count has decided to take a sample of company accounts and trace each through the company to make sure it is correctly accounted for. From his experience with other firms, Count has found that *every* company, through mistakes, once in a while miscredits an account. So, Count must determine the proportion, p, of these improper accounts. He feels p will be 0.01 if the

company is only making mistakes, but 0.1 if the books are being juggled.

Through many (delicate) conversations with Acme management, Count has determined that the consequences of his actions on company stockholders would be:

Event \ Count's Action	Certify the Annual Report	Do Not Certify the Annual Report
$p = 0.01$	+$5M	−$20M
$p = 0.1$	−$8M	−$3M

where M stands for millions of dollars. Furthermore, Count feels that $P(p = 0.01) = 0.8$; $P(p = 0.1) = 0.2$.

a. Which decision should Count make if he cannot sample?
b. What is the *maximum* stockholders would be willing to pay Count to take his sample?
c. If Count takes a sample of size 50, and this sample can be expected to be approximately binomially distributed, what strategy would Count adopt? (Ignore any consideration of sampling costs.)

11. The advertising manager for SOGGIES, a children's breakfast cereal, is trying to decide whether to direct a TV campaign toward mothers or toward children. The object, of course, is to appeal to the member(s) of the household who make the purchase decisions for children's breakfast cereals. Since the decision maker is not the same in all households, the advertising manager would like to determine the proportion, p, of households in which children's breakfast cereal decisions are made by children. Toward that end, he proposes to survey a random sample of households in which children's breakfast cereals are purchased. The survey is designed so that each household will indicate the decision maker for that household. The manager also knows: (1) The overall net profit from a campaign directed toward mothers is $10 per receptive mother (i.e., those mothers who make the cereal purchase decisions). Designing the content of an adult campaign would cost $150,000; (2) The overall net profit from a campaign directed toward children would be only $5 per receptive household. (There may be more than one child in a household.) On the other hand, designing the content of the campaign would only require $50,000.

There are 50,000 households that buy children's breakfast cereal. (To avoid confusion, assume every household has a mother and at least one child.) The advertising manager feels the values of p will be either 0.2, 0.6, or 0.8, with probabilities 0.5, 0.2, and 0.3, respectively.

a. What are the payoff and loss matrices for this problem? Which action should be taken if no sampling occurs?
b. What is the value for c^* if $n = 5$? $n = 10$? $n = 20$?

12. Consider Problem 5 of Chapter 5. If Hi can conduct the test as many times as he wants, with the sampling distribution of each trial being the same, and the outcome of each trial being (probabilistically) independent of all other outcomes, what is his best strategy if he runs four tests instead of one?

13. The marketing manager of a firm that markets nationwide is trying to decide whether to market a product recently developed in its laboratories. Having considerable experience with similar products, the manager knows that 25% of such products are considered successes, and continue to be marketed, while 75% are failures, and are discontinued shortly after introduction. The manager also knows he faces the following opportunity losses:

Actions / Events	Market the Product	Don't Market the Product
Successful Product	0	$3,000
Unsuccessful Product	$4,700	0

The manager can either make his decision immediately or use one of two market research plans. The more expensive market research scheme proposes to conduct extensive personal interviews with a random sample of residents in one or more large cities. The scheme is expensive, although it is less so because a similar interview is already being made for another new product in one city. Hence, the cost of the interview scheme is:

$$\text{Sample cost} = \begin{cases} \$100 & \text{if } n = 1 \\ \$100 + \$250(n-1) & \text{if } n \geq 2 \end{cases}$$

where n is the number of cities in which interviews take place. To compensate for its cost, of course, the scheme is quite accurate. It has been shown in the past that surveys of this type have an accuracy of:

$P(\text{test says market} \mid \text{successful product}) = 1 - (0.1)^n$
$P(\text{test says don't market} \mid \text{unsuccessful product}) = 1 - (0.2)^n$

The alternative market research scheme involves test marketing the product and purchasing consumer panel data to determine whether the product will be a success or not. Of course, the consumer panel data gives only an indication of whether the panel members purchased the product or not. The marketing manager can assume that panel members act independently with an equal probability of purchase, and the probability of purchase is $p = 0.5$ if the product will be successful, and $p = 0.04$ if the product will *not* be successful. Finally, consumer panel data costs:

$$\text{Sample cost} = \$50 + \$20n$$

where n is the number of consumers sampled.

Which is the best decision for the manager—sample three cities using the first sampling plan, or sampling 20 panel members? What is the cost of uncertainty of the best plan?

14. One of the difficulties many people have in applying Bayesian decision theory is in determining the probabilities of events. This problem shows a way in which this can be (partially) avoided. Assume for the Playful Monarch problem, Problem 9, that the subject is not quite sure of the value of p, the prior probability of a *balanced* coin. If 50 tosses yield 30 heads, what is the range of p for which the subject will state that the coin is unbalanced?

15. Suppose you are playing a game with a friend. He has two dice, one of which is fair and one of which is "loaded" so that the outcome six will never occur. The friend randomly picks one of the two dice, allows you to roll it any number of times you want, and then you must state whether he has chosen the fair die or the loaded one. If your decision is correct, you win \$5. If your decision is wrong, you pay \$5. Furthermore, you pay your friend 50¢ each time you roll the die. Show that $c^* = 1$ for all n in this problem.

16. For the New Drug problem, can you develop an expression giving the best value of c for *any* given n? (Hint: Consider a decision tree approach to this problem). Can you solve this expression; i.e., isolate c^*? (Requires knowledge of logarithms).

17. A company has a machine that manufactures bolts. Each time the machine is cleaned the company must decide whether an expert should adjust it or whether the operator has done a sufficiently good job. The opportunity loss matrix is:

Actions / Events	Call in the Expert	Accept the Operator's Setup
$p = 0.2$	4	0
$p = 0.5$	0	2

and it has been found that $P(p = 0.2) = 0.6$ and $P(p = 0.5) = 0.4$.

a.   What is the best decision if the company cannot sample?

Suppose the company decided to use the following sampling scheme: Sample until the first defective bolt is observed. The random variable in this case is the number of bolts observed (to *and including* the first defective bolt), N. Furthermore, N obeys a geometric probability distribution, and:

$$\left. \begin{array}{l} P(N = n|p) = p(1 - p)^{n-1} \\ P(N \geq n|p) = (1 - p)^{n-1} \end{array} \right\} \quad \text{for } n = 1,2,3, \ldots .$$

$$\text{and } E(N|p) = 1/p$$

where p is the probability of a defective bolt.

b. What do you conjecture the *form* of a strategy would be for this sampling plan?

c. Using your conjectured form, and the distribution of p in part (*a*), develop an expression for UEL in terms of the (as yet undetermined) strategy values.

18. The Nadir Mining and Manufacturing Company has an option to purchase the mineral rights to some land with possible uranium deposits. The company is trying to determine which of three possible courses of action to take. If the proportion, p, of high grade uranium ore is low enough, of course, the company should let their option lapse. If there is a large proportion of high grade ore, the company will immediately start construction for a processing plant on the site. The fixed cost for this operation is $500,000. The profit from each ton of *high grade ore* is $50, and there are 20,000 tons of material that can be processed.

Finally, if the proportion of high grade ore is neither very high nor very low, a third course of action involves removing the material from the site to the nearest port (20 miles) and shipping the ore to the current plant, which can process lower grade material. The fixed cost of removal equipment to the site is $150,000. For this scheme, it has been estimated that the profit per ton for high grade ore will be $25, since there will be additional transportation and processing costs.

From previous experience on similar sites, Nadir feels that the proportion of high grade ore will be either 0.1, 0.3, 0.5, 0.7, or 0.9, with corresponding probabilities 0.1, 0.2, 0.3, 0.3, and 0.1.

a. List the actions and events for this problem.

b. Construct a loss table for this problem.

c. Which of the terminal actions is best?

A sampling scheme has been devised by Nadir. Since high grade uranium ore occurs in relatively homogeneous strata, drilling to obtain core samples at random locations and random depths will yield cores that are either high grade or not. n core samples of material will be (randomly) taken from the field, and each will be analyzed to determine whether or not it is high grade ore.

d. If $n = 3$, list *all* the strategies Nadir might consider. Judging from your experience with two action binomial sampling problems, which strategies would you think are dominant? Why do you think they are dominant?

Consider only the dominant set of strategies for the remaining questions, and let $n = 3$ for parts (*e*) and (*f*).

e. As a function of the parameters of your proposed strategy, develop a *concise* expression for conditional expected loss and overall expected loss.

f. Find the best strategy for $n = 3$.

Binomial Sampling Problems—II

IN THE LAST CHAPTER we began our study of binomial sampling problems. The problems we discussed were restricted to two actions and a finite (small) number of values for p. This chapter continues the discussion of these problems, and addresses itself to the major question facing a decision maker who is concerned with such a problem: Should a sample be taken and if so, what size sample should it be? The techniques of the previous chapter can be used to determine the best strategy (cutoff point) for a given sample size, and we will find that these techniques are needed to determine the best sample size as well.

7.1 THE COST OF SAMPLING

As in our previous problems, we will assume that sampling costs something, and the major objective is then to balance the additional information obtained from the sample against its cost. Presumably, if the sample didn't cost anything, it would pay us to take a very large sample, since the larger the sample the closer we could estimate the true value of p, and we would then know which decision was optimal. So, we will assume that each problem we deal with has a sample cost. In particular, for the Valley Sisters problem we will assume that

$$\text{Sample Cost} = \$0.10 + 0.06n,$$

where n = sample size.

The above formula, in combination with the UEL calculation described in Chapter 6, allows us to determine the total opportunity loss for *the best strategy* for any sample size. In Chapter 5 we pointed out that the total opportunity loss for a sampling strategy is the *sum* of the sample cost and the unconditional expected loss of the strategy. Thus, for binomial sampling problems we have:

Total Opportunity Loss for given n = Sample Cost
$$+ \text{UEL for strategy using } c^*, \text{ given } n.$$

So, for the Valley Sisters problem with $n = 3$ we found $c^* = 1$ and UEL = 0.885, and

Total Opportunity Loss = $0.10 + 0.06 \times 3$
$$+ 0.885 = 1.165, \text{ for } n = 3.$$

For $n = 6, c^* = 1$, UEL = 0.740, and

Total Opportunity Loss = $0.10 + 0.06 \times 6$
$$+ 0.740 = 1.20, \text{ for } n = 6.$$

Total Opportunity Loss is used extensively in this chapter, and it shall henceforth be abbreviated TL.

7.2 DETERMINATION OF THE BEST SAMPLE SIZE

Once we can evaluate the total opportunity loss for the best strategy for any sample size, we are ready to find the best sample size (which may be zero—i.e., do not sample). Unfortunately, there is no simple formula from which we can calculate the optimal value of n. A trial and error procedure must be employed. Fortunately, since we know how to find the optimal strategy for fixed n, the trial and error procedure is essentially a search for the optimal value of one variable (n) only. The basic procedure we shall adopt is

Fix n, find the corresponding c^*, then vary n (and c^* as necessary) to find the overall best value.

Of course, c^* will change as n changes, so one of the complications of the procedure is that a new c^* will need to be determined for each new n that is chosen.

There are many questions that arise when one considers such a process. One concerns the upper limit on the values of n which will have to be searched. If a reasonable upper bound does not exist, the task is essentially hopeless. A second question concerns a more precise specification of the procedure itself. Some readers probably feel, after reading the above statement, that they know no more than they did before they read it. This feeling is understandable, but the specification of a precise algorithm[1] has been purposely omitted so that the reader feels free to try any trial and error method he might want to solve the problem. One specific algorithm is given below, but there is no guarantee that it will be an efficient one in terms of the number of calculations required. All we can guarantee is that it will solve any problem in a systematic way.

7.2.1 Determining an Upper Bound for *n*

Let us turn first to the question of an upper bound on *n*. Since

Total Opportunity Loss = Sample Cost + UEL for the best strategy

and UEL is always greater than or equal to zero, it follows that a sampling plan whose sample cost alone is greater than the Total Opportunity Loss for some other plan could never be optimal. This concept allows us to calculate an upper bound on the *n* values which must be searched. The sample cost for a particular sample size is compared with the TL for the best strategy (known at the time) and that sample is then either included or eliminated depending on the relation between its sample cost and the best TL. This idea can be formulated mathematically in a slightly more general and much more useful way. If we solve the equation

Sample Cost = best TL

for *n*, the value of *n* obtained is the maximum value that can be considered. An example will make this clear. Before any strategies for any *n*'s have been determined, the best TL in the Valley Sisters problem is the one associated with the terminal action, *N*, and $\mathcal{E}(N) = 1.20$. The expression equating sample cost with best TL becomes

$$0.10 + 0.06n = 1.20,$$

which is a simple equation in *n*. Solving this equation yields

$$0.06n = 1.20 - 0.10$$
$$n = \frac{1.20 - 0.10}{0.06} = 18.33.$$

Thus, when $n = 18.33$ the sample cost *exactly* equals the best TL[2]. Any *n* larger than 18.33 will have a sample cost (and, hence, a TL)

---

[1] An algorithm is just a specific set of rules for solving a problem. A simple example of an algorithm is the method we have all learned to multiply two multidigit numbers together.

[2] $\mathcal{E}(N) = 1.20$ is the best TL known at this time. However, there may be even better TLs obtained as we begin the search for the optimal *n*.

larger than 1.20. Furthermore, of course, the sample size can be only an integer value. Therefore, the maximum sample size that needs to be considered is 18. This upper bound on the sample size for any problem will be designated n_{max}. Thus, we have found for the Valley Sisters problem that $n_{max} = 18$.

Unfortunately, 18 potential values for n means there will be a large amount of work associated with the trial and error procedure for finding the best n. However, as we enter into our search routine we will usually find we have certain sampling schemes (sample sizes) that have lower TLs than one of the terminal actions. These better values can then be used in a calculation similar to that above, and the upper bound value for n can be decreased. For instance, we know that TL for $n = 3$ is better than $\mathcal{E}(N)$, and when that value is used in the upper bound calculation

$$0.10 + 0.06n = 1.165$$

or

$$n = 17.75$$

and a new, "tighter," upper bound on n is 17. This particular improvement is minimal, but it serves to illustrate the point. Perhaps other, significantly better, TLs will be found as the search (for the best n) progresses, and any one of these can be used in a similar calculation.

7.2.2 The Algorithm

In this section we will present a specific algorithm for finding the optimal sample size. The algorithm is guaranteed to find the optimal answer to any problem, but *not* with a minimum number of calculations. Since the calculations associated with solving these problems are quite tedious, the student is urged to develop different algorithms—ones that might cut down on the total number of calculations necessary to arrive at the answer. The student is also cautioned, of course, to make sure the algorithm really does work. The algorithm we propose in this section is:

1. Fix $n = 1$, and find the corresponding c^*.
2. Increment n by 1, and find the new c^*.
3. Continue step 2 until the sample cost for the current n exceeds the best TL found.

On first inspection this algorithm seems to involve a lot of work. The best strategy for every value of n between $n = 1$ and $n = n_{max}$ must be determined, and remember from Chapter 6 that to determine the best strategy for a fixed n requires a trial and error search procedure. Fortunately, we have two rules that significantly decrease the amount of work that must be done. The first is:

> c^* will not decrease as n increases.

For example, in the Valley Sisters problem for $n = 3$, we found $c^* = 1$. Then, with the above rule, we would know that $c = 0$ cannot be optimal for $n = 6$. The second rule is:

> c^* can increase *at most* one as n increases by one.

The combination of the two rules means that, except for $n = 1$, we have only to evaluate the UEL associated with two strategies for each n. For example, in the Valley Sisters problem, when we have found that $c^* = 1$ for $n = 6$, the only two candidates for c^* we need to consider for $n = 7$ are $c = 1$ and $c = 2$. The first rule would be violated by $c = 0$ and $c = 3$ would violate the second rule.

Finding c^* for $n = 1$ the situation is even easier: $c = 0$ represents the simple strategy corresponding to the terminal action A, and $c = 2$ corresponds to the terminal action N. Thus for $n = 1$ only $c = 1$ has to be evaluated. In all (that is, for all n) each n has to have two strategies (c values) evaluated except $n = 1$, and there are thus $2n_{max} - 1$ total strategies that must be evaluated.

7.2.2.1 A Demonstration of the Algorithm Applied to the Valley Sisters Problem. For the Valley Sisters problem we have

$$\mathcal{E}(N) = 1.20; \; \mathcal{E}(A) = 3.24; \; \text{Sample Cost} = 0.10 + 0.06n.$$

For $n = 1$ and $c = 1$

$$
\begin{aligned}
\text{UEL} &= 1.92 \times P(B \geq 1 | n = 1, p = 0.01) \\
&+ 1.08 \times P(B \geq 1 | n = 1, p = 0.02) \\
&+ 0.24 \times P(B \geq 1 | n = 1, p = 0.04) \\
&+ 1.2 \times P(B < 1 | n = 1, p = 0.15) \\
&= 1.92 \times 0.01 + 1.08 \times 0.02 + 0.24 \times 0.04 + 1.2 \times 0.85 \\
&= 1.07;
\end{aligned}
$$

thus, for $n = 1$,

$$
\begin{aligned}
\text{UEL} &= 3.24 \text{ for } c = 0 \\
\text{UEL} &= 1.07 \text{ for } c = 1 \\
\text{UEL} &= 1.20 \text{ for } c = 2,
\end{aligned}
$$

and therefore $c^* = 1$. The Total Opportunity Loss for the best $n = 1$ strategy is

$$
\begin{aligned}
\text{TL} &= \text{UEL} + \text{Sample Cost} \\
&= 1.07 + 0.10 + 0.06 \times 1 \\
&= 1.23.
\end{aligned}
$$

Now that c^* is known for $n = 1$ we can go on to $n = 2$. For $n = 2$ and $c = 1$

$$
\begin{aligned}
\text{UEL} &= 1.92 \times P(B \geq 1 | n = 2, p = 0.01) \\
&\quad + 1.08 \times P(B \geq 1 | n = 2, p = 0.02) \\
&\quad + 0.24 \times P(B \geq 1 | n = 2, p = 0.04) \\
&\quad + 1.2 \times P(B < 1 | n = 2, p = 0.15) \\
&= 1.92 \times 0.0199 + 1.08 \times 0.0396 + 0.24 \times 0.0784 + 1.2 \times 0.7225 \\
&= 0.967,
\end{aligned}
$$

and for $c = 2$

$$
\begin{aligned}
\text{UEL} &= 1.92 \times P(B \geq 2 | n = 2, p = 0.01) \\
&\quad + 1.08 \times P(B \geq 2 | n = 2, p = 0.02) \\
&\quad + 0.24 \times P(B \geq 2 | n = 2, p = 0.04) \\
&\quad + 1.2 \times P(B < 2 | n = 2, p = 0.15) \\
&= 1.92 \times 0.0001 + 1.08 \times 0.0004 + 0.24 \times 0.0016 + 1.2 \times 0.9775 \\
&= 1.174,
\end{aligned}
$$

and these are the only c values that must be considered. Therefore, $c^* = 1$ for $n = 2$, and

$$
\begin{aligned}
\text{TL} &= \text{UEL} + \text{Sample Cost} \\
&= 0.967 + 0.1 + 0.06 \times 2 \\
&= 1.187.
\end{aligned}
$$

Now that c^* is known for $n = 2$ we know the two values of c to consider for $n = 3$, and the algorithm can proceed.

To write out all the calculations associated with the algorithm would be tedious and take up far too many pages of this book. Therefore, only a summary of the calculations will be given, and that is contained in Table 7.1. Continuing on, we find that $c^* = 1$ for $n = 3$ and the associated Total Opportunity Loss is 1.165. The value of c^* continues to be 1 for all values of n less than or equal to 9. Then, at $n = 10$ we find that the UEL for $c = 2$ is smaller than the UEL for $c = 1$. Using the principle that c^* can increase by at most one, we know, *without determining the UEL for $c = 3$,* that $c^* = 2$ when the sample size is 10. The calculations continue in this manner until the upper bound, $n_{\max} = 18$, is reached.

An intermediate step in this algorithm is to determine the best strategy for each sample size and its associated UEL. To these best UELs are added the sample costs, and the resulting Total Opportunity Losses are given in the rightmost column of Table 7.1. The optimal sample size is then found by finding the minimum TL. In this case, the optimal sample size, which shall be denoted by n^*, is 4, and the associated TL is 1.162. Comparing this value with the expected opportunity losses for the terminal

TABLE 7.1
A Summary of the Calculations Used to find the Best *n* in the
Valley Sisters Problem

Sample Size	Value of c	UEL	Sample Cost	TL
1	0	3.24		
	1*	1.07	0.16	1.23
	2	1.20		
2	1*	0.967	0.22	1.187
	2	1.174		
3	1*	0.885	0.28	1.165
	2	1.13		
4	1*	0.822	0.34	1.162
	2	1.074		
5	1*	0.775	0.40	1.175
	2	1.012		
6	1*	0.740	0.46	1.20
	2	0.946		
7	1*	0.717	0.52	1.237
	2	0.879		
8	1*	0.703	0.58	1.283
	2	0.814		
9	1*	0.697	0.64	1.337
	2	0.752		
10	1	0.698		
	2*	0.693	0.70	1.393
11	2*	0.638	0.76	1.398
	3	0.938		
12	2*	0.588	0.82	1.408
	3	0.888		
13	2*	0.543	0.88	1.423
	3	0.836		
14	2*	0.503	0.94	1.443
	3	0.785		
15	2*	0.468	1.00	1.468
	3	0.734		
16	2*	0.437	1.06	1.497
	3	0.684		
17	2*	0.410	1.12	1.530
	3	0.637		
18	2*	0.387	1.18	1.567
	3	0.591		

* Denotes the optimal value of c for that n.

actions, $\mathcal{E}(N)$ and $\mathcal{E}(A)$, we find it is cheaper to sample and the strategy should be:

> Sample four cans. If one or more are improperly filled, stop the machine and adjust it. If none are improperly filled, continue the run without adjustment.

We have found that $n^* = 4$ and $c^* = 1$ in the Valley Sisters problem.

7.2.2.2 *A Demonstration of the Algorithm Applied to the New Drug Problem.* We will conclude the discussion of this algorithm with an application to the New Drug problem. This problem is different enough from the Valley Sisters problem to give an interesting contrast.

The New Drug problem is again a two-action problem with actions:

M = Market the new drug
D = Don't market the new drug,

and two possible events, p (the probability of curing any person) = $\frac{3}{4}$ or $p = \frac{1}{2}$. The analysis of this problem in Chapter 6 found

$$\mathcal{E}(M) = 16,000; \; \mathcal{E}(D) = 10,000,$$

and if we let K be the number of people (out of a sample of size n) who were treated with the drug and cured, the composite strategy is

$$\{\text{If } K < c \text{ then } D, \text{ if } K \geq c \text{ then } M\}$$

and the associated, reduced UEL expression is

$$\text{UEL} = 10,000 \times P(K < c|n, p = \tfrac{3}{4}) + 16,000 \times P(K \geq c|n, p = \tfrac{1}{2}).$$

The final expression needed to solve this problem is the sample cost function. In this case assume it costs $450 for each patient who is treated. Then

$$\text{Sample Cost} = \$450n,$$

and the upper bound on n can be obtained by equating the sample cost with the best opportunity loss known at this point. In this problem this is:

$$450n = 10,000$$
$$n = \frac{10,000}{450} = 22.22,$$

and thus $n_{max} = 22$.

The next step is to find the best strategy (c^*) for each value of n between 1 and 22. For $n = 1$ and $c = 1$ we have

$$\begin{aligned}
\text{UEL} &= 10,000 \times P(K < 1|n = 1, p = \tfrac{3}{4}) \\
&+ 16,000 \times P(K \geq 1|n = 1, p = \tfrac{1}{2}) \\
&= 10,000 \times 0.25 + 16,000 \times 0.5 \\
&= 10,500.
\end{aligned}$$

Furthermore, $c = 0$ and $c = 2$ correspond to the terminal actions M and D respectively, and we find that $c^* = 2$ for $n = 1$ (since $\mathcal{E}(D) = 10,000$). Continuing on, for $n = 2$ and $c = 2$:

$$\begin{aligned}
\text{UEL} &= 10,000 \times P(K < 2|n = 2, p = \tfrac{3}{4}) \\
&+ 16,000 \times P(K \geq 2|n = 2, p = \tfrac{1}{2}) \\
&= 10,000 \times 0.4375 + 16,000 \times 0.25 \\
&= 8,375.
\end{aligned}$$

Again, $c = 3$ corresponds to the terminal action D, whose expected opportunity loss is larger than $\$8,375$, and therefore $c^* = 2$ for $n = 2$ as well as for $n = 1$.

For $n = 3$ and $c = 2$

$$
\begin{aligned}
\text{UEL} &= 10{,}000 \times P(K < 2 | n = 3, p = \tfrac{3}{4}) \\
&\quad + 16{,}000 \times P(K \geq 2 | n = 3, p = \tfrac{1}{2}) \\
&= 10{,}000 \times 0.1563 + 16{,}000 \times 0.5 \\
&= 9{,}563,
\end{aligned}
$$

and for $n = 3$ and $c = 3$

$$
\begin{aligned}
\text{UEL} &= 10{,}000 \times P(K < 3 | n = 3, p = \tfrac{3}{4}) \\
&\quad + 16{,}000 \times P(K \geq 3 | n = 3, p = \tfrac{1}{2}) \\
&= 10{,}000 \times 0.5781 + 16{,}000 \times 0.125 \\
&= 7{,}781,
\end{aligned}
$$

so $c^* = 3$ for $n = 3$.

Continuing in the same manner would again be too tedious and space consuming. The calculations for this problem were continued, and those for n values between 1 and 10 are contained in Table 7.2. After c^* was calculated for $n = 10$ it was decided to obtain a tighter upper bound on

TABLE 7.2
A Summary of the Calculations Used to Find the Optimal Sample Size for the New Drug Problem

$(1 \leq n \leq 10)$

Sample Size	Value of c	UEL	Sample Cost	TL
1	0	16,000		
	1	10,500		
	2*	10,000	450	10,450
2	2*	8,375	900	9,275
	3	10,000		
3	2	9,563		
	3*	7,781	1,350	9,131
4	3*	7,617	1,800	9,417
	4	7,836		
5	3	9,035		
	4*	6,672	2,250	8,922
6	4	7,194		
	5*	6,411	2,700	9,111
7	5*	6,061	3,150	9,211
	6	6,551		
8	5	6,951		
	6*	5,527	3,600	9,127
9	6	5,720		
	7*	5,431	4,050	9,481
10	7*	4,991	4,500	9,491
	8	5,619		

n_{max}. The best TL at this point is 8,922 and equating this to the sample cost function yields

$$450n = 8,922$$

$$n = \frac{8,922}{450} = 19.83,$$

so the new n_{max} will be 19. With this value the calculations were continued, and these values are summarized in Table 7.3.

TABLE 7.3
A Summary of the Calculations Used to Find the Optimal Sample Size for the New Drug Problem
$$(11 \leq n \leq 19)$$

Sample Size	Value of c	UEL	Sample Cost	TL
11	7	5,537		
	8*	4,679	4,950	9,629
12	8*	4,678	5,400	10,078
	9	4,680		
13	8	5,451		
	9*	4,195	5,850	10,045
14	9	4,508		
	10*	4,021	6,300	10,321
15	10*	3,898	6,750	10,648
	11	4,083		
16	10	4,432		
	11*	3,577	7,200	10,777
17	11	3,729		
	12*	3,495	7,650	11,145
18	12*	3,293	8,100	11,393
	13	3,596		
19	12	3,649		
	13*	3,085	8,550	11,635

When all the TL values are compared, we find the minimum occurs at $n = 5$, and the corresponding Total Opportunity Loss is 8,922. Furthermore, this value is lower than the expected opportunity loss of the best terminal action, so the optimal policy is:

> Treat five patients. If four or more are cured, market the drug. Otherwise, do not market it.

There are two ways in which the outcomes of this problem differ from those of the Valley Sisters problem, and it will help our understanding of these types of problems to point these differences out. First notice that, while c^* had only two values in the Valley Sisters problem, its value ranged from 2 to 13 in the New Drug problem.

The second characteristic of the New Drug problem is that the TL value, as a function of n, does not have a single local minimum. That is, there are several values of n (3, 5, 8, and 13) for which the TL values for neighboring values of n are both larger. It would be nice if any local optimum was also a global optimum. Then we could say that the best n was found whenever we found one whose neighbors ($n - 1$ and $n + 1$) had higher TLs. The point of discussing this is to say that it is *not* true, and cannot form the basis for an algorithm. Unfortunately, any algorithm must (at least implicitly) search all values of n in order to find the one with the best TL.

7.3 SUMMARY

This chapter has completed the discussion of the binomial sampling problem (when we have only a finite number of events) by discussing a method for finding the optimal sample size. Unfortunately, the model does not have any properties that make the solution of this problem easy. Instead, the suggested algorithm really consists of a complete enumeration (all values of n) of the total opportunity losses, and a selection of the best of these.

PROBLEMS

1. For the Valley Sisters problem, find the best strategy for:

    a. Sample Cost $= 0.01 + 0.06n$
    b. Sample Cost $= 0.10 + 0.04n$
    c. Note the similarities between these cost functions and the one used in the text, and compare the optimal strategies and TLs for the three. What conclusions do you see?

2. If Count Cash (Problem 10, Chapter 6) faces the following sample cost function

$$\text{Sample Cost} = \$500,000 + 25,000n$$

    what is his best strategy?

3. For the Spark Ling Co., (Problem 8, Chapter 6), what is the best strategy if

    a. Sample Cost $= 0.08n$
    b. Sample Cost $= 1.5 + 0.1n$

4. For the SOGGIES breakfast cereal problem (Problem 11 of Chapter 6) find the best strategy if

$$\text{Sample Cost} = 60,000 + 500n$$

5. For Problem 13, Chapter 6, find the best strategy.

6. For Problem 15, Chapter 6

    a. How many times should you roll the die? (that is, what is n^*?)
    b. If no sampling is used, the game is a fair game. How much do you expect to win (or lose) from your friend if you sample n^* times?
    c. After sampling n^* times, what is the maximum you would pay for perfect information as to which die had been chosen?

7. For Problem 17, Chapter 6, suppose the sample cost function is

    $$\text{Sample Cost} = \$0.05 + 0.06N$$

    a. How would this function be used in such a problem, since N is a random variable?
    b. Indicate the steps needed to determine the best strategy. Do not do any calculations.

8. It can be shown that to find the optimal sampling rule, you should start with $n = 1$, $c = 1$ and increase n one at a time. This implies that a decision rule with $c = 0$ will never be optimal for any n. Show that such a decision will always be more costly than one of the terminal decisions without sampling, where sampling cost $= a + bn$, and $a \geq 0$, $b > 0$.

8

Suspension of Judgment in Binomial Sampling Problems

UP TO THIS POINT we have considered binomial sampling problems in which the analysis of the problem (that is, how much to sample and what strategy to adopt) is conducted first. Many times, however, the analyst is not brought into the problem in the beginning, but only after a sample (of some arbitrarily determined size) has been taken and its outcome is known. This chapter discusses the concepts that underlie analyzing such samples. There are two basic approaches we consider. First, if a terminal action must be chosen with the given sample outcome, which action will be best to choose? Second, *if it is possible,* should we consider taking another sample before making our final decision? We will find that the method we use to approach the first problem is very closely related to the decision tree techniques we discussed in Chapter 5, and the methods we use to solve the second problem are the same as those in Chapters 6 and 7.

8.1 ANALYSIS OF A PREVIOUSLY OBTAINED SAMPLE

In the case in which we have a previously obtained sample, the cost of having taken that sample is no longer of concern to us, since the money has already been spent. What is important, of course, is to determine which is the best terminal action to choose for any given sample outcome. For example, in the Valley Sisters problem, suppose the foreman comes to you and says, "I took a sample of six cans and found one defective. What action should I take?" If you had completed the analysis of the Valley Sisters problem described in Chapter 7, you would know the answer of course. There we found that for a sample of size 6

$(n = 6)$, the optimal cutoff point was one $(c^* = 1)$. Let us suppose, however, that this is the first time you have ever faced this particular problem. One way to solve it, of course, is to complete an analysis like that in Chapter 7. However, we will find there is an easier way to solve the problem, and this new method will naturally lead into the larger question of whether we should consider taking an *additional* sample. This easier method is based upon a partial decision tree analysis of the Valley Sisters problem.

Consider the decision tree for the Valley Sisters problem when $n = 6$, which is given in Figure 8.1. A complete analysis of this tree would be quite time consuming. However, we don't have to analyse the tree completely. Recall that we know there was one bad can in our sample of

FIGURE 8.1
The Decision Tree for the Valley Sisters Problem when $n = 6$

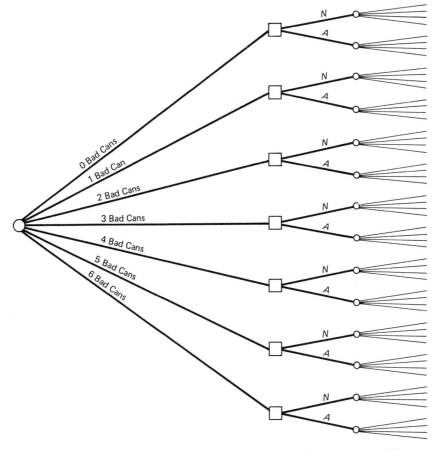

Note: Each of the ⊙⟨ at the right of the tree indicates the four events: $p = 0.01$; $p = 0.02$; $p = 0.04$; and $p = 0.15$.

six cans. Therefore, we need only choose between the actions N and A for that *one* branch of the tree. In Chapter 5 we learned that to calculate the expected value of the right-most nodes in the tree, we used the probabilities of the events ($p = 0.01$ to $p = 0.15$) *conditioned on* the sample outcome. That is, we need $P(p = 0.01 | B = 1, n = 6)$, etc. These can be calculated using Bayes' rule. For instance,

$$P(p = 0.01 | B = 1, n = 6) = \frac{P(B = 1 | n = 6, p = 0.01)P(p = 0.01)}{P(B = 1 | n = 6)},$$

and the probability in the denominator, $P(B = 1 | n = 6)$ can be expressed as a sum of products of probabilities:

$$\begin{aligned} P(B = 1 | n = 6) = {} & P(B = 1 | n = 6, p = 0.01)P(p = 0.01) \\ & + P(B = 1 | n = 6, p = 0.02)P(p = 0.02) \\ & + P(B = 1 | n = 6, p = 0.04)P(p = 0.04) \\ & + P(B = 1 | n = 6, p = 0.15)P(p = 0.15). \end{aligned}$$

In this case we have

p-value	P(p-value)	P(B = 1|n = 6, p value)
0.01	0.4	0.0570
0.02	0.3	0.1085
0.04	0.2	0.1956
0.15	0.1	0.3994

so,

$$P(p = 0.01 | B = 1, n = 6)$$

$$= \frac{0.4 \times 0.0570}{0.4 \times 0.0570 + 0.3 \times 0.1085 + 0.2 \times 0.1956 + 0.1 \times 0.3994}$$

$$= \frac{0.0228}{0.0228 + 0.03255 + 0.03912 + 0.03994}$$

$$= \frac{0.0228}{0.13441}$$

$$= 0.170.$$

In a similar manner we have

$$P(p = 0.02 | B = 1, n = 6) = \frac{P(B = 1 | n = 6, p = 0.02)P(p = 0.02)}{P(B = 1 | n = 6)}$$

and since $P(B = 1 | n = 6)$ has the same value as before, we have

$$P(p = 0.02 | B = 1, n = 6) = \frac{0.3 \times 0.1085}{0.13441}$$

$$= 0.242.$$

The other two updated probabilties, $P(p = 0.04|B = 1, n = 6)$ and $P(p = 0.15|B = 1, n = 6)$ are calculated in the same way. The important thing to notice about these calculations is that each conditional event probability is obtained by taking one of the terms of the denominator and dividing it by the sum of all the other terms. Knowing this, and the fact that the conditional probabilities of all four events are needed, the following tabular method of calculation of event probabilities is compact and helpful.

1. List (in columns) the p values, their unconditional probabilities, and the probabilities of the sample outcome given these p values.
2. Multiply the respective elements in columns 2 and 3 to get column 4.
3. Add the values in column 4.
4. Create column 5 by dividing each element in column 4 by the sum of all elements in column 4. The column 5 values are the conditional event probabilities.

This tabular method is given (for the problem we have just been discussing) in Table 8.1. Notice that the sum of the values in column (4)

TABLE 8.1
Calculating the Probabilities of Events Conditional on the Sample Outcome

p-values	P(p)	P(B = 1 | n = 6,p)	Col. (2) × Col. (3)	Conditional Event Probabilities
0.01	0.4	0.0570	0.02280	0.170
0.02	0.3	0.1085	0.03255	0.242
0.04	0.2	0.1956	0.03912	0.291
0.15	0.1	0.3994	0.03994	0.297
		Sum	0.13441	1.000

is the denominator in each of the Bayesian calculations given previously, and that the conditional event probabilities, column (5), sum to 1, as they should since they are probabilities.

Once we have these new event probabilities, we are ready to choose the best action. Recall that the matrix of opportunity losses for this problem is:

	A	N
$p = 0.01$	4.80	0
$p = 0.02$	3.60	0
$p = 0.04$	1.20	0
$p = 0.15$	0	12

and the expected opportunity losses for the two actions are:

$$\mathcal{E}(A) = 4.80 \times 0.170 + 3.60 \times 0.242 + 1.20 \times 0.291 + 0 \times 0.297$$
$$= 2.036,$$
$$\mathcal{E}(N) = 0 \times 0.170 + 0 \times 0.242 + 0 \times 0.291 + 12 \times 0.297$$
$$= 3.564.$$

Hence the best action is to adjust the machine before continuing the run.

This concludes our analysis of this problem. Given a particular sample outcome we have determined (from looking at the decision tree) that we merely need to obtain the probabilities of the events conditioned upon the sample outcome, and use these conditional probabilities to determine which of the actions to take. Although the calculation of the conditional event probabilities is not particularly stimulating or easy, notice how much easier it is to apply this technique to solve this problem than to apply the technique discussed in Chapter 6. We will illustrate this technique with another example, this one from the New Drug problem, and that will be given below. Before we do that, however, we need to establish some new terminology.

In the terminology of decision theorists, the two sets of event probabilities we have been dealing with are called the *prior* and *posterior* distributions. These are illustrated in Figure 8.2. The prior distribution

FIGURE 8.2
An Illustration of Prior and Posterior Distributions

Events			
$p = 0.01$	0.4	Sample of	0.170
$p = 0.02$	0.3	⎯⎯⎯⎯⟶	0.242
$p = 0.04$	0.2	6 cans,	0.291
$p = 0.15$	0.1	1 defective	0.297
	Prior Distribution		Posterior Distribution

is the distribution *before* (prior to) the sample, and the posterior distribution is the distribution *after* the sample outcome is known. It is important to realize that prior and posterior are always designations of the events probability distribution *relative to* a sample. Thus, if we had updated the events probability distribution following the sample of six cans in which one was defective, and then obtained another sample of, say, ten cans with no defectives, the *posterior* distribution given in Figure 8.1 would become the *prior* distribution for the new sample of ten cans.[1] This notion of using the posterior distribution as a new prior will be crucial to us when we consider taking an additional sample.

Before we consider the larger question of an additional sample, let us conclude this section with another example. Suppose in the New Drug problem of Chapter 6 ten patients have been treated with the drug and six were cured. Which action should be taken in the light of this evidence? As before, we must first use Bayes' rule, either formally or through the tabular technique proposed above to obtain the posterior distribution of events. The prior distribution is:

$$P(p = \tfrac{1}{2}) = 0.8 \text{ and } P(p = \tfrac{3}{4}) = 0.2.$$

Using these numbers the tabular calculation is:

p-values	P(p)	P(K = 6 |n = 10,p)	Col. (3) × Col. (4)	Conditional Event Probabilities
0.75	0.2	0.1460	0.0292	0.151
0.5	0.8	0.2051	0.1641	0.849
	(Prior)		0.1933	(Posterior)

and, using the opportunity loss table:

	M (Market)	D (Don't Market)
$p = \tfrac{3}{4}$	0	$50,000
$p = \tfrac{1}{2}$	$20,000	0

the expected opportunity losses are:

$$\mathcal{E}(M) = 0 \times 0.151 + 20,000 \times 0.849 = 16,980$$
$$\mathcal{E}(D) = 50,000 \times 0.151 + 0 \times 0.849 = 7,550.$$

Therefore, the best action is D; that is, not to market the drug.

This concludes the example of applying the technique to the New Drug problem, and you can see that the ideas and mechanics are quite straightforward. Before we go on to study the more complex problem of considering another sample, we should point out one important thing about the answers we have obtained. *They are consistent with the results obtained in Chapters 6 and 7.* For instance, in Chapter 6 we found that for $n = 6$ in the Valley Sisters problem the optimal cutoff, c, is one. An optimal cutoff point of one implies that the best strategy is to adjust the machine whenever the number of defective cans is one or more. When

---

[1] The reader may realize that, since the outcomes of a binomial sampling process are independent, we can combine the six and ten can samples and, using the original prior—$P(p = 0.01) = 0.4$, etc.—obtain the same posterior as that of the two-step procedure discussed in this section.

we used the specific outcome of one defective can in six and the posterior distribution analysis method given in this chapter, we found that the best action was to adjust the machine. Similarly, in Chapter 7 we found that $c^* = 7$ for the New Drug problem when $n = 10$. This is consistent with the conclusion reached in this chapter that, for six cures in ten patients the best decision is not to market the product.

It should be of no surprise to the thoughtful reader that these two techniques provide outcomes that are consistent with one another. The techniques of Chapters 6 and 7 are based upon the enumeration of strategies approach to solving decision theory problems, and the posterior analysis technique of this chapter is based upon a decision tree approach. We stated in Chapter 5 that the two techniques are equivalent, so we should expect the specialized versions of these techniques applied to binomial sampling problems to be consistent with each other.

8.2 SUSPENSION OF JUDGMENT, OR THE CONSIDERATION OF TAKING ANOTHER SAMPLE WHEN THE RESULTS OF ONE ARE KNOWN

Up to this point in this chapter we have only considered the possibility of making a terminal decision, given a particular sample outcome. However, you must realize that this is not the only set of actions open to you as an analyst. You also have the option of considering an additional sample. In this section we shall present the concepts and mechanics by which this is done. These concepts and mechanics are collectively called *suspension of judgment,* because that is exactly what we are doing—suspending the choice of a terminal action until an additional sample has been taken and analyzed.

The concepts underlying suspension of judgment are very simple, given what you have previously learned. What we must do is analyze a new sample using the techniques discussed in Chapters 6 and 7, *while taking the information we already have (i.e., the first sample outcome) into account.* This can easily be done by using the posterior distribution. The information from the sample outcome is incorporated with the prior distribution to create a posterior distribution. This posterior distribution is then used in the analyses we studied in Chapters 6 and 7 to make a decision on whether further sampling should occur, and if so how much.

8.2.1 An Example of Suspension of Judgment Analysis

Suppose you, as an analyst for the Valley Sisters Coffee Company, are approached by the foreman of the can-filling line and asked to make a decision. The foreman tells you that ten cans have been sampled, and of these ten, one defective has occurred. The questions you want to answer for yourself are:

1. Should another sample be taken and, if so, what should the size of this sample be? *or*
2. Should an immediate terminal action be chosen and, if so, which one?

In this section we will use the technique of posterior distribution analysis, in combination with the techniques of Chapters 6 and 7, to demonstrate how to answer these questions.

Let's first consider the second question, which terminal action should be taken, since it is (mechanically) easier to answer, and its answer must be known in order to fully answer the question of whether an additional sample would be useful. In order to determine which terminal action is best, we need to obtain the posterior distribution for the outcome given. The calculations for the posterior distribution are presented in Table 8.2. We can use this posterior distribution to determine which

TABLE 8.2
The Posterior Probability Distribution for the Foreman's Sample of One Defective Can in Ten

p-values	Prior Probability Distribution	Probability of Sample Outcome	Product of Cols. (2) and (3)	Posterior Probability Distribution
0.01	0.4	0.0913	0.03652	0.207
0.02	0.3	0.1667	0.05001	0.283
0.04	0.2	0.2770	0.05540	0.313
0.15	0.1	0.3474	0.03474	0.197
			0.17667	1.000

of the terminal actions should be chosen. If the machine is adjusted, the expected loss is

$$\mathcal{E}(A) = 4.8 \times 0.207 + 3.6 \times 0.283 + 1.2 \times 0.313 + 0 \times 0.197$$
$$= 2.39,$$

while if the run is continued, the expected loss is

$$\mathcal{E}(N) = 0 \times 0.207 + 0 \times 0.283 + 0 \times 0.313 + 12 \times 0.197$$
$$= 2.36.$$

Therefore, it is less expensive to continue the run without adjustment.

Consider now the larger question of whether an additional sample should be taken and, if so, how big this additional sample should be, and what the optimal strategy associated with it is. In order to answer this question we shall analyze this problem exactly as we analyzed the sampling problems in Chapters 6 and 7, *except* that we shall use the posterior distribution rather than the prior distribution as the probability distribution of events.

For example, if we should choose an *additional* sample of size 6, then the expression for the Unconditional Expected Loss (UEL) for $n = 6, c = 1$, is

$$\begin{aligned}
\text{UEL} = &\ \text{loss}(A|p = 0.01)P(B \geq 1|n = 6, p = 0.01)P(p = 0.01) \\
&+ \text{loss}(A|p = 0.02)P(B \geq 1|n = 6, p = 0.02)P(p = 0.02) \\
&+ \text{loss}(A|p = 0.04)P(B \geq 1|n = 6, p = 0.04)P(p = 0.04) \\
&+ \text{loss}(N|p = 0.15)P(B < 1|n = 6, p = 0.15)P(p = 0.15)
\end{aligned}$$

and when the above expressions are replaced with their values, we have

$$\begin{aligned}
\text{UEL} = &\ 4.8 \times 0.0585 \times 0.207 + 3.6 \times 0.1142 \times 0.283 \\
&+ 1.2 \times 0.2172 \times 0.313 + 12 \times 0.3771 \times 0.197 \\
= &\ 1.15.
\end{aligned}$$

To determine if $c = 1$ is the optimal strategy, we must compare its UEL with the UEL of neighboring values. For $c = 0$ we have a pure strategy equivalent to always choosing A, so

$$\text{UEL} = 2.39 \text{ for } c = 0,$$

while for $c = 2$ we have

$$\begin{aligned}
\text{UEL} = &\ 4.8 \times 0.0015 \times 0.207 + 3.6 \times 0.0057 \times 0.283 \\
&+ 1.2 \times 0.0216 \times 0.313 + 12 \times 0.7765 \times 0.197 \\
= &\ 1.85.
\end{aligned}$$

Therefore, by a comparison of the three UEL values we find that $c = 1$ is the optimal cutoff value when the *new* (additional) sample size is $n = 6$.

Notice that the above calculation is exactly the same as the kind of calculations carried out in Chapter 6. The only difference is that for the calculations we have just completed, the posterior rather than the prior is used as the probability distribution of events.

We now know the best strategy for the additional sample of size 6. However, we really want to answer the larger question of whether any additional sample should be taken. To do that we will use the techniques of Chapter 7. Recall that the first quantity we discussed in Chapter 7 was the sample cost function. In order to determine whether an additional sample should be taken, we needed to weigh the additional benefits of the sample (in lowering the unconditional expected loss) against its costs. Let us suppose in this case that the foreman estimates the additional sample cost will be 17¢ plus 11¢ per unit sampled, that is

$$\text{Sample Cost} = 0.17 + 0.11n \text{ (in dollars)}.$$

It is this cost function we shall use in determining whether any additional sampling should take place.

It is important to notice here that we do not consider the cost of the sample already taken. The fact that the foreman already knew the outcome of the sample of ten has no bearing on the sample cost, because we only want to consider the *potential* costs of our decision. The cost of the sample already obtained is a *sunk* cost (one already incurred) and should have no bearing on what the best policy is *from here on*. In order to determine the best policy from here on, we are only going to consider *future* costs.

Consider now the overall problem of finding the best sample size. Just as in Chapter 7 we proceed by trial and error. The first thing we can calculate is the upper ceiling on the sample size we will need to consider. This can be done by realizing that the sample cost (alone) certainly cannot exceed the expected loss of the best action or strategy found to date. In this case we know that the best terminal action is N, and its expected loss is 2.36. Therefore, we have

$$0.17 + 0.11n \leq 2.36,$$

which when solved yields

$$n \leq 19.9,$$

and we know that the maximum sample size we need to consider is 19.

Using this upper limit on the sample size, we still need to perform the step-by-step calculations given in the algorithm in Section 7.2.2. Thus, we start with $n = 1$, and find the best c, then work our way on up, increasing n one at a time, until the upper limit of 19 is reached. For each value of n we calculate the best value of c, and the corresponding UEL and TL (Total Loss). The result of these calculations applied to this problem are illustrated in Table 8.3. From this table we see that the best sample size is $n = 6$, the corresponding optimal cutoff point is $c = 1$, and the Total Loss of that strategy is 1.978. Knowing this, we are still not quite finished, however. *If* we sample, then a sample of size 6 is optimal, but we still haven't answered the question of whether we should sample at all. Fortunately, this last question is easy to answer. All we need to do is compare the best Total Loss for sampling (1.98) with the expected loss of the best terminal action without further sampling (2.36). Since the best TL for sampling is less in this case, it is better to take an additional sample than to take an immediate terminal action. Therefore, *after* a sample of size 10 is observed, which contains one bad can, the optimal decision is to sample an *additional* six cans. If one or more of these additional cans is defective, then the machine should be adjusted. Otherwise, the run should be continued without adjustment to the machine.

TABLE 8.3
Analysis of Various Sample Sizes in Suspension of
Judgment for the Valley Sisters Problem

n	c	UEL	Sample Cost	TL
1	0	2.388		
	1*	2.055	0.28	2.335
	2	2.364		
2	1*	1.798	0.39	2.188
	2	2.312		
3	1*	1.585	0.5	2.085
	2	2.224		
4	1*	1.409	0.61	2.019
	2	2.111		
5	1*	1.265	0.72	1.985
	2	1.985		
6	1*	1.148	0.83	1.978†
	2	1.851		
7	1*	1.053	0.94	1.993
	2	1.715		
8	1*	0.978	1.05	2.028
	2	1.581		
9	1*	0.918	1.16	2.078
	2	1.452		
10	1*	0.873	1.27	2.143
	2	1.329		
11	1*	0.838	1.38	2.218
	2	1.215		
12	1*	0.814	1.49	2.304
	2	1.108		
13	1*	0.798	1.6	2.398
	2	1.011		
14	1*	0.788	1.71	2.498
	2	0.923		
15	1*	0.784	1.82	2.604
	2	0.843		
16	1	0.785		
	2*	0.772	1.93	2.702
17	2*	0.709	2.04	2.749
	3	1.245		
18	2*	0.654	2.15	2.804
	3	1.152		
19	2*	0.606	2.26	2.866
	3	1.065		

* Denotes the optimal cutoff point for that value of n.
† Denotes the overall best Total Loss.

8.2.2 A Comparison of Two Sampling Schemes

It is interesting to compare the results we just obtained with those obtained for the Valley Sisters problem in Chapter 7. There we also found that sampling was better than not sampling, but the optimal sample size was $n = 4$, the optimal cutoff point was $c = 1$, and the associated Total Loss was 1.162. Here, by comparison, we have a *combined* sample size of 16, a combined cutoff point of 2, and associated

Total Loss of 1.98. While some of the difference is due to a different sample cost function, it can be shown that using the original cost function $(0.1 + 0.06n)$ on the problem in this chapter yields an optimal *additional* sample of size 8, an optimal cutoff point of 1, and an associated TL of 1.56. This is equivalent to a combined sample of size 18 with a combined cut off point of 2.

Why does this difference occur? One would hope, if anything, that knowing a sample outcome would lead to a better decision (one with a lower Total Loss), whereas this shows just the opposite situation. Unfortunately, our intuition about a sample always helping us is naive. Sometimes, and this example is a good illustration of it, the sample outcome makes the situation (at least in terms of the losses involved) more uncertain rather than more certain. One easy way to notice this is to notice how, for the original Valley Sisters problem the expected loss of the best terminal action was 1.20, while after the sample of size 10 with one defective can the expected loss of the best terminal action has jumped to 2.36. It is good for the reader to carefully study these two examples. They can provide a surprising insight into just how complicated binomial sampling problems can be.

8.2.3   Another Example of Suspension of Judgment

Let's consider another example of suspension of judgment, this time applied to the New Drug problem. If we want to analyze additional samples after the outcome has occurred in which six out of ten patients were cured, we proceed as follows. First, the posterior distribution is obtained. This posterior distribution was calculated in Section 8.1, and it is

$$P(p = 0.5) = 0.849 \text{ and } P(p = 0.75) = 0.151$$

The second step is to determine which of the two immediate actions is best. This was also done in Section 8.1, and we found that the Don't Market (D) action was the best, and its associated expected opportunity loss (using the posterior distribution) is 7,550. The third step is to determine the maximum bound on additional sampling. This can be done by determining the sample size, n, for which the sample cost equals the expected opportunity loss of the best immediate action. If we assume the same sample cost as in Chapter 7 ($450 per patient with no fixed cost) then we have

$$450n = 7,550$$

or

$$n = \frac{7,550}{450}$$
$$= 16.8,$$

and thus the maximum sample we need to consider is $n = 16$.

Once all these quantities have been obtained, the final step is to find the sample size and corresponding optimal cutoff point that has the least TL of all sample sizes considered. The calculations for this step are summarized in Table 8.4. We find from these calculations that the

TABLE 8.4
Analysis of Various Sample Sizes in Suspension of Judgment for the New Drug Problem

n	c	UEL	Sample Cost	TL
1	0	16980		
	1	10378		
	2*	7550	450	8,000
2	2*	7548	900	8,448
	3	7550		
3	2	9670		
	3*	6487	1,350	7,837†
4	3	7282		
	4*	6222	1,800	8,022
5	4*	5956	2,250	8,206
	5	6289		
6	4	7116		
	5*	5376	2,700	8,076
7	5	5686		
	6*	5252	3,150	8,402
8	6*	4881	3,600	8,481
	7	5375		
9	6	5563		
	7*	4540	4,050	8,590
10	7	4611		
	8*	4510	4,500	9,010
11	8*	4088	4,950	9,038
	9	4669		
12	8	4482		
	9*	3891	5,400	9,291
13	9*	3821	5,850	9,671
	10	3922		
14	9	4442		
	10*	3476	6,300	9,776
15	10	3682		
	11*	3373	6,750	10,123
16	11*	3216	7,200	10,416
	12	3444		

* Denotes the optimal cutoff point for each *n*.
† Denotes the best TL.

minimum TL occurs when $n = 3$ and $c^* = 3$, and its value is \$7,837. If we definitely were going to continue sampling, it would be best to sample three more patients, and market the drug only if all three are cured. *However,* this strategy has a higher expected opportunity loss than the immediate action of not marketing. In this case, it is less expensive to make an immediate decision rather than suspend judgment while another sample is taken.

8.3 SUMMARY

We have seen that the analysis of binomial sampling problems when a sample outcome is known is basically the same as the analysis when no sample information is known. The basic difference comes in the probability distribution of events that is used. In the terminology of this chapter, a problem in which no sample information is known is analyzed using the *prior* probability distribution of events, while a problem in which some sample information is already known is analyzed using the *posterior* probability distribution of events. This posterior distribution is obtained by applying Bayes' rule to combine the probabilities of the sample outcome with the prior probabilities of events.

PROBLEMS

1. For the Valley Sisters example, suppose another sample is taken *after* the outcome of the first sample ($n = 6$, $B = 1$) is known. Thus, the *prior* is $P(p = 0.01) = 0.170$, etc. If the additional sample is of size 4 ($n = 4$) and has zero defective cans ($B = 0$), what is the new posterior distribution of p values?

2. Suppose in the Valley Sisters problem you are taking an initial sample, so the prior is $P(p = 0.01) = 0.4$, etc.

    a. What is the posterior distribution if $n = 10$ and $B = 1$?
    b. Your answer to part (*a*) should be the same as your answer to Problem 1. Explain why this is so.

3. Suppose in the New Drug example that no sample has been taken. Thus, the prior is $P(p = 0.5) = 0.8$, etc. What is the posterior distribution after a sample of 15 patients have been treated with the drug and eight are cured?

4. Consider the Playful Monarch problem, Problem 9 of Chapter 6. Suppose the subject tosses the coin eight times and three heads appear. What is the posterior probability distribution?

5. For the Spark Ling Co., Problem 8 of Chapter 6, find the posterior distribution if a sample of size 10 is taken and one box is misfilled.

6. Consider Problem 17 of Chapter 6, except assume the prior distribution is $P(p = 0.2) = 0.3$ and $P(p = 0.5) = 0.7$.

    a. What is the posterior distribution if the fifth bolt is the first defective?
    b. One advantage to the decision tree format for analyzing sampling problems is that they can verify forms of strategies. In Chapter 6 we could only conjecture the form of the optimal sampling strategy. Using a decision tree like Figure 8.1 will help verify our

intuition (or correct it if it is wrong). Analyze enough (at least up to $N = 5$) of the branches on the decision tree for the bolt problem to verify what the form of the optimal sampling strategy is.

7. Suppose for Problem 13 of Chapter 6, both tests are conducted at once. In the first, one city is surveyed and the outcome indicates the product should be marketed. In the second (and independent of the first), six panel members were randomly selected and only one purchased the product.

   a. What is the posterior distribution?
   b. Draw a representative decision tree (à la Figure 8.1) for the *joint* sampling plan indicated in this problem.
   c. Instead of conducting both experiments jointly, suppose the company considered conducting them *sequentially*. Draw a representative decision tree for *this* sampling plan. (Don't forget to include the order of the experiments in your decision tree!)

8. Which action should be taken in the Valley Sisters problem if a sample of size 12 yields no defectives? (Assume the prior is $P(p = 0.01) = 0.4$, etc.)

9. If in the New Drug example 15 patients have been treated and eight cured (as in Problem 3 above), what action should be taken?

10. If in the New Drug example ten people have been treated and eight cured, which action should be taken?

11. For the Playful Monarch problem (Problem 9 of Chapter 6), which action should the subject take if the coin has been tossed ten times and six heads have appeared?

12. Suppose in the New Drug example, that in a sample of ten patients eight were cured. If the company wants to consider taking another sample, what is the maximum size it needs to consider for such a sample?

13. In the Playful Monarch problem (Problem 9 of Chapter 6), ten tosses of the coin has produced six heads. If for three copper pieces, the subject can buy another 20 tosses, should he do so? What is the optimal value of c for these 20 additional tosses?

14. Consider the Count Cash problem (Problem 10 of Chapter 6). Answer the questions in that problem *posterior* to observing a sample of ten accounts of which two have been incorrectly accounted for.

15. Find the optimal *additional* sample size for the SOGGIES problem (Problem 11 of Chapter 6) if an initial sample of ten households yields six in which the children's breakfast cereal decisions are made by children, and the sample cost function is $5,000 + 200n$.

16. Find the optimal *additional* sample size for the Spark Ling Co. prob-
     lem (Problem 8 of Chapter 6) if an initial sample of five boxes yields
     no defectives, and the sample cost function is $0.90 + 0.05n$.

17. For the marketing manager of Problem 13, Chapter 6, assume that
     the personal interview market research plan has already been con-
     ducted in one city, and the conclusion of that test is to market the
     product. The manager is considering taking an additional sample from
     the consumer panel before making his decision. If the cost of the con-
     sumer panel is $800 + 50n$, should he conduct this additional test?
     If so, what are the optimal values of n and c?

18.[2] Verify that for the Valley Sisters problem the use of the original
     sample cost function yields an *additional* optimal sample of size 8, an
     optimal cutoff point of 1, and an associated TL of 1.56. (See Section
     8.2.2.)

---

[2] This problem requires the use of the computer routines accompanying this text
for a complete analysis.

An Introduction to Continuous Probability Distributions and Their Use in Decision Theory Problems

UP TO THIS POINT we have considered only problems whose probability distributions had a finite and small number of outcomes. For instance, in Chapter 6 the sampling distributions had $n + 1$ possible outcomes where n, the potential sample size, was usually smaller than 20. Furthermore, even the prior distributions of events were limited to a small number—four possible p values in the Valley Sisters problem and two possible p values in the New Drug problem. At the time we adopted these prior distributions we acknowledged that to assume p takes on only a small number of values seemed wrong. It seemed much more likely that p should be allowed to take on a whole spectrum of values between 0 and 1. In this chapter we will discuss the concept of a probability distribution for a random variable that can take on a whole spectrum of values. Such a probability distribution is called a *continuous probability distribution*. We will also discuss some of the techniques by which these continuous probability distributions can be used in binomial sampling problems. Unfortunately, a thorough understanding of these techniques requires a knowledge of integral calculus. Therefore, the development of techniques given in this chapter will be in the sections marked with an asterisk (*), and the reader is urged to avoid these if he does not understand integral calculus. Because of the calculus background needed to understand much of the material when continuous prior distributions are used with binomial sampling, the range of problems you will be able to solve when you finish reading this chapter will not be as great as those covered in Chapters 6, 7 and 8. Chapter 10 will continue the development of binomial sampling problems with continuous prior distributions, but will require a knowledge of integral calculus throughout. For the reader interested in solving such problems but without the integral calculus background needed for Chapter 10, Section 13.1 provides a good way to use the methods of Chapters 6, 7, and 8 on problems with continuous priors.

We have many times emphasized the fact that there are two kinds of probability distributions used in decision theory problems—the prior, or probability distribution of events, and the sampling distributions. Up to this point we have discussed problems in which both prior and sampling distributions are finite; that is, take on only a finite number of values. In this chapter and Chapter 10 we will keep the sampling distributions finite (the binomial distribution), but combine them with continuous prior distributions. Then in Chapters 11 and 12 we will discuss situations in which the sampling distribution is continuous, specifically the normal probability distribution. So, continuous probability distributions will be used throughout the rest of this book, and it is important that you understand the concepts in this chapter.

9.1 GENERAL CONCEPTS OF CONTINUOUS DISTRIBUTIONS

When we speak of continuous distributions we are really speaking of the probability distribution of some random variable, X, whose state space (set of values it can take on) is the set of all real numbers between a and b. For example, in the Valley Sisters problem we would like to allow our random variable (p) to take on any value between 0 and 1.

When we use these random variables we must develop some new notions and mathematics to work with them. The most important of these is the notion that we always express the probability of our random variable X being contained in an interval, rather than the probability of its having a specific value. Thus, we speak of

$$P(c \leq X \leq e)$$

rather than

$$P(X = d)$$

because the latter has no meaning for a continuous random variable.[1]

When we work with continuous probability distributions we use a helpful (mathematical) device called a *probability density function*. The probability density function is a mathematical function that has the property that the *area underneath it* between any two values of the

---

[1] That $P(X = d)$ has no meaning is certainly not obvious, but its verification would require mathematical capabilities beyond the average reader. Therefore we present the statement without proof.

random variable is the probability that an outcome of the random variable will occur within that range of values.

Let's take an example. The probability distribution for a binomial sampling problem might have a probability density function

$$f(p) = \begin{cases} 3(1-p)^2 & \text{if } 0 < p < 1 \\ 0 & \text{otherwise} \end{cases}.$$

This function is graphed in Figure 9.1, and the probability that p will

FIGURE 9.1

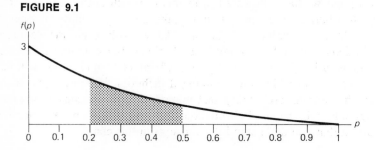

lie between 0.2 and 0.5, $P(0.2 \le p \le 0.5)$, is represented by the shaded area. Using integral calculus, it can be shown that the value of this probability is 0.387, that is:

$$P(0.2 \le p \le 0.5) = 0.387.$$

There are two important points to remember about this technique. First, the probability density function allows us to determine the probability of p lying in *any* interval of values between 0 and 1. Thus it is a very powerful tool. Furthermore, the probability density function is used to calculate other characteristics of the distribution, such as mean and variance. These techniques will be demonstrated below.

The second point to remember is that the probability within an interval will vary with the probability density function. For instance, another probability distribution for p might be one whose probability density function is:

$$f(p) = \begin{cases} 1 & \text{if } 0 < p < 1 \\ 0 & \text{otherwise} \end{cases}.$$

This function is graphed in Figure 9.2, and the probability that p lies between 0.2 and 0.5 is indicated by the shaded area. In this case, the shaded portion is a rectangle, so its area is the product of the length times the height, or $(0.5 - 0.2) \times 1 = 0.3$. Thus for this probability distribution we have:

$$P(0.2 \le p \le 0.5) = 0.3,$$

FIGURE 9.2

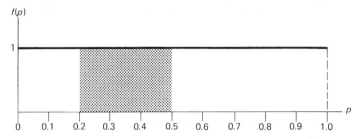

and this is, of course, different from $P(0.2 \leq p \leq 0.5)$ for the probability distribution whose probability density function is depicted in Figure 9.1.

The probability distribution we have just studied, the one whose probability density function is

$$f(p) = \begin{cases} 1 & \text{if } 0 < p < 1 \\ 0 & \text{otherwise} \end{cases},$$

is called the *uniform* (or rectangular) distribution. The uniform distribution is quite useful in decision theory. If it is used, the decision maker in establishing the prior is saying that each value of p is as likely as every other value of p; that is, the decision maker has no a priori felling that one value for p is any more likely than any other.

*9.2 OBTAINING PROBABILITIES FROM PROBABILITY DENSITY FUNCTIONS

For the reader who knows integral calculus, the probability of the random variable, p, lying between 0.2 and 0.5 is given by the definite integral of the probability density function, $f(p)$, between 0.2 and 0.5. In mathematical symbols this is:

$$P(0.2 \leq p \leq 0.5) = \int_{0.2}^{0.5} f(p)\, dp.$$

Thus, if $f(p)$ is as depicted in Figure 9.1,

$$f(p) = \begin{cases} 3(1 - p)^2 & \text{if } 0 < p < 1 \\ 0 & \text{otherwise} \end{cases},$$

then

$$P(0.2 \leq p \leq 0.5) = \int_{0.2}^{0.5} 3(1 - p)^2\, dp = -(1 - p)^3 \Big|_{0.2}^{0.5} = 0.387.$$

Similarly, when $f(p)$ is uniform

$$P(0.2 \leq p \leq 0.5) = \int_{0.2}^{0.5} 1\, dp = p \Big|_{0.2}^{0.5} = 0.3.$$

This property holds in general, of course, and the probability of a continuous random variable X lying in any interval is given by the definite integral of $f(x)$ from the lower end of the interval to the upper end of the interval, where $f(x)$ is the probability density function of X; that is,

$$P(c \leq X \leq e) = \int_c^e f(x)\, dx.$$

9.3 THE MEAN AND VARIANCE OF CONTINUOUS RANDOM VARIABLES

Just as with the finite probability distributions we discussed in Chapter 2, the probability distributions of continuous random variables have a measure of location, the mean (or expected value), and two very closely related measures of dispersion, the variance and standard deviation. These quantities are obtained using the probability density function and integral calculus, so we can only mention here that they exist, and not show how they are derived. As an example, we can give the values for the mean and variance of the two distributions we have previously studied. For the random variable whose probability density function is

$$f(p) = \begin{cases} 3(1-p)^2 & \text{if } 0 < p < 1 \\ 0 & \text{otherwise} \end{cases},$$

the value of the mean is $\frac{1}{4}$, and the value of the variance is $\frac{3}{80}$. For the random variable whose probability density function is

$$f(p) = \begin{cases} 1 & \text{if } 0 < p < 1 \\ 0 & \text{otherwise} \end{cases},$$

the value of the mean is $\frac{1}{2}$ (which should be apparent from Figure 9.2) and the value of the variance is $\frac{1}{12}$.

Nothing more can be said about the mean and variance for continuous probability distributions at this point. Section 9.4 will give the method for obtaining them for those who understand integral calculus, and Section 9.5 will discuss two "general" continuous probability distributions, and give formulas from which the mean and variance can be calculated, knowing the parameter values. The important point of this section is that means and variances exist for continuous probability distributions, and that they are, respectively, the measures of location and dispersion for these distributions.

*9.4 DERIVATIONS OF MEANS AND VARIANCES FOR CONTINUOUS PROBABILITY DISTRIBUTIONS

The formula for calculating the mean is closely related to the formula for calculating a mean for a finite probability distribution, which we discussed in Chapter 2. There we stated that the mean is obtained as the sum of products of values times probabilities. Here we replace probabilities with the probability density function, and summation with integration, both because there is a continuum of values of the random variable. Thus, if the random variable X has a probability density function $f(x)$, then

$$E(X) = \int_{-\infty}^{+\infty} xf(x)\,dx.$$

For example, the random variable p, which has the probability density function

$$f(p) = \begin{cases} 3(1-p)^2 & \text{if } 0 < p < 1, \\ 0 & \text{otherwise} \end{cases},$$

has a mean that is

$$E(p) = \int_{-\infty}^{+\infty} pf(p)\,dp = \int_0^1 p \times 3(1-p)^2\,dp = \tfrac{1}{4}.$$

In a similar manner the variance is calculated by weighting the squared deviation from the mean by the probability density function and integrating over all possible values. Thus:

$$\text{Var}(X) = \int_{-\infty}^{+\infty} [x - E(X)]^2 f(x)\,dx,$$

and for the probability density function

$$f(p) = \begin{cases} 3(1-p)^2 & \text{if } 0 < p < 1, \\ 0 & \text{otherwise} \end{cases},$$

the variance is

$$\text{Var}(p) = \int_{-\infty}^{+\infty} [p - E(p)]^2 f(p)\,dp$$
$$= \int_0^1 (p - \tfrac{1}{4})^2 \times 3(1-p)^2\,dp = \tfrac{3}{80}.$$

9.5 USEFUL CONTINUOUS PROBABILITY DISTRIBUTIONS

In Chapter 2 we discussed specific random variables and their probability distributions. Each value of the random variable had a specific probability, and there was very little, if any, relationship between the distributions of different random variables. Then in Chapter 6 we introduced a new concept in probability distributions, the binomial distribution. While we call it by a singular name, the binomial distribution really represents many distinct (in the sense of specific values for probabilities) distributions. The binomial distribution is a mathematical *formula* that allows us to *generate* these distinct probability distributions once specific values for the *parameters n* and *p* are given. That is, we can use the mathematical formula known as the binomial distribution and get an entirely different distribution when $n = 5$ and $p = 0.4$ from the distribution when $n = 15$ and $p = 0.7$.

Just as the binominal distribution is one case (there are many) of a formula that lets us calculate many distinct finite probability distributions, there are similar formulas for obtaining many distinct continuous probability distributions. There are two we shall study in this book because they are the most useful to the branches of decision theory we shall cover; but, again, there are many other formulas that exist. The two we will study are called the *beta distribution* and the *normal distribution*. Those of you who go on to Chapter 10 will find the beta distribution very useful for binomial sampling problems. The normal distribution is the most widely used distribution in the field of statistics. One of the reasons for this is a special property of sampling known as the central limit theorem. We shall discuss the results of the central limit theorem in Chapter 12, where it will form the heart of the discussions on *normal sampling*.

One of the properties of the binomial distribution is that the values of the mean and variance of any specific distribution derived from this formula can be obtained from (rather simple) formulas containing only the parameters n and p; that is, if X is a binomially distributed random variable, then

$$E(X) = np$$
$$\text{Var}(X) = np(1 - p).$$

This same property holds true for any of these general formulas. In order to find the mean and variance of the specific distribution we are working with, we merely need to plug the values of the parameters into some (usually simple) formulas to obtain the values of the mean and the variance, rather than having to find the value of a complicated sum or some definite integral. This result is very helpful when one works with these general formulas.

9.5.1   The Beta Distribution

The beta distribution is a formula that allows us to obtain many distinct continuous probability distribution on the spectrum of values between 0 and 1. The general formula for the probability density function is

$$f(x) = \begin{cases} (a + 1)\binom{a}{b} x^b (1 - x)^{a-b} & \text{if } 0 < x < 1, \\ 0 & \text{otherwise} \end{cases}$$

where a and b are the parameters whose values must be specified in order to obtain a specific probability density function. It is necessary that the value of a always be greater than or equal to the value of b.

Furthermore, for the work in this book we will restrict the values of a and b to be nonnegative integers, although the beta distribution is in general defined for all values of a and b that satisfy $-1 < b < a + 1$.

A word of caution is important at this point. The above formula looks very much like the binomial probability formula

$$P(X = k) = \binom{n}{k} p^k (1 - p)^{n-k}$$

(and, as we will see in Chapter 10, there are good reasons why it should), but be careful to distinguish between the two. In the binomial formula n and p are the parameters (whose values must be known beforehand) and k is the variable which takes on several values ($k = 0$, $1, 2, \ldots, n$). On the other hand, in the beta distribution, a and b are the parameters and x is the variable that takes on several values (specifically, every value between 0 and 1, $0 < x < 1$). Furthermore, the binomial formula allows us to calculate probabilities, whose values must lie between 0 and 1, while the beta formula is used to calculate points on a probability density function, and these are not restricted to values less than or equal to 1. For instance, if $a = 5$, $b = 2$, and we calculate the value of $f(x)$ when $x = 0.3$, we have

$$f(x) = (5 + 1) \binom{5}{2} (0.3)^2 (1 - 0.3)^{5-2} = 1.85,$$

a value greater than 1.

To make matters even more confusing between the binomial and beta formulas, the easiest way to calculate specific values for the beta probability density function is to use the binomial probabilities from Table I. For example, the easy way to calculate the value for $f(x)$ given above:

$$f(x) = (5 + 1) \binom{5}{2} (0.3)^2 (1 - 0.3)^{5-2}$$

is to realize that most of the expression,

$$\binom{5}{2} (0.3)^2 (1 - 0.3)^{5-2}$$

is a binomial probability, which can be obtained from Table I. Using that table we find that

$$\binom{5}{2} (0.3)^2 (1 - 0.3)^{5-2} = 0.4718 - 0.1631 = 0.3087,$$

and thus

$$f(x) = 6 \times 0.3087 = 1.8522.$$

Let us again emphasize, however, that in spite of this close numerical relationship the two formulas represent very different concepts.

9.5.2 Properties of the Beta Distribution

As we mentioned above, the values of the mean and variance of the beta distribution can be calculated from certain formulas if the values of a and b are known. In this case, if X is a beta distributed random variable, then

$$\mathrm{E}(X) = \frac{b+1}{a+2} \text{ and } \mathrm{Var}(X) = \frac{ab+a+1-b^2}{(a+2)^2(a+3)}.$$

For instance, if X is beta distributed with $a = 5$ and $b = 2$, then

$$\mathrm{E}(X) = \tfrac{3}{7} \text{ and } \mathrm{Var}(X) = {}^{12}\!/_{392}.$$

The beta distribution can take on three basic shapes. One occurs in the special case when both a and b have a value of zero. The probability density function formula then reduces to

$$f(x) = \begin{cases} 1 & \text{if } 0 < x < 1 \\ 0 & \text{otherwise} \end{cases},$$

which is the probability density function for the uniform distribution. We already discussed this distribution in Section 9.1 and it is depicted in Figure 9.2.

The other probability distribution we introduced in Section 9.1,

$$f(p) = \begin{cases} 3(1-p)^2 & \text{if } 0 < p < 1 \\ 0 & \text{otherwise} \end{cases},$$

is also a beta distribution (with parameter values $a = 2$, $b = 0$) and this represents the second basic shape of the beta distribution. Whenever $b = 0$ or $b = a$, the probability density function looks like the letter "J" lying on its side, and these types of probability distributions are called "J-shaped." One of these J-shaped distributions is depicted in Figure 9.1, and another one for $a = b = 6$ is depicted in Figure 9.3.

FIGURE 9.3
The Beta Probability Density Function When $a = 6$ and $b = 6$

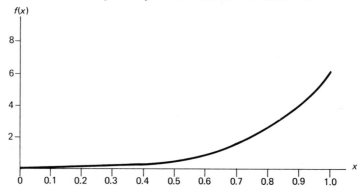

For values of the parameters other than those we discussed above, the beta probability density function is roughly bell shaped. The maximum value of the function occurs some place between 0 and 1 (specifically at b/a), and the function looks somewhat like that depicted in Figure 9.4. Furthermore, the probability density function generally be-

FIGURE 9.4
The Beta Probability Density Function When $a = 5$ and $b = 2$

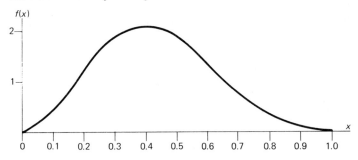

comes "tighter" (smaller variance) and more symmetric about the maximum value as a and b both increase. This behavior is depicted in Figure 9.5, where two probability density functions with the same maximum value are graphed.

FIGURE 9.5
The Beta Probability Density Functions When $a = 5$, $b = 2$ and $a = 50$, $b = 20$

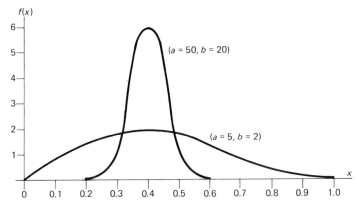

9.5.3   The Normal Distribution

The second continuous distribution we shall study in this course is the normal distribution. It is also variously known as the "bellshaped curve" and the Gaussian distribution, and the range of potential values is the whole spectrum of values from $-\infty$ to $+\infty$. On this range, the probability density function has the rather complicated formula:

$$f(x) = \frac{1}{\sqrt{2\pi}\,\sigma}\,e^{-\frac{1}{2}\left(\frac{x-\mu}{\sigma}\right)^2},$$

where μ and σ are the parameters of the distribution, x is the variable that ranges over the values from $-\infty$ to $+\infty$, and e is a numerical constant (like π) whose value is approximately 2.72.

When this probability density function is plotted, the graph shows the familiar bell-shaped form shown in Figure 9.6. The curve is always

FIGURE 9.6
A Probability Density Function for a Normal Distribution

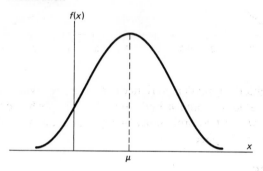

symmetric about the value of μ. How the shape changes as the values of μ and σ change will be shown below.

Just as with the beta distribution, the mean and variance of the normal distribution can be expressed as functions of the parameters μ and σ. In this case, the functions are very simple. If X is normally distributed with parameters μ and σ, then

$$\mathrm{E}(x) = \mu \text{ and } \mathrm{Var}(x) = \sigma^2.$$

Thus, for the normal distribution, one parameter is the mean and the other is the standard deviation.[2]

Because of the simple relationships between the parameters and the mean and variance for a normal distribution, it is easy to depict how changes in the parameters affect the probability density function. Figure 9.7 shows two normal probability density functions with different values for μ and the same value for σ. Since μ is the mean, or measure of location, it seems reasonable that the two distributions should have the

---

[2] Recall from Chapter 2 that the standard deviation is the square root of the variance for any probability distribution.

FIGURE 9.7

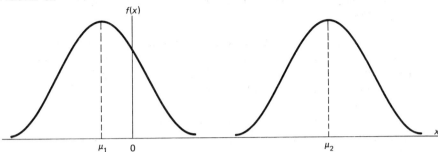

same shape, but should be centered around different values. Therefore, we conclude that changing μ has the effect of moving the distribution about on the horizontal axis but not changing its shape.

On the other hand, if we increase σ the variance will be increased. Figure 9.8 depicts two normal distributions with the same value of μ

FIGURE 9.8
Two Normal Distributions with the Same Mean and Different Values of σ

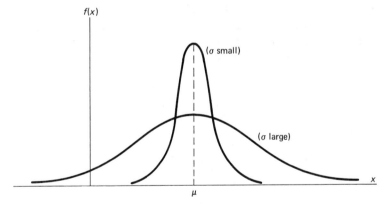

and different values of σ. Notice that as the value of σ becomes larger, the distribution becomes more spread out; i.e., there are higher probabilities of more diverse values. The distribution with the smaller variance has a very peaked curve—most of the values of the distribution lie close to the mean—whereas the distribution with the large variance has a very disperse curve—values can be far away from the mean.

This concludes our discussion of the normal distribution for now. We will reexamine it in much greater detail in Chapter 11, when we consider normal sampling. It is presented here merely to give another example of a continuous probability distribution.

9.6 MAKING DECISIONS WHEN THE PRIOR DISTRIBUTION IS CONTINUOUS

Now that you understand the concept of a probability distribution for a random variable that can take on a whole spectrum of values, we are ready to discuss how to make decisions when the prior distribution is continuous. Many of the ideas that were developed in Chapter 3 will apply to the situations discussed here. The major difference occurs in the mechanics of obtaining the answer. Just as when working with the continuous distribution, the analysis of decision problems with continuous priors requires a knowledge of integral calculus, so the results will be stated without proof in the unstarred sections, and the verification of the results will be contained in the starred sections. So, in concept, the reader will find this material much like Chapter 3 while the mechanics will be much different and more complicated.

9.6.1 Continuous Payoff and Loss Functions

When we move to a set of events that includes a whole spectrum of values, we must also change our specification of the payoffs and losses associated with each event. We will need to know the payoff for each action for *every possible value* of the event. The technique of Chapter 3 in which we developed a payoff (or loss) table listing the actions along the top margin and the events along the left margin as illustrated here

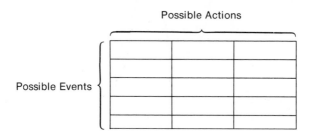

Possible Actions

Possible Events

will no longer work because an infinite number of events are possible. For instance, in the Valley Sisters problem, if we allow p to take on *every* value between 0 and 1, we would never be able to even *list* all these p values, let alone calculate the payoffs associated with each action for every p value.

Fortunately, mathematics provides an easy way out of this dilemma. We *implicitly* list the payoff for every event-action pair by describing a set of *functions*, one for each action. These functions then allow us to calculate the payoff for any particular value of p we care to specify.

Development of payoff (or cost) functions is quite straightforward.

As an example, consider the Valley Sisters problem. The cost of one action, adjusting (denoted A), is $6 no matter *what* the current event (value for p) is. Thus, the cost function for action A is the very simple

$$\text{Cost}(A) = \$6.$$

The development of the cost function for continuing, N, is only slightly more difficult. Recall that each can cost the company 6¢ to replace, and the number of cans in a production run was 2,000. Thus the expected number of defective cans in the run would be 2,000p, and the corresponding expected cost is

$$\text{Cost}(N) = \$0.06 \times 2{,}000p = \$120p.$$

Once these functions are known, of course, we can determine the cost of either action for any specified value of p. For example, if $p = 0.1$

$$\text{Cost}(A) = \$6 \text{ (as it is for all values of } p),$$

and

$$\text{Cost}(N) = 120 \times 0.1 = \$12.$$

One of the things we need to know for these functions is which action has the best (lowest) cost for any value of p. An easy way to see the relationship between the cost functions is to graph them. When the Cost(A) function is plotted, it is a straight, horizontal line, while the Cost(N) function is a linear function with a positive slope. Both of

FIGURE 9.9
A Comparison of the Two Cost Functions in the Valley Sisters Problem

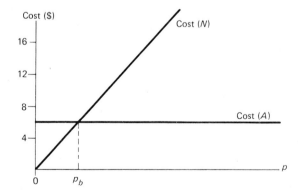

these functions are plotted in Figure 9.9. Since we are interested in least cost, notice that action N has the least cost for any value of p to the *left* of the point p_b, and action A has the least cost for any point to the *right* of p_b.

The point p_b, called the *break-even point,* will be important in future calculations, so we must find its value. Since it occurs at the point of intersection of the two cost lines, it is the value of p for which the two actions have the same cost. This value is easily found by equating the two cost functions and solving for the corresponding value for p. Thus

$$\text{Cost}(N) = \text{Cost}(A)$$

or

$$120p = 6$$

which implies

$$p_b = {}^{6}\!/_{120} = 0.05.$$

Once we have made this calculation we know that the cost of action N is less than the cost of action A for all values of p less than 0.05, and the cost of action A is less than the cost of action N for all values of p greater than 0.05. This knowledge can be used to obtain opportunity loss functions (functions are needed because we have an entire spectrum of events) for each action. Recall that opportunity loss is defined as:

> Opportunity Loss: The difference between the payoff (or cost) of a particular action for a given event, and the payoff (or cost) for the *best* action for that same event.

In this case an event is a specific value of p. Figure 9.9 is copied in Figure 9.10 with the addition of a graphical representation of the opportunity loss for action N when $p = 0.1$. At this event (value of p), action A is the best (has the lowest cost) and the opportunity loss for action N is the amount by which $\text{Cost}(N)$ exceeds $\text{Cost}(A)$. We can calculate the amount of the opportunity loss by using the cost functions. We previously calculated, for $p = 0.1$,

$$\text{Cost}(A) = \$6 \text{ and Cost}(N) = \$12.$$

Therefore, the opportunity loss for N at $p = 0.1$ is $\$12 - \$6$, or $\$6$. Similar calculations can be made for any specific p value (event).

An important thing to notice about Figure 9.10 is that one action is the best over a spectrum of values. Action A has the best (lowest) cost for any value of p greater than p_b, and action N has the lowest cost for any value of p less than p_b. It follows from our concept of opportunity loss that the opportunity loss for action A is zero for values of p greater than p_b and the opportunity loss for action N is zero for values of p less than p_b. To obtain the opportunity loss functions where the values are not zero we simply subtract the best cost from the cost of the action we are considering. Thus for p greater than p_b, the opportunity loss for action N is the cost of action N minus the cost of action A. Expressed

FIGURE 9.10

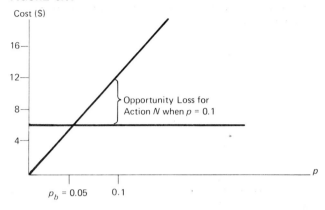

Cost ($)

16—

12—

8—

> Opportunity Loss for
Action N when $p = 0.1$

4—

$p_b = 0.05$ 0.1

p

mathematically, this is

$$\text{Loss}(N) = \text{Cost}(N) - \text{Cost}(A) \text{ for } p > p_b$$

or

$$\text{Loss}(N) = 120p - 6 \text{ for } p > p_b.$$

Combining this expression with the range over which the opportunity loss for action N is zero, we get the overall opportunity loss expression for action N:

$$\text{Loss}(N) = \begin{cases} 0 & \text{if } 0 \leq p \leq p_b \\ 120p - 6 & \text{if } p_b < p \leq 1 \end{cases}.$$

By similar reasoning we obtain the opportunity loss function for action A:

$$\text{Loss}(A) = \begin{cases} 6 - 120p & \text{if } 0 \leq p < p_b \\ 0 & \text{if } p_b \leq p \leq 1 \end{cases}.$$

These two functions are plotted in Figures 9.11 and 9.12.

FIGURE 9.11
The Opportunity Loss Function for Action A in the Valley Sisters Problem

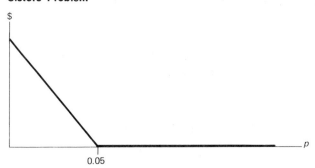

$

p

0.05

FIGURE 9.12
The Opportunity Loss Function for Action *N* in the Valley Sisters Problem

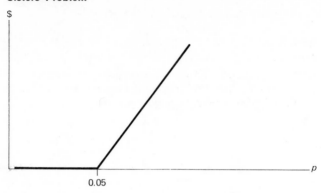

9.6.2 Analysis of Problems with Continuous Priors when No Sampling Occurs

Now that we have the tools—specifically the payoff (cost) and opportunity loss functions—that we need, we are ready to consider how to choose the best action in problems with continuous prior distributions. We will consider only the no sampling case, because the analysis of binomial sampling problems requires mathematics beyond the level of the average reader, and its discussion is confined to the advanced material of Chapter 10.

In Chapter 3 we chose the best action by calculating the expected payoff (or cost or opportunity loss) for each action and chosing the action with the best expected value. We use the same concept to compare actions in this section. Only the technique for obtaining the expected values is changed. It can be shown (see Section 9.6.3) that if some action *A* has a linear payoff or cost function:

$$\text{Payoff}(A) = a + bp$$

then the expected payoff for taking action *A* is

$$E(A) = a + bE(p),$$

where $E(p)$ is the mean or expected value of the prior distribution. For example, in the Valley Sisters case we have

$$\text{Cost}(N) = 120p,$$

so the expected cost for taking action *N* is

$$E(N) = 120\,E(p).$$

Thus if we have a prior distribution of p whose mean is 0.07, the expected cost for taking action N is

$$E(N) = 120\,E(p) = 120 \times 0.07 = \$8.40.$$

Thus we can use this simple formula, $E(A) = a + b\,E(p)$, to calculate the expected payoff of any action with a linear payoff function. In order to determine the best action we can calculate the expected payoffs (or costs) for all the other actions and find the best of these. As an example, for the Valley Sisters problem the only other action is adjusting, A, and since

$$\text{Cost}(A) = \$6,$$

a constant, its expected cost is the same value, $E(A) = \$6$. This fact can be obtained from common sense (the cost of A is the same for all values of p) or from the formula $E(A) = a + b\,E(p)$ where $b = 0$. Once we have calculated the expected cost of both actions when $E(p) = 0.07$, we find that A is the best action since its expected cost is less than the expected cost of action N.

One of the interesting aspects of what we have just done is that the decision of which action is best depends only upon the *mean* of the prior distribution. We could have two prior distributions with widely

FIGURE 9.13
Two Very Different Distributions with the Same Mean

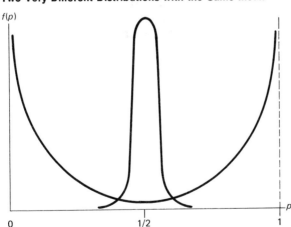

different shapes, such as in Figure 9.13, but if their means were the same the conclusion of which action was best would be the same. To take this concept one step further, a simple algebraic derivation (which is shown in Section 9.6.3) will demonstrate that the following simple rule can be applied to *two-action*[3] *problems with linear payoff (or cost) functions:*

> For any two-action problem with linear payoff functions, the best action can be found by comparing the values of $E(p)$ and p_b. If $E(p) > p_b$, take one action; if $E(p) < p_b$ take the other action.

The interesting property of this rule is that it compares a *single* aspect of the prior distribution, its mean, and a *single* aspect of the payoff functions, the break-even point, to determine the best decision.

Unfortunately, as it stands this is a very ambiguous rule. We are told to take one action if $E(p) > p_b$, but which specific action (say in the Valley Sisters problem) should be associated with each outcome of the test? We can answer this question by making use of common sense, and we will demonstrate how to do this for the Valley Sisters problem. At the same time we shall provide a heuristic argument for why the rule works.

Suppose in the Valley Sisters problem we have a prior distribution which is beta with parameters $a = 14$, $b = 0$. Then from our discussion of the beta distribution, we know that

$$E(p) = \frac{b + 1}{a + 2} = \frac{1}{16} = 0.0625.$$

Furthermore, we have previously calculated the break-even point of the Valley Sisters problem as $p_b = 0.05$. Therefore, in this situation we find that $E(p) > p_b$. Which action should we take as a result of knowing this? The answer can be found in Figure 9.14, which compares the

FIGURE 9.14
The Cost Functions for the Two Actions in the Valley Sisters Problem

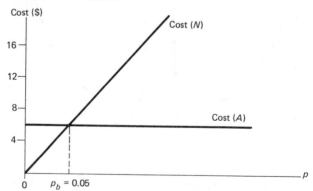

---

[3] The requirement of only two actions is not essential here. The thoughtful reader should be able to quickly generalize this rule when there are more than two actions, each with a linear payoff.

cost functions for the two actions in the Valley Sisters problem. Notice that action A is best (has the lowest cost) for any value of p greater than the break-even point, p_b. Our analysis of the prior distribution indicates that, *on the average,* the p value will be greater than p_b. Since action A has the lowest cost in this range, it follows that *on the average* action A will have a lower overall cost than action N, and therefore action A is the best action. (It is easy to verify that A is the best action in this case by using the expected value method to show that $E(A) < E(N)$ for a prior distribution whose mean is 0.0625.) By similar reasoning, if our distribution had been such that $E(p) < p_b$, then N would have been the best action.

Thus we have justified the rule by arguing that we choose the action which is, *on the average,* the best. Any time $E(p) > p_b$, we choose action A, since action A is the best action for all values of p greater than p_b; and any time $E(p) < p_b$, we choose action N, which is the best action for all values of p less than p_b. Each new problem of this type will require the reader to make a similar kind of common sense judgement about how to apply the $E(p)$ versus p_b rule.

It is important to emphasize that although we used a beta distribution as a prior just above, the ideas we have developed do not depend in any way upon the *form* of the prior distribution. The examples from this section have been for binomial sampling problems, but we will see that the same ideas will be used in Chapter 11 for normal sampling problems. We can *even* use the $E(p)$ versus p_b rule for problems with finite prior distributions, such as those in Chapter 6, providing we have enough information to calculate p_b.

Now that we have a simple rule for determining the best action for the problems we have been discussing, let us turn to a determination of the expected opportunity loss for each action. Unfortunately, while the expected payoff for actions with linear cost functions are easy to calculate, the expected loss is quite difficult. Only in the case when the prior distribution is a beta distribution can we obtain a closed form expression for the expected loss. Furthermore, this expression is different for the action whose loss function is zero for *low* values of p, $(p < p_b)$, from that for the action whose loss function is zero for *high* values of p $(p > p_b)$. Specifically, if the prior distribution is beta with parameters a and b, and

$$\text{Loss}(A) = \begin{cases} K + kp & \text{if } p < p_b, \\ 0 & \text{if } p > p_b \end{cases}$$

then the expected loss of Action A is

$$\mathcal{E}(A) = KP(B \geq b + 1 | n = a + 1, p = p_b)$$
$$+ k \left(\frac{b+1}{a+2} \right) P(B \geq b + 2 | n = a + 2, p = p_b),$$

and if the loss function is

$$\text{Loss}(A) = \begin{cases} 0 & \text{if } p < p_b \\ K + kp & \text{if } p > p_b \end{cases}$$

then the expected loss is

$$\mathcal{E}(A) = KP(B < b + 1 \,|\, n = a + 1, p = p_b) \\ + k\left(\frac{b+1}{a+2}\right) P(B < b + 2 \,|\, n = a + 2, p = p_b),$$

where the probabilities are from Table I, the table of cumulative binomial probabilities, at the back of this text.

Let's take an example of the calculations in these formulas in the Valley Sisters problem. Again assume that p is beta distributed with parameters $a = 14$ and $b = 0$. From Figure 9.12 we see that action N has a zero opportunity loss for low values of p ($p < p_b$), and its opportunity loss function is

$$\text{Loss}(N) = \begin{cases} 0 & \text{if } p < p_b. \\ 120p - 6 & \text{if } p > p_b \end{cases}$$

Therefore to calculate $\mathcal{E}(N)$, we should use the second of the above expected opportunity loss formulas, and we have:

$$K = -6; \, k = 120; \, a = 14; \, b = 0,$$

and

$$\begin{aligned} \mathcal{E}(N) &= -6 \times P(B < 1 \,|\, n = 15, p = 0.05) \\ &\quad + 120 \times \tfrac{1}{16} \times P(B < 2 \,|\, n = 16, p = 0.05) \\ &= -6 \times 0.4633 + 120 \times \tfrac{1}{16} \times 0.8108 \\ &= 3.3012. \end{aligned}$$

The calculation for action A is similar. In this case we see from Figure 9.11 that A has a zero opportunity loss for high values of p ($p > p_b$), and its opportunity loss function is

$$\text{Loss}(A) = \begin{cases} 6 - 120p & \text{if } p < p_b. \\ 0 & \text{if } p > p_b \end{cases}$$

so $\mathcal{E}(A)$ is calculated using the first expected opportunity loss formula. Thus:

$$K = 6; \, k = -120; \, a = 14; \, b = 0,$$

and

$$\begin{aligned} \mathcal{E}(A) &= 6 \times P(B \geq 1 \,|\, n = 15, p = 0.05) \\ &\quad - 120 \times \tfrac{1}{16} \times P(B \geq 2 \,|\, n = 16, p = 0.05) \\ &= 6 \times 0.5367 - 120 \times \tfrac{1}{16} \times 0.1892 \\ &= 1.8012. \end{aligned}$$

Therefore we see that $\mathcal{E}(A) < \mathcal{E}(N)$, which implies the best action is A, confirming the results we obtained from the $E(p)$ versus p_b rule.

Clearly these expected opportunity loss formulas are much more difficult to use and make the restrictive assumption of requiring a beta prior, so it is unlikely that they would be used instead of the much simpler $E(p)$ versus p_b rule for choosing the best action. However, there are situations in which a best action has been chosen, and it is necessary to determine the expected value of perfect information so that it can be compared with the cost of a potential sample. It is *always* true that the expected opportunity loss for the best action is the expected value of perfect information for the problem, so once the best action is known we might need to use one of the expected opportunity loss formulas.

*9.6.3 Some Derivations of Formulas in Section 9.6.2

The first formula presented without proof in Section 9.6.2 is the formula for the expected payoff of an action whose payoff function is linear; i.e., if the payoff function of A is

$$\text{payoff}(A) = a + bp,$$

then it is easy to show that $E(A) = a + b\, E(p)$. If the prior distribution of p has a probability density function, $f(p)$, then from the formula for expected value we have:

$$E(A) = \int_{-\infty}^{+\infty} (a + bp)f(p)\, dp,$$

which is

$$= a \int_{-\infty}^{+\infty} f(p)\, dp + b \int_{-\infty}^{+\infty} pf(p)\, dp$$
$$= a + bE(p),$$

since

$$\int_{-\infty}^{+\infty} f(p)\, dp = 1 \text{ and } \int_{-\infty}^{+\infty} pf(p)\, dp = E(p).$$

The derivation of the $E(p)$ versus p_b rule requires more algebra, but is equally straightforward. Consider a problem with two actions, A_1 and A_2, whose associated payoff functions are:

$$\text{Payoff}(A_1) = K_1 + k_1 p; \text{ Payoff}(A_2) = K_2 + k_2 p.$$

If we were to compare these actions to determine which is the best, we would first calculate their expected payoffs. For A_1 we have

$$E(A_1) = K_1 + k_1 E(p),$$

and for A_2 we obtain

$$E(A_2) = K_2 + k_2 E(p).$$

Then, A_1 is a better action than A_2 if $E(A_1) > E(A_2)$, or if

$$K_1 + k_1 E(p) > K_2 + k_2 E(p).$$

Solving this last expression for $E(p)$ we get

$$(k_1 - k_2)E(p) > K_2 - K_1$$

and

$$
E(p) \begin{cases} > \dfrac{K_2 - K_1}{k_1 - k_2} & \text{if } k_1 - k_2 > 0 \\[2mm] < \dfrac{K_2 - K_1}{k_1 - k_2} & \text{if } k_1 - k_2 < 0 \end{cases}
$$

since the sense of an inequality is changed if we divide both sides by a negative number.

The above distinction is a bit cumbersome. We can make things easier by determining what the ratio $K_2 - K_1 / k_1 - k_2$ is.

Consider the problem of determining the break-even point for the general problem given above. It is found by equating the two payoff functions and solving for the value of p:

$$K_1 + k_1 p = K_2 + k_2 p$$

or

$$(k_1 - k_2)p = K_2 - K_1$$

or

$$p_b = \frac{K_2 - K_1}{k_1 - k_2}.$$

Now if we look back to the expression for $E(p)$, we find that what we are really doing is comparing $E(p)$ to p_b. Thus our general rule can be stated as:

> For any problem with linear payoff functions, compare $E(p)$ with p_b. If $E(p) > p_b$, take one action; if $E(p) < p_b$, take the other action.

And this, of course, is the $E(p)$ versus p_b rule. The ambiguity in it arises because for the general statement we don't know whether $k_1 - k_2$ is positive or negative.

The final derivation we want to make in this section is that of the formulas for the expected losses for each action. The calculation is straightforward but messy. Unlike situations in previous chapters, when the presence of the zeros associated with opportunity losses helped us, here we will find the derivation of the expected opportunity losses much more difficult. In the following material we will show how the expected opportunity loss for any action can be derived.

Consider two actions, A_1 and A_2, whose opportunity losses are:

$$\text{Loss}(A_1) = \begin{cases} J_1 + j_1 p & \text{if } p < p_b \\ 0 & \text{if } p > p_b \end{cases}$$

$$\text{Loss}(A_2) = \begin{cases} 0 & \text{if } p < p_b \\ J_2 + j_2 p & \text{if } p > p_b, \end{cases}$$

where J_1, j_1, J_2, and j_2 are known constants.

The associated expressions for the expected losses are

$$\mathcal{E}(A_1) = \int_0^{p_b} (J_1 + j_1 p) f(p)\, dp; \; \mathcal{E}(A_2) = \int_{p_b}^1 (J_2 + j_2 p) f(p)\, dp.$$

Consider integrating the expression for $\mathcal{E}(A_1)$. We have

$$\mathcal{E}(A_1) = \int_0^{p_b} (J_1 + j_1 p) f(p)\, dp = J_1 \int_0^{p_b} f(p)\, dp + j_1 \int_0^{p_b} p f(p)\, dp.$$

We can carry the above integration no further without assuming a functional form for the probability distribution of p values. If we assume that the p values are beta distributed then the two integrals can be evaluated. In particular it can be shown[4] that if the p values are beta distributed with parameters a and b then

$$\int_0^{p_b} f(p)\, dp = P(B \geq b + 1 | n = a + 1, p = p_b).$$

Thus, again we see that the beta and binomial distributions are very closely related. Knowing the relationship between the area under the curve of a beta probability density function and the cumulative binomial probabilities also allows us to determine the value of the second integral in the above expected opportunity loss expression. In the next section we will show that

$$\int_0^{p_b} p f(p)\, dp = \left(\frac{b+1}{a+2}\right) P(B \geq b + 2 | n = a + 2, p = p_b).$$

Knowing alternative expressions for these two integrals gives us an alternative expression for the expected opportunity loss of action A_1:

$$\mathcal{E}(A_1) = J_1 P(B \geq b + 1 | n = a + 1, p = p_b)$$
$$+ j_1 \left(\frac{b+1}{a+2}\right) P(B \geq b + 2 | n = a + 2, p = p_b).$$

Thus, knowing values for J_1, j_1, a, and b, and by using Table I, we can determine a value for $\mathcal{E}(A_1)$.

In a similar fashion, we find that

$$\mathcal{E}(A_2) = J_2 P(B < b + 1 | n = a + 1, p = p_b)$$
$$+ j_2 \left(\frac{b+1}{a+2}\right) P(B < b + 2 | n = a + 2, p = p_b),$$

---

[4] The proof of this statement goes beyond the level of this book.

and one of these two expressions can be used to find the expected loss of either action.

*9.6.4 Derivation of the Expected Loss Integral

We will conclude this section with a derivation of the integral

$$I = \int_0^{p_b} pf(p)\, dp.$$

Given that p is beta distributed with parameters a and b, we have

$$f(p) = (a + 1)\binom{a}{b}p^b(1 - p)^{a-b} = \left(\frac{(a + 1)!}{b!(a - b)!}\right)p^b(1 - p)^{a-b}$$

and

$$I = \int_0^{p_b} pf(p)\, dp = \int_0^{p_b} p\left(\frac{(a + 1)!}{b!(a - b)!}\right)p^b(1 - p)^{a-b}\, dp.$$

Now if we multiply and divide the integral by $\dfrac{b + 1}{a + 2}$, and combine the p terms, we have

$$I = \frac{b + 1}{a + 2}\int_0^{p_b} \frac{a + 2}{b + 1}\left(\frac{(a + 1)!}{b!(a - b)!}\right)p^{b+1}(1 - p)^{a-b}\, dp$$

$$= \frac{b + 1}{a + 2}\int_0^{p_b} (a + 2)\binom{a + 1}{b + 1}p^{b+1}(1 - p)^{a-b}\, dp$$

and then we finally notice that $a - b = a + 1 - (b + 1)$, and the integral becomes the integral of the probability density function of a beta distribution with parameters $a + 1$ and $b + 1$. Using the similarity between the cumulative beta and the cumulative binomial, we have

$$\int_0^{p_b} (a + 2)\binom{a + 1}{b + 1}p^{b+1}(1 - p)^{a+1-b-1}\, dp = P(B \geq b + 2|n = a + 2,$$

$$p = p_b),$$

so,

$$I = \frac{b + 1}{a + 2}P(B \geq b + 2|n = a + 2, p = p_b),$$

which is the expression we need to evaluate the expected opportunity loss expression.

9.7 SUMMARY

This chapter has discussed the basic concepts of a continuous distribution, and how to solve decision problems in which the prior probability distribution is continuous. The major emphasis throughout has been binomial sampling problems in which the set of events is the spectrum of p values between 0 and 1. Many of the techniques discussed in this chapter also apply to the normal sampling problem, which is discussed in Chapters 11 and 12.

PROBLEMS

Note: For several of these problems it is important for the reader to know the formula for the area of a trapezoid. A trapzoid is a planar figure with two sides parallel, e.g.,

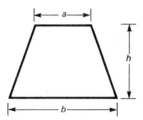

The formula for the area of a trapezoid is the average length of the parallel sides times the distance between them, or using the notation of the figure above:

$$\text{Area} = \left(\frac{a + b}{2}\right) \times h$$

1. For the uniform distribution whose density function is

$$f(x) = \begin{cases} 1 & \text{if } 0 < x < 1 \\ 0 & \text{otherwise} \end{cases}$$

find the following probabilties:

a. $P(X \geq 0.6)$
b. $P(0.1 \leq X)$
c. $P(0.1 \leq X \leq 0.6)$
d. $P(X \leq 0.1)$
e. $P(0.582 \leq X \leq 0.6897)$
f. $P(X \leq -1)$

2. Consider the beta distribution with parameters $a = 1$, $b = 0$; i.e.,

$$f(x) = \begin{cases} 2(1 - x) & \text{if } 0 < x < 1 \\ 0 & \text{otherwise} \end{cases}.$$

For this distribution find the following probabilities:

a. $P(X \geq 0.8)$
b. $P(X \geq 0.2)$
c. $P(0.2 \leq X \leq 0.8)$
d. $P(X \leq 0.36)$
e. $P(0.25 \leq X \leq 0.683)$

3. Consider a random variable, X, with the following probability density function:

$$f(x) = \begin{cases} \frac{2}{15}x & \text{if } 0 < x \le 3 \\ 1 - \frac{2}{10}x & \text{if } 3 < x < 5. \\ 0 & \text{otherwise} \end{cases}$$

 a. Graph this probability distribution.
 b. Find the following probabilities:
 (1) $P(X \le 2)$
 (2) $P(2 \le X \le 4)$
 (3) $P(X \le 3)$
 (4) $P(0.3 \le X \le 5)$

4. The uniform distribution is defined on intervals other than between 0 and 1. For instance, the random variable, X, whose probability density function is

$$f(x) = \begin{cases} \frac{1}{3} & \text{if } 1 \le x \le 4 \\ 0 & \text{otherwise} \end{cases}$$

is also said to have a uniform distribution. For this distribution find:

 a. $P(X \ge 2)$
 b. $P(X \le 3)$
 c. $P(1.67 \le X \le 3.86)$
 d. $P(X \ge 6)$

*5. Using integral calculus, find $P(0.2 \le X \le 0.6)$ for the beta distribution with the following parameters:

 a. $a = 0, b = 0$
 b. $a = 2, b = 0$
 c. $a = 0, b = 2$
 d. $a = 5, b = 3$
 e. $a = 1, b = 1$
 f. $a = 3, b = 2$

*6. Using integral calculus, find the mean and variance of the probability distributions given in problems 3 and 4.

7. Graph $f(p)$ for the beta distributions with the following parameters:

 a. $a = 0, b = 0$
 b. $a = 5, b = 2$
 c. $a = 50, b = 20$

8. Graph $f(p)$ for the two beta distributions

 a. $a = 5, b = 1$
 b. $a = 5, b = 4$.

What do you notice about these distributions, both from the values used to plot them and their appearance?

9. Determine the mean and variance for the following beta distributions, and indicate which of the three "shape" classifications they fall into.

   a. $a = 0, \ b = 0$
   b. $a = 6, \ b = 3$
   c. $a = 20, \ b = 10$
   d. $a = 5, \ b = 5$
   e. $a = 4, \ b = 1$
   f. $a = 4, \ b = 3$
   g. $a = 4, \ b = 0$
   h. $a = 6, \ b = 0$

10. What are the values for the mean and variance of normal distributions with the following parameters?

    a. $\mu = 3, \ \sigma = 1$
    b. $\mu = 1, \ \sigma = 3$
    c. $\mu = -3, \ \sigma = 16$
    d. $\mu = 16, \ \sigma = 3$

11. For the following problems, state the actions, derive a payoff or cost function for each action, determine the break-even point(s), and derive the opportunity loss functions for each action.

    a. The Spark Ling Co., Problem 8 of Chapter 6
    b. The SOGGIES problem, Problem 11 of Chapter 6
    c. The Nadir Mining and Manufacturing Co., Problem 18 of Chapter 6.

12. For the Spark Ling Co. (Problem 8 of Chapter 6), find the best action for the following prior distributions:

    a. A prior whose $E(p) = 0.28$
    b. A prior whose $E(p) = 0.47$
    c. A prior whose $E(p) = 0.63$
    d. A beta distribution with $a = 6, \ b = 3$
    e. A beta distribution with $a = 6, \ b = 6$.

13. For the SOGGIES problem (Problem 11 of Chapter 6) find

    a. The best action for a beta prior with parameters $a = 6, \ b = 4$.
    b. The expected payoff for each action with this prior.
    c. The expected value of perfect information with this prior.

14. State the generalization of the $E(p)$ versus p_b rule when the problem has three actions, each with a linear payoff. Also give the specific action rule in this case for the Nadir Mining and Manufacturing Co. (Problem 18 of Chapter 6).

*Binomial Sampling Problems—III

IN CHAPTERS 6, 7, and 8 we discussed binomial sampling problems in which the set of events was some finite (small) number of possible values of p. At the time we stated that the assumption of p taking on only a few values was questionable. In Chapter 9 we partially removed that restriction and spent some time choosing between terminal actions when the probability distribution of p values is continuous. This chapter will continue to discuss solutions to such problems. The first part of the chapter will consider updating a *continuous* prior distribution in order to make a decision between terminal actions. In the process we shall see how intimately the beta and binomial distributions are related. The final sections will then use many of these ideas to discuss how to solve sampling problems when the prior distribution is continuous. Throughout the chapter we will assume the reader understands and can work with integral calculus, since its use is vital to the applications we will be considering here.

10.1 UPDATING A CONTINUOUS PRIOR DISTRIBUTION

We want to first consider a problem similar to that discussed at the beginning of Chapter 8. Knowing a prior distribution and a sample outcome, which terminal action should be chosen? Recall that in Chapter 8 we took a decision tree approach toward solving this problem and we shall do the same thing here. Recall further that the way we solved the problem was to use Bayes' rule to combine the prior and the sample information into a *posterior* distribution, which was then used—just as the prior would have been used in the absence of sampling—to deter-

---

* A thorough understanding of the techniques in this chapter requires a knowledge of integral calculus.

mine the best action. We shall use *exactly* the same procedure here—only the mechanics will change.

The reason our mechanics need to change is that the version of Bayes' rule, which we presented in Chapter 2 and used in Chapters 5 and 8, applies only when all the probability distributions involved are discrete. In the work in this chapter we will need to use Bayes' rule in situations where the prior distribution is continuous. To fill this need we will give a different version of Bayes' rule, and discuss its use in binomial sampling problems. In the process we will see the beta distribution rediscovered.

The version of Bayes' rule we presented in Chapter 2 was

$$P(B_k|A_i) = \frac{P(A_i|B_k)P(B_k)}{\sum_j P(A_i|B_j)P(B_j)}.$$

The version which we shall use now is exactly analogous if we adopt the following changes:

1. Replace $P(B_k)$ with a probability density function, $f(b)$
2. Replace summation, Σ, with integration, $\int$.

The version of Bayes' rule that results is:

$$f(b|A_i) = \frac{P(A_i|B = b)f(b)}{\int_{-\infty}^{+\infty} P(A_i|B = b)f(b)\,db}.$$

Let us apply this formula to a specific example. Suppose in the Valley Sisters problem we assume that p can take on any value between 0 and 1, and that the distribution of p values is uniform over that interval. The formula for the probability density function of a uniform distribution on the interval from 0 to 1 is

$$f(p) = \begin{cases} 1 & \text{if } 0 < p < 1 \\ 0 & \text{otherwise} \end{cases}.$$

This function is depicted in Figure 10.1.

FIGURE 10.1

If the above density function indicates our *prior* (before any sampling) attitude toward the distribution of p values, how would our attitude change if we observed one can and found that it was a defective can? To answer this question we would use the new version of Bayes' rule:

$$f(p|B = 1) = \frac{P(B = 1|p)f(p)}{\int_{-\infty}^{+\infty} P(B = 1|p)f(p)\, dp},$$

where

$f(p)$ = our prior attitude about the distribution of p values;

$P(B = 1|p)$ = the probability of seeing a bad can, given the value of p;

$f(p|B = 1)$ = our posterior (after sample observation) attitude about the distribution of p values.

Our objective is to use the above formula to calculate $f(p|B = 1)$. In order to do so we must obtain specific values for each of the quantities on the right-hand side of the above expression. We already have expressed $f(p)$. Furthermore, $P(B = 1|p) = p$, and

$$\int_{-\infty}^{+\infty} P(B = 1|p)f(p)\, dp = \int_{-\infty}^{+\infty} pf(p)\, dp$$

$$= \int_{-\infty}^{0} p \cdot 0 \cdot dp + \int_{0}^{1} p \cdot 1 \cdot dp + \int_{1}^{+\infty} p \cdot 0 \cdot dp$$

$$= \frac{p^2}{2}\bigg|_{0}^{1} = \tfrac{1}{2}.$$

Combining these we get

$$f(p|B = 1) = \frac{p}{\tfrac{1}{2}} \cdot f(p) = 2pf(p)$$

$$= \begin{cases} 2p & \text{if } 0 < p < 1 \\ 0 & \text{otherwise} \end{cases}.$$

This function is depicted in Figure 10.2, and expresses just the relation-

FIGURE 10.2

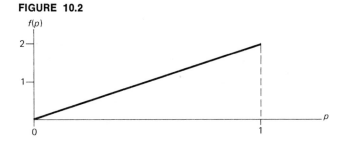

ship we would expect. If we initially think each value of p is equally likely (a uniform prior) and we then observe a bad can, our posterior distribution is going to be more heavily weighted in favor of high values of p rather than low values.

Consider another example of this type of updating. Suppose we have a uniform prior, as before, but we observe a good can instead of a bad can. What does our posterior distribution then look like? We have

$$f(p|B = 0) = \frac{P(B = 0|p)f(p)}{\int_0^1 P(B = 0|p)f(p)\, dp}.$$

(The above expression implicitly acknowledges the fact that the nonzero values of $f(p)$ lie between 0 and 1 only.) To evaluate this we have

1. $f(p)$ is uniform, as before
2. $P(B = 0|p) = 1 - p$

3. $\int_0^1 P(B = 0|p)f(p)\, dp = \int_0^1 (1 - p)\, dp = -\frac{(1 - p)^2}{2}\Big|_0^1 = \frac{1}{2};$

hence,

$$f(p|B = 0) = \frac{(1 - p)}{\frac{1}{2}} \cdot f(p) = 2(1 - p) \cdot f(p)$$

$$= \begin{cases} 2(1 - p) & \text{if } 0 < p < 1 \\ 0 & \text{otherwise} \end{cases}.$$

This function is depicted in Figure 10.3 and again verifies our intuition

FIGURE 10.3

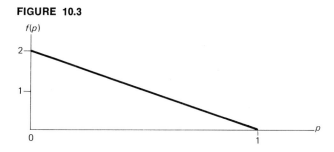

that the observation of one good can should make smaller values of p more probable and higher values of p less probable. Notice also the symmetry between Figures 10.2 and 10.3. The observation of a bad can makes larger values of p more probable *to the same degree that* the observation of a good can makes smaller values of p more probable.

10.2 THE BETA DISTRIBUTION REVISITED

Consider the two posterior distributions developed in the preceeding section:

$$f(p|B = 0) = 2(1 - p); \text{ and } f(p|B = 1) = 2p.$$

Each of these is a beta distribution. The first one,

$$f(p) = 2(1 - p),$$

is a beta distribution with parameter values of $a = 1$ and $b = 0$, and the second one,

$$f(p) = 2p,$$

is a beta distribution with parameter values of $a = 1$ and $b = 1$. We will now show that this relationship holds for *any* binomial sample outcome.

If we take a binomial sample of size n and observe r successes, we have

$$P(B = r|n, p) = \binom{n}{r} p^r (1 - p)^{n-r}.$$

Combining this sample outcome with a uniform prior distribution, we have

$$f(p|B = r, n) = \frac{P(B = r|n, p)f(p)}{\int_0^1 P(B = r|n, p)f(p)\, dp}$$

and

$$\int_0^1 P(B = r|n, p)f(p)\, dp = \int_0^1 \binom{n}{r} p^r (1 - p)^{n-r}\, dp$$

$$= \binom{n}{r} \int_0^1 p^r (1 - p)^{n-r}\, dp.$$

This last integral is one we will encounter many times in this chapter. Fortunately, we can show (by integration by parts) that it has a closed form expression, which is a ratio of factorial expressions.

$$\int_0^1 p^r (1 - p)^{n-r}\, dp = \frac{r!(n - r)!}{(n + 1)!}.$$

Using this fact we find that the denominator of our Bayes' rule expression is

$$\int_0^1 P(B = r|n, p)f(p)\, dp = \binom{n}{r} \frac{r!(n - r)!}{(n + 1)!} = \frac{1}{n + 1}.$$

Therefore

$$f(p|B = r, n) = \frac{\binom{n}{r} p^r (1 - p)^{n-r}}{\dfrac{1}{n + 1}} \cdot f(p)$$

$$= \begin{cases} (n + 1)\binom{n}{r} p^r (1 - p)^{n-r} & \text{if } 0 < p < 1 \\ 0 & \text{otherwise} \end{cases}.$$

The final expression on the right-hand side of the above equation is the probability density function for a beta distribution, with parameters $a = n$ and $b = r$.

Thus, we see that if we start with a uniform prior and perform binomial sampling, the posterior distribution is beta distributed with parameters $a = n$ and $b = r$. We have a shorthand diagram for expressing this fact, which is

$$\text{Uniform Prior} \xrightarrow[n,\ r]{\text{Binomial Sampling}} \text{Beta Posterior} \atop n,\ r$$

Unfortunately, a uniform distribution does not provide a great deal of flexibility in choosing a prior. However, there is a direct generalization of the above rule that makes the assignment of a realistic prior possible. Using the same method as we used above, the reader can easily verify for himself that the following, more general statement is true.

$$\begin{array}{c} \text{Beta Prior} \\ a,\ b \end{array} \xrightarrow[n,\ r]{\text{Binomial Sampling}} \begin{array}{c} \text{Beta Posterior} \\ a + n,\ b + r \end{array}$$

Thus, if we start with *any* beta prior, and perform binomial sampling, the posterior will also be beta.

10.3 MAKING POSTSAMPLE DECISIONS WITH A BETA PRIOR

Given what we have learned above, we are ready to analyze problems for which a sample outcome is known. In order to use the power of the above shorthand expression we will *always* assume that the prior distribution is beta. In fact, throughout the rest of this chapter we will always assume a beta prior, because of its intimate relationship with binomial sampling.[1] The reader who wants to use a prior that cannot be closely approximated with a beta distribution will have to forsake the elegance of the mathematics used in this chapter for the "brute force" methods discussed in Chapter 13.

Once we assume a beta prior, the analysis of problems in which a sample outcome is known is very simple. The posterior expected payoffs for the two actions can easily be determined by using the formula given in Chapter 9, and the best action is the one with the optimum payoff. For example, in the Valley Sisters problem we know that

$$\text{Cost}(A) = \$6; \quad \text{Cost}(N) = \$120p,$$

---

[1] A prior distribution (in combination with some sampling distribution) that yields a posterior distribution of the same type is called a *conjugate* prior. Thus, the beta distribution is a conjugate prior to the binomial sampling distribution.

and since these are linear functions we know from Chapter 9 that

$$E(A) = \$6; \quad E(N) = \$120E(p),$$

where $E(p)$ is the expected value of the probability distribution of events. We found in Chapter 9 that if the prior is beta with $a = 14$ and $b = 0$, then without sampling we have

$$E(A) = \$6 \text{ and } E(N) = 120 \times \tfrac{1}{16} = 7.5$$

so A is the best action.

If, however, we have the same prior distribution, and in addition we know for the particular run that a sample of five cans has yielded no defectives, then the posterior distribution is beta with parameters $a = 14 + 5 = 19$ and $b = 0 + 0 = 0$. Using this posterior distribution, whose mean is

$$E(p) = \frac{b+1}{a+2} = \frac{1}{21}$$

the expected costs for the two actions are

$$\text{E}(A) = \$6 \text{ and } E(N) = 120 \times \tfrac{1}{21} = 5.71.$$

Therefore, for this particular run, N is the best action.

This result can be obtained in another way. In the previous chapter we had a simple rule for deciding which action is best. Recall that we compared the value of the mean of the prior distribution with the value of the breakeven point to determine which action should be chosen. The same rule can be used here, except now, since we have a sample outcome, we will use the mean of the *posterior* distribution to compare with the breakeven point. Using this technique in this case we see that the mean of the posterior distribution, which is $\tfrac{1}{21}$ or 0.0476, is smaller than the breakeven point of 0.05. Hence, the optimal action is the action whose cost is best for low values of p (below p_b), and this is action N.

10.4 PROBLEMS INVOLVING SAMPLING

Now that we have analyzed problems in which no sampling occurs, and those for which a specific sample outcome is known, let us turn to the more difficult (in a mechanical sense only) problem in which we must determine the best sizes for a sample that has not yet been taken.

Many of the concepts that were developed in Chapters 6 and 7 will be used in this chapter. For instance, the types of strategies we will find are optimal are cutoff point strategies:

$$\{\text{If } B < c \text{ then } A_1; \text{ if } B \geq c \text{ then } A_2\},$$

and the objective will be to find the best values for n and c. In some ways our task is easier (for instance we will be able to calculate c^* from a formula rather than obtain it by trial and error), but the overall task is quite difficult, mainly because the determination of the total cost for a strategy is so difficult. As in Chapters 6 and 7 we will first study the problem of finding c^* for fixed n, then consider the problem of finding the best value for n.

10.4.1   Finding c* with n Fixed

For this problem it is again convenient to approach it from a decision tree point of view. We will limit ourselves to problems in which the prior is a beta distribution. For these problems, the concept developed in Section 10.2

$$\text{Beta Prior} \xrightarrow[n, r]{\text{Binomial Sampling}} \text{Beta Posterior}$$
$$a, b \qquad\qquad\qquad a + n, b + r$$

is very powerful, and it makes the decision tree approach very useful.

Consider the $E(p)$ versus p_b decision rule we developed in Chapter 9:

If $E(p) > p_b$ then choose one action, otherwise choose the other,

and consider its application *after* a sample has been observed. For the posterior beta distribution

$$E(p) = \frac{b + r + 1}{a + n + 2}$$

where a and b represent the parameters of the *prior* beta distribution.

Our decision rule says to always choose one action if

$$\frac{b + r + 1}{a + n + 2} > p_b.$$

If we take this expression and isolate r we find the following rule:

Always choose one action if $r > p_b(a + n + 2) - b - 1$.

Now consider the sampling situation: The value of n is fixed, a, b, and p_b are known, and one action is always chosen when r is greater than some calculated quantity. The above rule verifies that a cutoff point strategy is best, and furthermore allows us to calculate c^*. Thus, instead of having to calculate c^* by trial and error, as we did when the prior was discrete, we can now quickly calculate what c^* should be for any n.

As an example, consider the Valley Sisters problem when $a = 14$, $b = 0$, $p_b = 0.05$. We will calculate the best value for c when $n = 20$. We have

$$p_b(a + n + 2) - b - 1 = 0.05 \times (14 + 20 + 2) - 0 - 1 = 0.8,$$

and the decision rule is

Always choose one action if $r > 0.8$.

Since r (and c) can have only integer values, it follows that $c^* = 1$ for $n = 20$.

The question still remains as to which action should be chosen for $B \geq 1$. However, this is the same problem we faced in Chapter 6, and the solution is the same. High values of r indicate high values of p, and A is the best action for high values of p. Therefore, the strategy for $n = 20$ is

$$\{\text{If } B < 1 \text{ choose } N; \text{ if } B \geq 1 \text{ choose } A\}.$$

10.4.2   Finding the Optimal Sample Size

Once c^* is known for each n, the optimal n must be found by trial and error, just as it was in the discrete case. The algorithm presented in Chapter 7 can be used, with minor modifications, to find the best value for n. One important change that will be made is that we will be determining the total expected payoff (or cost) for any strategy rather than the total expected opportunity loss because we found in Chapter 9 that the expected payoff for any action is much easier to calculate than the expected opportunity loss. Therefore, in the remainder of this chapter we shall abbreviate total expected payoff as TEP. Using this, the algorithm given in Chapter 7 can be restated for the continuous problem as:

1. Fix $n = 1$, calculate c^* and the TEP of the corresponding strategy
2. Increment n by 1, and calculate the corresponding c^* and TEP
3. Continue step 2 until the sample cost alone would make any larger values of n not as good as the current best one.

While this algorithm is quite straightforward, it does involve a number of tedious calculations. Furthermore, the calculation burden is compounded by the fact that it is quite difficult to calculate TEP in the continuous case. We will discuss its calculation below. However, the totality of the computational burden for solving an optimal sample size problem when the prior is beta makes the algorithm painful to execute unless one has the aid of a computer.[2]

10.4.3   Determining the Value of Total Expected Payoff (TEP)

This is best accomplished by considering the decision tree approach, because of the power of the prior-posterior rule in this situation. We will demonstrate the procedure for $n = 3$, but it will apply for any n. For $n = 3$ we have four possible sample outcomes, $r = 0, 1, 2,$ and 3, and the decision tree is:

---

[2] Interactive computer programs in APL and BASIC are available with this text.

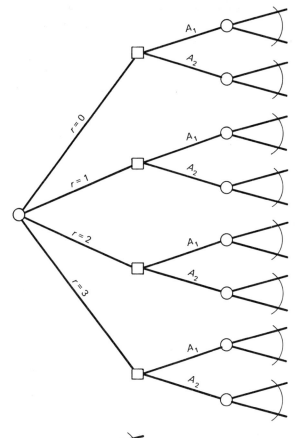

The special notation indicates that the event space is continuous, and it would be impossible to depict enough branches at that node.

The normal analysis of such a tree would involve:

1. Calculate the expected value at each of the right chance nodes (the ⟨node symbol⟩ nodes).

2. Choose the best of the two actions at each decision node.

3. Weight these (best) values at each decision node by the *unconditional* probability of the corresponding sample outcome and sum. The resulting value is the overall expected value of the best strategy.

Fortunately, steps 1 and 2 above can be shortened in this case, since c^* is so easy to calculate. Suppose A_1 is the best action for low values of p. Then, the optimal strategy for a fixed sample size is:

$$\{\text{If } B < c^* \text{ then } A_1; \text{ if } B \geq c^* \text{ then } A_2\}$$

and the value of c^* can be easily calculated, as we saw in Section 10.4.1.

What has the value of c^* to do with the decision tree analysis? Recall that the decision tree and enumeration of strategies approaches are equivalent *in every respect*. Thus, not only will the overall expected value be the same, but the strategy will be the same. Realization of this fact, plus the ease with which c^* can be obtained, allows us to know, *prior to any decision tree calculations,* whether A_1 or A_2 should be chosen at any decision node. Thus, the calculations in step 1 of the decision tree analysis are halved, and step 2 is eliminated. For example, if we found $c^* = 1$ for a particular problem, the decision tree presented above could be reduced (for calculation purposes) to

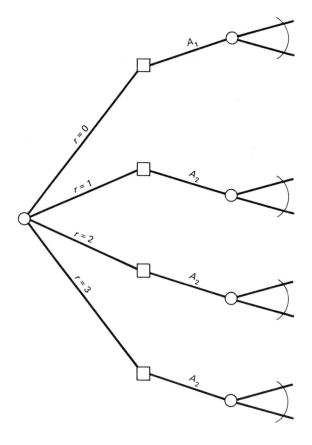

Once this reduction has been made the expected values must be obtained. Calculating the expected values at the right-most chance nodes is quite easy. Recall that we will use expected payoff, because the calculations are so much simpler. We have previously found that

$$E(A_1) = K_1 + k_1 E(p); \; E(A_2) = K_2 + k_2 E(p)$$

and

$$E(p) = \frac{b + r + 1}{a + n + 2}$$

so that the calculations at the right-most chance nodes are very straight-forward.

Unfortunately, the calculation at the left (final) chance node is quite difficult. The difficulty arises in the determination of the unconditional probabilities of the sample outcomes. The conditional probabilities are the standard binomial expression:

$$P(B = r|n, p) = \binom{n}{r} p^r (1 - p)^{n-r}.$$

To obtain unconditional probabilities we must take the above expression, weight it by $f(p)$, and integrate over all p values between 0 and 1:

$$P(B = r|n) = \int_0^1 P(B = r|n, p) f(p) \, dp$$

$$= \int_0^1 \binom{n}{r} p^r (1 - p)^{n-r} (a + 1) \binom{a}{b} p^b (1 - p)^{a-b} \, dp.$$

This last integral can be evaluated using the rule given in Section 10.2, and we get

$$P(B = r|n) = \frac{(a + 1) \binom{a}{b} \binom{n}{r}}{(a + n + 1) \binom{a + n}{b + r}},$$

whose simplest form for hand calculation is probably

$$P(B = r|n)$$

$$= (a + 1) \binom{a}{b} \frac{[(r + 1)(r + 2) \cdots (r + b)] [(n - r + 1)(n - r + 2) \cdots (n - r + a - b)]}{(n + 1)(n + 2) \cdots (n + a + 1)}$$

and where it is understood, for any of the last three sequences, that if the last term is *less* than the first term the entire sequence is replaced by 1. Thus, if $b = 0$ then $r + 1 > r + b$, and

$$(r + 1)(r + 2) \cdots (r + b) = 1.$$

So, the calculation of the overall expected value for the optimal strategy and fixed n then is obtained by taking these unconditional probabilities and multiplying them by the conditional expected values for the best action *given* a particular sample outcome.

An example is imperative at this point. Suppose in the Valley Sisters problem we choose to establish a beta prior with $a = 18$ and $b = 0$. We have previously calculated $p_b = 0.05$. Assume that we take a sample of size 5. The first thing we need to know is the value of c^*. For a

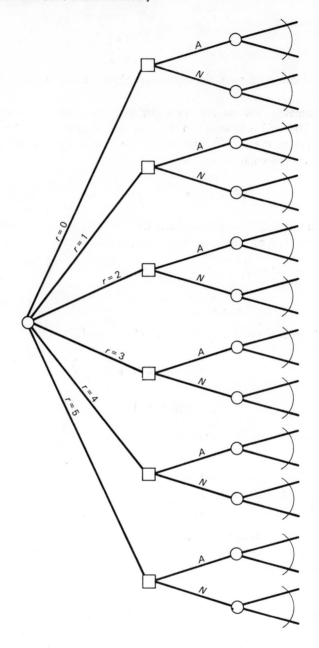

sample of size 5 we have

$$p_b(a + n + 2) - b - 1 = 0.05 \times (18 + 5 + 2) - 0 - 1 = 0.25.$$

Therefore, we should choose one action (which will be A) whenever $r > 0.25$, and this implies that $c^* = 1$. Using this, we see that the original decision tree for the sample size 5 problem is as depicted on page 230, and this reduces to:

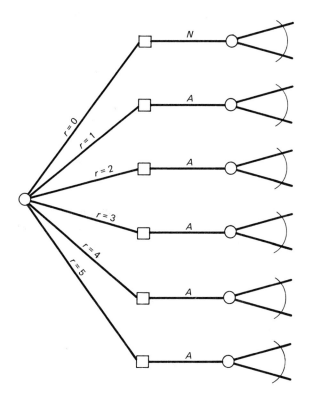

Now, for the rightmost branches of the reduced tree, we need to calculate $E(N)$ (using a posterior distribution) when $r = 0$, and $E(A)$ when $r = 1, 2, 3, 4,$ and 5. Thus, we have

For $r = 0$: $E(N) = 120E(p) = 120 \times \dfrac{0 + 0 + 1}{18 + 5 + 2} = 4.8$

For $r = 1$ through 5: $E(A) = 6$ (This is a special case where the expected value of one action does not depend on p.)

With these our tree becomes:

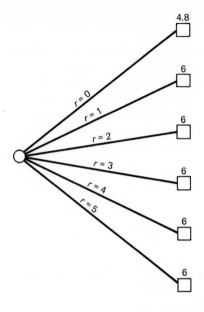

and the only step remaining is to calculate the probabilities of each of the outcomes and determine the overall expected cost of the tree. Using the formula given above for $P(B = r|n = 5)$, we have:

$$P(B = 0|n = 5) = (19)\binom{18}{0} \times$$

$$\frac{[(0+1)(0+2) \cdots (0+0)][(5-0+1)(5-0+2) \cdots (5-0+18-0)]}{(5+1)(5+2) \cdots (5+18+1)}$$

$$= 19 \times 1 \times \frac{[1][6 \times 7 \times \cdots \times 23]}{6 \times 7 \times \cdots \times 24} = \frac{19}{24} = 0.7917,$$

$$P(B = 1|n = 5) = (19)\binom{18}{0} \times$$

$$\frac{[(1+1)(1+2) \cdots (1+0)][(5-1+1)(5-1+2) \cdots (5-1+18-0)]}{(5+1)(5+2) \cdots (5+18+1)}$$

$$= 19 \times 1 \times \frac{[1][5 \times 6 \times \cdots \times 22]}{6 \times 7 \times \cdots \times 24} = \frac{19 \times 5}{23 \times 24} = 0.1721,$$

and the others can be similarly calculated. Their values are:

$$P(B = 2|n = 5) = 0.0313$$
$$P(B = 3|n = 5) = 0.0045$$
$$P(B = 4|n = 5) = 0.0004$$
$$P(B = 5|n = 5) = 0$$

Using these probabilities, the overall expected cost for this strategy is

$$4.8 \times 0.7917 + 6 \times 0.1721 + 6 \times 0.0313 + 6 \times 0.0045$$
$$+ 6 \times 0.0004 + 6 \times 0 = 5.05.$$

Once this number is obtained, we must combine it with the sample cost for a sample of size 5. At this step the user must be careful. If you are using cost figures, as we are in the Valley Sisters case, the sample cost should be *added* to the overall expected value obtained from the decision tree analysis. If, on the other hand, you are using payoff figures, the sample cost must be subtracted. It is important to carefully consider the appropriate combination of sample cost and value from the tree for any particular problem. In the Valley Sisters case this is:

TEP = Sample Cost + Overall Expected Value from Decision Tree
   = 0.10 + 0.06 × 5 + 5.05
   = 5.45,

if we use the sample cost function, $0.10 + 0.06n$, as we used in Chapter 7.

The reader can quickly see that the calculation of TEPs is an extremely tedious process, especially when n gets large. The above example illustrates all the steps which must be taken to obtain values for the total expected payoffs.

10.5 SUMMARY

This chapter has dealt with the solution of binomial sampling problems when the prior distribution (on p) is continuous. The concepts used are exactly the same as those in Chapters 6 and 7—only the techniques are different. We still find that the optimal strategy will have a single cutoff point, and that the overall best strategy is found by trial-and-error search on the potential values of n.

PROBLEMS

1. Using the continuous version of Bayes' rule, derive the posterior distributions from a uniform prior and the following binomial sampling outcomes:

   a. One success and one failure
   b. Two successes
   c. Three successes
   d. Two successes and two failures

2. You are playing a game with a friend. He takes a spinner on a card and randomly chooses two points along the circumference of the card. Thus, the card is partitioned into two segments; that is,

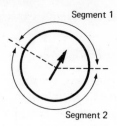

Segment 1

Segment 2

Your friend then spins the spinner, and announces whether it stopped in Segment 1 or Segment 2. Let p = (Length of Segment 1)/(Circumference). Describe why, at this point (before any data is known), the distribution of p is uniform. What is the probability distribution of p if the announced outcome is Segment 1? Segment 2? Suppose the spinner is spun twice, and the outcomes are Segment 1, then Segment 2: What now is the probability distribution of p?

3. Show, by derivation, that the rule

$$\text{Beta Prior} \xrightarrow[n,\ r]{\text{Binomial Sampling}} \text{Beta Posterior}$$
$$a,\ b \qquad\qquad\qquad a+n,\ b+r$$

is correct.

4. Two people are betting on the flip of a thumbtack. The game is played by flipping the thumbtack once. If a "points up" occurs, the players each win \$1. Otherwise they win nothing. The players can be identified as:

    Player 1: A person with a rectangular prior on $0 \le p \le 1$ for p, the probability of a "points up."
    Player 2: A person with a beta prior, and $a = 6$, $b = 2$.

    a. What is the maximum each player would pay to play the above game?
    b. Suppose the players knew that on 12 previous tosses, eight "points up" had occurred. With this information, what is the maximum each would be willing to pay?

5. The manager of the gift shop in the local hotel is trying to decide which of two items he should stock this week. The two items are cigars and fresh flowers. He knows that an important factor in his decision is the male and female composition of the forthcoming National High School Teacher's Convention. If a high proportion of the attendees are men, the cigars would sell better, while if there is a high proportion of women, the flowers will sell better. If p is the proportion of men at the convention the manager feels his profit functions will be:

$$\text{Profit from flowers} = \$500 - \$2{,}500p$$
$$\text{Profit from cigars} = \$500p$$

and from prior teachers' conventions he has observed that the proportion of men is beta distributed with $a = 5$, $b = 3$.

   a.   Which decision should the manager make if he must make an immediate decision? What is the corresponding expected payoff?
   b.   Suppose a random sample of five preregistered attendees yields four women. Which decision should he now make? What is the corresponding expected payoff?
   c.   Suppose instead the sample of five has not been taken, but the manager is considering it. If he takes the sample, what strategy should he adopt? What is the value of the sample to him?

6.   The sales manager for Butterflylarva Tractor Co. is trying to develop a procedure for evaluating new salesmen. Although sales ability is a highly individual trait, the manager has found that, as far as he is concerned, the criterion can be reduced to the proportion of sales per call for each man. Since tractor sales are highly seasonal, the company has developed the following compensation scheme for salesmen: (1) A base salary of $5,000 per year; (2) A commission of $100 per tractor sold.

   The company receives a profit of $350 (before the salesman's salary and commission) on each tractor sold.

   Assuming a salesman can make 100 calls during a year, and that the probability of a sale on any call is constant and independent of previous successes:

   a.   Derive the payoff and loss functions *for the company* on considering a new salesman.
   b.   In the past, the sales manager has found the proportion of sales per call is distributed over prospective salesmen as beta with $a = 12$, $b = 1$. Should a salesman be hired right off the street (without testing his ability)?
   c.   Suppose Joe Slick applies for a job as a salesman, is given six calls to make, and sells two tractors. Should Joe be hired?
   d.   A psychological testing company has proposed a battery of screening tests to determine whether or not a prospective salesman will be profitable to the company. The testing company claims their procedure will give *perfect* information. That is, every salesman they reject will be unprofitable. *However,* the screening process is quite expensive. If field testing of salesmen is infeasible, how much would the company be willing to pay for this screening service? (Verbally explain your answer. A mere statement is *not* sufficient.)
   e.   Suppose Joe Slick, having already sold two tractors in six calls. has an opportunity to take the test. How much would Butterflylarva be willing to pay for (perfect) information on Joe?

7.   Consider a problem for which:

$$\text{Cost}(A_1) = 5 + p; \quad \text{Cost}(A_2) = 5\tfrac{1}{2}$$

and there is a beta prior on p with $a = 2, b = 1$.

   a.   What is the best c when $n = 3$?

   b.   Suppose the sample has not been taken yet. For the best strategy when $n = 3$, find the *overall* expected loss or the *overall* expected cost.

8.   You are shopping in a local stationery store close to closing time one evening, when you suddenly realize you have been locked in the store with the fiendish owner, Mr. Mephisto. Mr. Mephisto will release you only after you have played a game with him. He will select a thumbtack at random from a box of thumbtacks, and flip it. The thumbtack will either land in a points-up position, $\curvearrowright$, or lying on its side, $\downarrow$. Before the thumbtack is flipped you must guess which outcome will occur. If, after the flip, you have guessed correctly, Mr. Mephisto will pay you $90. On the other hand, if you have guessed incorrectly, you must pay Mr. Mephisto $10. Analyze this problem by:

   a.   Using your knowledge of the beta distribution to establish a prior distribution for p, the probability of "points up." Limit your range of a values to $1 \leq a \leq 5$, and be sure to justify your choice.

   b.   Listing the actions available to you, and deriving the payoff functions for the actions.

   c.   Use the above to determine which action to take. What is the opportunity loss for this action?

   d.   Suppose Mr. Mephisto tells you he has previously flipped this particular thumbtack, and three "points up" appeared in eight tosses. Which action should you take given this information?

   e.   Suppose instead of the sample information in part (d), Mr. Mephisto allows you to flip the thumbtack any number of times, but each flip will cost you 50¢. Should you take some preliminary flips? If so, how many, and what will your strategy be?

   f.   Suppose Mr. Mephisto gives you *both* the information in part (d) and the opportunity for further sampling, discussed in part (e), except now each additional flip will cost 25¢. Should more sampling be taken, or should an immediate action be taken? If more sampling is optimal, how much, and what is the strategy?

9.   Show that the rule:

$$\text{Beta Prior} \xrightarrow{\text{Geometric Sampling}} \text{Beta Posterior}$$
$$a, b \qquad\qquad\qquad\qquad a + n, b + 1$$

is correct.

Note: Problems 10 and 11 depend upon knowing the rule stated in Problem 9.

10.   Suppose in the Valley Sisters case the foreman knows the probability of a defective can, p, is beta distributed with $a = 5, b = 1$. One morning he decides to sample until he sees the first defective. Which

decision should he make if the first can is defective? if the tenth can is the first defective?

11. For Problem 17 of Chapter 6, assume instead of the distribution given in part (a), that every value of p can occur.

    a. Suppose the prior distribution is uniform (rectangular) on $0 < p < 1$. What is the posterior distribution, having observed a sample outcome of $N = n$?

    b. Using a beta prior with $a = 2$, $b = 1$, what is the best decision if no sampling occurred? Assume the cost for the expert is $8 + 5p$ and the cost for accepting the operator's setup is $25p$.

    c. Suppose $N = 5$. What is the best terminal decision given this sample outcome? (Using $a = 2$, $b = 1$.)

    d. As a continuation of Problem 7, Chapter 7, suppose $N = 5$. Should you consider taking another sample if the cost of the first sample is $0.04 + 0.03N$, and the cost of the second sample is $0.03N$? Note: Do *not* give the optimal size of this additional sample, just whether or not the additional sample should be taken. (Hint: Very little calculation has to be done for this problem. Consider very carefully your answers to parts [b] and [c].)

11

Decision Making when Means
Are Events

UP TO THIS POINT in the text we have considered two kinds of event ranges. In the earlier chapters (Chapters 3, 4, 5, 6, 7, and 8) we considered problems in which the number of events was small. Then later (Chapters 9 and 10) we considered problems in which the event could be any value in a range from 0 to 1. In this chapter and Chapter 12 we will consider a different class of problems for which the event can be any value over a much larger range. We will find in this case that the important measure of the event will be the mean, m. We will begin the chapter with a discussion of two examples typical of those in which the mean value is the event, and then discuss how the ideas of decision theory can be applied toward solving such problems. We will find that many of the ideas developed in Chapter 9 will also apply to the decision problems discussed in this chapter. Unlike the binomial sampling situation, however, it *will* become apparent that the student who has no knowledge of calculus will be able to master the concepts necessary to solve decision problems involving the mean when sampling is used to aid the decision. However, the discussion of sampling for these problems will be deferred to Chapter 12. This chapter will merely introduce such problems and discuss how to solve them when no sampling occurs.

11.1 TWO EXAMPLES

To give the student a feeling of comfort with such problems, we begin by stating and discussing two examples typical of the general class of problems encountered. One example will be from manufacturing, and one from marketing.

Mining: The Nadir Mining and Manufacturing Co. has an option on an iron ore field in Wisconsin, and must make a decision whether to mine the land or let their option lapse. The ore contained in the field is magnetite (an oxide of iron whose chemical formula is Fe_3O_4), which does not occur in layers (strata) but is dispersed throughout the field. Therefore, Nadir would like to know the mean amount (in pounds) of magnetite per ton of material taken from the field. If the yield of magnetite per ton is high enough, it will pay Nadir to buy the land and start mining it.

If Nadir lets the option lapse, they will incur no costs and receive no profit. On the other hand, if they decide to buy the field, it will cost $500,000. In addition, the fixed cost of moving mining equipment to the field would be $200,000, and the cost of moving the material to the processing plant would be $26 per ton. The net profit (after all refining costs have been included) per pound of magnetite is 25¢. There are 50,000 tons of usable material in the field.

This example is typical of the problems encountered in practice, although many of the accounting details have been simplified. The quantity of interest to Nadir is the mean number of pounds of magnetite per ton of field material. The actual value of the mean is unknown, of course, and becomes the event in our decision problem. We will label it m, since it is a mean. The value of m has some natural boundaries in this problem, as it does in most decision problems. Its value cannot be less than zero (there cannot be less than no magnetite per ton of material) nor more than 2,000 (the total ton of material weighs only 2,000 pounds). However, within these boundaries it can take on any value.

Now let us turn to the actions for this problem. There are two actions:

L = Let the option lapse
M = Mine the field

and we want to develop payoff functions for each of these. Notice that we are going to develop payoff *functions,* (rather than a payoff table) because the event can be any value of m between 0 and 2,000.

For the first action the payoff function is easy. Since no costs are incurred, and no profits are gained, we have

$$\text{Profit}(L) = 0.$$

The payoff fuction of M is only slightly more complicated. The costs for removing all the material from the field will be $500,000 for the land, plus \$200,000 fixed cost for the mining equipment, plus $26 \times 50,000 = \$1,300,000$ variable cost, or a total of \$2,000,000. The profit received will depend on the mean amount of ore per ton. The profit per ton of material is $0.25m$, so the overall profit is $0.25m \times 50,000 = 12,500m$. Therefore, we have

$$\text{Profit}(M) = 12,500m - 2,000,000.$$

Each of the above payoff functions are linear in the value of the event. This will be another restriction on the problems we will deal with— namely, that they will have linear payoff functions.

How we use these payoff functions will be discussed in Section 11.2. Suffice it to say that we will be using these payoff functions in ways very similar to the methods we developed in Chapter 9. We will discuss the concept of a breakeven point, give formulas for calculating the expected payoff for each action, discuss how to obtain and use the opportunity loss functions, and discuss what prior distributions can be used with these problems.

In closing we should emphasize that this problem has only two actions. As with binomial sampling problems, we will restrict our discussions to two-action problems throughout this chapter and the next because the mechanics are much easier when we are only considering two actions. However, the concepts we will develop can be applied (with, admittedly, much more work) to problems with any number of actions.

Let us now turn to the other example, and discuss it in the same vein as the mining problem we just discussed.

Coffee South: The Valley Sisters Coffee Co. is currently marketing its coffee only in the northeastern portion of the United States. However, it is considering expanding its market to include the southeast. Whether or not it will be profitable to do this depends on the amount of coffee consumed in households in the southeastern portion of the country. The amount of coffee consumed (in ounces per year) for households in the southeast will, of course, vary from household to household. However, there are enough households (10 million) in this area so that the quantity of interest to Valley Sisters is the *average* consumption per year, m.

If Valley Sisters decide not to market in the southeast, they will neither gain nor loose anything. If they decide to enter the southeastern market, they will incur a fixed marketing cost of \$250,000 per year. As a result of this level of marketing activity the decision analysis group in the company assumes that Valley Sisters' market share in the southeast will be the same as their current market share, 8%. In addition to the marketing costs, there will be fixed production costs for meeting the new higher level of demand of \$150,000 per year. The selling price of

the coffee will be 41¢ per pound (wholesale) and the variable production, marketing, and distribution costs will be 37¢ per pound.

This problem is again a two-action problem, with actions:

D = Don't market in the South
M = Do market in the South.

The corresponding payoff functions are

$$\text{Profit}(D) = 0,$$

$$\text{Profit}(M) = (0.41 - 0.37) \times \frac{m}{16} \times 10,000,000 \times 0.08$$

$$- 250,000 - 150,000$$

$$= 2,000m - 400,000.$$

Again we have a problem where, because of the large number of
units involved, a mean is an appropriate quantity to represent the event.
Notice that this problem has many of the same characteristics as the
other one. There are two actions, each with a linear payoff function.
The event is an unknown quantity that can take on a whole spectrum
of values. Here also the set of events has some natural boundaries.
Clearly the value of m cannot be less than zero (implying the average
family *gives up* coffee rather than consuming it) and there is also certainly some upper bound on the value of m. However, unlike the
previous example, it is not so obvious what this upper bound should
be. It is clear, however, that the average coffee consumption per household cannot have an infinite value.

We have discussed above two examples of problems in which some
mean is a reasonable event, and developed the payoff functions for
these problems. In the next section we will consider how to use these
payoff functions to make decisions about which action to choose.

11.2 ANALYSIS OF PAYOFF FUNCTIONS

In this section we shall consider several ways in which the payoff
functions for the problems we consider can help us. First, since they
are functions, we can plot a graph of them, and it will be helpful to
have a graph with both payoff functions on it. Figure 11.1 is such a
graph for the Nadir Mining and Manufacturing problem. Since the
action L (let the option lapse) incurs no costs and generates no profits,
its payoff function is a horizontal line at the zero profit level. On the
other hand, action M has a payoff of $-\$2,000,000$ when m is zero, and
the payoff steadily improves. At some point (value of m) the profit
from action M becomes positive, and hence exceeds the profit from

FIGURE 11.1
A Graph of the Payoff Functions in the Nadir Mining and Manufacturing Problem

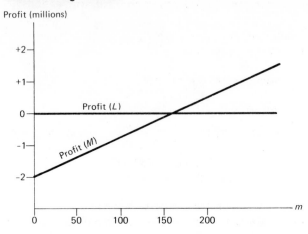

action L. This value is called the breakeven point, just as it was in Chapter 9. However, since the value of m is now the event, we will denote the breakeven point as m_b.

The breakeven point can be easily calculated by finding the value of m for which the payoffs of the two actions are equal. In this case we have

$$\text{Profit}(M) = \text{Profit}(L)$$

or

$$12,500m - 2,000,000 = 0$$

when

$$m = \frac{2,000,000}{12,500} = 160.$$

Thus, the breakeven point is 160, or in symbols,

$$m_b = 160.$$

Once the value of the breakeven point is known, we can determine opportunity loss functions for each action. Again recall that the opportunity loss for any action is the amount by which that action's payoff is worse than the payoff of the *best* action for the same event (value of m in this case). Thus, a glance at Figure 11.1 will show that for values of m less than m_b, L is the action with the best profit, whereas M is the action with the best profit for values of m *greater* than m_b. For values of m less than m_b the opportunity loss of M is the difference between the profit of action L (the best action) and the profit of action M, or

$$0 - (12{,}500m - 2{,}000{,}000) = 2{,}000{,}000 - 12{,}500m.$$

Similarly, for values of m greater than m_b the opportunity loss of action L is the difference between its profit and the profit of action M at the same value of m, or

$$12{,}500m - 2{,}000{,}000 - 0 = 12{,}500m - 2{,}000{,}000.$$

Collecting all the above discussion into a pair of mathematical formulas, we have

$$\text{loss}(L) = \begin{cases} 0 & \text{if } m \le m_b \\ 12{,}500m - 2{,}000{,}000 & \text{if } m > m_b \end{cases}$$

$$\text{loss}(M) = \begin{cases} 2{,}000{,}000 - 12{,}500m & \text{if } m < m_b \\ 0 & \text{if } m \ge m_b \end{cases}$$

These opportunity loss functions will prove useful to us when we analyze the decision problems in this chapter.

The techniques we have applied above can also be applied to the Valley Sisters marketing problem, Coffee South. In this case we have developed the two payoff functions:

$$\text{Profit}(D) = 0$$

and

$$\text{Profit}(M) = 2{,}000m - 400{,}000.$$

These two functions are graphed in Figure 11.2, and you can see that D is the best action for small values of m, while M is the best action for large values of m.

FIGURE 11.2
The Two Payoff Functions for Coffee South

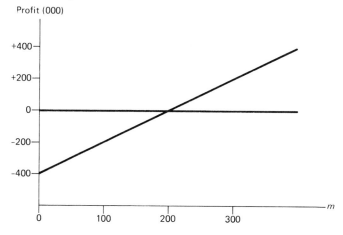

The breakeven point, m_b, can be obtained by finding the value of m for which the payoffs are equal. In this case, the algebra is:

$$\text{Profit}(M) = \text{Profit}(D),$$

which is

$$2{,}000m - 400{,}000 = 0,$$

and this occurs when

$$m = \frac{400{,}000}{2{,}000} = 200.$$

Thus, the breakeven point is $m_b = 200$.

Once we have the breakeven point and a graph like Figure 11.2, which shows which payoff function is best over which range of m, the loss functions can be obtained. In this case, when $m > m_b$ M is the best action, and the opportunity loss of D relative to this is

$$\text{Profit}(M) - \text{Profit}(D)$$
$$\text{or}$$
$$2{,}000m - 400{,}000 - 0,$$
$$\text{or}$$
$$2{,}000m - 400{,}000.$$

Similarly, for $m < m_b$ D is the best action and M has an opportunity loss function which is

$$\text{Profit}(D) - \text{Profit}(M)$$
$$\text{or}$$
$$0 - (2{,}000m - 400{,}000),$$
$$\text{or}$$
$$400{,}000 - 2{,}000m.$$

Therefore, the overall opportunity loss functions are

$$\text{loss}(D) = \begin{cases} 0 & \text{if } m \leq m_b \\ 2{,}000m - 400{,}000 & \text{if } m > m_b \end{cases}$$
$$\text{loss}(M) = \begin{cases} 400{,}000 - 2{,}000m & \text{if } m < m_b \\ 0 & \text{if } m \geq m_b \end{cases}$$

11.3 MAKING A DECISION FOR THESE PROBLEMS

Now that we have analyzed the payoff functions for each action in these problems, and the relationship between the payoff functions, it is time to consider how to make optimal decisions. The first and most important (and probably most confusing) aspect is to remember clearly what the events are in this case. *The events are values of m.* Clearly m has only one value, but before making the decision we do not know precisely what this value is. Therefore, in order to make an intelligent decision we must determine probabilities that various events (values of *m*) will occur. Since *m* can take on any value (usually within a specified range, such as 0 to 2,000 in the Nadir problem), the probability distribution of events which we adopt will be *continuous.* The first question we need to address in this section concerns what kinds of probability distributions make sense in terms of their applicability to this problem. In this context we will discuss two, the uniform and the normal distributions.

11.3.1   The Uniform Distribution as a Prior

The probability distribution which might, at first glance, seem the simplest to use for these problems is the uniform distribution, which we first studied in Chapter 9. The most general form for the probability density function of the uniform distribution is

$$f(x) = \begin{cases} \dfrac{1}{b-a} & \text{if } a \le x \le b, \\ 0 & \text{otherwise} \end{cases}$$

and the graph of this function is given in Figure 11.3. When this probability distribution is applied to the mean, *m,* we see that the

FIGURE 11.3
A Graph of the Uniform Probability Density Function

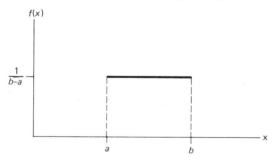

distribution assumes there is some lower bound, *a, below* which the value of *m* will never fall, and some upper bound, *b, above* which the value of *m* will never fall. Furthermore, within the range of values between *a* and *b* it is assumed that *m* will equally likely take on any value.

While the uniform prior might appear to be simple to use, it has properties that contradict any rational feelings one might have about a prior distribution for this problem. The major contradiction arises because of the uniformity and finite boundaries of the distribution. Suppose, for example, a uniform prior is chosen for the Nadir problem with a lower boundary of 100 ($a = 100$) and an upper boundary of 200 ($b = 200$). An implication of using this prior would be that the probability that m lies between 190 and 200 is 0.1, while the probability that m lies between 200 and 210 is 0. For most applications this is clearly an absurd property and argues strongly against the use of the uniform distribution as a prior. Clearly what is needed is a prior distribution of a different form. One distribution that has good properties is the normal distribution, which will be discussed in the next section.

11.3.2   The Normal Distribution as a Prior

It must be said at the outset that the properties of the normal distribution are not exactly those needed when it is used as the prior distribution for the mean. However, for most real decision theory problems the misalignment is very small, while the benefits of using the normal distribution as a prior are numerous. We will see in this chapter that it provides much more appealing characteristics as a prior than the constant and all-or-nothing characteristics of the uniform distribution. Then in Chapter 12 we will see that the normal prior distribution is very closely related to the sampling distribution that applies to decision problems involving the mean, just as in Chapter 9 we saw that the beta distribution is very intimately related to binomial sampling. For these two reasons we will adopt the normal distribution as our prior distribution for all decision problems involving the mean.

We mentioned above that the normal distribution does not meet all of the characteristics necessary for a prior for these problems. Where then does it fail to meet them? The answer is in the range of values that are allowed. A normally distributed random variable is allowed to take on any value over the entire spectrum of values from minus infinity to plus infinity. On the other hand, the mean (which is the random, or unknown, variable) is usually restricted by the physical limitations of the problems.[1] We saw in the Nadir problem that m must be no smaller than zero and no larger than 2,000. In the Coffee South problem m was constrained to be greater than zero, and while there was no *explicit* upper bound, we had the feeling that there is some *implicit* one. So, the range allowed for a normal random variable is incompatible with the physical limitations of the problems we plan to use it on.

How serious a problem is this incompatibility? Usually it causes almost no problem. To understand where the problem arises, and how serious it is, we must study the characteristics of the decision problems when we apply various normal priors.

---

[1] This characteristic is so universal that it is very difficult to think of a *single* problem in which it is not true.

Recall from Chapter 9 that the normal distribution has two parameters, μ and σ, and that these parameters are very closely related to the expected value and variance of the normal probability distribution. If X is a random variable whose probability distribution is normal with parameters μ and σ, then the expected value of X is mu,

$$E(X) = \mu,$$

and the variance of X is the square of sigma,

$$\text{Var}(X) = \sigma^2.$$

That is, σ is the standard deviation of X. If we use the normal distribution as a prior distribution of m, the mean, then we *expect* the value of m to be μ, and the variance of our expectations about that μ value is σ^2, that is:

$$E(m) = \mu \text{ and } \text{Var}(m) = \sigma^2.$$

It is very important in this chapter and Chapter 12 to distinguish between the event variable, m, and the expected value of the prior distribution, μ. Both are means, and could be so labeled. However, we will follow the convention of calling the *event, m,* the mean, and $E(m)$ the expected value. More important than the literary distinction, however, is the distinction the reader should have in his mind about the difference between the two. The event, m, is the mean for a varying outcome *over a specified area,* or *for a specified population.* In the Nadir problem m is the mean iron ore per ton taken from the field in question. Clearly the iron ore yield will vary from ton to ton of material within the field. The event m gives the overall average yield for all 50,000 tons of material in the field. In contrast to this, $E(m)$ is determined by the manager asking himself (or the analyst asking him): What are the probabilities of various values of the events, m, occurring? This question can be answered from historical data, completely subjectively, or by some combination of the two. The expected value of this probability distribution, $E(m)$, then is the *average* value of m that the manager would expect to see *over all fields* that had the same characteristics as the field in question.

To completely specify a normal distribution as a prior for m, we must not only specify that it *is* normal, but specify values for μ and σ. In the discussion that follows, we assume that the work necessary to do this has already been done. *How* to make this specification is discussed in Chapter 13, and the reader interested in knowing these techniques can study them there.

One final subject must be discussed before we pass on to a thorough analysis of how to use a normal prior distribution and what the consequences of its incompatibility with the realities of the problem are. This is the subject raised in Section 11.3.1 when we were talking about using a uniform prior. We found, for instance, that if we assumed a prior distribution on m that is uniform with boundaries of 100 and 200, then the probability that m will lie between 190 and 200 is 0.1, while the probability that m will lie between 200 and 210 is 0. This abrupt cutoff phenomenon does not occur if the normal distribution is used as a prior. If, for instance, we use a normal prior on m whose excepted value and variance are the same as the uniform distribution with boundaries 100 and 200, we find that the probability that m lies between 190 and 200 is 0.041, while the probability that m lies between 200 and 210 is 0.023. This demonstrates the property of the normal distribution that equal length intervals have positive probabilities, rather than the all-or-nothing probability characteristics of the uniform distribution. The probabilities we have been discussing are illustrated in Figure 11.4, where A demonstrates that the area underneath the probability density function (which is the probability for the interval) for the uniform distribution makes an

FIGURE 11.4
A Comparison of Prior Probabilities from Two Distributions with the Same Expected Value (150) and Variance (833)

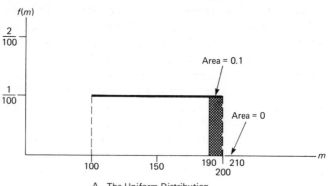

A. The Uniform Distribution

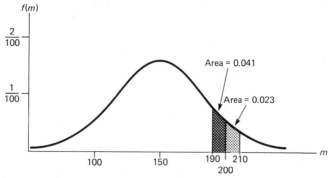

B. The Normal Distribution

abrupt change from 0.1 to 0, while B demonstrates that over the same ranges the probabilities from the normal distribution decline gradually.

11.4 USING THE NORMAL DISTRIBUTION AS A PRIOR

In all of the discussion in this section we will assume that the prior distribution is normal, and that the values of its parameters, μ and σ are known. The major questions we want to explore in this section are: (1) How to use the normal distribution as a prior for decision problems involving the mean, and (2) What are the results of changing the specification of the normal prior on the problem. It is not until the reader understands the answers to these questions that we can return to an analysis of the incompatibility between the normal distribution and the physical realities of the problem. Therefore, a discussion of the incompatibility problem will be deferred to Section 11.5.

11.4.1 Determining Which Action is Best

The most interesting result in using prior distributions to solve problems in which the mean is the event variable is that the best action is determined only by the expected value of the prior distribution, and *not* by its functional form (i.e., whether it is normal, or uniform, or anything else) nor any other characteristics about the distribution. This is illustrated in Figure 11.5, which displays four very different distributions, two normal, one uniform, and one distribution of another form, yet since each has an expected value of 150, the best action for each of these will be the same. Why then did we spend so much time discussing the relative advantages and disadvantages of the uniform and normal distributions as potential priors? We will find later in this section that when we analyze other aspects of the problem, such as the expected value of perfect information, EVPI, that the form and other characteristics of the prior *do* make a difference. It is for this reason that we discussed the relative merits of normal and uniform priors.

Let us now consider an analysis of the decision problem of the mean to determine which action is best. Using integral calculus, it can be shown that if an action, A, has a linear payoff function

$$\text{Payoff } (A) = a + bm,$$

then the expected payoff for taking this action is

$$E(A) = a + b\, E(m).$$

Therefore, in order to compare actions to determine which one is best, all we have to do is use the parameters of the payoff function, a and b,

FIGURE 11.5
Four Different Distributions, Each with the Same Expected Value (150)

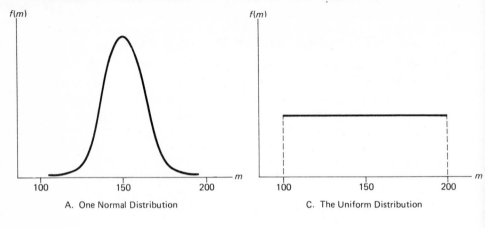

A. One Normal Distribution

C. The Uniform Distribution

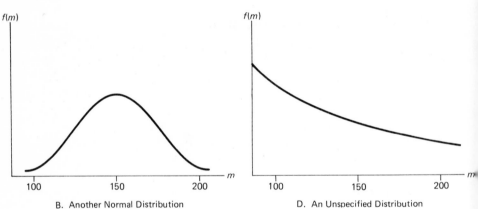

B. Another Normal Distribution

D. An Unspecified Distribution

in combination with the expected value of the prior distribution, $E(m)$, to calculate the expected payoff for each action.

Let's take an example. In the Nadir problem the payoff functions are

$$\text{Profit } (L) = 0 \text{ and Profit } (M) = 12{,}500m - 2{,}000{,}000.$$

If the prior distribution of m values has an expected value of 150—i.e., $E(m) = 150$—then,

$$E(L) = 0 + 0 \times 150 = 0$$

and

$$E(M) = 12{,}500 \times 150 - 2{,}000{,}000 = -125{,}000.$$

Since the expected profit for action L is greater than the expected profit for action M, action L is the best action to take for a prior with an expected value of 150.

This general result, that the expected payoff for each action depends only on the parameters of the payoff function and the expected value of the prior distribution, was also obtained in Chapter 9. Because of this we found that there was an easy rule to use to make a choice between the actions. This rule compared the expected value of the prior with the breakeven point. There is an exactly analogous rule in this case, which may be stated as:

> The $E(m)$ versus m_b rule: Compare the value of $E(m)$ with the value of m_b. If $E(m) > m_b$, then one action is optimal, while if $E(m) < m_b$, then the other action is optimal.

As with the rule in Chapter 9, this rule is ambiguous as to *which* action is optimal for $E(m) > m_b$, etc. However, just as in Chapter 9, we can use common sense to make this determination for any particular problem. For example, in the Nadir problem we know that $m_b = 160$. If we establish a prior whose expected value is 150, we know the optimal action is the action which has the highest payoff for values of m less than 150. For Nadir, this action is L. Similarly, suppose we establish a prior in the Coffee South example which has an expected value of 210. Since $m_b = 200$ in this case, we know the optimal action is the one whose payoffs are best for values of m above m_b. Looking at Figure 11.2 we see that the action M—market in the southeast—is best in this range of m values. Hence, with a prior distribution whose expected value is 210 (or anything above 200), M is the optimal action. (This fact can be verified by using $E(m) = 210$ and calculating the expected payoff for the two actions, D and M, in this problem.)

11.4.2 The Expected Opportunity Losses

Unfortunately, while it is extremely easy to choose between terminal actions using an expected payoff analysis, this analysis tells us nothing about the potential benefits that might accrue to a particular problem from taking a sample. In order to consider whether a sampling scheme is worthwhile we must know the expected value of perfect information, EVPI, for the problem being considered. Since EVPI is equivalent in value to the expected opportunity loss for the best action, we must learn how to calculate expected opportunity losses for problems like Nadir and Coffee South. Unfortunately, while this is conceptually easy it is mechanically more difficult than calculating the expected payoff for the same action. Furthermore, unlike the calculation of expected payoffs, the calculation of expected opportunity losses is very dependent upon the *form* of the distribution. *In all the work that follows, we will assume that the prior distribution is normal.*

The expected opportunity analysis formula is hard to derive, even for those who know calculus, so it will be given without verification in this text. It can be shown that, *for the optimal action A,* the expected opportunity loss is

$$\mathcal{E}(A) = |k|\sigma(m)L_{N*}(D),$$

where

|k| is the absolute value of the *slope* of the nonzero portion of A's opportunity loss function;

$E(m)$ is the mean of the prior distribution on m;

$\sigma(m)$ is the standard deviation of the prior distribution (it is distinguished $\sigma(m)$ because we will encounter another standard deviation in Chapter 12);

$L_{N*}(D)$ is a value obtained from Table II at the back of the text;

and

$$D = \frac{|m_b - E(m)|}{\sigma(m)},$$

a calculated value. Certainly this formula is not easy to understand. We will explain how it works and how the numbers are obtained so that the reader can get a better feel for using it.

Let's first consider how it works. Figure 11.6 shows two graphs for the Nadir problem. In A we have graphed the opportunity loss function for action L, and the probability density function for a normal prior on m whose expected value is 150. In B is graphed this same normal prior distribution and the opportunity loss function for action M. In Chapter 3 we calculated expected opportunity loss by multiplying the magnitudes of the losses by their probabilities and summing. While we cannot get into the details without a knowledge of integral calculus, the concept is very similar for a continuous random variable. In this case the magnitude of the opportunity loss is multiplied by the value of the probability density function and the result is "summed." Using this concept it is easy to see in Figure 11.6 why L has the lowest expected opportunity loss. The portion of the m spectrum where its loss function is *not* zero is multiplied by smaller values of $f(m)$ than the loss function for m. Since the prior distribution is symmetrical about its mean, and the loss functions are symmetrical about m_b, these kinds of visual comparisons can be easily made.

The symmetry of the loss functions in these problems is very useful. In this case we say that the loss functions are symmetrical with each other because they are mirror images of one another about the point m_b. Since the zero portion of the opportunity loss curves contributes nothing to the expected opportunity loss, the only relevant section of the loss curves are those where the loss is not zero. Notice that the symmetry of the functions in these regions results in the loss function

FIGURE 11.6
Graphs of the Loss Functions for Nadir with a Normal
Prior Whose Expected Value is 150

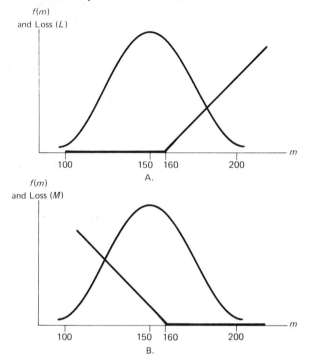

for L rising to the right *at the same rate* that the loss function for M is rising to the left. The mathematical label for this rate of change is called the *slope* of the line. In terms of the oportunity loss functions for the Nadir problem:

$$\text{loss}(L) = \begin{cases} 0 & \text{if } m \leq m_b \\ 12{,}500m - 2{,}000{,}000 & \text{if } m > m_b \end{cases}$$

$$\text{loss}(M) = \begin{cases} 2{,}000{,}000 - 12{,}500m & \text{if } m < m_b \\ 0 & \text{if } m \geq m_b \end{cases}$$

the slope of the nonzero portions of these functions is the numerical value multiplying the variable m. Thus, for the loss(L) function the slope of the nonzero portion is 12,500, while for loss(M) the slope of the nonzero portion is $-12{,}500$. One slope is the negative of the other, which is another way of stating that the loss functions are the mirror images of one another.

This discussion on the slopes of the loss functions has a purpose. The constant k in the expected opportunity loss expression,

$$\mathcal{E}(A) = |k|\sigma(m)L_{N*}(D),$$

is the slope of *either* of the loss functions. The vertical lines surrounding k mean that we must use the absolute value of k in our expressions, and the absolute value of either slope in the Nadir problem is 12,500. Therefore, we always get the same multiplier for the expected opportunity loss expression no matter which loss function we use to obtain the slope.

Now that all the parts of the expected opportunity loss expression have been described, let us give two examples of the use of this expression. First, for the Nadir problem we have L being the best decision, so

$$\mathcal{E}(L) = |k|\sigma(m)L_{N*}(D).$$

Suppose that we choose a normal prior distribution whose mean is 150 and whose standard deviation is 20. That is, our prior is normal with

$$E(m) = 150, \text{ and } \sigma(m) = 20.$$

Using these and the breakeven point, $m_b = 160$, we can calculate the value for D,

$$D = \frac{|m_b - E(m)|}{\sigma(m)} = \frac{|160 - 150|}{20} = 0.5,$$

and with this value we find from Table II that

$$L_{N*}(D) = L_{N*}(0.5) = 0.1978.$$

Finally, we have discussed above that

$$|k| = 12,500,$$

so that

$$\begin{aligned} \mathcal{E}(L) &= |k|\sigma(m)L_{N*}(D) \\ &= 12,500 \times 20 \times 0.1978 \\ &= 49,450. \end{aligned}$$

Thus, if one took action L in the Nadir problem the expected opportunity loss for this action would be about \$49,450. Since the expected opportunity loss for the best immediate action is also the expected cost of perfect information, the \$49,450 puts a ceiling on the amount Nadir would be willing to spend on a sample to obtain additional information about the field.

Let us also use this formula to find the expected opportunity loss of the best action in the Coffee South example. Suppose we establish a prior distribution that is normal with mean 240 and standard deviation 25, that is,

$$E(m) = 240 \text{ and } \sigma(m) = 25.$$

Once this is known we must first determine which action, D or M, is best. We have prevously calculated the breakeven point as $m_b = 200$, so with the proposed prior we have $E(m) > m_b$. Looking at Figure

FIGURE 11.7
The Two Payoff Functions for Coffee South

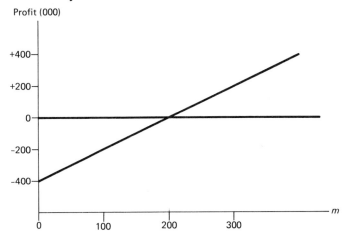

11.7, which is a reproduction of Figure 11.2, we see that M is the best action for values of m greater than m_b, and therefore is the optimal action when $E(m) > m_b$. Therefore, we know that the expected opportunity loss for M can be calculated using the formula given above:

$$\mathcal{E}(M) = |k|\sigma(m)L_{N*}(D).$$

For this problem, the loss function for M is

$$\text{loss}(M) = \begin{cases} 400{,}000 - 2{,}000m & \text{if } m < m_b \\ 0 & \text{if } m \geq m_b \end{cases}$$

so

$$|k| = |-2{,}000| = 2{,}000.$$

Then, since $E(m) = 240$ and $\sigma(m) = 25$,

$$D = \frac{|m_b - E(m)|}{\sigma(m)} = \frac{|200 - 240|}{25} = 1.6,$$

and from Table II we find

$$L_{N*}(D) = L_{N*}(1.6) = 0.02324.$$

We now have all the numbers needed to calculate the expected opportunity loss, and

$$\begin{aligned} \mathcal{E}(M) &= |k|\sigma(m)L_{N*}(D) \\ &= 2{,}000 \times 25 \times 0.02324 = 1{,}162. \end{aligned}$$

As always, this expected opportunity loss is also the expected value of perfect information. In this case we see that the Valley Sisters Company is confident enough of their potential market that they would be willing to pay very little for a sample to improve their idea of what the distribution of m is.

We have presented above the method for calculating the expected opportunity loss of the *best* action for any two-action problem with linear payoffs and a normal prior on the events (values of m). Although calculating this expected opportunity loss is not as easy as calculating the expected payoffs, it does allow the decision maker to calculate the magnitude of the uncertainty in the problem. Knowing this is important, because it will give an indication of whether sampling should be considered before a final decision is made. The mechanics of analyzing a sample will be discussed in Chapter 12, but the first indication is always whether it would pay to engage in sampling, and that is the question we are now partially able to answer, using the idea of the expected value of perfect information. We will be able to answer it even more fully when we consider how much information a sample will give us. This quantity, the expected value of sample information, EVSI, will be calculated in Chapter 12. Even now, however, we have a value for EVPI, which will allow us to roughly determine whether any sampling is worthwhile.

One final note before we close this section. While the $E(m)$ versus m_b rule only considers the relationship between one measure of the prior—$E(m)$—and one measure of the payoff functions—m_b, the expected opportunity loss analysis, especially through the value of D, accounts not only for the relative values of $E(m)$ and m_b, but how the value of their difference relates to the measure of uncertainty in the prior, $\sigma(m)$. Thus, as far as the expected opportunity loss calculation is concerned, it is not how far apart $E(m)$ and m_b are, but how far apart they are *relative to* $\sigma(m)$. This relative uncertainty is what is important (as it should be) in calculating an upper limit on the value of a sample to us.

*11.4.3   An Exploration of the L_{N*} (D) Table

For those readers with a knowledge of integral calculus, it is instructive to explore $L_{N*}(D)$ to determine exactly what it expresses. Consider, as an example, the opportunity loss function for the action L in the Nadir problem:

$$\text{loss}(L) = \begin{cases} 0 & \text{if } m \leq m_b \\ 12{,}500m - 2{,}000{,}000 & \text{if } m > m_b \end{cases}.$$

A more convenient way to express this loss function is:

$$\text{loss}(L) = \begin{cases} 0 & \text{if } m \leq m_b \\ 12{,}500(m - m_b) & \text{if } m > m_b \end{cases}.$$

Using this, and a prior distribution of m values whose probability density function is $f(m)$, it is easy to see that

$$\mathcal{E}(L) = \int_{m_b}^{\infty} 12{,}500(m - m_b)f(m)\, dm.$$

In the case when $f(m)$ is the probability density function of a normal distribution:

$$f(m) = \frac{1}{\sqrt{2\pi}\,\sigma}\, e^{-\frac{1}{2}\left(\frac{m-\mu}{\sigma}\right)^2},$$

then it can be shown[2] that the integral expression for $\mathcal{E}(L)$ is

$$\int_{m_b}^{\infty} 12{,}500(m - m_b)f(m)\, dm$$

$$= 12{,}500\sigma \left\{ \frac{1}{\sqrt{2\pi}}\, e^{-\frac{1}{2}\left(\frac{m_b - \mu}{\sigma}\right)^2} - \frac{m_b - \mu}{\sigma} P\left[Z \geq \frac{m_b - \mu}{\sigma} \right] \right\}$$

where Z is a standardized normal random variable, that is, one whose mean is 0 and whose standard deviation is 1. Therefore, we see by comparing this formula to the original expected opportunity loss formula,

$$\mathcal{E}(L) = |k|\sigma(m)L_{N*}(D),$$

that

$$L_{N*}(D) = \frac{1}{\sqrt{2\pi}}\, e^{-\frac{1}{2}D^2} - DP[Z \geq D],$$

where, of course,

$$D = \frac{|m_b - \mu|}{\sigma}.$$

While knowing the precise formula for $L_{N*}(D)$ may be important for some readers, the concept of what it is is probably more important. Those who solve Problem 11 at the end of this chapter will see that it can be used to calculate expected losses for problems with normal priors and more than two actions.

11.5   THE TROUBLE WITH THE NORMAL DISTRIBUTION IS . . .

In Section 11.4 we advocated using the normal distribution as a prior for decision problems involving the mean largely because it did not have the counter-intuitive properties that the uniform distribution had. *However,* the normal distribution is not completely free of problems. Its major methodological problem is that the range of values it takes on is $-\infty$ to $+\infty$, and we previously argued that to have an event with an unrestricted range is unrealistic. Fortunately, however, for *reasonable*

---

[2] This is left as an exercise for the reader.

specifications of the standard deviation, $\sigma(m)$, relative to $E(m)$ and the absolute range of m values the mis-specification caused by assuming m can take on *any* value is very slight. For instance, the prior distribution we assumed for the Nadir problem had a mean of 150 and a standard deviation of 20. From a probability analysis of the normal distribution (a subject we have not covered in this text), it can be shown that the probability that m will lie between 40 and 260 is 0.9999998. Stated another way, the probability we will find a value (for m) less than 40 or greater than 260 is 0.0000002. Thus, even though the normal distribution technically allows values outside the permissable (0 to 2,000) range of the Nadir problem, the chances of observing a value outside that range are miniscule. So, the normal as a prior makes practical sense even though its properties do not absolutely coincide with the needs of mean value problems.

11.6 A POSTSCRIPT ON COFFEE SOUTH

Suppose, after the analysis presented above had been completed for the Coffee South problem, the results were presented at a meeting attended by the company's top management and some marketing personnel. One of the people attending was Don Sharp, a market research analyst. After hearing the structure of the study and the results, Don's comments were as follows.

"I appreciate the skill required to solve this problem, and the hard work the Decision Analysis Group has put into solving it, but the problem's structure is wrong. I can quote you five secondary sources that give the per capita coffee consumption by any demographic breakdown you could ever conceivably think of. Total coffee consumption now and in the near future is known with great accuracy. The thing that makes life uncertain in this business is that we do not know market share."

This hypothetical situation occurs, unfortunately, all too often in practice. Statistical and decision theory studies are wasted because the people with the technical expertise to carry out these studies lack a real understanding of what the major issue is. All the sophisticated analysis in the world will not make up for an improperly defined problem. In this case the uncertainty in per capita consumption was an illusion, and the result was a wasted study.

How could this study have been made appropriate? First, of course, the structure of the problem must be correct. If it is market share which the company is unsure about, then market share must become the uncertain event. Second, testing would probably take place. In the next chapter we shall talk about sampling to obtain a better idea of what the mean will be. Companies interested in determining market share for their product in a new market often conduct test marketing—actually selling the product in one small segment (usually one city) of the new market to determine the level of consumer response. Unfortunately, test marketing is fraught with problems. Competitors like to spoil the results of a test market by intensifying their own marketing efforts in the test market. Salesmen tend to be overzealous with a new product. The company may conduct promotional efforts in the test market that cannot be duplicated (usually because of cost) over the entire new market. Whatever the situation, "good" market tests are hard to design and conduct.

The major point here is not that test marketing is difficult, however. One of the most successful early applications of decision theory was to a new product introduction.[3] The reason for raising this issue in this text is to emphasize that studies with the wrong design are worthless. Both the manager with the problem and the person with the capability to solve the problem need to interact closely throughout the project. Such close interaction will prevent the disastrous situation that occurred in the Coffee South problem.

11.7 SUMMARY

In this chapter we have discussed problems in which the unknown event is a mean. We have further restricted our discussion to two-action problems and normal prior distributions. For problems with this structure we have developed a rule for determining which action is best, and the expected opportunity loss associated with that action. Chapter 12 will now build upon the concepts discussed in this chapter, and present a method for analyzing these problems when sampling is undertaken.

PROBLEMS

1. Show that for the uniform distribution given by the following probability density function:

$$f(m) = \begin{cases} \dfrac{1}{2,000} & \text{if } 0 \le m \le 2,000 \\ 0 & \text{otherwise} \end{cases}$$

   a. The probability that m lies between 100 and 200 is 0.05.
   b. The probability that m lies between 0 and 160 is 0.08.

2. Verify the symmetry of loss functions about m_b.

   a. For the Coffee South example.
   b. In general.

---

[3] Paul E. Green, "Bayesian Decision Theory in Pricing Strategy," *Journal of Marketing,* January 1963, pp. 5–15.

*3. Show that $E(m) = \dfrac{a+b}{2}$ for a uniform prior distribution.

*4. Show that if Payoff $(A) = a + bm$, then the expected payoff of A, $E(A)$, is $a + bE(m)$.

5. Prove the $E(m)$ versus m_b rule.

6. In the Coffee South example, verify that M is the optimal action if the prior has an expected value of $210 by calculating the expected profits for both actions at this value of $E(m)$.

7. Find the best action and the expected opportunity loss for this action if you establish a normal prior in:

    a. The Nadir problem with $E(m) = 150$, $\sigma(m) = 30$;
    b. The Nadir problem with $E(m) = 170$, $\sigma(m) = 20$;
    c. The Coffee South problem with $E(m) = 195$, $\sigma(m) = 25$.

8. It is instructive to see how the expected opportunity loss changes as $E(m)$, $\sigma(m)$, and $|k|$ change. In the Nadir problem assume the prior distribution is normal and

    a. Let $\sigma(m) = 20$, $|k| = 12{,}500$, and sketch a graph of the expected opportunity loss for the best action as a function of $E(m)$ in the range $E(m) = 110$ to $E(m) = 210$.
    b. Let $E(m) = 150$, $|k| = 12{,}500$, and sketch a graph of the expected opportunity loss for the best action as a function of $\sigma(m)$ in the range $\sigma(m) = 5$ to $\sigma(m) = 50$.
    c. Let $E(m) = 150$, $\sigma(m) = 20$, and sketch a graph of the expected opportunity loss for the best action as a function of $|k|$ in the range $|k| = 0$ to $|k| = 25{,}000$.

9. American Steel Corp. has a problem in converting pig iron, a raw material, into steel. The process involves burning out carbon (and other impurities) from a molton mixture of pig iron. The process (called the Bessemer process) is quite variable in its output, however. The point at which the carbon burning is stopped critically affects the final quality of the steel. High carbon steel is less valuable than low carbon steel. Furthermore, if not enough carbon is burned off, the end product is cast iron, a material with very few of the appealing properties of steel.

    The company's problem is the following. At the end of the carbon burn they must decide whether to process the molten material as steel or as cast iron. The price per ton for steel is $150 - \$5m$, where m is the mean carbon content (in pounds). (There are 100 tons of molten material in each batch.) If the material is processed as steel, the processing costs are $5,000. If the material is processed as cast iron, the cost is only $1,000. The selling price for cast iron is $38 - \$0.2m$ per ton.

    a.   Determine the profit functions for American's two actions.

    b.   What is m_b in this case?

    c.   What are the opportunity loss functions?

    d.   If the company establishes a prior on m that has a mean of 16 and a standard deviation of 3, which action is best for each batch? What is the expected opportunity loss for this action?

*10.   Verify that

$$\int_{m_b}^{\infty} 12{,}500(m - m_b)f(m)\,dm$$

$$= 12{,}500\sigma \left\{ \frac{1}{\sqrt{2\pi}}\, e^{-\frac{1}{2}\left(\frac{m_b - \mu}{\sigma}\right)^2} - \frac{m_b - \mu}{\sigma} P\left[Z \geq \frac{m_b - \mu}{\sigma} \right] \right\}$$

if $f(m)$ is from a normal distribution. (See Section 11.4.3.)

*11.   Consider a problem in which a mean, m, is the event and there are three possible actions, A_1, A_2, and A_3 whose *profit* functions are:

    Profit $(A_1) = 5 + \frac{1}{2}m$; Profit $(A_2) = m$; Profit $(A_3) = -5 + \frac{4}{3}m$,

and assume the prior distribution on m is normal with $E(m) = 13$ and $\sigma(m) = 2$.

    a.   Derive the loss functions for the three decisions

    b.   Write the integral expressions for the expected losses for each action.

    c.   Find the *value* of the expected opportunity losses for each action by using the $L_{N^*}(D)$ table.

12.   Joe Smith, a resident of Phoenix, Arizona, is getting worried about the cost of heating the hot water for his home. Fuel costs have been rising steadily, and Joe has every indication that, with the decreasing world energy supply, the trend will continue. Therefore, Joe has been investigating the possibility of installing a solar hot water heater in his home. He is particularly interested in the two units manufactured by the Sun Temp Corporation, and needs to make a decision on which size he should choose.

    The basic concept of a solar hot water heater is illustrated in Figure 11.8. When the temperature of the water in the storage tank falls below a certain point, the pump is activated that pumps the water through the solar panel. In the solar panel the water is heated by the sun, and the hotter water returns to the storage tank. If the water cannot be sufficiently heated in this manner, the control valve changes the direction of flow from the solar panel to the regular hot water heater, where the water is heated by natural gas or electricity. Thus, the system is termed an augmented system, because the sun provides only 70 to 90 percent of the total heat needed. The rest is supplied by the energy source in the regular hot water heater. Joe's problem is one of determining the size of solar unit to install; that is, he needs to decide whether to install a small solar

FIGURE 11.8
A Basic Diagram of An Augmented Solar Hot Water Heater

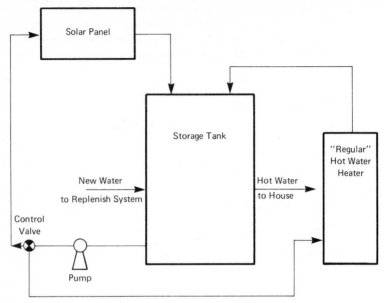

panel and a small storage tank, or a large solar panel and a large storage tank. A larger system would cost more to install, but would use the regular hot water heater less, hence the energy cost would be less, while a smaller system would require less initial capital outlay but require more water heating by the conventional method. Which system would be best depends on how much hot water Joe and his family use on an average day, and unfortunately Joe doesn't know what this is. He is willing, however, to state his beliefs on what the prior probability distribution of average consumption is.

After a thorough analysis of the cost and installation time and expected life of the solar systems, and the anticipated future costs for energy for his conventional water heater, Joe developed the following cost functions for his two actions:

Buy the small system: Cost = $1 + 0.0225m$,
Buy the large system: Cost = $2.2 + 0.0075m$,

and m is the average daily consumption (in gallons) of hot water. In addition to these cost functions, Joe is willing to establish a prior distribution on m which is normally distributed with an expected value of 65 and a standard deviation of 10.

a. What is the breakeven point, m_b, for these cost functions? As a result of this calculation, which action should Joe take?

b. Calculate the expected payoffs for each of Joe's actions.

c. Determine Joe's opportunity loss functions and cost of uncertainty.

d. One of the quantities Joe had to guess at in calculating the variable costs in his cost functions (0.0225 and 0.0075) was the future price of conventional energy, and the variable costs directly reflect this quantity. For example, Joe guessed his future bills (if he did not install the solar water heater) would be $6 per month, and this figure, in combination with others, resulted in the 0.0225 and 0.0075 figures. Joe is interested in doing some sensitivity analysis on this figure, since it is, at best, only an educated guess. He knows that because the numbers are directly related, if he halves his guess of future conventional water heating costs (to $3 per month) then the variable costs in his cost functions will be half of 0.0225 and 0.0075 or 0.01125 and 0.00375, while if conventional heating costs will be double what Joe estimated, or $12 per month, then the variable cost coefficients will be doubled, or 0.045 and 0.015. Consider in the following questions a range of monthly conventional water heating costs from $3 to $12.

(1) Determine which of Joe's two actions is best for each value in this range of costs.

(2) Calculate enough values of the cost of uncertainty to be able to sketch a graph of the relationship between monthly conventional heating costs and Joe's associated cost of uncertainty. How can you explain the behavior of this curve?

Decisions Involving Means
when Sampling Occurs

IN CHAPTER 11 we discussed problems in which the mean was the event of interest to us, and discussed the use of a normal prior distribution in connection with such problems. In this chapter we shall extend the analysis of the problems involving means to include sampling—both decisions made after a sample outcome is known and the more important category of considering taking a sample. The objective of taking a sample is, of course, to get a better idea of what the true mean is in the problem.

In presenting the techniques for such an analysis, we will find it important to discuss the rudiments of the science of statistics, so a great deal of the beginning of this chapter will deal with what statistics is, and how it relates to the science of decision theory. Once the reader has a basic understanding of statistics, the remainder of the chapter will be devoted to the major topic—that of analyzing problems in which the unknown mean is the event.

12.1 A STATISTICS PRIMER

The science of statistics can be used whenever a quantity of interest varies over a population of subjects. For example, in the Nadir Mining and Manufacturing problem, which was discussed in Chapter 11, the concentration of iron ore (magnetite) varies over the various tons of material in the ore field. The quantity of interest in this case is the concentration of iron ore, and the population is the collection of one ton segments of material in the field. If the field were absolutely homogeneous in its iron ore concentration, then there would be no variation in the quantity of interest, and no need to use statistics. The fact that the variation exists makes the decison problem regarding the field more difficult, and yet more challenging.

Because we have a quantity whose value varies over a population in this example, we can say that the quantity of interest has some *probability distribution* over the members of the population. The concept that this probabilty distribution exists is central to obtaining an understanding of what statistics is and how it works. Therefore, we urge the reader to think about this concept until he is convinced that quantities that vary over populations have probability distributions.

Now, the important aspect of the probability distribution to Nadir is the single quantity known as the *expected value, or mean.* The company is not interested in the specific character of the distribution, only in what happens *on the average.* If the precise character of the probability distribution is known, however, the expected value can easily be calculated using the tools given in Chapter 2. Unfortunately of course, the precise character of the distribution is *not* known (usually little more is known that the fact that the quantity of interest varies over the popluation) and other means of obtaining the expected value must be used.

Given that we do not known the precise character of the probability distribution we are interested in, we have two options. The most obvious one is to take a complete census of the population, and thus establish the precise character of the probability distribution. Complete censuses are rare in practical situations. The U.S. Bureau of the Census comes close to obtaining a census of the U.S. population every ten years, but even this activity misses certain citizens—especially residents of inner cities and very rural areas.

A much more common approach to dealing with these situations is to use the science of statistcs to make a "guess" at the expected value (or whatever other characteristics of the population probability distribution we are interested in). Statistics has the advantage of not requiring an evaluation of the entire population, as a census does. Therefore, using statistics costs less than taking a census. However, we have to settle for less information as a result. If a census is taken, the expected value of the probability distribution can be calculated exactly, whereas the science of statistics only gives us an *estimate* (a good guess) of the expected value. So, just as in Chapter 6 and 7, we will find that we will be weighing the cost of obtaining an additional sample against the added value that sample can give.

The process and concepts of the science of statistics are given in Figure 12.1. In the upper left hand corner of the diagram is a box that represents the population we are dealing with, and it notes the fact that the quantity of interest varies over the members of the population. Since

FIGURE 12.1
A Diagram of the Statistical Process

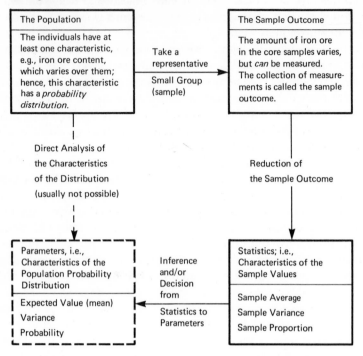

we are not taking a census of this population, not all members will be measured, yet the heart of the statistical process is taking a *representative* small group of individuals from the population, and measuring the quantity of interest for these individuals. This representative small group is called the *sample*. The outcomes that result from the measurements of the individuals in the sample is called, not surprisingly, the *sample outcome*. The basic difference between the science of statistics and taking a census is that in statistics we analyze the sample outcome, while for a census we analyze the population probability distribution. The sample outcome is represented by the box in the upper right of Figure 12.1.

How the sample is taken is very important, as you may imagine. The most important aspect is that the sample is *representative* of the population from which it is drawn. The mechanics of how to do that are too involved to discuss in this text. Suffice it to say that entire books and career specialties of some statisticians are built upon the ideas of obtaining a representative sample. Examples abound in statistics of incorrect conclusions drawn because the sample was not representative of the population. A rather well known one involves an election poll taken by the *Literary Digest* in the 1932 presidential election. The sample was taken from telephone subscribers, and the prediction was that Roosevelt would lose the election. As we all know, of course, Roosevelt won the election. The problem with the *Literary Digest*'s poll was that telephone subscribers, in 1932, were not a representative sample of the electorate.

Let's take an example of obtaining a sample. In the Nadir problem, a sample could be a small group of one ton segments taken from scattered points and at various depths within the field. However, it is easy to see that such a sampling scheme is infeasible because, for instance, it would cost a lot of money to extract and analyze one ton of material from a point, say, 96.7 feet below the surface. Instead, analysts of land formations obtain core samples, which are much smaller and more easily obtained and analyzed. Suppose Nadir obtained five scattered core samples from the field and, upon analysis, discovered that these samples contained 157, 182, 123, 148 and 164 pounds of magnetite per ton of material. In this case the *sample* is of size 5, and consists of the five core samples. The *sample outcome* is the five values 157, 182, 123, 148, and 164.

Now the reason for taking the sample is to obtain some idea about some characteristic of the population probability distribution. In Nadir's case, the management is interested in knowing the expected value of the population probability distribution. Although it is not a *precise* use of the word, we shall call the characteristic we are interested in a *parameter* of the distribution. Some parameters (the mean, variance, and a probability) are represented by the lower left-hand box of Figure 12.1. This box has a dotted line around it to indicate that the exact numerical values for these parameters are not known. (If they were known, of course, taking a sample would not be necessary!) However, in order to *use* the sample outcome, we must know something about the structure of probability distributions in general, and the fact that certain parameters of probability distributions can be defined. (That we need to know something about the structure of probability distributions is why probability theory and random variables is such an important part of statistics.) Thus, we enclose this box with a dotted line to indicate that we know about the *structure* of probability distributions enough to know that these parameters exist without knowing the *precise values* of these in the particular problem we are dealing with.

Now that you have a feeling for three of the boxes in Figure 12.1, we come to the most important one, which is at the lower right. The objective of the statistical process is to take the sample outcomes, for which the exact values are known, and make *inferences* about a particular parameter of the population, which is the real quantity of interest to us. In order to do this, we have to have some way of *reducing* the sample data to give us an *estimate* of the population quantity of interest. Deciding how to do this is usually accomplished by a combination of intuition and mathematical skill. We do not have the time, nor is it the purpose of this text, to develop the mathematical underpinnings of this branch of statistics, yet our common sense will serve us very well in deciding what measure (from the sample) should be used to estimate a certain parameter of the population.

In the problems we will be facing in this chapter, the population mean is the parameter whose value we would like to know. The question in your mind should now be—What is an appropriate measure from the sample that will give us a good estimate of the population mean? The answer is the sample average—the sum of all the sample values divided by the size of the sample (the number of values we have). Thus, in the Nadir problem where the values 157, 182, 123, 148, and 164 were obtained, the sample average is

$$\frac{157 + 182 + 123 + 148 + 164}{5} = 154.8.$$

Historically, the sample average has proven to be a good choice to represent the expected value of an unknown probability distribution,[1] and it is the estimate we shall use in this text.

The measures that are obtained from the sample and used to estimate parameters of the population are known as *statistics*. These are the quantities represented in the lower right-hand box of Figure 12.1, and it is these statistics we use to make inferences about the value of the corresponding parameter. (That we must have a statistic that *corresponds* to the parameter of interest cannot be emphasized strongly enough, yet this point is easy to gloss over. Perhaps an absurd example, such as using the sample average to make inferences about the population variance will emphasize the importance of this correspondence!)

The four boxes in Figure 12.1 have now all been described, and you should have a good feeling for the relationship between them and how they describe the statistical process. The process begins in the upper left-hand corner with a quantity that is varying over some population, and about which something is needed to be known. Since the varying quantity has a probability distribution, we know that this distribution has some characteristics—i.e., an expected value, a variance, and a probability, at least one of which is of interest but whose value is unknown. Since a complete census of the population is infeasible, we turn instead toward obtaining a sample and analyzing that sample. The numbers we get as a result of combining the sample outcomes in various ways

---

[1] Recent research is showing, however, that other more complicated estimates of the mean may be better than the sample average. Suffice it to say, however, that for the work in this text the sample average provides an *extremely* adequate representation of the unknown expected value.

are called statistics, and if we make a careful choice, one statistic is closely related to the population parameter we are interested in knowing. This appropriate statistic is then used as an *estimate* of its corresponding *parameter,* and its value is used to help make decisions involving the parameter.

Before we go on to the very important idea of statistics as random variables, we need to give the formula for the sample average. If there are n members in the sample, and the value of the ith sample member is x_i, then the sample average, denoted $\bar{x}$, is

$$\bar{x} = \frac{x_1 + x_2 + \cdots + x_n}{n}$$

For example, in the Nadir sample, the first outcome was 157, so we let $x_1 = 157$, the second outcome was 182, so we let $x_2 = 182$, etc., until we have

$$x_1 = 157, \ x_2 = 182, \ x_3 = 123, \ x_4 = 148, \ x_5 = 164, \ n = 5$$

and

$$\bar{x} = \frac{157 + 182 + 123 + 148 + 164}{5} = 154.8.$$

12.1.1 Statistics as Random Variables

The most important concept in the science of statistics is that the statistics (the various reductions of the sample outcomes, such as $\bar{x}$) are random variables. This is often a hard concept for students to understand. They are likely to say—How can anything about the calculation

$$\frac{157 + 182 + 123 + 148 + 164}{5} = 154.8$$

be random? This is absolutely true, yet if we think of the value of the sample average *before* the sample is taken, we do not know for sure that the outcomes will yield an $\bar{x}$ of 154.8. In fact, if we took *another* sample of size 5 from the field Nadir is considering, we would be very *unlikely* to get another sample average whose value is 154.8. The reason for both of these, of course, is that the individual cores we sample have varying concentrations of iron ore. It is in this broader context that we say the sample average (or any statistic) is a random variable. *Before* the sample is taken we do not know what value the sample average will have.

To fix some points for discussion, let's suppose Nadir took another sample of five cores from the field and found that the corresponding iron ore concentrations were 138, 167, 182, 134, and 155. The sample average for this sample outcome is

$$\frac{138 + 167 + 182 + 134 + 155}{5} = 155.2,$$

a number which is not the same as (although it is *close* to) the first sample average of 154.8.

That these two values, 154.8 and 155.2 are not the same emphasizes the point we have made above, namely that statistics are random variables. We took two samples and got two different values for the sample average. On the other hand, the fact that these values are close to one another illustrates another point about statistics—that although statistics are random variables, we would expect different values of the statistic to be relatively "close" to one another. Furthermore, an appealing property of a good statistic is that its value be "close to" the value of the corresponding parameter. Both of these concepts can be expressed in much more mathematical detail, which we won't do here. We merely mention them so that the reader will be aware such problems are being considered. Furthermore, we need to state that the sample average obeys both of these properties when it is used as an estimator of the population expected value.

12.1.2   The Probability Distribution of the Sample Average

Once we have established that the sample average is a random number, the probabilitists among us will immediately ask what its probability distribution is. For we learned in Chapter 2 that every random number has a probability distribution, and we will find in this chapter that knowledge of the probability distribution of the sample average is *essential* to being able to use it in our decision problems. (It is analogous to the fact that in order to solve the problems in Chapters 6, 7, 8, and 9 we had to know that the sampling distribution was binomial.) So if we need to know the probability distribution of the sample average, then what is it? Unfortunately, things aren't as simple as we would like them to be. While each sample average has a probability distribution, the *form* of the probability distribution for the sample average depends upon the *form* of the probability distribution for the original random variable. Let's take simple examples of this, and in the process introduce a new type of figure that will be helpful in conceptually viewing the problem.

If the probability distribution of the quantity of interest (the upper left-hand box of Figure 12.1) is known, then the probability distribution of any statistic of a sample drawn from that distribution can also, at least conceptually, be obtained. A simple example will illustrate this point. Suppose we take a fair coin, and think of the outcome heads (H)

as a 1, and the outcome tails (T) as a 0. Then we have a random variable (outcomes 0 and 1, each with probability $\frac{1}{2}$) and we can easily take a random sample of any size from this "population" and calculate any statistic from the sample outcomes. Let's suppose the size of the sample is 3. Then the possible sample outcomes are three zeroes, two zeroes and a one, two ones and a zero, and three ones. Furthermore, since the process by which we would obtain samples satisfies the conditions for binomial sampling, we know that

$$P(\text{Three 0s}) = \binom{3}{0} (\tfrac{1}{2})^0 (1 - \tfrac{1}{2})^{3-0} = \tfrac{1}{8}$$

$$P(\text{Two 0s, One 1}) = \binom{3}{1} (\tfrac{1}{2})^1 (1 - \tfrac{1}{2})^{3-1} = \tfrac{3}{8}$$

$$P(\text{One 0, Two 1s}) = \binom{3}{2} (\tfrac{1}{2})^2 (1 - \tfrac{1}{2})^{3-2} = \tfrac{3}{8}$$

$$P(\text{Three 1s}) = \binom{3}{3} (\tfrac{1}{2})^3 (1 - \tfrac{1}{2})^{3-3} = \tfrac{1}{8}.$$

Finally, if we are interested in the *average* outcome, we can see that three zeroes will yield an average of 0, two zeros and a one will give an average of $\frac{1}{3}$, etc., and the probability distribution of the sample average for a sample of size 3 is given in Table 12.1.

TABLE 12.1
The Probability Distribution of $\bar{x}$, when a Fair Coin is Flipped Three Times

Value of $\bar{x}$	Probability
0	$\frac{1}{8}$
$\frac{1}{3}$	$\frac{3}{8}$
$\frac{2}{3}$	$\frac{3}{8}$
1	$\frac{1}{8}$

It is interesting to explore this probability distribution a bit. First, notice that the expected value of the original distribution from which we are sampling is

$$E(X) = 0 \times \tfrac{1}{2} + 1 \times \tfrac{1}{2} = \tfrac{1}{2},$$

a value that isn't even *attained* by the sample average, $\bar{x}$. On the other hand, the most probable values of $\bar{x}$ are "close to" $\frac{1}{2}$, verifying our feeling that the sample average is a good estimator (but can never, at least for a sample of size 3, have the exact value) of the population expected value.

Now for some illustrative graphics. Let us graph (using the techniques given in Chapter 2) both the original distribution for the population, which we shall call the *parent* distribution, and the distribution for the sample average, which shall be called the *sampling* distribution. The graph of the parent distribution for the problem we discussed above is given in Figure 12.2, and the graph of the sampling distribu-

FIGURE 12.2
The Probability Distribution of the Number of Heads in One Flip of a Fair Coin

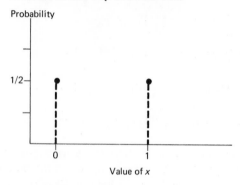

FIGURE 12.3
The Probability Distribution of $\bar{x}$ in a Sample of Size 3 from the Distribution in Figure 12.2

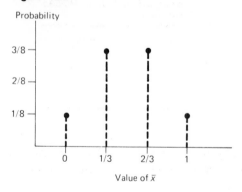

tion is given in Figure 12.3. In Figure 12.4 these are combined in a manner we shall adopt throughout the rest of this book. In this figure, the parent distribution is given along with the sampling distribution, so that the reader can understand their correspondence.

We have illustrated the determination of the sampling distribution for $\bar{x}$ in a very simple case above, and introduced the idea of showing the parent and sampling distributions in the same graph. These graphs

FIGURE 12.4
A Combination of Figures 12.2 and 12.3

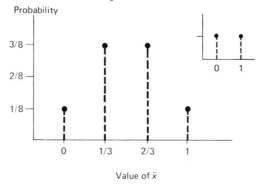

Value of $\bar{x}$

will be used below to illustrate how the sampling distribution changes as the parent distribution changes.

Suppose as a parent distribution we have the U-shaped distribution given in Table 12.2. Then the sampling distribution for $\bar{x}$ in a sample of size 3 can be derived, and both are shown in Figure 12.5. The im-

TABLE 12.2
A Hypothetical U-Shaped Distribution

Value of x	Probability
0	3/8
1	1/8
2	1/8
3	3/8

portant thing to notice is the comparison between Figures 12.5 and 12.4. The parent distributions are different, and thus the sampling distributions, *even for the same sample size,* are different. Therefore, the *form* (i.e., what it looks like and the relationship between the possible values) of the sampling distribution depends upon the form of the parent distribution.

Unfortunately, the fact that the form of the parent distribution dictates the form of the sampling distribution makes life (for the decision theory analyst) much more complicated. Sometimes the form of the parent distribution is known, or can be inferred from the properties of the situation, but much more frequently it is not known. Are most problems then intractable? Fortunately not. There is a very powerful result, known as the *central limit theorem,* which allows the sampling

FIGURE 12.5
The Graph of the Distribution in Table 12.2 and the Sample Average
Distribution for a Sample of Size 3

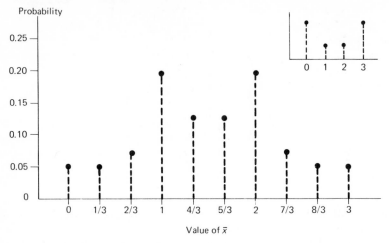

distribution of the sample average to be approximated by a normal probability distribution, *regardless* of the form of the parent population. The only requirement we need to invoke this result is that the sample size is "large enough." Illustrations of the central limit theorem and a discussion of exactly how large a sample size is needed will be given in the next section.

12.1.3   The Central Limit Theorem

As we learned in the previous section, the central limit theorem, which we will state and illustrate in this section, allows us to divorce the sampling distribution of the sample average, $\bar{x}$, from the parent distribution. Since in the real world the form of the parent distribution (i.e., whether it is binomial or normal or whatever) is seldom known, the central limit theorem proves to be a very powerful result.

The central limit theorem can be stated as:

> No matter what the form of parent distribution is, the sampling distribution of $\bar{x}$, the sample average, is approximately normal as n, the sample size, becomes large.

This statement is a powerful result, yet there is a conditional clause in it, which we must explore. We must ask what is meant by the requirement of a large sample size. If a sample size of a million is required before the sampling distribution of $\bar{x}$ is approximately normal, then the central limit theorem must be designated only as a mathematically interesting fact with no practical value. Fortunately, as you can guess from the fact that we are discussing it, just the opposite is true. We will find that the normal distribution provides a good approximation to the sampling distribution of $\bar{x}$ for quite small sample sizes, on the order of $n = 10$ to $n = 30$. Therefore, in most practical sampling situations the central limit theorem can be invoked, and the normal distribution used as a good approximation to the sampling distribution of $\bar{x}$.

Let's take a look at some examples of the true sampling distribution of $\bar{x}$ for various sample sizes, to see (visually) when the normal approximation can be safely used. The first example is that of rolling a fair die. We saw in Chapter 2 that there are six outcomes, 1 through 6, and each has a probability of outcome of $\frac{1}{6}$. In symbols, this is:

$$P(1) = P(2) = P(3) = P(4) = P(5) = P(6) = \tfrac{1}{6}.$$

This parent distribution is graphed in Figure 12.6. Notice that it is a discrete version of the uniform distribution.

FIGURE 12.6
The Probability Distribution for Rolling a Fair Die

Using this parent distribution, let's look at the distribution of the sample average if the fair die is rolled three times. This distribution is given in Figure 12.7. Although you have the ability to calculate this distribution, the calculations are tedious so only the results will be given. Those students who are interested in finding out how this distribution was derived can use the concepts given in Problem 2 to calculate the exact sampling distribution shown here.

The distribution shown in Figure 12.7 clearly has many of the characteristics of a normal distribution. It is symmetrical, high in the middle, and tapers off on both sides. However, in one important aspect it is quite different from the normal distribution. Whereas this distribution can only take on the discrete values 1, $\frac{4}{3}$, $\frac{5}{3}$, 2, . . . , 6, the normal distribution is used for a continuous random variable, and can

FIGURE 12.7
The Sampling Distribution of x̄ When a Fair Die is Rolled 3 Times

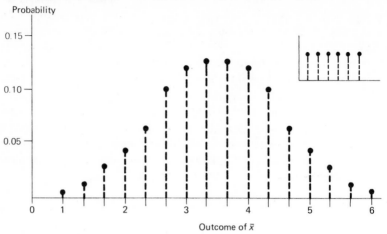

Probability

Outcome of x̄

take on all values between $-\infty$ and $+\infty$. Because of this disparity between the actual and approximate sampling distributions, how can we possibly use the normal distribution as an approximation? The answer lies in considering the probabilities of various intervals. When we do that we will discover that they are essentially the same, and thus the normal distribution is a good approximation to the sampling distribution of x̄, even if the true distribution is discrete and the approximate distribution is continuous.

A good method to show that the true and approximate sampling distributions are equivalent is to consider probability statements of the form:

$$P(\bar{x} \geq a)$$

for both the true and approximate distributions. If the values we get for each are roughly the same we will say that one distribution is a good approximation of the other. For example, from the true distribution the probability that the sample mean with be $3\frac{1}{2}$ or more,

$$P(\bar{x} \geq 3\frac{1}{2})$$

is $\frac{1}{2}$. (It is easy to see that this is so because the distribution is symmetrical, and $3\frac{1}{2}$ is the midpoint of the distribution.)

In order to compare what the value of $P(\bar{x} \geq 3\frac{1}{2})$ is for the normal approximation, we must know the mean, μ, and standard deviation, σ, of the approximating distribution. We establish these values in an absolutely sensible way. *We choose a mean and standard deviation for the approximating distribution that are equivalent to the mean and standard deviation for the true distribution.* Thus, if we were to analyze the sampling distribution represented in Figure 12.7 we would find

$$E(\bar{x}) = 3\tfrac{1}{2}$$
$$\text{Var}(\bar{x}) = \tfrac{35}{36}.$$

Therefore, for our normal approximation we should set

$$\mu = 3\tfrac{1}{2} \text{ and } \sigma = \sqrt{\frac{35}{36}} = 0.986.$$

Using these values the probability that $\bar{x}$ is greater than or equal to $3\tfrac{1}{2}$, *using the normal approximation is* $\tfrac{1}{2}$.[2] Thus in this case the true and approximate sampling distributions have the same cumulative probabilities.

What about the comparative probabilities for other intervals? Table 12.3 gives the values for $P(\bar{x} \geq a)$ for various values of a for both

TABLE 12.3
A Comparison of $P(\bar{x} \geq a)$ between the True Sampling Distribution of $\bar{x}$ and the Approximate Normal Sampling Distribution of $\bar{x}$ for Various Values of a

Value of a	True $P(\bar{x} \geq a)$	Approximate $P(\bar{x} \geq a)$
$\tfrac{1}{2}$	1	0.9988
$1\tfrac{1}{2}$	0.9815	0.9788
$2\tfrac{1}{2}$	0.8380	0.8450
$3\tfrac{1}{2}$	0.5	0.5
$4\tfrac{1}{2}$	0.1620	0.1550
$5\tfrac{1}{2}$	0.0185	0.0212
$6\tfrac{1}{2}$	0	0.0012

the true and approximate distributions. You can see that the two sets of probabilities are quite similar, and this verifies that the normal distribution provides a good approximation to the sampling distribution of $\bar{x}$ in this case.

Although we got somewhat sidetracked by a demonstration that the normal distribution provided a good approximation to the true sampling distribution, we can now return to the main theme of this section, which is an investigation of at what point (i.e., at what minimum sample size) does the normal distribution become a good approximation to the true sampling distribution of $\bar{x}$? The startling results for this case are: *When the parent distribution is uniform, as in Figure 12.6, the normal approximation holds for a sample as small as size 3.* This is indeed a

---

[2] We have not discussed in this text how to find this probability, so the reader will have to accept this answer without justification.

comforting confirmation that the central limit theorem can be used as a practical tool. While we will show that other parent distributions require larger sample sizes before the normal approximation can be used, we will find that the minimum sample size never becomes excessive.

Let us now consider two other illustrations of the applicability of the central limit theorem. Since the probabilistic verification is cumbersome, we will confine this discussion to looking at graphs. Therefore, we will only be able to get a "feel" for when the normal distribution would be an adequate approximation to the true sampling distribution, yet, just as in the previous example, we will find that our graphical ability is correct, and could be verified by extensive probability calculations if we were so inclined.

Suppose a loaded die is rolled. This die is weighted so that the outcomes are no longer equally probable. Instead, the probability of the outcomes 1 and 6 is $\frac{1}{4}$, the probability of 2 and 5 is $\frac{1}{6}$, and the probability of 3 and 4 is $\frac{1}{12}$. The probability distribution of this random variable, which will be the parent distribution for this example, is shown in Figure 12.8.

FIGURE 12.8
The Probability Distribution of Rolling a Loaded Die

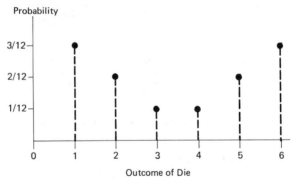

Now let's see what the true sampling distribution of $\bar{x}$ looks like. Figure 12.9 shows the true sampling distribution of $\bar{x}$ for a sample of size 3. Unfortunately, unlike the previous example, this distribution cannot be approximated by a normal distribution. For example, notice that the middle values are actually lower than some of the more extreme values, and this behavior is *not* true of the normal distribution. However, as Figure 12.10 illustrates, if we increase the sample size to 7, you see that the true sampling distribution is very close to a normal distribution. Therefore, when we start with a parent distribution like that illustrated in Figure 12.8, a sample of size 7 is big enough so that the central limit theorem can be used.

FIGURE 12.9
The Sampling Distribution of x̄ When the Loaded Die is Rolled 3 Times

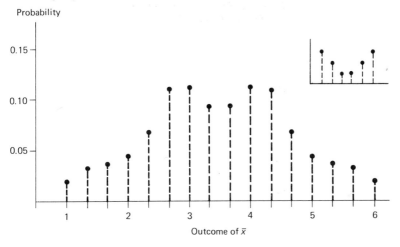

FIGURE 12.10
The Sampling Distribution of x̄ When the Loaded Die is Rolled 7 Times

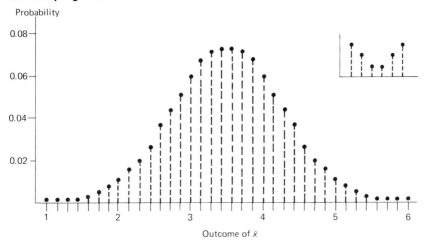

As a final parent distribution we will choose the probability distribution of the number of sixes that occur when two fair dice are rolled. In this case, the probability of no sixes is $^{25}\!/_{36}$, the probability of one six is $^{10}\!/_{26}$, and the probability of two sixes is $^{1}\!/_{36}$. Therefore our parent distribution will be

$$P(0) = {}^{25}\!/_{36}, \; P(1) = {}^{10}\!/_{36}, \; P(2) = {}^{1}\!/_{36},$$

and this distribution is graphed in Figure 12.11.

FIGURE 12.11
The Probability Distribution of the
Number of Sixes That Appear When
Two Fair Dice are Rolled

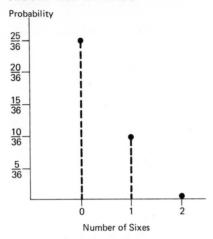

Consider taking a sample of size 7 from this distribution. The true distribution of the sample average is shown in Figure 12.12. Ignoring

FIGURE 12.12
The Sampling Distribution of $\bar{x}$ When Two Fair Dice are Rolled 7 Times

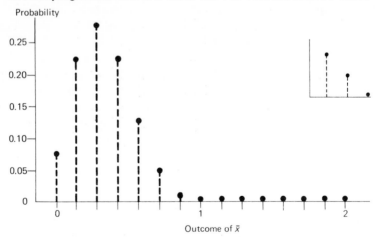

the values with very small probability between $\bar{x} = 1$ and $\bar{x} = 2$, the remainder of the distribution looks roughly like a normal distribution. However, the approximation is probably not really close because the left-hand side of the distribution is different from the right-hand side.

That is, the distribution is not symmetrical. Therefore, we will consider larger sample sizes.

If the sample size is increased to 11, as illustrated in Figure 12.13,

FIGURE 12.13
The Sampling Distribution of x̄ When Two Fair Dice are Rolled 11 Times

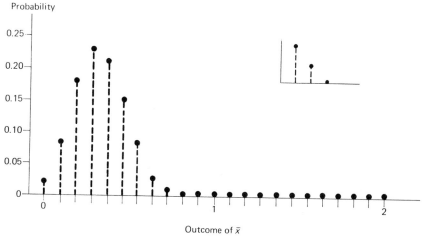

Outcome of x̄

we see that, although the true sampling distribution retains some of its asymmetry, it now looks very much like a normal distribution, and it seems reasonable that the central limit theorem can be used.

There are several conclusions that can be drawn from these examples. First, and most importantly, the sample size needed before we can use the normal approximation is usually quite small—say $n \leq 15$. Furthermore, the form of the true sampling distribution depends upon the form of the parent distribution from which the sample was drawn, and the rapidity with which this true sampling distribution becomes similar to a normal distribution depends upon the form of the parent distribution. Finally, we should emphasize that the normal approximation becomes better and better as the sample size increases. Thus, if the normal distribution is a good approximation for the distribution of x̄ when the sample size is ten ($n = 10$), it will be an even better approximation for a sample of size fifteen ($n = 15$), etc.

12.1.4 A Recap

Since we have been heavily involved in the science of statistics in this section, and statistics is peripheral to the objective of this book, it is helpful to summarize what we have discussed, and to give a prognosis of what lies ahead.

We have found that whenever we are interested in knowing the value of a *parameter* of a population probability distribution, the science of statistics comes into play. This science says that instead of taking a complete censes of the population we will take a *sample,* which is a representative small group of the population, and perform our measurements on this small group. From the sample data we gather we will take one value (which usually results from a reduction of the data in some way, viz., the sample average) and use that value to "represent" the parameter of interest in the population. Thus, the sample average is taken as the representative of the population mean, a sample proportion is taken as representative of some population probability, etc. Furthermore, since the sample value will vary from sample to sample, we say that it is a random variable, and seek its probability distribution, because its probability distribution must be known for us to be able to use it in our decision problems. *Fortunately,* for the situation we are studying in this chapter, namely, that of making a decision based upon an unknown *mean,* the problem in many cases becomes vastly simplified because we have a result known as the central limit theorem, which says that for a sufficiently large sample, and *any* population distribution, the normal distribution will be a good approximation to the probability distribution of the sample average.

12.2 UPDATING A NORMAL PRIOR WITH NORMAL SAMPLING

Now that the reader understands the rudiments of statistics we can turn back to the problem discussed at the beginning of the chapter, namely how to solve problems in which the mean is the unknown event. In Section 12.1 we learned two important things that will allow us to tackle such problems. The first is that the relevant way to reduce the sample outcome data when the mean is the unknown quantity of interest is to calculate the sample average. Throughout the rest of this chapter the sample average will be used as the sole representative of the sample outcome. The other important tool we have obtained from Section 12.1 is that the sample average is approximately normally distributed, no matter what the form of the distribution from which the sample is obtained. Thus, we have a situation in which, for all intents and purposes, the sampling distribution is always normal. Furthermore, in Chapter 11 we saw that the normal distribution provides a reasonable form for the prior distribution in these problems. Therefore, for all the problems we will consider in the remainder of this chapter we will assume that *both* the prior distribution and the sampling distribution are normal. While these assumptions make the problem very tractable to analysis, and are very reasonable, they do lead to confusion. It is important in all that follows that the reader carefully distinguish between the *prior* normal distribution, and its parameter values, and the *sampling* normal distribution and its parameter value.

In this section the problem of making a terminal decision when a sample outcome is already known will be analyzed. The reader will discover that the approach is exactly the same as in Chapters 5 and 8. Then the final section will discuss how to obtain an optimal sample when sampling is being considered.

A very powerful result, which we cannot verify, can be represented by the following diagram:

$$\text{Normal Prior} \xrightarrow[\text{Distribution of } \bar{x}]{\text{Normal Sampling}} \text{Normal Posterior;}$$
$$\text{on } m \hspace{6.5cm} \text{on } m$$

that is, if we have a normal prior on our unknown quantity (the mean) and if the sampling distribution of the sample average is normal, then the posterior distribution of m is also normal. This very important fact, coupled with the formulas given below for the values of the posterior parameters, will be all that we need to make decisions when a sample outcome is known.

When a sample outcome is known, we assume the following information is available:

About the prior distribution:
    Its expected value: $E_o(m)$
    Its variance: $\sigma_o{}^2(m)$

About the parent distribution from which the sample is obtained:
    Its variance: s^2

About the sample outcome:
    Its average: $\bar{x}$
    Its size: n.

This is just the information one would expect to have, perhaps with the exception of the variance of the parent distribution. While it seems to be restrictive to require this information to be known, the decision problem would be much more complex if it were not known (it would become a problem with *two* uncertain events), and we will limit ourselves to a discussion of problems where only the mean is unknown. Such an assumption is not unreasonable in some situations, especially those in which the mean is likely to vary between decision problems but the variance is not. For instance, we will assume in solving the Nadir problem that the mean yield of iron ore will vary from field to field, but that the variation of iron ore content *within* a field will not vary across fields. Thus, if Nadir has analyzed other fields in the past they may have found that they can guess quite accurately how much the iron ore content will vary within any field by knowing the similarity in variances among previously explored fields.

Given these five quantities, and the assumptions of normality for the prior and sampling distributions, the posterior distribution is normal with: An expected value, $E_1(m)$, of

$$E_1(m) = \frac{\dfrac{E_0(m)}{\sigma_0{}^2(m)} + \dfrac{n\bar{x}}{s^2}}{\dfrac{1}{\sigma_0{}^2(m)} + \dfrac{n}{s^2}}$$

and a variance, $\sigma_1{}^2(m)$, of

$$\sigma_1{}^2(m) = \frac{1}{\dfrac{1}{\sigma_0{}^2(m)} + \dfrac{n}{s^2}}.$$

Let's take an example. Recall from Chapter 11 that the prior distribution selected by Nadir management was a normal distribution with an expected value, $E_0(m)$, of 150 and a standard deviation, $\sigma_0(m)$, of 20. Thus, the variance, $\sigma_0{}^2(m)$, is 400. Suppose Nadir decided to perform sampling in the field on which they have the option, and they are willing to assume that the variance of iron ore content within fields is constant, and has a value of 550. Then if a sample of size 20 yields a sample average of 164, the posterior distribution of the mean, m, is normal and has an expected value of:

$$E_1(m) = \frac{\dfrac{E_0(m)}{\sigma_0{}^2(m)} + \dfrac{n\bar{x}}{s^2}}{\dfrac{1}{\sigma_0{}^2(m)} + \dfrac{n}{s^2}} = \frac{\dfrac{150}{400} + \dfrac{20 \times 164}{550}}{\dfrac{1}{400} + \dfrac{20}{550}} = 163.1,$$

and a variance of

$$\sigma_1{}^2(m) = \frac{1}{\dfrac{1}{\sigma_0{}^2(m)} + \dfrac{n}{s^2}} = \frac{1}{\dfrac{1}{400} + \dfrac{20}{550}} = 25.73.$$

Before we discuss how to use these numbers in a decision problem, it is helpful to look at the values to get a feeling for how the posterior distribution is affected by the prior and sampling distributions. Let's first consider the posterior mean. The mean of the prior (150) is lower than the sample average (164), so the mean of the posterior is forced upward as a result of the sample outcome. How close to 164 the value comes depends upon the relative values of the variances. In this case the variance of the prior (400) is large relative to the variance of the field (adjusted for sample size; 550/20). The result of this is a drastic decrease in the posterior variance and a posterior mean which is very close to the sample mean.

Now let us turn to the decision aspects of such a problem. If the prior and sampling occurred as stated above, which decision—let the option lapse (L), or start mining (M)—should Nadir make? In Chapter 11 we learned that the expected value of the prior distribution can be compared to the breakeven point $(m_b = 160$ in this case) to determine which action should be taken. *However,* if a sample outcome is known, then the expected value of the posterior distribution replaces the expected value of the prior in the decision rule. In this case we have $E_1(m)$ greater than m_b, and the best action for large values of m is to mine the field (M). Therefore, once we have calculated the expected value of the posterior (163.1 in this case) the decision of which action to take is easily determined.

As a final analysis, let us consider the cost of uncertainty at this point. Recall (from Chapter 11) that the cost of uncertainty with only the prior information is $\mathcal{E}(L) = \$49,450$, and the formula for the cost of uncertainty is

$$\mathcal{E}(A) = |k|\sigma(m)L_{N*}(D)$$

where:

A is the best action;

$|k|$ is a constant obtained from the slopes of the loss functions (12,500 in this problem);

$\sigma(m)$ is the standard deviation of the normal distribution, which expresses the uncertainty about the value of m;

D is the number of standard deviations between the expected value and m_b,

$$= \frac{|E(m) - m_b|}{\sigma(m)}; \text{ and}$$

$L_{N*}(D)$ is obtained from Table II at the back of this text.

In this case the best action is M, and the values of $E(m)$ and $\sigma(m)$ will be those from the posterior distribution, $E_1(m)$ and $\sigma_1(m)$. Thus,

$$D = \frac{|E_1(m) - m_b|}{\sigma_1(m)} = \frac{|163.1 - 160|}{\sqrt{25.73}} = 0.6111,$$

$$L_{N*}(D) = 0.1656,$$

and

$$\mathcal{E}(M) = 12,500 \times \sqrt{25.73} \times 0.1656$$
$$= \$10,500,$$

and the cost of uncertainty has dropped considerably as a result of taking the sample.

Unfortunately, it is not always true that sampling will decrease the cost of uncertainty. We first encountered a situation in which a sample increased the uncertainty in Section 8.2.2. We will give another example here to demonstrate the principle again.

Suppose we again take a sample of size 20 from the field, and the sample average is 164, but the variance of the field is 7,500 instead of 550. Given this change, the posterior distribution has an expected value of

$$E_1(m) = \frac{\dfrac{150}{400} + \dfrac{20 \times 164}{7,500}}{\dfrac{1}{400} + \dfrac{20}{7,500}} = 157.2,$$

and a variance of

$$\sigma_1{}^2(m) = \frac{1}{\dfrac{1}{400} + \dfrac{20}{7,500}} = 193.55.$$

With these values

$$D = \frac{|157.2 - 160|}{\sqrt{193.55}} = 0.2013,$$

and

$$L_{N*}(D) = L_{N*}(0.2013) = 0.3064.$$

Therefore, the expected opportunity loss for the best action (L) is

$$\begin{aligned}\mathcal{E}(L) &= 12,500 \times \sqrt{193.55} \times 0.3064 \\ &= \$53,280.\end{aligned}$$

Thus, here we have a situation that has increased the expected opportunity loss instead of decreasing it. It is characteristic of samples that this situation will sometimes arise, and it is important to analyze these situations to understand better the mechanisms contributing to expected opportunity loss.

It would be easy in this case to attribute the difference to the change in variance, yet the real reason is more subtle than that. No matter how large the variance within the field is, the result of taking any sample is that the posterior variance is smaller than the prior variance. In this case the variance of m decreased from 400 to 193.55. On the other hand, the sample outcome caused the posterior expected value to move toward the breakeven point. The effect of this move is to increase the expected opportunity loss. In this case the increase in $L_{N*}(D)$ value more than compensated for the decrease in $\sigma(m)$ value, and the net result was that the expected opportunity loss of the best action increased. Thus, the increase in expected opportunity loss is caused by the posterior expected value being much closer to the breakeven point than the prior expected value was.

12.3 DETERMINING STRATEGIES WHEN THE SAMPLE SIZE IS FIXED

Given the material we have discussed above, we are now ready to consider a situation in which a sample is to be considered, and we will want to know *if* sampling is appropriate, and if so, how large the sample should be. We will begin in this section by considering a fixed sample size, to show how the optimal strategy and the expected value of sample information can be calculated. Then in Section 12.4, we consider the larger problem of the determination of an optimal sample size.

What happens when the sample size is fixed? Before the sample is taken we can talk about a strategy, which in this case is a decision rule about which action to take for various values of the sample outcome, $\bar{x}$. The easiest way to see how to derive this strategy is to consider the $E(m)$ versus m_b rule in relation to the posterior distribution, which could be obtained after the sample outcome is known. It is helpful to work with an example, so let's consider what strategy Nadir would develop for their problem if they had decided on a sample of size 9. *If* the value of $\bar{x}$ were known (which it is not at this point), then the best action could be determined by calculating the expected value of the posterior distribution:

$$E_1(m) = \frac{\dfrac{E_0(m)}{\sigma_0{}^2(m)} + \dfrac{n\bar{x}}{s^2}}{\dfrac{1}{\sigma_0{}^2(m)} + \dfrac{n}{s^2}},$$

and then comparing the value of $E_1(m)$ to m_b to obtain a decision rule. Since we don't know the value of $\bar{x}$ we cannot carry through these calculations. However, we can do them conceptually and obtain a strategy for this sampling situation.

In this case the action M is taken whenever $E_1(m) > m_b$. When $E_1(m)$ is reexpressed in terms of the prior and sample values this relation becomes: Choose M whenever

$$\frac{\dfrac{E_0(m)}{\sigma_0{}^2(m)} + \dfrac{n\bar{x}}{s^2}}{\dfrac{1}{\sigma_0{}^2(m)} + \dfrac{n}{s^2}} > m_b.$$

The above expression can be rearranged to isolate $\bar{x}$ and we have:
Choose M whenever

$$\bar{x} > \frac{\dfrac{m_b}{\sigma_1^2(m)} - \dfrac{E_0(m)}{\sigma_0^2(m)}}{\dfrac{n}{s^2}},$$

and where

$$\sigma_1^2(m) = \frac{1}{\dfrac{1}{\sigma_0^2(m)} + \dfrac{n}{s^2}}.$$

Now if n is fixed, then the value of the right-hand side of the above inequality can be calculated. Let

$$c^* = \frac{\dfrac{m_b}{\sigma_1^2(m)} - \dfrac{E_0(m)}{\sigma_0^2(m)}}{\dfrac{n}{s^2}},$$

and the strategy becomes the simple statement:

Choose M whenever $\bar{x} > c^*$.

Now this is really only half a strategy, because it does not tell us what action to choose when $\bar{x} \leq c^*$, but it should be fairly obvious to the reader that the complete strategy is again (just as in Chapters 6–10) a cutoff point strategy, viz.:

Choose M if $\bar{x} > c^*$ and choose L if $\bar{x} < c^*$.

Therefore, the cutoff point part of the strategy is easy to obtain.

Let's consider some numbers. For the sample of size 9, and assuming again that $E_0(m) = 150$, $\sigma_0^2(m) = 400$, $m_b = 160$, and $s^2 = 550$, we have

$$\sigma_1^2(m) = \frac{1}{\dfrac{1}{400} + \dfrac{9}{550}} = 53.01,$$

and

$$c^* = \frac{\dfrac{160}{53.01} - \dfrac{150}{400}}{\dfrac{9}{550}} = 161.5.$$

Thus, whenever a sample of size 9 has an $\bar{x}$ greater than 161.5, the optimal action is M, while if $\bar{x}$ is less than 161.5, the best action is L.

In order to compare various sample sizes we need methods for calculating both the form and value of the optimal strategy. Fortunately, a formula exists for calculating the strategy's value. It can be shown that the expected value of sample information (EVSI) of the strategy can be calculated by

$$\text{EVSI} = |k|\lambda L_{N*}(F),$$

where:

$|k|$ is obtained from the slopes of the loss functions;
λ is calculated from the variances of the prior and the parent distribution and the sample size, and

$$\lambda = \frac{\sigma_0^2(m)}{\sqrt{\sigma_0^2(m) + \dfrac{s^2}{n}}};$$

and

$$F = \frac{|m_b - E_0(m)|}{\lambda}.$$

If we are trying to determine whether a sample of a particular size should be taken, we can compare this value of the sample to it's cost. This will be the procedure followed in the next section.

Let's take an example of calculating the value of a strategy. For the Nadir problem, if the sample is of size 9, then

$$\lambda = \frac{\sigma_0^2(m)}{\sqrt{\sigma_0^2(m) + \dfrac{s^2}{n}}}$$

$$= \frac{400}{\sqrt{400 + \dfrac{550}{9}}} = 18.63,$$

and

$$F = \frac{|160 - 150|}{18.63} = 0.5368,$$

so

$$L_{N*}(F) = 0.1867,$$

and

$$\begin{aligned}
\text{EVSI} &= |k|\lambda L_{N*}(F)\\
&= 12{,}500 \times 18.63 \times 0.1867 = \$43{,}480.
\end{aligned}$$

This represents a significant savings, considering that the cost of uncertainty for the prior distribution is \$49,450. The net savings realized will depend upon the sample cost, of course, but the potential looks very good in this case.

12.4 FINDING THE OPTIMAL SAMPLE SIZE

Now that we know how to determine the form of the optimal strategy for any fixed sample size and determine its value, we are ready to consider the larger question of how big a sample (if any) should be taken. To do this we merely consider the net value of the sample after the sample cost has been subtracted, and then determine the optimal sample size by trial and error on all potential sample sizes.

In order to discuss an example we need a sample cost function. Suppose in the Nadir problem we assume the sample cost function is

$$\text{Sample Cost} = \$30,000 + \$1,000n.$$

Then the optimal sample size is obtained by first considering a sample of size one ($n = 1$) and calculating its value (EVSI) relative to its cost. Then the value versus cost for $n = 2$ is calculated, etc. The process is continued until the cost of the sample alone would exceed the expected opportunity loss of the best immediate action (without sampling). Then all the values obtained are searched to find the optimal sample size; i.e., the one whose net value,

$$\text{EVSI} - \text{Sample Cost},$$

is highest. If this net value is negative, then we know it is better not to sample, while if it is positive then sampling is better and the optimal sample size is the one with the highest net value.

Figure 12.14 graphically illustrates this idea. If EVSI is considered as a function of sample size, n, it is usually S-shaped, as shown in part A of the figure. Although linearity is not a requirement for the solution of these problems, we shall consider only linear sample cost functions. Two such cost functions are displayed in part B of the figure.

The net value of a sampling plan is the difference between the EVSI for a strategy and the cost of that strategy. Part C of Figure 12.14 graphs the EVSI curve of part A with sample cost function (1). There is a range of sample sizes for which EVSI is greater than sample cost. Therefore, in this situation it is worthwhile to sample, and the sample size which maximizes the difference between EVSI and sample cost will be the optimum sample size.

In contrast to the situation depicted in part C, part D shows the EVSI curve compared with sample cost function (2). Here there is no value of n for which EVSI is greater than sampling cost. Hence, no

FIGURE 12.14

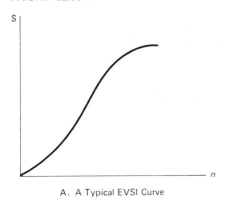

A. A Typical EVSI Curve

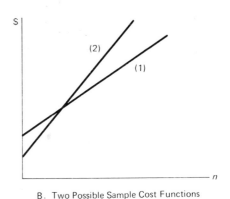

B. Two Possible Sample Cost Functions

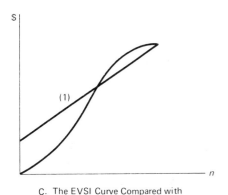

C. The EVSI Curve Compared with
Sample Cost Function (1)

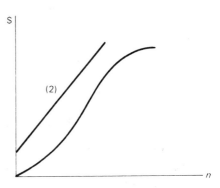

D. The EVSI Curve Compared with
Sample Cost Function (2)

sample should be taken. Instead, the optimal terminal action should be chosen.

For the Nadir problem we would begin by calculating an upper bound on the number of n values we would have to search by comparing the sample cost function to the expected opportunity loss of making a decision with only the prior information. In this case we have

$$30,000 + 1,000n > 49,450,$$

and this is true when

$$n > 19.45.$$

Therefore, we need not consider samples larger than 19, since any of these would have a sample cost alone that would exceed the cost of making an immediate decision.

For all values of n between 1 and 19 the net value of sampling must be determined. Clearly this will be a tedious procedure, best done by computer. We will illustrate three such calculations in the text, then summarize the results of all the calculations in Table 12.4. For $n = 1$ we have:

$$\lambda = \frac{400}{\sqrt{400 + \dfrac{550}{1}}} = 12.98,$$

$$F = \frac{|160 - 150|}{12.98} = 0.7704,$$

$$L_{N*}(F) = 0.1266,$$

and

$$\text{EVSI} = 12,500 \times 12.98 \times 0.1266 = \$20,540.$$

The sample cost for $n = 1$ is

$$\text{Sample Cost} = 30,000 + 1,000 \times 1 = \$31,000.$$

Therefore, the net value is

$$20,540 - 31,000 = -\$10,460.$$

Unfortunately, just because the net value of a sample of size 1 is negative we cannot quit and say that no sample would be profitable. For example, we have already found that the EVSI for a sample of size 9 is \$43,480, while the cost of this sample is only \$39,000. Thus, this sample would yield a net positive benefit, and the fact that the net value for $n = 1$ is negative is not enough to stop our analysis.

Continuing the analysis, for $n = 2$ we have

$$\lambda = \frac{400}{\sqrt{400 + \dfrac{550}{2}}} = 15.40,$$

$$F = \frac{|160 - 150|}{15.4} = 0.6494,$$

$$L_{N*}(F) = 0.1556,$$

and

$$\text{EVSI} = 12,500 \times 15.4 \times 0.1555 = \$29,950$$

Therefore, the net value is

$$29,950 - 32,000 = -\$2,050.$$

Finally, we will illustrate the calculations for $n = 3$. For this sample size we have

$$\lambda = \frac{400}{\sqrt{400 + \dfrac{550}{3}}} = 16.56,$$

$$F = \frac{|160 - 150|}{16.56} = 0.6039,$$

$$L_{N*}(F) = 0.1676,$$

and

$$EVSI = 12,500 \times 16.56 \times 0.1676 = 34,690.$$

Therefore, the net value for $n = 3$ is

$$34,690 - 33,000 = \$1,690.$$

This obviously tedious set of calculations will not be continued here. Instead, the set of sample sizes, EVSIs, and net value is given in Table

TABLE 12.4
Analysis of the Nadir Data to Determine the Optimum Sample Size

Sample Size (n)	Expected Value of Sample Information (EVSI)	Sample Cost	Net Value of Sample
1	$20,540	$31,000	$-10,460
2	29,950	32,000	-2,050
3	34,690	33,000	1,690
4	37,590	34,000	3,590
5	39,550	35,000	4,550
6	40,940	36,000	4,940
7	41,990	37,000	4,990
8	42,800	38,000	4,800
9	43,460	39,000	4,460
10	44,000	40,000	4,000
11	44,450	41,000	3,450
12	44,840	42,000	2,840
13	45,160	43,000	2,160
14	45,450	44,000	1,450
15	45,700	45,000	700
16	45,920	46,000	-80
17	46,110	47,000	-890
18	46,280	48,000	-1,720
19	46,440	49,000	-2,560

12.4. From the table we see that the sample size with the maximum net value is $n = 7$. Furthermore, since the net value for a sample of size 7 is positive, we know it is better to sample than to take an immediate action without sampling.

There is one additional calculation we must do to complete our analysis of the Nadir sampling problem, and that is to determine what the optimum strategy for a sample of size 7 will be. The optimum strategy is specified by the value of the cutoff point, c^*. In this case we have:

$$c^* = \frac{\dfrac{m_b}{\sigma_1{}^2(m)} - \dfrac{E_0(m)}{\sigma_0{}^2(m)}}{\dfrac{n}{s^2}},$$

and we know that $m_b = 160$, $E_0(m) = 150$, $\sigma_0{}^2(m) = 400$, $n = 7$, and $s^2 = 550$; so,

$$\sigma_1{}^2(m) = \frac{1}{\dfrac{1}{400} + \dfrac{7}{550}} = 65.67,$$

and

$$c^* = \frac{\dfrac{160}{65.67} - \dfrac{150}{400}}{\dfrac{7}{550}} = 162.0.$$

Therefore, the optimal strategy for Nadir is:

> Take 7 core samples randomly from the field. If the average yield of iron ore is 162 lbs. per ton of ore or more, then mine the field. Otherwise (i.e., if $\bar{x} < 162$) let your option lapse.

There is one more topic that will aid in finding the optimal sample size. This topic concerns the possibility of obtaining a tighter bound on the maximum number of samples that must be considered. We saw in the binomial sampling problems of Chapter 7 that the upper bound on n could be tightened if better expected losses (than those for the immediate actions) were encountered as the various sample sizes were analyzed. We will find we can do the same thing here. Before we do this, however, we must give the relationship between the EVSI of a sampling plan and its expected loss. Up to this point we have considered only the value of taking a sample relative to its cost, and have not discussed what its overall expected loss would be.

The formula for the overall expected loss for any sample is very straightforward. It is the expected loss of the best immediate action (the cost of uncertainty) minus the net value of the sample. For the Nadir problem the best immediate action is L, and

$$\mathcal{E}(L) = \$49,450.$$

Thus, for the optimal sample size of 7, whose net value is $4,990, the expected loss is $49,450 minus $4,990, which is $44,460. This figure, or the expected loss for any "good" sample, can then be used to decrease the number of sample sizes that need to be considered. In this case, using the expected loss for a sample of size 7, we have

$$30,000 + 1,000n > 44,460$$
$$\text{if } n > 14.5.$$

Therefore, after finding that a sample of size 7 has good potential, we could have used its overall expected loss to lower the total number of samples considered to 14.

The procedure illustrated above for finding the optimal sample size works well if the range of potential sample sizes that must be searched is relatively small. If this is not the case, then other procedures must be used. One method which could be used would be to have a computer routine that would determine the optimal sample size. Except for the fact that the $L_{N*}(D)$ table would have to be part of the program, efficient search techniques, lucidly described in Wilde's book,[3] could be used to quickly find the optimum sample size. The other method would be to use a nomographic technique, such as the one described in Schlaifer.[4]

12.5 SUMMARY

We have found in this chapter that problems in which the value of the mean is the unknown event can be solved quite simply if the prior distribution is assumed to be normal, and if the sample size is large enough so that the sampling distribution of $\bar{x}$, the relevant statistic in this case, is approximately normal also. We began with a long discussion of the science of statistics, and why it is important to know statistics in order to do advanced work in decision theory. Solving any problem beyond the simple binomial sampling problems requires enough knowledge of statistics to determine a good estimator for the unknown event. In the problems of this chapter, the value of the mean is the unknown event, and we spent a good portion of the chapter discussing the use of the sample average as an appropriate statistic, and its approximate sampling distribution, the normal.

The remainder of the chapter was devoted to solving problems with normal priors and normal sampling distributions. While the calculations are messy and tedious, the concepts are very straightforward. The most important concept used in working these problems is that a normal

---

[3] Douglass J. Wilde, *Optimum Seeking Methods* (Prentice-Hall, Inc., 1964).

[4] Robert Schlaifer, *Introduction to Statistics for Business Decisions,* (McGraw-Hill, 1961), pp. 333–35.

prior combined with a normal sampling distribution yields a normal posterior distribution. This fact, plus the concept of an exhaustive search to find the optimum sample size form the core of all the ideas used to solve normal problems.

PROBLEMS

1. Consider the simple random process discussed in Section 12.1.3, in which a fair coin is flipped and the outcome heads is given the value 1, and the outcome tails is given a value of zero.

   a. Determine the sampling distribution of $\bar{x}$ if the coin is flipped four times.

   b. Determine the sampling distribution of $\bar{x}$ if the coin is flipped five times.

   c. Suppose the coin is not fair, and the probability of a head occurring is 0.7. Now what is the sampling distribution of $\bar{x}$ if the coin is flipped five times?

2. A straightforward method that can be used to generate some sampling distributions is to develop a series of joint probability tables. For instance, for the data in Table 12.2,

Value of x	Probability
0	⅜
1	⅛
2	⅛
3	⅜

   the probability distribution for two outcomes from this distribution can be obtained by making a two-way table in which the values of the first outcome are listed along one margin, and the values of the second outcome are listed along the other. The body of the table then contains the joint probability that both of these outcomes will occur, and this joint probability is the product of the two individual probabilities, since the two outcomes are (assumed to be) independent. Thus, the upper right-hand box in the table below gives the probability that the first outcome is a zero and the second a 3, and the value of this probability is ⅜ times ⅜, or %₆₄.

Second Outcome

	0	1	2	3
0	⅜ × ⅜	⅜ × ⅛	⅜ × ⅛	⅜ × ⅜
1	⅛ × ⅜	⅛ × ⅛	⅛ × ⅛	⅛ × ⅜
2	⅛ × ⅜	⅛ × ⅛	⅛ × ⅛	⅛ × ⅜
3	⅜ × ⅜	⅜ × ⅛	⅜ × ⅛	⅜ × ⅜

First Outcome

The probability of the *sum* of the values of the two outcomes can be easily obtained from the table by realizing that each table event is mutually exclusive (and thus their probabilities are additive) and that all combinations of first and second outcomes that make up any value of the sum occur on the same diagonal of the table. Thus, the overall probability that the sum of the two outcomes is 2 is $\frac{1}{8} \times \frac{3}{8} + \frac{1}{8} \times \frac{1}{8} + \frac{3}{8} \times \frac{1}{8}$, the sum of the probabilities of the various outcomes (2 and 0, 1 and 1, and 0 and 2, respectively) whose sum is 2.

This process can be continued beyond two outcomes by creating successive tables in which one of the margins contains the *sum* of all previous outcomes. Thus, if we were interested in the sampling distribution for the sum of three outcomes from this distribution a second table would be constructed with one margin containing the sum of the first two outcomes as values and the other margin would contain the values of the third outcome.

a. Use the method outlined above to derive the sampling distribution (as given in Table 12.1) of $\bar{x}$ when a fair coin is flipped three times.

b. Use this method to obtain the sampling distribution which is graphed in Figure 12.5.

c. Using the population distribution

Value of x	Probability
5	$\frac{1}{3}$
6	$\frac{1}{3}$
7	$\frac{1}{3}$

use the above method to find the sampling distribution of $\bar{x}$ for a sample of size 3.

3. Graph the sampling distributions of $\bar{x}$ in problems 1 and 2(*c*). Which would you say could be adequately approximated by a normal distribution?

4. Compare the graph of the probability distribution obtained in problem 2(*c*) with Figures 12.4 and 12.7 as to the likelihood that the normal distribution could be used as an approximation to these sampling distributions. If you feel that some of these three distributions can be adequately approximated by the normal distribution while others cannot, how do you reconcile this finding with the fact that all three distributions have uniform parent distributions, and are for a sample of size 3?

5. Calculate the sample average for the following sample outcomes.

a. 13, 15, 3, −5, 2

b. 1, 2, 4, 5, 3, 4, 4, 100

6. The heights of a random sample of men from the Los Angeles Heart Study are: 69, 67, 68, 70, 66, 70, 65, 69, and 68. What number

would you use as an estimate of the mean height of the population from which this sample was taken?

7. Suppose in the Nadir problem the prior distribution has an expected value—$E_0(m)$—of 150 and a variance—$\sigma_0^2(m)$—of 400. Determine the expected value and variance of the posterior distribution for sample outcomes with the following characteristics:

   a. $\bar{x} = 150$ with $n = 20$, $s^2 = 550$
   b. $\bar{x} = 160$ with $n = 2$, $s^2 = 550$
   c. $\bar{x} = 160$ with $n = 1,000,000$, $s^2 = 550$.

   Discuss why you obtained the answers you did.

8. Show that when $s^2 = 0$ for any problem, EVSI = EVPI. Why is this so? What does $s^2 = 0$ mean?

9. It is instructive to consider the relationship between $E_0(m)$ and $E_1(m)$ as n and s^2 change. Let $E_0(m) = 150$; $\sigma_0^2(m) = 400$, and $\bar{x} = 164$. Graph the value of $E_1(m)$ as a function of

   a. n for n between 0 and 50, with $s^2 = 550$;
   b. s^2 for s^2 between 0 and 1,500, with $n = 20$.

10. If, in the Nadir problem, $E_0(m) = 150$, $\sigma_0^2(m) = 400$, $s^2 = 2,000$, and for a sample of size 10, $\bar{x} = 162$, what is the best action, knowing this sample outcome, and what is its associated cost of uncertainty?

11. In previous chapters the overall expected loss of a sampling strategy is made up of two components—the expected opportunity loss of the sampling plan and the sample cost. The same is true for normal sampling problems. Using the relationships discussed in Section 12.4, show that the expected opportunity loss of a normal sampling plan is the difference between the expected loss of the best immediate action and the EVSI of the sample.

12. Consider the situation described in Problem 10, except that the sample of size 10 has not yet been taken, so the value of $\bar{x}$ is not known. For this case determine:

   a. The optimal strategy
   b. The EVSI of this strategy
   c. Using the results of Problem 11, calculate the expected opportunity loss for this strategy. Why is this value not the same as the cost of uncertainty obtained in Problem 10?

13. Suppose all numbers for the Nadir problem are the same as those used in Section 12.4, except the sample cost function is

$$\$35,000 + \$750n.$$

Find the optimal sample size for this problem. What is the overall expected loss for this sample size? Hint: Look carefully at Table 12.4 before doing a lot of calculations in this problem.

14. Suppose in the Nadir problem you have $E_0(m) = 150$, $\sigma_0^2(m) = 400$, $s^2 = 2,000$, and a sample cost function of $35,000 + $750n$. What is the optimal strategy in this case?

15. Suppose in the Nadir problem you have the same values as given in Problem 14, except the cost function is $2,500n$. What is the optimal strategy in this case?

16. In the American Steel problem (Problem 9 of Chapter 11), suppose samples can be taken from the molten material and analyzed for carbon content. If the standard deviation of carbon content within any batch is known to be 6 $(s = 6)$, and the sample cost function is

$$\text{Sample Cost} = \$275 + \$4.20n$$

    what is American's optimal strategy?

17. In the Joe Smith solar water heater problem (Problem 12 of Chapter 11) suppose Joe has the option, in order to gather better data on his family's daily hot water consumption, of installing a small water meter on the outlet pipe of his hot water heater. There is a fixed cost of $15 to have this done, plus Joe will need to spend about a minute a day reading the meter. Joe is not willing to cost such a small part of his time, and on the same depreciation basis as his other capital items the water meter would cost 0.0625. Should Joe gather some data before making a decision? If so, how much? The standard deviation for daily hot water use in Joe's family is 14.

18. In part (*d*) of Problem 12 in Chapter 11 we considered some sensitivity analysis on Joe's cost functions. Answer the questions posed in Problem 17 above if the true future estimate of conventional hot water costs is:

    a. $12 per month;
    b. $3 per month.

chapter

13

Toward a Practical Science

THE PREVIOUS CHAPTERS of this text dealt with two concepts. The first, exemplified by Chapters 3 through 5, dealt with establishing the basic concepts of decision theory. The second, expressed in Chapters 6 through 12, dealt with applying these concepts to the two most basic kinds of analysis that would be faced, namely the estimation of either a probability (Chapters 6 through 9) or a mean (Chapters 9 through 12). In both cases, the most elegant results, and those amenable to hand (as opposed to computer aided) solutions, had at their very core the following assumptions:

1. The payoff (cost) functions are linear;
2. The form (either binomial or normal) of the sampling distribution is known;
3. The prior distribution is conjugate to the sampling distribution.

These situations are discussed in Chapter 10 for the binomial sampling distribution, and in Chapters 11 and 12 for the normal sampling distribution.

One of the goals of this chapter is to give the student techniques by which he can divorce himself from the rigidity of these assumptions. The other goal is to discuss how prior distributions can be established. In all previous work they have been given to us, one might think, by divine providence. In the reality of life, of course, divine providence gives us nothing—we must labor for all that we have and want. The same is true for prior distributions, and the first section of this chapter will discuss how to establish usable prior distributions.

The second part of the chapter will then consider what happens when the assumptions given above are relaxed. Every problem must have some structure, or it cannot be solved. Therefore, one assumption will be retained, that of the sampling distribution form being known. The other two are the more likely to be uncertain, and that is where we will focus our time. As the reader may have already guessed, the assumption most often violated is the third one. Usually the prior distribution is not conjugate to the sampling distribution. Therefore, a large part of this chapter will be devoted to discussing how to solve such problems. We will find the mechanics quite complicated, but the concepts easy. The remainder of the chapter will then discuss the first assumption, that the payoff costs are linear, and explore how much that can be changed.

13.1 ESTABLISHING PRIOR DISTRIBUTIONS

In discussing prior distributions there are several divisions of the subject it will be useful to acknowledge. The first deals with the *number* of values the event can take on. If there are a finite number of events possible, such as the states of the weather in John's problem of Chapter 3, then the prior distribution used for the problem is *discrete*. On the other hand, if the event can take on any one of a range of values, such as the probability of a defective can in the Valley Sisters problem of Chapter 6, then the prior distribution is *continuous*. Therefore, the two characterizations of the prior distribution, discrete and continuous, refer to the number of events possible.

The second division of prior distributions is by the *source* of the distribution. Sometimes there is data that has been collected on the occurrence of the events in question. If this data can be considered reliable—i.e, if the future can be expected to follow the same relative occurrence patterns as the past—then this data can be used to establish a prior distribution. We will call the source of such data *historical*. The other option for obtaining data, when no valid historical data is available, is to obtain the "best guess" from the decision maker in the problem. In this case, there may be no historical data, and the decision maker must establish the prior distribution in a way consistent with his prior beliefs. Such a source will be called *subjective*. Clearly, if you were to ask two people for prior distributions concerning the same set of events, you would be likely to get two different distributions. This is the reason for the term "subjective." Realizing this, you may question whether decision theory can be used in this case. However, recall that decision theory is not a theory in the abstract sense the way physics determines the theory (laws) of nature. Rather, it is a set of procedures through whose use the decision maker can establish his uncertainties and use them in combination with his sample outcomes and payoff functions to make a rational decision. Therefore, eliciting a subjective distribution from the decision maker is absolutely consistent with decision theory.

When a subjective prior distribution is used in decision theory, it is the decision maker's "best guess" in the sense that it is consistent with his beliefs and assumptions. This is not the same as a guarantee that the after-the-fact correct action will always be selected by those who apply decision theory. It may be, in spite of the fact the decision maker is acting on his best guess as to beliefs and assumptions, that these beliefs and assumptions are wrong. Totally separate from this is the fact that uncertainty is inherent in these problems, and this too can lead to a situation in which the after-the-fact correct action is not the one chosen by decision theory.

Once the prior distributions have been classified in the above two ways we have four categories. Each category must be treated somewhat differently. Figure 13.1 illustrates the steps that must be taken to trans-

FIGURE 13.1
Establishing Prior Distributions and Making Them Useful

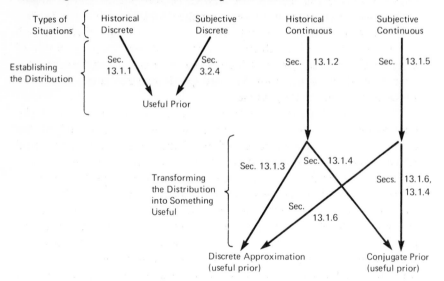

form the data in a certain situation into a form that can be used to solve a decision problem. In the case of discrete priors, there is a one-step process to the establishment of a useful prior. However, when one has continuous priors, there is a fairly distinct two-step process. The first involves *establishing* the prior, and the second involves *transforming* it into a useful form. In this case the usefulness of the prior is limited by our mathematical skills, and we must either develop from the data a conjugate prior (the *only* useful theoretical form) or, failing that, a discrete approximation to which we can apply numerical analysis techniques.

Figure 13.1 also indicates the subsections in which the various techniques will be discussed. All save the establishment of a subjective discrete prior will be illustrated in this chapter. The reader who needs to establish a subjective discrete prior can reread Section 3.2.4.

13.1.1 Using Historical Data to Establish a Discrete Prior

This situation is by far the easiest to understand and implement. It will serve as a good introduction and also set some ideas that will be used in the more complicated situations that follow. It is best to base the discussion on an example. We shall use the second example problem of Chapter 3 to illustrate the technique. In that problem, Mike was trying to choose between buying a new car or a used car, and the events were:

L = The used car will last less than one year
B = The used car will last between one and four years
M = The used car will last more than four years

We are assuming in this section that historical data is available. In this case, assume that Mike has polled enough of his friends and their experiences with used cars *similar to the ones he is considering* to obtain the following results:

Event	Frequency
L	28
B	65
M	12

That is, of all the experiences Mike's friends have had with used cars, 28 of these cars lasted less than a year, etc.

The development of a useful prior distribution from such data is very straightforward. The probability of each event is taken as the *relative frequency* of occurrence of the event in the historical data. Thus,

$$P(L) = \frac{28}{28 + 65 + 12} = \frac{28}{105} = 0.267,$$

$$P(B) = \frac{65}{105} = 0.619,$$

and

$$P(M) = \frac{12}{105} = 0.114.$$

Once these numbers are obtained, they can be used in any of the calculations in which a prior is required.

How does the total amount of experience affect this situation? Let's take the absurd case in which Mike is going to use data only on similar used cars *he* has bought, and he has bought only one used car in the past. Let's suppose that particular used car lasted less than one year. In this case, using historical data, Mike's prior would be:

$$P(L) = 1; \; P(B) = 0; \; P(M) = 0,$$

which is unrealistic. The error comes from Mike having too little relevant data to establish a realistic prior. In this case, Mike should use a subjective prior instead.

Unfortunately, there are no rules to tell an analyst when there is enough historical data so that it can be used to establish the prior distribution. The case with only one data point is absurdly obvious, but what about the case with five data points, or the case with 15 data points? We must stress that in reality all future projections are subjective. Every time historical data is used there is an implicit subjective judgment that the future will be the same as the past. The blind use of historical data is a false security blanket. Each situation must be evaluated for the adequacy of past data and its relevance to the future. There are no rules in this area. The best we can do is to warn the reader to consider carefully the adequacy and applicability of his historical data before using it to establish a prior.

13.1.2 Data Reduction to Establish a Frequency Distribution for a Historical Continuous Prior

Much work has been done in the field of statistics on the problem of establishing a continuous probability distribution from a given set of data. Unfortunately, we do not have the time, nor can we assume that the reader has the appropriate background to go into a complete analysis of these techniques. We will outline some possible approaches, and suggest references for the student who is interested in learning more about this field. Before that is done, however, we must start with an example of a set of data.

Suppose in the Valley Sisters problem that the company has collected data on 250 runs of their coffee-can filling machine. (That is about one year's worth of working days, if one run per day is made.) For each run they have determined the number of bad cans in that run. (Remember that each run consisted of 2,000 cans.) The results of this data collection are given in Table 13.1.

TABLE 13.1
The Number of Defectives in 250 Valley Sisters Runs

101	54	143	2	113	157	13	59	60	108
83	46	64	200	112	154	20	38	65	67
67	37	45	164	63	80	126	33	63	110
104	24	87	182	11	84	41	61	66	70
25	49	87	169	90	193	75	109	20	89
5	34	52	64	60	11	61	39	54	29
34	21	17	27	105	187	65	168	269	93
56	113	175	125	29	286	126	26	15	38
152	66	107	109	124	70	104	9	66	24
90	53	115	151	85	182	24	35	83	89
26	147	96	114	52	42	32	96	130	124
30	71	37	86	25	122	70	32	85	23
225	57	272	99	54	40	89	125	38	94
122	29	53	52	8	81	24	152	46	120
46	42	43	8	167	175	155	80	150	73
61	18	34	33	32	32	24	69	18	91
69	109	27	15	85	54	136	103	193	72
41	64	53	72	56	55	174	16	40	52
55	119	87	35	90	187	86	37	102	50
92	71	62	136	131	127	131	60	29	53
94	6	186	227	106	16	9	57	28	105
54	57	28	25	16	29	158	69	72	68
7	14	171	86	112	221	22	108	54	48
19	36	125	59	58	102	64	65	77	27
56	12	117	288	44	57	68	31	127	47

Thus, the first run had 101 defective cans, the second run had 54 defective cans, etc.

The first thing to do with a mass of data like this is to collect it in some set of categories so it is more managable. In this case, the categories

0–20, 21–40, 41–60, . . . , etc. . . . 261–280, More than 280

were selected, since most of the data points (all but two) are below 280. The *number* of categories selected (15 in this case) is arbitrary. We shall see later that the particular intervals chosen in this case are computationally convenient.

Once the categories are chosen, we must determine how many of the outcomes fall in each category. For the first category, 0–20 defective cans, there are 24 instances in which the machine produced 20 or fewer defective cans. Continuing in this manner, we obtain Table 13.2. Once the data is in this form it is much easier to use. The use of this historical distribution is illustrated in the following two sections.

TABLE 13.2
The Valley Sisters Data Collected into Categories

Number of Defective Cans in the Run	Number of Runs in which This Occurred
0–20	24
21–40	46
41–60	43
61–80	36
81–100	27
101–120	25
121–140	16
141–160	10
161–180	8
181–200	8
201–220	0
221–240	3
241–260	0
261–280	2
More than 280	2

13.1.3 Using Historical Data in a Discrete Approximation to a Continuous Prior

There are two things that can be done with historical data once it is collected in categories such as in Table 13.2. One is to use the data to develop a discrete approximation to the continuous prior. This technique will be illustrated in this section. The other method involves fitting a conjugate prior to the data. This fitting of a conjugate prior will be illustrated in the following section.

The process of taking historical data and making a discrete approximation to the true continuous distribution is surprisingly easy. First, the boundaries of the categories into which we grouped the data must be translated into values of the relevant event. In the Valley Sisters case the event is a p value. The boundaries of the categories represent the number of defective cans in a run of 2,000, so to get the *proportion* of defective cans in any run, *or in the categories*, the number of defective cans must be divided by 2,000. Thus, the category 0–20 represents any situation in which the *proportion* of defective cans is between $\dfrac{0}{2,000}$ and $\dfrac{20}{2,000}$, or between 0 and 0.01. We must distinguish here between the true probability, p, of a defective can on any trial of a particular run and the observed proportion of defectives in a run of 2,000. The proportion will not necessarily be exactly the same as the p value, but should be quite close for a run size as large as 2,000.

Once the boundaries of the categories have been translated into values of the relevant event, the observed frequency must be converted to an estimate of the prior probability. For example, in the Valley Sisters case the relative frequency of occurrences between 0 and 20 defective cans is $\frac{24}{250}$ = 0.096. Just as in the case of a discrete prior with historical information, we shall use this value of 0.096 as the probability that p will lie between 0 and 0.01. That is, through a conversion of the boundaries of the categories and the frequencies we have developed the following statement:

$$P(0 \leq p \leq 0.01) = 0.096.$$

When similar calculations are performed on the other intervals into which the observed data was grouped, the resulting approximate distribution is given in Table 13.3. Notice that the lower boundaries of the

TABLE 13.3
A Probability Distribution Obtained from the Historical Valley Sisters Data

Range of p Values	Probability
0–0.01	0.096
0.01–0.02	0.184
0.02–0.03	0.172
0.03–0.04	0.144
0.04–0.05	0.108
0.05–0.06	0.100
0.06–0.07	0.064
0.07–0.08	0.040
0.08–0.09	0.032
0.09–0.10	0.032
0.10–0.11	0.0
0.11–0.12	0.012
0.12–0.13	0.0
0.13–0.14	0.008
More than 0.14	0.008

intervals are made to coincide with the upper boundaries of the previous interval. While this is not consistent with the interval transformation procedure discussed above, it is consistent with the reality of the situation; i.e., that p can take on *any* value in the interval between 0 and 1.

While we have now developed a probability distribution from the historical data, it cannot be used in its present form. We must next discuss how to transform the distribution of Table 13.3 into something that can be used in calculations. There are basically two modes—numerical and mathematical—by which the problem can be solved, and the mathematical approach is tractable only if the prior is conjugate to the sampling distribution. The mathematical technique will be illustrated in the next section. The numerical technique will be illustrated below.

In order to have a workable discrete approximation to a continuous prior, there must be a specific value of p to assign a probability, rather than the intervals given in Table 13.3. For example, in Chapter 6 the discrete distribution of p values was

$$P(p = 0.01) = 0.4; P(p = 0.02) = 0.3;$$
$$P(p = 0.04) = 0.2; P(p = 0.15) = 0.1$$

and a similar definitive statement is needed here.

This definiteness can easily be accomplished by choosing a discrete approximation in which the probability of an interval is concentrated at the *midpoint* of that interval. Thus,

$$P(0 \leq p \leq 0.01) = 0.096$$

becomes

$$P(p = 0.005) = 0.096,$$

and similar changes are made to the other intervals. The result of these changes is given in Table 13.4, and this distribution can be used exactly

TABLE 13.4
**A Useful Discrete Approxima-
tion to the Prior Distribution
for Valley Sisters Using the
Historical Data**

p Value	Probability
0.005	0.096
0.015	0.184
0.025	0.172
0.035	0.144
0.045	0.108
0.055	0.100
0.065	0.064
0.075	0.040
0.085	0.032
0.095	0.032
0.105	0.0
0.115	0.012
0.125	0.0
0.135	0.008
0.570	0.008

as the much simpler distribution

$$P(p = 0.01) = 0.4; P(p = 0.02) = 0.3;$$
$$P(p = 0.04) = 0.2; P(p = 0.15) = 0.1$$

was used in Chapters 6 and 7 to solve the Valley Sisters problem.

One point that should be made concerning the transformation illustrated here is the last category in the table. Since p values lie between

0 and 1, the implicit boundaries on the final category are 0.14 to 1. Thus, the midpoint is 0.57.

While the calculation of the midpoint of the open-ended category in this case is easy, it is not possible to use this technique when the event space has no known and finite bounds. This situation occurs in the testing of a mean, as in Chapters 11 and 12. In this case we must ignore open-ended categories. This technique is illustrated in Section 13.1.6, where numerical techniques for analyzing such problems is discussed.

13.1.4   Fitting a Conjugate Prior to Historical Data

Much work has been done in statistics to take a set of data, such as the historical data we have for the Valley Sisters problem, and fit a theoretical distribution to it. A complete exploration of this field would be too complicated to undertake in this text. Therefore, we will demonstrate only two representative techniques that have been used. The techniques will be demonstrated for the Valley Sisters data, which was previously presented, but the same kinds of techniques can be applied to fitting a normal prior as well. Since the sampling distribution in the Valley Sisters problem is binomial, the conjugate prior which will be fitted to the data is the beta distribution.

There are two basic techniques used to fit a distribution of a given form (in our case the beta distribution) to a set of data. Since the *form* of the distribution is known, the problem really becomes one of choosing the "best" values of the parameters of the distribution. Since there can be many different definitions of exactly what "best" means, there are many different techniques for determining the values of the parameters. All of these techniques, however, fall into two general categories, and we will demonstrate a technique from each category.

The first group of techniques attempts to look at the *entire* data distribution and compare it with an entire theoretical distribution. This can best be illustrated graphically, although in practice the results are obtained numerically. In the Valley Sisters problem, for example, the historical data given in Table 13.2 is graphed as a *histogram* in Figure 13.2. This histogram will be compared to a similar graph that can be developed for the beta distribution. (The details of doing this will not be discussed here, since the object is to demonstrate the technique, not give the details for how to perform it. Suffice it to say that such a development can be made.) The results of doing so for a beta distribution with $a = 20$, $b = 0$ are shown in Figure 13.3 along with the historical distribution. Notice that while the relative heights of the two histograms are close for $p \geq 0.07$, the height of the beta distribution is much higher for the $0 \leq p \leq 0.01$ interval, and the beta consistently

FIGURE 13.2
A Histogram of the Valley Sisters Historical Data

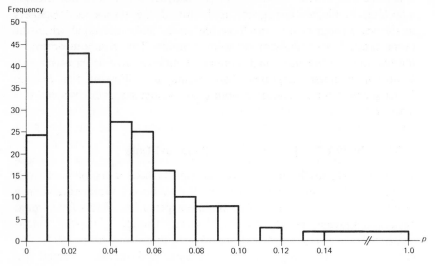

FIGURE 13.3
The Histogram for the Valley Sisters Historical Data (striped) plus the Histogram for a Beta Distribution with $a = 20$, $b = 0$ (solid)

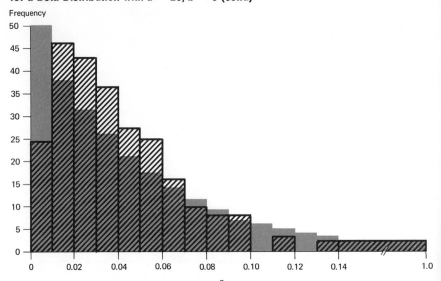

underestimates the observed frequencies for the intervals between $p = 0.01$ and $p = 0.07$. Therefore, this beta distribution does not provide a good fit; that is, the histogram for the beta distribution does not closely match the histogram for the historical data. Since the whole point of this exercise is to find a conjugate distribution that *closely* matches the observed data, we would have to reject the values of $a = 20$ and $b = 0$ as providing an appropriate conjugate prior.

As we mentioned above, we are studying a class of techniques that attempt to match an entire historical distribution to a proposed theoretical distribution. Mathematically, this is accomplished by forming a numerical measure of the goodness-of-fit between the two distributions. The various techniques that have been proposed differ in how this goodness-of-fit criterion is determined. The technique we shall discuss is called the minimum chi-square technique. It is the most popular of the techniques, and the estimates of the parameters obtained from it have appealing properties.

The goodness-of-fit criterion for the minimum chi-square technique is a sum of normalized squared deviations between the observed frequency in a cell and the frequency predicted by a particular mathematical distribution. In symbols:

$$\text{Goodness-of-fit criterion} = D = \sum_{\substack{\text{all} \\ \text{ranges}}} \frac{(\text{observed-expected})^2}{\text{expected}}$$

where:

observed = frequency of occurrence from the historical data
expected = frequency of occurrence from the conjugate distribution.

As an example of how this criterion is applied, the first range of p values, $0 \leq p \leq 0.01$, contains 24 observations from the historical data, while the beta distribution with $a = 20$, $b = 0$ predicts 50 observations in this category. Thus, we have for the first term in the summation expression for D:

observed = 24
expected = 50

$$\frac{(\text{observed} - \text{expected})^2}{\text{expected}} = \frac{(24 - 50)^2}{50} = 13.5.$$

Similarly, for the second category, $0.01 \leq p \leq 0.02$,

observed = 46
expected = 38

$$\frac{(\text{observed} - \text{expected})^2}{\text{expected}} = \frac{(46 - 38)^2}{38} = 1.68.$$

Similar calculations are carried out for each of the ranges of p values. The goodness-of-fit criterion, D, is then the sum of all of these normalized discrepancy values.

The procedure outlined above gives the value for D for one particular set of values of a and b. However, the objective is to find the "best" values of a and b, and in this case "best" means those that minimize the value of D. Therefore, a search over all values of a and b must be carried out. Many technical details and computational work is involved. We do not have time to discuss these here. The result, however, is that the "best" values of a and b are $a = 49$, $b = 1$. The beta distribution that results from these parameter values and the histogram of the original data are graphed in Figure 13.4, and we see that this beta distribution does indeed provide a good fit to the historical data.

FIGURE 13.4
The Histogram for the Valley Sisters Historical Data (striped) plus the Histogram for a Beta Distribution with $a = 49$, $b = 1$ (solid)

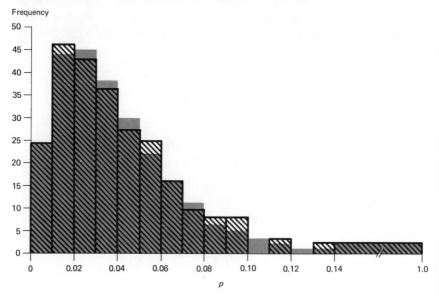

The other major technique used to estimate parameters is to solve sets of simultaneous equations involving the parameters to be estimated and certain reductions of the data. The most widely used and most powerful of these techniques is the method of maximum likelihood. It will not be demonstrated, however, since the application of the concept requires a large amount of mathematical ability—much more than that assumed of the readers of this text. Therefore we will demonstrate the technique with another approach called the method of moments. While it is not a good statistical technique (the estimates obtained, at times, can be quite bad), it is simple and will serve for purposes of illustration.

The method of moments is simplistic in concept. When a probability distribution with two parameters needs to be estimated, two quantities from the sample—the mean and the variance—are calculated and equated with the corresponding expressions from the probability distribution. For example, for the Valley Sisters data, the sample mean, expressed in terms of p values, is:

$$\bar{p} = \frac{p_1 + p_2 + \cdots + p_{250}}{250}$$

$$= \frac{101/2{,}000 + 54/2{,}000 + \cdots + 47/2{,}000}{250}$$

$$= 0.0395.$$

The sample variance, a quantity we have not discussed before, is a measure of dispersion within the sample. Its calculation is designed to correspond as closely as possible to the calculation of variance described in Chapter 2. Each data point's squared deviation from the sample mean is first obtained. For instance, with the Valley Sisters data, the squared deviation of the first data point is

$$\left(\frac{101}{2{,}000} - 0.0395\right)^2 = 0.000121.$$

The squared deviations for each data point are then added together, and the sum is divided by the sample size, n, minus 1. The resulting quantity is called the sample variance. Thus, in the Valley Sisters case the sample variance is

$$\frac{\left[\left(\frac{101}{2{,}000} - 0.0395\right)^2 + \left(\frac{54}{2{,}000} - 0.0395\right)^2 + \cdots + \left(\frac{47}{2{,}000} - 0.0395\right)^2\right]}{250 - 1}$$

$$= 0.000761.$$

The probability distribution we are interested in fitting to the data in this case is the beta distribution. We learned in Chapter 9 that for the beta distribution

$$E(p) = \frac{b + 1}{a + 2}; \text{ and}$$

$$\text{Var}(p) = \frac{ab + a + 1 - b^2}{(a + 2)^2(a + 3)}.$$

Then the method of moments prescribes that we equate the theoretical and observed means and variances

$$\frac{b+1}{a+2} = 0.0395$$

$$\frac{ab + a + 1 - b^2}{(a+2)^2(a+3)} = 0.000761$$

and solve these equations simultaneously for the values of the parameters, a and b.[1]

Clearly this is not an easy calculation to make, and it is further complicated by the fact that as far as we have studied the beta distribution in this book, the values of a and b must be integers. However, the point of this discussion is not to train the reader in how to make these calculations, but rather to illustrate the other class of techniques for estimating parameters of distributions. These techniques generally result in equating expressions involving the parameters of the distribution (in this case the expressions for the mean and variance of the beta distribution) with some reductions of the original data (in this case $\bar{p}$ and the sample variance) and solving simultaneously for the values of the parameters.

Before we conclude this section we should point out that for the normal distribution (which is the conjugate prior for normal sampling) the method of moments and the maximum likelihood method for obtaining the estimates of the parameters are essentially the same, and no other method is in general use for estimating the parameters of a normal distribution. Recall that the parameters of the normal distribution, μ and σ^2, are, respectively, the mean and variance. Therefore the method of moments would set μ equal to $\bar{x}$ and σ^2 equal to the sample variance. This system of equations needs no solution to isolate the values of μ and σ^2. Therefore, the method is computationally very easy and the results have good statistical properties.

13.1.5 Establishing a Subjective Prior

Subjective priors express the feelings of a particular decision-maker about the "odds" of various events happening. It is the job of the decision theory analyst in this case to interact with the decision maker, usually through a dialogue. The objective of this interaction is to get the decision maker to express his prior beliefs. We will illustrate the procedure below by giving a hypothetical dialogue between two people—the decision theory analyst and a decision maker. The problem they are facing is that of establishing a prior distribution for the Nadir Mining

---

[1] It is interesting to note that when this is done the best values of a and b are $a = 49$ and $b = 1$.

and Manufacturing example, which was first discussed in Chapter 11. We will assume in this case that the person capable of making an accurate determination of the probability distribution of m is the company geologist.

ANALYST: I want to have a dialogue with you to determine what chances there are of various concentrations of high-grade ore in the field whose lease you are making a decision on. You have years of experience in this position, and that is exactly what you need to solve this problem.

GEOLOGIST: O.K., but don't throw any mathematics at me. My math is very rusty.

ANALYST: That is why I am here. The main thing I want from you is a framework upon which to make a decision. Let me worry about the mechanics of the mathematics. Now, let's set some boundaries on the problem. We will be talking about the *average* pounds of magnetite per ton of material *for the field as a whole*. Do you understand that?

GEOLOGIST: Yes.

ANALYST: Now, clearly, any ton of material can be at most pure magnetite, which is 2,000 pounds per ton, and must contain in the least no pounds of magnetite, which is 0 pounds per ton. Therefore, the boundaries on your value are 0 and 2,000, right?

GEOLOGIST: That is correct, but I have never seen a field that contained a contiguous ton of pure magnetite.

ANALYST: That kind of feeling is just what I want to elicit from you! Let's explore it further. If we let m represent the average pounds of magnetite per ton of material, then, as we have said, m lies between 0 and 2,000.

GEOLOGIST: And is never, in real life, 2,000.

ANALYST: Right! Now let me explore your feelings about the chances for m further. Considering the whole range of m values, how would you divide it so that the chances of m being on either side of this value are equal.

GEOLOGIST: I don't understand.

ANALYST: Let me put it another way. If I select a value of m of 300, would you say the chances are greater that m is below 300 or above 300?

GEOLOGIST: That's easy! m has a much greater chance of being below 300 than above it. But is this the same question as the last one you asked me?

ANALYST: You will see it leads to the same answer. Now let me pick a value of m of 150. Would you say the chances are greater that m is below 150 or above 150?

GEOLOGIST: That's a tough choice. But if I were pressed, I would say the chances are greater that it is above 150.

ANALYST: Fine! What if I choose 160 as the division point. Are the chances greater that m lies above 160 or are they greater that m lies below 160?

GEOLOGIST: I don't like these questions. They're too tough!

ANALYST: I need to know the answer in order to establish your feelings about the various chances of m occurring. Just remember that this is not a quiz. You and I are working together to establish a probability distribution. So, if you make a decision and later want to change it, that's perfectly OK with me. Also, you should know that I will keep giving you tougher and tougher questions of this sort until you cannot distinguish between the two parts of the range of m values! So, if 160 divides the range up into *equally likely* parts, just tell me.

GEOLOGIST: No, I don't quite feel that. I feel the chances are slightly higher that m is below 160 than above it. In fact, the point you are looking for—the one that divides the range into equally likely parts is probably 154 or 155. Let's say it is 154.

ANALYST: Good! Now in the process of determining relative chances, do you see that you have answered my first question, which was—How would you divide the range of m values so that the chances of m being on either side of that division line are equal?

GEOLOGIST: Of course! And, I am getting the hang of how to do this. But I must say that exploring potential divisional values of m helped me make a final decision.

ANALYST: It usually does. That is the process I want you to go through, mentally at least, to answer each of my questions.

GEOLOGIST: You mean there are more? I hoped we were finished.

ANALYST: On the contrary, we are just getting started. However, now that you have a feeling for the process, I think you will find each decision easier.

GEOLOGIST: OK. Where do we go from here?

ANALYST: Well, you have said that an m value of 154 divides the entire range of m values into two parts that are equally likely.
(Aside: This means that the median of his distribution, $m_{0.50}$, is 154.)
Now I would like you to consider only m values between 0 and 154. How would you divide this range of m values into two equally likely parts?

GEOLOGIST: What happens if the true m value is bigger than 154?

ANALYST: For the question we are considering, nothing. Suppose you must choose between the chances of m lying between 0 and 120 and the chances of m lying between 120 and 154. If m turns out bigger than 154, you neither win nor lose anything.

GEOLOGIST: Well, in that case I would pick the region between 120 and 154. That has much higher odds than the region below 120.

ANALYST: Can you pick a value for m that divides the region between 0 and 154 into two *equally likely* regions?

GEOLOGIST: Yes . . . let's see . . . I would pick a value of . . . 140.

ANALYST: Good! (Aside: That means the 25th percentile, $m_{0.25}$, is 140.) Now, please divide the region between 154 and 2,000 into two equally likely parts.

GEOLOGIST: That's a little harder to do. Sometimes we really get lucky with a field, and it has a high magnetite concentration. So let's say that it is 175.

ANALYST: OK. (Aside: That means that $m_{0.75} = 175$.) Now, just as a check, what you have told me so far is that the chances of m lying between 140 and 175 are equal to the chances that it lies outside this range.

GEOLOGIST: I said that? When?

ANALYST: This is just a consistency check. Remember that there are no incorrect answers here. I am just checking you to make sure I get the most accurate record of your feelings.

GEOLOGIST: OK. But I do feel that the chances are greater that m is inside the range 140 to 175 than outside it.

ANALYST: Fine. Then let's change the numbers. If you feel the range from 140 to 175 is more likely, how would you change the boundaries so that the region inside and the region outside are equally likely?

GEOLOGIST: Well, I feel pretty good about the 140. But I think I will change the 175 to 170. With that change I feel the chances are the same for m being inside or outside the range.

ANALYST: OK. How do you feel about 154 as a dividing line for the entire region?

GEOLOGIST: I still feel that is OK.

ANALYST: Then let's go on. (Aside: We now have $m_{0.25} = 140$, $m_{0.50} = 154$, $m_{0.75} = 170$.)
Take the region from 0 to 140. Where would you divide it so that the result is two equally likely regions?

GEOLOGIST: Boy, that's tough. I'm not sure I can do that!

ANALYST: Think, in your experience, of all the fields of magnetite under 140. Where did they divide up?

GEOLOGIST: Well, let's see. I'd say about 120.

ANALYST: (Aside: That means $m_{0.125} = 120$.) Now divide the range from 170 to 2,000 into two equally likely parts.

GEOLOGIST: I feel very shaky about this, but let's see . . . I would say 198.

ANALYST: (Aside: That means $m_{0.875} = 198$.) Let's try one more division
. . .

GEOLOGIST: Hold it! That's as much as I can do.

ANALYST: All right. I think I have enough data to construct a reasonable prior distribution.

Having completed this dialogue, we are ready to develop a distribution from it. Recall that the data the geologist gave was

$$m_{0.125} = 120; \ m_{0.25} = 140; \ m_{0.5} = 154; \ m_{0.75} = 170; \ m_{0.875} = 198.$$

In order to obtain a complete distribution from this, realize that the percentiles are cumulative probabilities; that is, another way to write $m_{0.25} = 140$ is

$$P(m \leq 140) = 0.25.$$

These can be used as data points, then, to plot a cumulative probability curve. This curve is shown in Figure 13.5. Notice that, with some measure of liberty taken at the upper and lower extremities, a smooth curve can be drawn through the data points. This creates a cumulative probability distribution.

FIGURE 13.5
The Cumulative Subjective Distribution of the Nadir Geologist

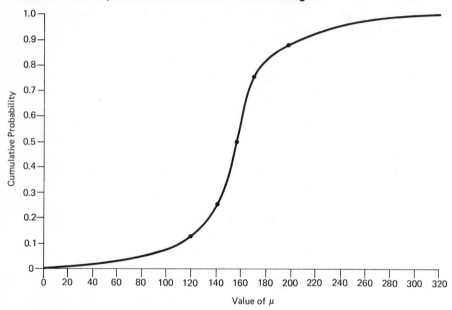

Just as with the historical data, there are two things we can do with this distribution. We can either transform it into a discrete approximation and use the distribution that way, or we can try to fit a conjugate prior to it. Making a discrete approximation of it will be discussed in the next section. If it seems advantageous to do so, a conjugate prior distribution can be fitted to the subjective distribution using a combination of the techniques discussed in the next section and the minimum chi-square technique.

13.1.6 Transforming a Subjective Continuous Prior into a Useful Distribution

If the subjective prior is in the graphical form, as in Figure 13.5, we will find it is an easy matter to develop a discrete approximation to it. The first thing to be done is to establish some reasonable *finite* boundaries beyond which we are willing to say the value of (in this case)

m will never lie. The necessity of this step will become obvious later. In this case, Figure 13.5 gives reasonable finite boundaries of 0 and 320. Assuming that m has a zero probability of lying outside this range, the values within this range must be discretized in some way. A convenient method for doing this is to take equal intervals on the vertical axis and determine the corresponding m values on the horizontal axis. For example, if the vertical axis is divided into 20 equal intervals (each of length 0.05), then the m value corresponding to 0.05 is 90, the m value corresponding to 0.10 is 112, the m value corresponding to 0.15 is 126, etc. Thus, we are saying the following:

$$P(m \leq 90) = 0.05$$
$$P(m \leq 112) = 0.10$$
$$P(m \leq 126) = 0.15$$
.
.
.
etc.

These probability statements can be reworked to give the probabilities of disjoint intervals:

$$P(0 \leq m \leq 90) = 0.05$$
$$P(90 \leq m \leq 112) = 0.05$$
$$P(112 \leq m \leq 126) = 0.05$$
.
.
.
etc.

When this process is completed, it results in a table of ranges of events and probabilities, like Table 13.5.

There is nothing magical about dividing the vertical axis into 20 parts, or in making each part equal. Any number of other divisions would work equally well, although we shall find having the same probabilities will make life (mechanically) a little easier for us in the next section. The only necessary requirement for dividing up the cumulative distribution is that it be divided into enough parts to make the discrete approximation representative of the original distribution. Unfortunately, there are no rules for doing this, so the reader has to use his own discretion in accomplishing it.

Once a division like the one represented by Table 13.5 has been accomplished, the step to a useful discrete distribution is trivial. As we did for the historical prior in Section 13.1.3, we merely take the midpoint of each interval and consider the probability as being concentrated

TABLE 13.5
Another Representation of the Nadir
Subjective Distribution

Range of m Values	Probability
0–90	0.05
90–112	0.05
112–126	0.05
126–134	0.05
134–140	0.05
140–144	0.05
144–147	0.05
147–150	0.05
150–152	0.05
152–154	0.05
154–156	0.05
156–158	0.05
158–161	0.05
161–165	0.05
165–170	0.05
170–178	0.05
178–190	0.05
190–207	0.05
207–232	0.05
232–320	0.05

at that point. Thus, we replace

$$P(0 \leq m \leq 90) = 0.05$$

with the discrete approximation:

$$P(m = 45) = 0.05.$$

Each of the other intervals is treated similarly, and the resulting distribution—which in this form can be used as a discrete approximation—is given in Table 13.6

If, instead of a discrete approximation, you wish to fit a conjugate prior to this data, the minimum chi square technique discussed in Section 13.1.4 can be used to do this. However, unlike the historical data, this subjective distribution cannot be fit to its appropriate conjugate prior using either the maximum likelihood method or the method of moments, since these both require individual data points rather than the cumulative probability distribution that is given.

13.2 SOLVING NORMAL SAMPLING PROBLEMS WITHOUT CONJUGATE PRIORS

Chapters 6 and 7 were devoted to a study of binomial sampling problems with discrete—and, hence nonconjugate—priors. Therefore, the foundation for nonconjugate priors in binomial sampling has been

TABLE 13.6
A Discrete Approximation to the
Nadir Subjective Distribution

m Value	Probability
45	0.05
101	0.05
119	0.05
130	0.05
137	0.05
142	0.05
145.5	0.05
148.5	0.05
151	0.05
153	0.05
155	0.05
157	0.05
159.5	0.05
163	0.05
167.5	0.05
174	0.05
184	0.05
198.5	0.05
219.5	0.05
276	0.05

thoroughly covered. This section will be devoted to presenting techniques for working with normal sampling problems with discrete priors. As always, we will first consider the problem without sampling and then consider the addition of sampling.

13.2.1 Decision Problems with Means as Events for Which No Sampling Occurs

We first considered these problems in Chapter 11. At that point the following rule was developed:

If Payoff(A) = $a + bm$,
then Expected Payoff(A) = $a + bE(m)$.

This rule still holds. The difference now is that the expected value of the prior distribution, $E(m)$, is not given as a parameter. Instead, it must be calculated from the discrete prior. For example, for the discrete distribution which was developed for the Nadir problem in the previous section (the distribution is given in Table 13.6), we have:

$$E(m) = m_1 P(m_1) + m_2 P(m_2) + \cdots + m_{20} P(m_{20})$$
$$= 45 \times 0.05 + 101 \times 0.05 + 119 \times 0.05 + \cdots + 276 \times 0.05$$
$$= 156.3.$$

Once this quantity is known, the expected payoffs of the two actions can be quickly calculated. In the Nadir problem the two actions are:

L = Let the option lapse
M = Mine the field

and the payoff functions are:

Profit(L) = 0
Profit(M) = 12,500m − 2,000,000.

Therefore, the expected payoffs of the two decisions are

$E(L)$ = 0
$E(M)$ = 12,500 × 156.3 − 2,000,000
      = −46,250,

and with this prior L is the best action.

In many problems, including the one we have just solved, it is helpful to know the expected opportunity loss of the best action. When the prior is discrete, it is probably easiest to calculate the expected opportunity loss by developing payoff and loss tables for the problem. Since we have discretized the prior, we are only considering a finite number of values for m. Hence, such a table can be developed. The payoff and loss tables for the Nadir problem are given in Table 13.7. Using the

TABLE 13.7
Payoff (A) and Opportunity Loss (B) Tables for the Discretized Nadir Problem

Value of m	A Payoff Table L	M	B Loss Table L	M
45	0	−1,438,000	0	1,438,000
101	0	−737,500	0	737,500
119	0	−512,500	0	512,500
130	0	−375,000	0	375,000
137	0	−287,500	0	287,500
142	0	−225,000	0	225,000
145.5	0	−181,300	0	181,300
148.5	0	−143,800	0	143,800
151	0	−112,500	0	112,500
153	0	−87,500	0	87,500
155	0	−62,500	0	62,500
157	0	−37,500	0	37,500
159.5	0	−6,250	0	6,250
163	0	37,500	37,500	0
167.5	0	93,750	93,750	0
174	0	175,000	175,000	0
184	0	300,000	300,000	0
198.5	0	481,300	481,300	0
219.5	0	743,800	743,800	0
276	0	1,450,000	1,450,000	0

opportunity loss table, the expected opportunity loss of action L is

$$\mathcal{E}(L) = 0 \times 0.05 + 0 \times 0.05 + \cdots$$
$$+ 743,800 \times 0.05 + 1,450,000 \times 0.05$$
$$= 164,100.$$

In this case the minimum expected opportunity loss is high, and it seems that it would be worth sampling. Procedures for analyzing a sample will be given in the next two sections.

13.2.2 Analysis of a Given Sample Outcome

The first problem we shall consider is that of a known sample outcome. For example, consider as in Chapter 12 that a sample of size 20 yields a sample average of 164, and the variance of the sampling distribution, s^2, is 550. Just as in Chapter 12 we will update the prior distribution to a posterior and use this posterior distribution to determine which action is best. *However,* the nice compact rule which we had in Chapter 12 for updating the prior

$$\text{Normal Prior} \xrightarrow[\text{Sampling}]{\text{Normal}} \text{Normal Posterior}$$

no longer holds, since the prior is no longer (necessarily) normal. Instead, we perform a computational update of the discrete prior, using an appropriate version of Bayes' rule.

The version of Bayes' rule we need to perform the update is different from the version used in previous chapters because the sampling distribution in this problem is continuous. In this version, the probability of the sample outcome given the event is replaced by the value of the *probability density function* for the sample outcome given the event, and Bayes' rule is

$$P(m_i|\bar{x}) = \frac{f(\bar{x}|m_i)P(m_i)}{f(\bar{x}|m_1)P(m_1) + f(\bar{x}|m_2)P(m_2) + \cdots + f(\bar{x}|m_{20})P(m_{20})}$$

where

$P(m_i|\bar{x})$ is the posterior probability of m_i occurring, having observed $\bar{x}$;

$f(\bar{x}|m_i)$ is the probability density value of $\bar{x}$, given the mean value m_i;

$P(m_i)$ is the prior probability of m_i occurring.

The unfamiliar quantity in this expression is $f(\bar{x}|m_i)$. It comes from the probability density function of the normal distribution, whose formula was given in Section 9.5.3:

$$f(x) = \frac{1}{\sqrt{2\pi}\,\sigma}\, e^{-\frac{1}{2}\left(\frac{x-\mu}{\sigma}\right)^2}.$$

In this case the random variable is x, and

$$\mu = m_i; \sigma = \sqrt{\frac{s^2}{n}}$$

The values for $f(x|m_i)$ would be difficult to calculate by hand. Table III at the end of the text contains values from which $f(x)$ can be obtained as a function of the normalized quantity $(x - \mu)/\sigma$. As an example of the use of this table, consider finding the value for $f(x|m_i)$ for the 13th (discretized) m value, $m_i = 159.5$: x is the random variable in this case, so

$$\mu = 159.5 \text{ and } \sigma = \sqrt{\frac{550}{20}} = 5.25.$$

The value of x is 164, so the normalized value which we use to find $f(x|m_i)$ is

$$\frac{x - 159.5}{5.25} = \frac{164 - 159.5}{5.25} = 0.857.$$

Using this value, the value from Table III is 0.2763. This value must then be divided by σ to obtain $f(x|m_i)$. Thus,

$$f(x|m_i) = \frac{1}{\sigma} \times \text{Value from Table III}$$

$$= \frac{1}{5.25} \times 0.2763 = 0.0526.$$

The $f(x|m_i)$ values for the other m_i can be calculated in a similar manner. In doing these calculations, whenever the value of the normalized variable,

$$(x - m_i) \Big/ \sqrt{\frac{s^2}{n}}$$

exceeds 4.99, the value from Table III is taken to be zero. The results of these calculations are given in the third column of Table 13.8. Whenever the value of the normalized variable,

$$(x - m_i) \Big/ \sqrt{\frac{s^2}{n}}$$

is negative in this calculation, a symmetry property of Table III was invoked. For instance, at $m_i = 174$ the normalized variable is

$$\frac{x - m_i}{\sqrt{\frac{s^2}{n}}} = \frac{164 - 174}{5.25} = -1.905.$$

Because of the symmetry of the function in Table III, the value corre-responding to -1.905 is the same as the value corresponding to $+1.905$. Therefore,

$$f(\bar{x}|m = 174) = \frac{1}{\sigma} \times \text{Value corresponding to } +1.905 \text{ from Table III}$$

$$= \frac{1}{5.25} \times 0.06500 = 0.01238.$$

Once these $f(\bar{x}|m_i)$ values are calculated, they can be multiplied by the prior probabilities, $P(m_i)$, and normalized to sum to 1. The result is the posterior distribution, and its calculation is also illustrated in Table 13.8. This table does nothing more than give an illustration of

TABLE 13.8
An Illustration of Bayes' Rule Applied to the Nadir Data

m Value	Prior Distribution	$f(\bar{x}|m_i)$	Column 2 × Column 3	Posterior Distribution
45	0.05	0	0	0
101	0.05	0	0	0
119	0.05	0	0	0
130	0.05	0	0	0
137	0.05	0	0	0
142	0.05	0.0000117	0.0000005854	0
145.5	0.05	0.0001550	0.000007748	0
148.5	0.05	0.0009796	0.00004898	0.004
151	0.05	0.003509	0.0001754	0.013
153	0.05	0.008377	0.0004189	0.032
155	0.05	0.01761	0.0008806	0.067
157	0.05	0.03137	0.001569	0.120
159.5	0.05	0.05260	0.002625	0.200
163	0.05	0.07463	0.003731	0.285
167.5	0.05	0.06070	0.003035	0.231
174	0.05	0.01238	0.0006250	0.048
184	0.05	0.00005352	0.000002676	0
198.5	0.05	0	0	0
219.5	0.05	0	0	0
276	0.05	0	0	0
Sum			0.01312	1.0

how to use the Bayes' rule formula given above.

Once the posterior distribution is obtained, it can be used in place of the prior to determine which action is best. For this posterior $E(m) = 162.1$. Since this value is higher than the breakeven point, M is the best action. When the expected payoffs and expected losses are calculated for this action we get

Expected payoff: $E(M) = 25,900$
Expected loss: $\mathcal{E}(M) = 14,800$.

13.2.3 Finding the Optimal Sample Size

If we are faced with a problem of *considering* taking a sample, then it would be helpful to know how to calculate the optimal sample size. As a preliminary to answering that question, we must investigate the form of strategy that is optimal. Fortunately, it can be shown that the form of the strategy is independent of the prior distribution. Therefore, as long as the payoff functions are linear, the optimal strategy for the Nadir problem, as an example, will be:

$$\{\text{If } \bar{x} < c^* \text{ then } L; \text{ while if } \bar{x} > c^* \text{ then } M\}.$$

Unfortunately, it is not easy to find the value of c^*, as it was in Chapter 12. In this case, when the prior distribution is nonconjugate, the value of c must be solved for by trial and error. Fortunately, as in the binomial sampling case, the total expected loss of a strategy as a function of c has a single minimum. Therefore, once a strategy has been found whose total expected loss is less than for neighboring values of c, the optimum is known.

Once the optimum value of c is known for a particular sample size, the value of the sample size, n, is changed, and a new optimal strategy is found. The analysis continues in this manner until, by trial and error, the optimal sample size is found. The entire procedure is tedious, time consuming, and requires a level of numerical analysis expertise not assumed of the readers of this text. Therefore, we will not discuss the details here. The student who is familiar with numerical analysis can take the concepts we have presented here and develop his own method of analysis. The student who knows no numerical analysis is wiser to be aware of the concepts involved in the problem, and leave the details of the calculation to a technical consultant.

13.3 HOW DOES CHANGING THE ASSUMPTION OF LINEAR PAYOFFS AFFECT THE PROBLEM?

It must be clear to the student by now that every time an assumption about the problems we discussed in Chapters 6 through 12 is relaxed, some of the elegant structure—which helped in the solution of the problem—is also lost. In this section, we will discuss ways in which the payoffs can become nonlinear and for which some of the helpful structure of the problem is retained. We will also discuss ways of solving problems under any circumstances.

In the previous (Chapters 6 through 12) investigation of problems, how was the assumption of linear payoff functions important to us? An analysis of these chapters will reveal two areas. The first is in the development of the expected value versus the breakeven point rules. When the payoff functions are nonlinear, these no longer hold.

The second area in which the linear payoff functions are important is in the development of the single cutoff point strategies. However, unlike the $E(m)$ versus m_b type of rule, some nonlinear payoff functions can be introduced here and the property still holds. The crucial property of linear payoff functions used here is the property that they have only one crossover point. However, many pairs of nonlinear payoff functions can be described that also satisfy this property. For example, Figure 13.6 shows two such pairs of functions. In mathematics beyond the level

GURE 13.6
ro Examples of Nonlinear Payoff Functions With a Single Cross-Over Point

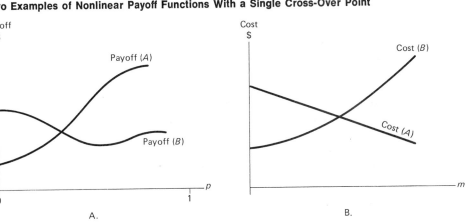

of this book it can be shown that anytime there is only one cross-over in the payoff functions, a strategy with a single cutoff point will be optimal. In symbols, for any binomial sampling problem, a strategy of the form:

$$\{\text{If } B < c^* \text{ then } A_1, \text{ while if } B \geq c^* \text{ then } A_2\}$$

will always be optimal whenever there is only one cross-over point in the payoff functions. Similarly, for normal sampling, a strategy of the form:

$$\{\text{If } \bar{x} < c^* \text{ then } A_1, \text{ while if } \bar{x} > c^* \text{ then } A_2\}$$

will always be optimal whenever there is only one cross-over point in the payoff functions.

What happens when there is *more* than one cross-over point in the payoff function? How would we handle a problem whose payoff functions are like those in Figure 13.7? The answer is to go back to first principles. We learned in Chapter 5 that by using a decision tree approach, no form of strategy need be assumed best. Instead, the optimal

FIGURE 13.7
A Pair of Payoff Functions for Which the Single
Cutoff Point Strategy Is *Not* Best

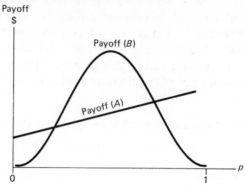

strategy emerges from the calculations on the tree. Therefore, the way a problem whose payoff functions are like those in Figure 13.7 should be approached is to develop the full decision tree for enough sample sizes so it becomes clear what the optimal form of the strategy is, and then use this optimal form in the remainder of the calculations.

13.4 SUMMARY

This chapter has dealt with several topics that move decision theory from a science to a useful tool. All of these techniques are important and useful, but probably the most important thing that can be said in closing the chapter is that first principles (those contained in Chapters 3 through 5) are the most important. The remainder of the book makes life easier only for those who apply decision theory toward solving certain specific problems.

PROBLEMS

1. The Circle-Gouger Co. manufactures do-it-yourself drain cleaning machines that are placed in hardware stores for rental to customers. In an effort to increase the placement of their units in the hardware stores, the company has made a survey of the number of requests per day for one of their units. This survey was done at several "average" hardware stores. The company defines an average hardware store as one with between 100 and 300 customers per day. The results of the survey show:

Number of Requests for Drain Cleaning Machines	0	1	2	3	4
Frequency of Days	91	75	22	9	3

a. Use this historical data to establish a prior distribution on demand for this product.

b. If you are the owner of a hardware store serving an average 250 customers per day, would you be willing to use the prior developed in part (*a*)? Why or why not?

c. If you are the manager of a hardware store serving an average of 1,500 customers per day would you be willing to use the prior developed in part (*a*)? Why or why not?

2. If your answer to parts (*b*) or (*c*) of Problem 1 were that you would not use it, can you suggest ways to modify the distribution given to develop an adequate prior for yourself?

3. Consider the Count Cash problem, Problem 10 of Chapter 6. Suppose Count summarizes his experiences in other firms he has suspected of juggling their books as follows. In each case Count has taken 100 accounts and traced each through to ascertain whether or not it is correctly accounted for. The resulting number of improper accounts for the 50 firms Count has investigated are given below.

9	0	1	1	7	9	0	0	0	10
1	0	8	9	1	10	2	1	2	1
0	4	0	0	0	1	0	9	8	1
1	13	1	8	0	0	0	0	0	1
8	8	2	0	2	1	2	10	8	1

a. Using any boundaries you think appropriate, collect this data into categories

b. Develop a probability distribution for this data like the distribution given in Table 13.3

c. Develop a useful discrete approximation from this data like the approximation given in Table 13.4

d. Draw a histogram for this data.

4. The frequencies for the $a = 20$, $b = 0$ and $a = 49$, $b = 1$ beta distributions shown in Figures 13.3 and 13.4 are:

Range of p Values	$a = 20, b = 0$ Frequency	$a = 49, b = 2$ Frequency
0–0.01	50	24
0.01–0.02	38	44
0.02–0.03	31	45
0.03–0.04	26	38
0.04–0.05	21	30
0.05–0.06	17	22
0.06–0.07	14	16
0.07–0.08	11	11
0.08–0.09	9	7
0.09–0.10	7	5
0.10–0.11	6	3
0.11–0.12	5	2
0.12–0.13	4	1
0.13–0.14	3	1
More than 0.14	8	1

Calculate the goodness-of-fit value, D, for each of these potential representations of the historical data. Verify that the $a = 49$, $b = 1$ distribution provides a much better fit than the $a = 20$, $b = 1$ distribution.

5. For the American Steel problem, Problem 9 of Chapter 11, suppose that the analysis of a number of batches yields the following mean carbon content, m.

17.44	14.86	15.56	12.09
16.57	18.78	18.47	12.00

a. Use these data points to estimate the expected value and variance of the prior distribution of m, $E_0(m)$ and $\sigma_0^2(m)$, if it can be reasonably asumed that the prior is normally distributed.
b. Using this prior, which action is optimal? What is the expected opportunity loss for this action?
c. Suppose, as in Chapter 12, the standard deviation of carbon content within batches is 6. If a sample of size 5 from the current batch yields an $\bar{x}$ of 13.8, which action should American take? What is the expected payoff and opportunity loss for this action?

6. Consider the process of flipping a thumbtack, which has two possible outcomes, points up, $\downarrow$, and lying on its side, $\nwarrow$. Through a dialogue with yourself, or with the help of a friend, establish your own subjective probability distribution for p, the probability of points up. Use this distribution to obtain a useful discrete approximation for your prior like the approximation given in Table 13.4.

7. Answer parts (b), (c), (d), (e), and (f) of Problem 8 in Chapter 10 using the prior developed in Problem 6 above. (This problem does not require knowledge of the material in Chapter 10 for its solution.)

8. Using the subjective prior distribution for the Nadir problem which is displayed in Figure 13.5, which action should Nadir take if a sample of 4 yields a sample average, $\bar{x}$, of 162.5? (Assume s^2 is still 550.)

9. Suppose an analysis of a manager at American Steel (Problem 9 of Chapter 11) reveals the following percentiles for a subjective distribution:

$$m_{0.125} = 11; \quad m_{0.25} = 13; \quad m_{0.5} = 16; \quad m_{0.75} = 18.5; \quad m_{0.875} = 20.$$

a. Using these points, develop a discrete approximation (similar to Table 13.6) that can be used to solve American's problem.
b. Using this prior, which action is best for American? What are its expected payoff and expected loss?
c. Suppose a sample of size 5 yields an average for the current batch of 13.8. Which action should American take? What are the expected payoff and expected opportunity loss associated with this action?

10. Consider a problem in which the mean, m, is the event and the payoffs for the two actions are

$$\text{Payoff } (A_1) = m^2; \quad \text{Payoff } (A_2) = 150 + 5m.$$

Supose that the company trying to solve this problem is willing to establish a normal prior whose variance, $\sigma_0^2(m)$ is 9.

a. Verify for this problem that there is only one cross-over point for the payoff functions in the range of m values greater than zero, and that $m_b = 15$.

b. Calculate the expected payoffs for both actions in this problem when $E(m) = 14$, 15, and 16. (Hint: For a normal prior $E(m^2) = \sigma^2 + \mu^2$.) Explain how the numerical answers you have obtained show that the $E(m)$ versus m_b rule no longer holds.

c. Suppose this company is considering taking a sample of size 7 from a sampling distribution whose variance, s^2, is 293.6. What will be the variance of the posterior normal distribution?

d. Using this posterior variance, determine which of the two actions is best if the posterior mean is 14, 14.1, 14.2, 14.3, 14.4, . . . , 14.9, 15.0. Which of these eleven potential posterior means comes closest to being a cutoff point? Translate this cutoff point to a cutoff point for the $\bar{x}$ value. (These questions are designed to give the reader some experience with the procedure necessary to find the cutoff point in a problem where the payoff functions are not linear.)

11. Consider a two action binomial sampling problem with the following payoff functions:

$$\text{Payoff } (A_1) = 20p(1 - p); \quad \text{Payoff } (A_2) = 4p + 2.4$$

a. Graph these payoff functions to verify that there is more than one breakeven point for this problem in the range of p values between 0 and 1.

b. The possible values of p which can occur for this problem are 0.1, 0.3, 0.5, 0.7, and 0.9. The prior probabilities for these values are all 0.2. Consider taking a sample of size 4. Draw and analyze a decision tree for this problem. What is the optimal strategy?

c. Judging from the strategy for $n = 4$ which you obtained in part (b), can you guess what the general form of a strategy might be for this problem?

14

Where Are We Going?

THE PREVIOUS CHAPTERS have discussed, sometimes in excessive detail, the application of the techniques of decision theory to certain kinds of problems. It is worthwhile at this point to withdraw from that activity, contemplate our navels, and ask where we have been and where we are going. That is the purpose of this chapter. It begins with a general summary of the ideas and techniques discussed in previous chapters. It then discusses what subjects were *not* covered in this text, and the background required of the student in order to master these subjects. The chapter concludes with a prognosis of where the field of decision theory is going—what types of problems it should be able to solve in the future, and what minimum requirements are necessary for its survival.

14.1 WHAT YOU HAVE LEARNED

This text concentrated on two major aspects of decision theory. The first, contained mainly in Chapters 3 through 5, concerned the basic concepts of how to solve problems using decision theory. There we learned that the basic value used to make decisions was an expected value, determined by combining the chances of various events occurring with the values accruing to the actions if each of these events occurred. In Chapter 3 the values were simple quantities such as hours of enjoyment or dollars received. In Chapter 4 we recognized that in certain situations these quantities could not be used directly, so a method was developed to transform their values into utilities. These utilities were then used in place of the original values in the expected value calculations.

In Chapter 5 the concept of obtaining additional information through taking a sample was considered. The most important concept of this chapter is that sample information is not perfect. On the other hand it can be, as exemplified by the quote in Chapter 1, surprisingly powerful—much more powerful than most people are capable of understanding. Given this situation, Chapter 5 deals with techniques for properly treating sample information. Associated with this treatment is the concept that one must adopt a strategy when dealing with a sample. A strategy is an acknowledgement that different actions may be taken for different sample outcomes. The method of evaluation of a sampling plan then dealt with the evaluation of the best strategy for that plan.

Chapters 6 through 12 then discussed in great detail the application of these concepts to the two most prevalent kinds of sampling situations. The first of these, in which a probability is the unknown quantity, is dealt with in Chapters 6 through 10. Much of the material in these chapters deals with the mechanics and "tricks" of making this problem amenable to solution. This, unfortunately, is characteristic of decision theory applied to anything save the most simple minded kinds of problems.

The second part of these chapters, Chapters 11 and 12, dealt with the application of decision theory concepts to situations in which a mean is the quantity to be determined. As with the previous chapters, these too devote a great deal of time to the mechanics of solving these types of problems.

There is one clarion advantage both of the "realistic" situations dealt with in this book have over situations we have not discussed. That is the presence of a sampling distribution of known form. In the case in which we are trying to determine the value of a probability the sampling distribution is, under certain generally satisfied assumptions, binomial. When we are trying to determine the value of a mean, the powerful central limit theorem tells us that, given a sufficiently large sample, the sampling distribution is normal. These results are extremely powerful, and unique to the two situations we have studied. If some other characteristic of the population, say its variance, is the quantity of interest in the study, there is, unfortunately, no universal sampling distribution. A quick review of Chapters 6 through 12 will show the reader how utterly important the results obtained there depend upon knowing the form of the sampling distribution. When the form of the sampling distribution is not known, the situation is not hopeless. It is, however, a much more conceptually and methodologically difficult situation to deal with.

Chapter 13 is the only chapter remaining to be reviewed. There techniques are given so the reader can move from theory to practice. However, the assumption throughout that chapter is that the form of the sampling distribution is still known. Therefore, Chapter 13 is still limited to binomial and normal sampling situations. It does, however, give the reader good ideas on methods to solve decision theory problems when others of the assumptions in these problems are relaxed. It also gives the reader a flavor for the numerical analysis and empirical statistics techniques usually necessary to analyze problems in practice.

14.2 WHAT PROBLEMS YOU HAVE NOT LEARNED TO SOLVE

There are three major classifications of topics that have not been studied in this text. The first, a continuation of the study of topics like those in the text, is limited by the size of this text and the assumed mathematical sophistication of its readers. In spite of the fact that we cannot continue, ad infinitum, discussing decision theory problems with different characteristics, it is helpful to look at the dimensions of problems we did not discuss.

There are two ways we can make decision theory problems more difficult. The first is to consider problems in which the unknown quantity is not some probability or the mean of a distribution, but some other characteristic, say the variance. The difficulty of continuing our study in this direction has already been mentioned. Beyond the probability and the mean, no other characteristic has a universal sampling distribution. Therefore, although the reader may have thought binomial and normal sampling problems to be very difficult to solve, these other kinds of problems would be orders of magnitude more difficult.

The second dimension to increasing the difficulty of decision theory problems is to make more than one characteristic of the population distribution unknown. For example, in the normal sampling chapters we assumed that the mean of a varying quantity was unknown, but that the variance of this same quantity was known. Often this is an unrealistic assumption, and both the mean and the variance of a quantity are unknown. However, introducing a new event (the unknown variance) into a decision theory problem makes the problem much more difficult to solve. Therefore, these problems have not been treated in this text.

For the reader who is interested, and who has the appropriate mathematics and statistics background (see below), books by DeGroot[1] and Raiffa and Schlaifer[2] are recommended for further study in these areas.

---

[1] Morris H. DeGroot, *Optimal Statistical Decisions* (McGraw-Hill, 1970).

[2] Howard Raiffa and Robert Schlaifer, *Applied Statistical Decision Theory,* Division of Research, Graduate School of Business Administration, Harvard University, 1961.

The second major classification not covered in this text is that of multiattribute utility functions. If more than one outcome is relevant to the decision problem at hand, then these outcomes must be combined to provide a univariate measure of the utility of any event-action pair. As mentioned in Chapter 4, significant progress is being made in the development of techniques to make this combination, and in interactive computer programs to allow the decision maker to establish his own multiattribute utility function. Therefore, the reader can look forward to useful results in this field within five years.

The third major classification not covered is that of group decision making. In all the problems treated in this book the assumption has been that a single individual had total responsibility for making these decisions. The situation becomes much more muddied when a group has the responsibility for making a decision. Since a decision theory problem can potentially have many subjective aspects, what kind of a decision should be made if the individuals in the group differ (as they undoubtedly will) in their assessment of these quantities? Unfortunately, much work needs to be done in this area before good techniques are developed to solve the problem. The dilemma of this problem hinges on the question of the willingness of the group to work together, trust each other, and the group's ability to have a synergistic effect. Chapter 8 in Raiffa[3] succinctly presents the dilemma in this area. Until more work is done in this area we will have to rely on individuals (elected officials, corporate heads) as having a utility function that is reflective of the group they are serving.

14.3 WHAT THE TECHNOLOGIST NEEDS TO STUDY FURTHER

As the reader is probably already aware, the successful application of decision theory to any problem beyond the simplest requires a level of expertise in statistics and numerical analysis. Any further study in this field magnifies that need. The person who is interested in becoming a decision theory analyst needs additional experience in two widely divergent fields. One, which will be discussed below, is that of interaction with people, especially decision makers. Decision theory problems cannot be solved in a vacuum. Interaction is absolutely essential to successfully solving such problems. The second field in which the technologist needs more training is that of statistics and numerical analysis. In order even to read such previously mentioned books as DeGroot and Raiffa and Schalifer, the student needs comprehensive training in mathematical statistics. In order to successfully tackle the problems associated with the practical applications in this field the student needs a thorough grounding in applied statistics and numerical

---

[3] Howard Raiffa, *Decision Analysis* (Addison-Wesley, 1968).

analysis. It is very hard to continue in this field without this background. The serious student is urged to gain as much knowledge in these areas as possible.

14.4   WHERE IS THE FIELD OF DECISION THEORY GOING?

The prognosis for decision theory is good. New techniques, especially in the area of multiattribute utility theory, are being developed almost daily. Furthermore, with the new interest in interactive computing, many of the decision theory techniques, including the assessment of utility functions, are being programmed. Soon they will be available in software packages for all decision makers who have access to an interactive computer terminal. This development will put decision theory very much in the eyes of the decision makers, and should make it a tool used widely.

The computer packages will have their limitations, of course, and the forefront of development of the science depends upon individuals. Especially in the case of decision theory, the interaction between the technologist and the decision maker is vitally important. The practicing technologist realizes how vital this interaction is. However, the student who has never had any practical experience tends not to know how important interaction with management is. To put it simply, if you are reading this book and are interested in becoming a technologist in decision theory, your career future, and to a small extent the future of decision theory as a whole rests upon your ability and willingness to interact with decision makers.

If, on the other hand, you intend to become a manager, I hope this book has given you a basic understanding of decision theory, and that you understand in general *when* you can use it, and specifically when you can use it unaided, and when you need to call in an expert to help with the technical details. This book's main purpose is to stimulate its readers to try out decision theory, and adopt it as one of their tools when appropriate.

Tables

TABLE I
Cumulative Binomial Distribution

$$P(X \geq r|n, p)$$

$$n = 1$$

P R	01	02	03	04	05	06	07	08	09	10
1	0100	0200	0300	0400	0500	0600	0700	0800	0900	1000

P R	11	12	13	14	15	16	17	18	19	20
1	1100	1200	1300	1400	1500	1600	1700	1800	1900	2000

P R	21	22	23	24	25	26	27	28	29	30
1	2100	2200	2300	2400	2500	2600	2700	2800	2900	3000

P R	31	32	33	34	35	36	37	38	39	40
1	3100	3200	3300	3400	3500	3600	3700	3800	3900	4000

P R	41	42	43	44	45	46	47	48	49	50
1	4100	4200	4300	4400	4500	4600	4700	4800	4900	5000

$$n = 2$$

P R	01	02	03	04	05	06	07	08	09	10
1	0199	0396	0591	0784	0975	1164	1351	1536	1719	1900
2	0001	0004	0009	0016	0025	0036	0049	0064	0081	0100

P R	11	12	13	14	15	16	17	18	19	20
1	2079	2256	2431	2604	2775	2944	3111	3276	3439	3600
2	0121	0144	0169	0196	0225	0256	0289	0324	0361	0400

P R	21	22	23	24	25	26	27	28	29	30
1	3759	3916	4071	4224	4375	4524	4671	4816	4959	5100
2	0441	0484	0529	0576	0625	0676	0729	0784	0841	0900

P R	31	32	33	34	35	36	37	38	39	40
1	5239	5376	5511	5644	5775	5904	6031	6156	6279	6400
2	0961	1024	1089	1156	1225	1296	1369	1444	1521	1600

P R	41	42	43	44	45	46	47	48	49	50
1	6519	6636	6751	6864	6975	7084	7191	7296	7399	7500
2	1681	1764	1849	1936	2025	2116	2209	2304	2401	2500

$$n = 3$$

P R	01	02	03	04	05	06	07	08	09	10
1	0297	0588	0873	1153	1426	1694	1956	2213	2464	2710
2	0003	0012	0026	0047	0073	0104	0140	0182	0228	0280
3				0001	0001	0002	0003	0005	0007	0010

P R	11	12	13	14	15	16	17	18	19	20
1	2950	3185	3415	3639	3859	4073	4282	4486	4686	4880
2	0336	0397	0463	0533	0608	0686	0769	0855	0946	1040
3	0013	0017	0022	0027	0034	0041	0049	0058	0069	0080

P R	21	22	23	24	25	26	27	28	29	30
1	5070	5254	5435	5610	5781	5948	6110	6268	6421	6570
2	1138	1239	1344	1452	1563	1676	1793	1913	2035	2160
3	0093	0106	0122	0138	0156	0176	0197	0220	0244	0270

TABLE I (continued)

P	31	32	33	34	35	36	37	38	39	40
R										
1	6715	6856	6992	7125	7254	7379	7500	7617	7730	7840
2	2287	2417	2548	2682	2818	2955	3094	3235	3377	3520
3	0298	0328	0359	0393	0429	0467	0507	0549	0593	0640

P	41	42	43	44	45	46	47	48	49	50
R										
1	7946	8049	8148	8244	8336	8425	8511	8594	8673	8750
2	3665	3810	3957	4104	4253	4401	4551	4700	4850	5000
3	0689	0741	0795	0852	0911	0973	1038	1106	1176	1250

$$n = 4$$

P	01	02	03	04	05	06	07	08	09	10
R										
1	0394	0776	1147	1507	1855	2193	2519	2836	3143	3439
2	0006	0023	0052	0091	0140	0199	0267	0344	0430	0523
3			0001	0002	0005	0008	0013	0019	0027	0037
4									0001	0001

P	11	12	13	14	15	16	17	18	19	20
R										
1	3726	4003	4271	4530	4780	5021	5254	5479	5695	5904
2	0624	0732	0847	0968	1095	1228	1366	1509	1656	1808
3	0049	0063	0079	0098	0120	0144	0171	0202	0235	0272
4	0001	0002	0003	0004	0005	0007	0008	0010	0013	0016

P	21	22	23	24	25	26	27	28	29	30
R										
1	6105	6298	6485	6664	6836	7001	7160	7313	7459	7599
2	1963	2122	2285	2450	2617	2787	2959	3132	3307	3483
3	0312	0356	0403	0453	0508	0566	0628	0694	0763	0837
4	0019	0023	0028	0033	0039	0046	0053	0061	0071	0081

P	31	32	33	34	35	36	37	38	39	40
R										
1	7733	7862	7985	8103	8215	8322	8425	8522	8615	8704
2	3660	3837	4015	4193	4370	4547	4724	4900	5075	5248
3	0915	0996	1082	1171	1265	1362	1464	1569	1679	1792
4	0092	0105	0119	0134	0150	0168	0187	0209	0231	0256

P	41	42	43	44	45	46	47	48	49	50
R										
1	8788	8868	8944	9017	9085	9150	9211	9269	9323	9375
2	5420	5590	5759	5926	6090	6252	6412	6569	6724	6875
3	1909	2030	2155	2283	2415	2550	2689	2834	2977	3125
4	0283	0311	0342	0375	0410	0448	0488	0531	0576	0625

$$n = 5$$

P	01	02	03	04	05	06	07	08	09	10
R										
1	0490	0961	1413	1846	2262	2661	3043	3409	3760	4095
2	0010	0038	0085	0148	0226	0319	0425	0544	0674	0815
3		0001	0003	0006	0012	0020	0031	0045	0063	0086
4							0001	0002	0003	0005

P	11	12	13	14	15	16	17	18	19	20
R										
1	4416	4723	5016	5296	5563	5818	6061	6293	6513	6723
2	0965	1125	1292	1467	1648	1835	2027	2224	2424	2627
3	0112	0143	0179	0220	0266	0318	0375	0437	0505	0579
4	0007	0009	0013	0017	0022	0029	0036	0045	0055	0067
5				0001	0001	0001	0001	0002	0002	0003

P	21	22	23	24	25	26	27	28	29	30
R										
1	6923	7113	7293	7464	7627	7781	7927	8065	8196	8319
2	2833	3041	3251	3461	3672	3883	4093	4303	4511	4718
3	0659	0744	0836	0933	1035	1143	1257	1376	1501	1631
4	0081	0097	0114	0134	0156	0181	0208	0238	0272	0308
5	0004	0005	0006	0008	0010	0012	0014	0017	0021	0024

TABLE I (*continued*)

P	31	32	33	34	35	36	37	38	39	40
R										
1	8436	8546	8650	8748	8840	8926	9008	9084	9155	9222
2	4923	5125	5325	5522	5716	5906	6093	6276	6455	6630
3	1766	1905	2050	2199	2352	2509	2670	2835	3003	3174
4	0347	0390	0436	0486	0540	0598	0660	0726	0796	0870
5	0029	0034	0039	0045	0053	0060	0069	0079	0090	0102

P	41	42	43	44	45	46	47	48	49	50
R										
1	9285	9344	9398	9449	9497	9541	9582	9620	9655	9688
2	6801	6967	7129	7286	7438	7585	7728	7865	7998	8125
3	3349	3525	3705	3886	4069	4253	4439	4625	4813	5000
4	0949	1033	1121	1214	1312	1415	1522	1635	1753	1875
5	0116	0131	0147	0165	0185	0206	0229	0255	0282	0313

$$n = 6$$

P	01	02	03	04	05	06	07	08	09	10
R										
1	0585	1142	1670	2172	2649	3101	3530	3936	4321	4686
2	0015	0057	0125	0216	0328	0459	0608	0773	0952	1143
3		0002	0005	0012	0022	0038	0058	0085	0118	0159
4					0001	0002	0003	0005	0008	0013
5										0001

P	11	12	13	14	15	16	17	18	19	20
R										
1	5030	5356	5664	5954	6229	6487	6731	6960	7176	7379
2	1345	1556	1776	2003	2235	2472	2713	2956	3201	3446
3	0206	0261	0324	0395	0473	0560	0655	0759	0870	0989
4	0018	0025	0034	0045	0059	0075	0094	0116	0141	0170
5	0001	0001	0002	0003	0004	0005	0007	0010	0013	0016
6										0001

P	21	22	23	24	25	26	27	28	29	30
R										
1	7569	7748	7916	8073	8220	8358	8487	8607	8719	8824
2	3692	3937	4180	4422	4661	4896	5128	5356	5580	5798
3	1115	1250	1391	1539	1694	1856	2023	2196	2374	2557
4	0202	0239	0280	0326	0376	0431	0492	0557	0628	0705
5	0020	0025	0031	0038	0046	0056	0067	0079	0093	0109
6	0001	0001	0001	0002	0002	0003	0004	0005	0006	0007

P	31	32	33	34	35	36	37	38	39	40
R										
1	8921	9011	9095	9173	9246	9313	9375	9432	9485	9533
2	6012	6220	6422	6619	6809	6994	7172	7343	7508	7667
3	2744	2936	3130	3328	3529	3732	3937	4143	4350	4557
4	0787	0875	0969	1069	1174	1286	1404	1527	1657	1792
5	0127	0148	0170	0195	0223	0254	0288	0325	0365	0410
6	0009	0011	0013	0015	0018	0022	0026	0030	0035	0041

P	41	42	43	44	45	46	47	48	49	50
R										
1	9578	9619	9657	9692	9723	9752	9778	9802	9824	9844
2	7819	7965	8105	8238	8364	8485	8599	8707	8810	8906
3	4764	4971	5177	5382	5585	5786	5985	6180	6373	6563
4	1933	2080	2232	2390	2553	2721	2893	3070	3252	3438
5	0458	0510	0566	0627	0692	0762	0837	0917	1003	1094
6	0048	0055	0063	0073	0083	0095	0108	0122	0138	0156

$$n = 7$$

P	01	02	03	04	05	06	07	08	09	10
R										
1	0679	1319	1920	2486	3017	3515	3983	4422	4832	5217
2	0020	0079	0171	0294	0444	0618	0813	1026	1255	1497
3		0003	0009	0020	0038	0063	0097	0140	0193	0257
4				0001	0002	0004	0007	0012	0018	0027
5								0001	0001	0002

TABLE I (continued)

P	11	12	13	14	15	16	17	18	19	20
R										
1	5577	5913	6227	6521	6794	7049	7286	7507	7712	7903
2	1750	2012	2281	2556	2834	3115	3396	3677	3956	4233
3	0331	0416	0513	0620	0738	0866	1005	1154	1313	1480
4	0039	0054	0072	0094	0121	0153	0189	0231	0279	0333
5	0003	0004	0006	0009	0012	0017	0022	0029	0037	0047
6				0001	0001	0001	0002	0003	0004	

P	21	22	23	24	25	26	27	28	29	30
R										
1	8080	8243	8395	8535	8665	8785	8895	8997	9090	9176
2	4506	4775	5040	5298	5551	5796	6035	6266	6490	6706
3	1657	1841	2033	2231	2436	2646	2861	3081	3304	3529
4	0394	0461	0536	0617	0706	0802	0905	1016	1134	1260
5	0058	0072	0088	0107	0129	0153	0181	0213	0248	0288
6	0005	0006	0008	0011	0013	0017	0021	0026	0031	0038
7					0001	0001	0001	0001	0002	0002

P	31	32	33	34	35	36	37	38	39	40
R										
1	9255	9328	9394	9454	9510	9560	9606	9648	9686	9720
2	6914	7113	7304	7487	7662	7828	7987	8137	8279	8414
3	3757	3987	4217	4447	4677	4906	5134	5359	5581	5801
4	1394	1534	1682	1837	1998	2167	2341	2521	2707	2898
5	0332	0380	0434	0492	0556	0625	0701	0782	0869	0963
6	0046	0055	0065	0077	0090	0105	0123	0142	0164	0188
7	0003	0003	0004	0005	0006	0008	0009	0011	0014	0016

P	41	42	43	44	45	46	47	48	49	50
R										
1	9751	9779	9805	9827	9848	9866	9883	9897	9910	9922
2	8541	8660	8772	8877	8976	9068	9153	9233	9307	9375
3	6017	6229	6436	6638	6836	7027	7213	7393	7567	7734
4	3094	3294	3498	3706	3917	4131	4346	4563	4781	5000
5	1063	1169	1282	1402	1529	1663	1803	1951	2105	2266
6	0216	0246	0279	0316	0357	0402	0451	0504	0562	0625
7	0019	0023	0027	0032	0037	0044	0051	0059	0068	0078

$$n = 8$$

P	01	02	03	04	05	06	07	08	09	10
R										
1	0773	1492	2163	2786	3366	3904	4404	4868	5297	5695
2	0027	0103	0223	0381	0572	0792	1035	1298	1577	1869
3	0001	0004	0013	0031	0058	0096	0147	0211	0289	0381
4			0001	0002	0004	0007	0013	0022	0034	0050
5							0001	0001	0003	0004

P	11	12	13	14	15	16	17	18	19	20
R										
1	6063	6404	6718	7008	7275	7521	7748	7956	8147	8322
2	2171	2480	2794	3111	3428	3744	4057	4366	4670	4967
3	0487	0608	0743	0891	1052	1226	1412	1608	1815	2031
4	0071	0097	0129	0168	0214	0267	0328	0397	0476	0563
5	0007	0010	0015	0021	0029	0038	0050	0065	0083	0104
6		0001	0001	0002	0002	0003	0005	0007	0009	0012
7									0001	0001

P	21	22	23	24	25	26	27	28	29	30
R										
1	8483	8630	8764	8887	8999	9101	9194	9278	9354	9424
2	5257	5538	5811	6075	6329	6573	6807	7031	7244	7447
3	2255	2486	2724	2967	3215	3465	3718	3973	4228	4482
4	0659	0765	0880	1004	1138	1281	1433	1594	1763	1941
5	0129	0158	0191	0230	0273	0322	0377	0438	0505	0580
6	0016	0021	0027	0034	0042	0052	0064	0078	0094	0113
7	0001	0002	0002	0003	0004	0005	0006	0008	0010	0013
8									0001	0001

TABLE I (continued)

P\R	31	32	33	34	35	36	37	38	39	40
1	9486	9543	9594	9640	9681	9719	9752	9782	9808	9832
2	7640	7822	7994	8156	8309	8452	8586	8711	8828	8936
3	4736	4987	5236	5481	5722	5958	6189	6415	6634	6846
4	2126	2319	2519	2724	2936	3153	3374	3599	3828	4059
5	0661	0750	0846	0949	1061	1180	1307	1443	1586	1737
6	0134	0159	0187	0218	0253	0293	0336	0385	0439	0498
7	0016	0020	0024	0030	0036	0043	0051	0061	0072	0085
8	0001	0001	0001	0002	0002	0003	0004	0004	0005	0007

P\R	41	42	43	44	45	46	47	48	49	50
1	9853	9872	9889	9903	9916	9928	9938	9947	9954	9961
2	9037	9130	9216	9295	9368	9435	9496	9552	9602	9648
3	7052	7250	7440	7624	7799	7966	8125	8276	8419	8555
4	4292	4527	4762	4996	5230	5463	5694	5922	6146	6367
5	1895	2062	2235	2416	2604	2798	2999	3205	3416	3633
6	0563	0634	0711	0794	0885	0982	1086	1198	1318	1445
7	0100	0117	0136	0157	0181	0208	0239	0272	0310	0352
8	0008	0010	0012	0014	0017	0020	0024	0028	0033	0039

$$n = 9$$

P\R	01	02	03	04	05	06	07	08	09	10
1	0865	1663	2398	3075	3698	4270	4796	5278	5721	6126
2	0034	0131	0282	0478	0712	0978	1271	1583	1912	2252
3	0001	0006	0020	0045	0084	0138	0209	0298	0405	0530
4			0001	0003	0006	0013	0023	0037	0057	0083
5						0001	0002	0003	0005	0009
6										0001

P\R	11	12	13	14	15	16	17	18	19	20
1	6496	6835	7145	7427	7684	7918	8131	8324	8499	8658
2	2599	2951	3304	3657	4005	4348	4685	5012	5330	5638
3	0672	0833	1009	1202	1409	1629	1861	2105	2357	2618
4	0117	0158	0209	0269	0339	0420	0512	0615	0730	0856
5	0014	0021	0030	0041	0056	0075	0098	0125	0158	0196
6	0001	0002	0003	0004	0006	0009	0013	0017	0023	0031
7						0001	0001	0002	0002	0003

P\R	21	22	23	24	25	26	27	28	29	30
1	8801	8931	9048	9154	9249	9335	9411	9480	9542	9596
2	5934	6218	6491	6750	6997	7230	7452	7660	7856	8040
3	2885	3158	3434	3713	3993	4273	4552	4829	5102	5372
4	0994	1144	1304	1475	1657	1849	2050	2260	2478	2703
5	0240	0291	0350	0416	0489	0571	0662	0762	0870	0988
6	0040	0051	0065	0081	0100	0122	0149	0179	0213	0253
7	0004	0006	0008	0010	0013	0017	0022	0028	0035	0043
8			0001	0001	0001	0001	0002	0003	0003	0004

P\R	31	32	33	34	35	36	37	38	39	40
1	9645	9689	9728	9762	9793	9820	9844	9865	9883	9899
2	8212	8372	8522	8661	8789	8908	9017	9118	9210	9295
3	5636	5894	6146	6390	6627	6856	7076	7287	7489	7682
4	2935	3173	3415	3662	3911	4163	4416	4669	4922	5174
5	1115	1252	1398	1553	1717	1890	2072	2262	2460	2666
6	0298	0348	0404	0467	0536	0612	0696	0787	0886	0994
7	0053	0064	0078	0094	0112	0133	0157	0184	0215	0250
8	0006	0007	0009	0011	0014	0017	0021	0026	0031	0038
9				0001	0001	0001	0001	0002	0002	0003

P\R	41	42	43	44	45	46	47	48	49	50
1	9913	9926	9936	9946	9954	9961	9967	9972	9977	9980
2	9372	9442	9505	9563	9615	9662	9704	9741	9775	9805
3	7866	8039	8204	8359	8505	8642	8769	8889	8999	9102
4	5424	5670	5913	6152	6386	6614	6836	7052	7260	7461
5	2878	3097	3322	3551	3786	4024	4265	4509	4754	5000
6	1109	1233	1366	1508	1658	1817	1985	2161	2346	2539
7	0290	0334	0383	0437	0498	0564	0637	0717	0804	0898
8	0046	0055	0065	0077	0091	0107	0125	0145	0169	0195
9	0003	0004	0005	0006	0008	0009	0011	0014	0016	0020

TABLE I (continued)

$n = 10$

P	01	02	03	04	05	06	07	08	09	10
R										
1	0956	1829	2626	3352	4013	4614	5160	5656	6106	6513
2	0043	0162	0345	0582	0861	1176	1517	1879	2254	2639
3	0001	0009	0028	0062	0115	0188	0283	0401	0540	0702
4			0001	0004	0010	0020	0036	0058	0088	0128
5					0001	0002	0003	0006	0010	0016
6									0001	0001

P	11	12	13	14	15	16	17	18	19	20
R										
1	6882	7215	7516	7787	8031	8251	8448	8626	8784	8926
2	3028	3417	3804	4184	4557	4920	5270	5608	5932	6242
3	0884	1087	1308	1545	1798	2064	2341	2628	2922	3222
4	0178	0239	0313	0400	0500	0614	0741	0883	1039	1209
5	0025	0037	0053	0073	0099	0130	0168	.0213	0266	0328
6	0003	0004	0006	0010	0014	0020	0027	0037	0049	0064
7		0001	0001	0001	0001	0002	0003	0004	0006	0009
8									0001	0001

P	21	22	23	24	25	26	27	28	29	30
R										
1	9053	9166	9267	9357	9437	9508	9570	9626	9674	9718
2	6536	6815	7079	7327	7560	7778	7981	8170	8345	8507
3	3526	3831	4137	4442	4744	5042	5335	5622	5901	6172
4	1391	1587	1794	2012	2241	2479	2726	2979	3239	3504
5	0399	0479	0569	0670	0781	0904	1037	1181	1337	1503
6	0082	0104	0130	0161	0197	0239	0287	0342	0404	0473
7	0012	0016	0021	0027	0035	0045	0056	0070	0087	0106
8	0001	0002	0002	0003	0004	0006	0007	0010	0012	0016
9							0001	0001	0001	0001

P	31	32	33	34	35	36	37	38	39	40
R										
1	9755	9789	9818	9843	9865	9885	9902	9916	9929	9940
2	8656	8794	8920	9035	9140	9236	9323	9402	9473	9536
3	6434	6687	6930	7162	7384	7595	7794	7983	8160	8327
4	3772	4044	4316	4589	4862	5132	5400	5664	5923	6177
5	1679	1867	2064	2270	2485	2708	2939	3177	3420	3669
6	0551	0637	0732	0836	0949	1072	1205	1348	1500	1662
7	0129	0155	0185	0220	0260	0305	0356	0413	0477	0548
8	0020	0025	0032	0039	0048	0059	0071	0086	0103	0123
9	0002	0003	0003	0004	0005	0007	0009	0011	0014	0017
10								0001	0001	0001

P	41	42	43	44	45	46	47	48	49	50
R										
1	9949	9957	9964	9970	9975	9979	9983	9986	9988	9990
2	9594	9645	9691	9731	9767	9799	9827	9852	9874	9893
3	8483	8628	8764	8889	9004	9111	9209	9298	9379	9453
4	6425	6665	6898	7123	7340	7547	7745	7933	8112	8281
5	3922	4178	4436	4696	4956	5216	5474	5730	5982	6230
6	1834	2016	2207	2407	2616	2832	3057	3288	3526	3770
7	0626	0712	0806	0908	1020	1141	1271	1410	1560	1719
8	0146	0172	0202	0236	0274	0317	0366	0420	0480	0547
9	0021	0025	0031	0037	0045	0054	0065	0077	0091	0107
10	0001	0002	0002	0003	0003	0004	0005	0006	0008	0010

$n = 11$

P	01	02	03	04	05	06	07	08	09	10
R										
1	1047	1993	2847	3618	4312	4937	5499	6004	6456	6862
2	0052	0195	0413	0692	1019	1382	1772	2181	2601	3026
3	0002	0012	0037	0083	0152	0248	0370	0519	0695	0896
4			0002	0007	0016	0030	0053	0085	0129	0185
5					0001	0003	0005	0010	0017	0028
6								0001	0002	0003

TABLE I (continued)

P	11	12	13	14	15	16	17	18	19	20
R										
1	7225	7549	7839	8097	8327	8531	8712	8873	9015	9141
2	3452	3873	4286	4689	5078	5453	5811	6151	6474	6779
3	1120	1366	1632	1915	2212	2521	2839	3164	3494	3826
4	0256	0341	0442	0560	0694	0846	1013	1197	1397	1611
5	0042	0061	0087	0119	0159	0207	0266	0334	0413	0504
6	0005	0008	0012	0018	0027	0037	0051	0068	0090	0117
7		0001	0001	0002	0003	0005	0007	0010	0014	0020
8							0001	0001	0002	0002

P	21	22	23	24	25	26	27	28	29	30
R										
1	9252	9350	9436	9511	9578	9636	9686	9730	9769	9802
2	7065	7333	7582	7814	8029	8227	8410	8577	8730	8870
3	4158	4488	4814	5134	5448	5753	6049	6335	6610	6873
4	1840	2081	2333	2596	2867	3146	3430	3719	4011	4304
5	0607	0723	0851	0992	1146	1313	1493	1685	1888	2103
6	0148	0186	0231	0283	0343	0412	0490	0577	0674	0782
7	0027	0035	0046	0059	0076	0095	0119	0146	0179	0216
8	0003	0005	0007	0009	0012	0016	0021	0027	0034	0043
9			0001	0001	0001	0002	0002	0003	0004	0006

P	31	32	33	34	35	36	37	38	39	40
R										
1	9831	9856	9878	9896	9912	9926	9938	9948	9956	9964
2	8997	9112	9216	9310	9394	9470	9537	9597	9650	9698
3	7123	7361	7587	7799	7999	8186	8360	8522	8672	8811
4	4598	4890	5179	5464	5744	6019	6286	6545	6796	7037
5	2328	2563	2807	3059	3317	3581	3850	4122	4397	4672
6	0901	1031	1171	1324	1487	1661	1847	2043	2249	2465
7	0260	0309	0366	0430	0501	0581	0670	0768	0876	0994
8	0054	0067	0082	0101	0122	0148	0177	0210	0249	0293
9	0008	0010	0013	0016	0020	0026	0032	0039	0048	0059
10	0001	0001	0001	0002	0002	0003	0004	0005	0006	0007

P	41	42	43	44	45	46	47	48	49	50
R										
1	9970	9975	9979	9983	9986	9989	9991	9992	9994	9995
2	9739	9776	9808	9836	9861	9882	9900	9916	9930	9941
3	8938	9055	9162	9260	9348	9428	9499	9564	9622	9673
4	7269	7490	7700	7900	8089	8266	8433	8588	8733	8867
5	4948	5223	5495	5764	6029	6288	6541	6787	7026	7256
6	2690	2924	3166	3414	3669	3929	4193	4460	4729	5000
7	1121	1260	1408	1568	1738	1919	2110	2312	2523	2744
8	0343	0399	0461	0532	0610	0696	0791	0895	1009	1133
9	0072	0087	0104	0125	0148	0175	0206	0241	0282	0327
10	0009	0012	0014	0018	0022	0027	0033	0040	0049	0059
11	0001	0001	0001	0001	0002	0002	0002	0003	0004	0005

$$n = 12$$

P	01	02	03	04	05	06	07	08	09	10
R										
1	1136	2153	3062	3873	4596	5241	5814	6323	6775	7176
2	0062	0231	0486	0809	1184	1595	2033	2487	2948	3410
3	0002	0015	0048	0107	0196	0316	0468	0652	0866	1109
4		0001	0003	0010	0022	0043	0075	0120	0180	0256
5				0001	0002	0004	0009	0016	0027	0043
6							0001	0002	0003	0005
7										0001

P	11	12	13	14	15	16	17	18	19	20
R										
1	7530	7843	8120	8363	8578	8766	8931	9076	9202	9313
2	3867	4314	4748	5166	5565	5945	6304	6641	6957	7251
3	1377	1667	1977	2303	2642	2990	3344	3702	4060	4417
4	0351	0464	0597	0750	0922	1114	1324	1552	1795	2054
5	0065	0095	0133	0181	0239	0310	0393	0489	0600	0726
6	0009	0014	0022	0033	0046	0065	0088	0116	0151	0194
7	0001	0002	0003	0004	0007	0010	0015	0021	0029	0039
8					0001	0001	0002	0003	0004	0006
9										0001

TABLE I (continued)

P	21	22	23	24	25	26	27	28	29	30
R										
1	9409	9493	9566	9629	9683	9730	9771	9806	9836	9862
2	7524	7776	8009	8222	8416	8594	8755	8900	9032	9150
3	4768	5114	5450	5778	6093	6397	6687	6963	7225	7472
4	2326	2610	2904	3205	3512	3824	4137	4452	4765	5075
5	0866	1021	1192	1377	1576	1790	2016	2254	2504	2763
6	0245	0304	0374	0453	0544	0646	0760	0887	1026	1178
7	0052	0068	0089	0113	0143	0178	0219	0267	0322	0386
8	0008	0011	0016	0021	0028	0036	0047	0060	0076	0095
9	0001	0001	0002	0003	0004	0005	0007	0010	0013	0017
10						0001	0001	0001	0002	0002

P	31	32	33	34	35	36	37	38	39	40
R										
1	9884	9902	9918	9932	9943	9953	9961	9968	9973	9978
2	9256	9350	9435	9509	9576	9634	9685	9730	9770	9804
3	7704	7922	8124	8313	8487	8648	8795	8931	9054	9166
4	5381	5681	5973	6258	6533	6799	7053	7296	7528	7747
5	3032	3308	3590	3876	4167	4459	4751	5043	5332	5618
6	1343	1521	1711	1913	2127	2352	2588	2833	3087	3348
7	0458	0540	0632	0734	0846	0970	1106	1253	1411	1582
8	0118	0144	0176	0213	0255	0304	0359	0422	0493	0573
9	0022	0028	0036	0045	0056	0070	0086	0104	0127	0153
10	0003	0004	0005	0007	0008	0011	0014	0018	0022	0028
11				0001	0001	0001	0001	0002	0002	0003

P	41	42	43	44	45	46	47	48	49	50
R										
1	9982	9986	9988	9990	9992	9994	9995	9996	9997	9998
2	9834	9860	9882	9901	9917	9931	9943	9953	9961	9968
3	9267	9358	9440	9513	9579	9637	9688	9733	9773	9807
4	7953	8147	8329	8498	8655	8801	8934	9057	9168	9270
5	5899	6175	6443	6704	6956	7198	7430	7652	7862	8062
6	3616	3889	4167	4448	4731	5014	5297	5577	5855	6128
7	1765	1959	2164	2380	2607	2843	3089	3343	3604	3872
8	0662	0760	0869	0988	1117	1258	1411	1575	1751	1938
9	0183	0218	0258	0304	0356	0415	0481	0555	0638	0730
10	0035	0043	0053	0065	0079	0095	0114	0137	0163	0193
11	0004	0005	0007	0009	0011	0014	0017	0021	0026	0032
12				0001	0001	0001	0001	0001	0002	0002

$$n = 13$$

P	01	02	03	04	05	06	07	08	09	10
R										
1	1225	2310	3270	4118	4867	5526	6107	6617	7065	7458
2	0072	0270	0564	0932	1354	1814	2298	2794	3293	3787
3	0003	0020	0062	0135	0245	0392	0578	0799	1054	1339
4		0001	0005	0014	0031	0060	0103	0163	0242	0342
5				0001	0003	0007	0013	0024	0041	0065
6						0001	0001	0003	0005	0009
7									0001	0001

P	11	12	13	14	15	16	17	18	19	20
R										
1	7802	8102	8364	8592	8791	8963	9113	9242	9354	9450
2	4270	4738	5186	5614	6017	6396	6751	7080	7384	7664
3	1651	1985	2337	2704	3080	3463	3848	4231	4611	4983
4	0464	0609	0776	0967	1180	1414	1667	1939	2226	2527
5	0097	0139	0193	0260	0342	0438	0551	0681	0827	0991
6	0015	0024	0036	0053	0075	0104	0139	0183	0237	0300
7	0002	0003	0005	0008	0013	0019	0027	0038	0052	0070
8			0001	0001	0002	0003	0004	0006	0009	0012
9								0001	0001	0002

TABLE I (*continued*)

P R	21	22	23	24	25	26	27	28	29	30
1	9533	9604	9666	9718	9762	9800	9833	9860	9883	9903
2	7920	8154	8367	8559	8733	8889	9029	9154	9265	9363
3	5347	5699	6039	6364	6674	6968	7245	7505	7749	7975
4	2839	3161	3489	3822	4157	4493	4826	5155	5478	5794
5	1173	1371	1585	1816	2060	2319	2589	2870	3160	3457
6	0375	0462	0562	0675	0802	0944	1099	1270	1455	1654
7	0093	0120	0154	0195	0243	0299	0365	0440	0527	0624
8	0017	0024	0032	0043	0056	0073	0093	0118	0147	0182
9	0002	0004	0005	0007	0010	0013	0018	0024	0031	0040
10			0001	0001	0001	0002	0003	0004	0005	0007
11									0001	0001

P R	31	32	33	34	35	36	37	38	39	40
1	9920	9934	9945	9955	9963	9970	9975	9980	9984	9987
2	9450	9527	9594	9653	9704	9749	9787	9821	9849	9874
3	8185	8379	8557	8720	8868	9003	9125	9235	9333	9421
4	6101	6398	6683	6957	7217	7464	7698	7917	8123	8314
5	3760	4067	4376	4686	4995	5301	5603	5899	6188	6470
6	1867	2093	2331	2581	2841	3111	3388	3673	3962	4256
7	0733	0854	0988	1135	1295	1468	1654	1853	2065	2288
8	0223	0271	0326	0390	0462	0544	0635	0738	0851	0977
9	0052	0065	0082	0102	0126	0154	0187	0225	0270	0321
10	0009	0012	0015	0020	0025	0032	0040	0051	0063	0078
11	0001	0001	0002	0003	0003	0005	0006	0008	0010	0013
12							0001	0001	0001	0001

P R	41	42	43	44	45	46	47	48	49	50
1	9990	9992	9993	9995	9996	9997	9997	9998	9998	9999
2	9895	9912	9928	9940	9951	9960	9967	9974	9979	9983
3	9499	9569	9630	9684	9731	9772	9808	9838	9865	9888
4	8492	8656	8807	8945	9071	9185	9288	9381	9464	9539
5	6742	7003	7254	7493	7721	7935	8137	8326	8502	8666
6	4552	4849	5146	5441	5732	6019	6299	6573	6838	7095
7	2524	2770	3025	3290	3563	3842	4127	4415	4707	5000
8	1114	1264	1426	1600	1788	1988	2200	2424	2659	2905
9	0379	0446	0520	0605	0698	0803	0918	1045	1183	1334
10	0096	0117	0141	0170	0203	0242	0287	0338	0396	0461
11	0017	0021	0027	0033	0041	0051	0063	0077	0093	0112
12	0002	0002	0003	0004	0005	0007	0009	0011	0014	0017
13							0001	0001	0001	0001

$$n = 14$$

P R	01	02	03	04	05	06	07	08	09	10
1	1313	2464	3472	4353	5123	5795	6380	6888	7330	7712
2	0084	0310	0645	1059	1530	2037	2564	3100	3632	4154
3	0003	0025	0077	0167	0301	0478	0698	0958	1255	1584
4		0001	0006	0019	0042	0080	0136	0214	0315	0441
5				0002	0004	0010	0020	0035	0059	0092
6						0001	0002	0004	0008	0015
7									0001	0002

P R	11	12	13	14	15	16	17	18	19	20
1	8044	8330	8577	8789	8972	9129	9264	9379	9477	9560
2	4658	5141	5599	6031	6433	6807	7152	7469	7758	8021
3	1939	2315	2708	3111	3521	3932	4341	4744	5138	5519
4	0594	0774	0979	1210	1465	1742	2038	2351	2679	3018
5	0137	0196	0269	0359	0467	0594	0741	0907	1093	1298
6	0024	0038	0057	0082	0115	0157	0209	0273	0349	0439
7	0003	0006	0009	0015	0022	0032	0046	0064	0087	0116
8			0001	0001	0002	0003	0005	0008	0012	0017	0024
9						0001	0001	0002	0003	0004

TABLE I (continued)

P	21	22	23	24	25	26	27	28	29	30
R										
1	9631	9691	9742	9786	9822	9852	9878	9899	9917	9932
2	8259	8473	8665	8837	8990	9126	9246	9352	9444	9525
3	5887	6239	6574	6891	7189	7467	7727	7967	8188	8392
4	3366	3719	4076	4432	4787	5136	5479	5813	6137	6448
5	1523	1765	2023	2297	2585	2884	3193	3509	3832	4158
6	0543	0662	0797	0949	1117	1301	1502	1718	1949	2195
7	0152	0196	0248	0310	0383	0467	0563	0673	0796	0933
8	0033	0045	0060	0079	0103	0132	0167	0208	0257	0315
9	0006	0008	0011	0016	0022	0029	0038	0050	0065	0083
10	0001	0001	0002	0002	0003	0005	0007	0009	0012	0017
11						0001	0001	0001	0002	0002

P	31	32	33	34	35	36	37	38	39	40
R										
1	9945	9955	9963	9970	9976	9981	9984	9988	9990	9992
2	9596	9657	9710	9756	9795	9828	9857	9881	9902	9919
3	8577	8746	8899	9037	9161	9271	9370	9457	9534	9602
4	6747	7032	7301	7556	7795	8018	8226	8418	8595	8757
5	4486	4813	5138	5458	5773	6080	6378	6666	6943	7207
6	2454	2724	3006	3297	3595	3899	4208	4519	4831	5141
7	1084	1250	1431	1626	1836	2059	2296	2545	2805	3075
8	0381	0458	0545	0643	0753	0876	1012	1162	1325	1501
9	0105	0131	0163	0200	0243	0294	0353	0420	0497	0583
10	0022	0029	0037	0048	0060	0076	0095	0117	0144	0175
11	0003	0005	0006	0008	0011	0014	0019	0024	0031	0039
12		0001	0001	0001	0001	0002	0003	0003	0005	0006
13										0001

P	41	42	43	44	45	46	47	48	49	50
R										
1	9994	9995	9996	9997	9998	9998	9999	9999	9999	9999
2	9934	9946	9956	9964	9971	9977	9981	9985	9988	9991
3	9661	9713	9758	9797	9830	9858	9883	9903	9921	9935
4	8905	9039	9161	9270	9368	9455	9532	9601	9661	9713
5	7459	7697	7922	8132	8328	8510	8678	8833	8974	9102
6	5450	5754	6052	6344	6627	6900	7163	7415	7654	7880
7	3355	3643	3937	4236	4539	4843	5148	5451	5751	6047
8	1692	1896	2113	2344	2586	2840	3105	3380	3663	3953
9	0680	0789	0910	1043	1189	1348	1520	1707	1906	2120
10	0212	0255	0304	0361	0426	0500	0583	0677	0782	0898
11	0049	0061	0076	0093	0114	0139	0168	0202	0241	0287
12	0008	0010	0013	0017	0022	0027	0034	0042	0053	0065
13	0001	0001	0001	0002	0003	0003	0004	0006	0007	0009
14										0001

$$n = 15$$

P	01	02	03	04	05	06	07	08	09	10
R										
1	1399	2614	3667	4579	5367	6047	6633	7137	7570	7941
2	0096	0353	0730	1191	1710	2262	2832	3403	3965	4510
3	0004	0030	0094	0203	0362	0571	0829	1130	1469	1841
4		0002	0008	0024	0055	0104	0175	0273	0399	0556
5			0001	0002	0006	0014	0028	0050	0082	0127
6					0001	0001	0003	0007	0013	0022
7							0001	0002	0003	

P	11	12	13	14	15	16	17	18	19	20
R										
1	8259	8530	8762	8959	9126	9269	9389	9490	9576	9648
2	5031	5524	5987	6417	6814	7179	7511	7813	8085	8329
3	2238	2654	3084	3520	3958	4392	4819	5234	5635	6020
4	0742	0959	1204	1476	1773	2092	2429	2782	3146	3518
5	0187	0265	0361	0478	0617	0778	0961	1167	1394	1642
6	0037	0057	0084	0121	0168	0227	0300	0387	0490	0611
7	0006	0010	0015	0024	0036	0052	0074	0102	0137	0181
8	0001	0001	0002	0004	0006	0010	0014	0021	0030	0042
9					0001	0001	0002	0003	0005	0008
10									0001	0001

TABLE I (continued)

P	21	22	23	24	25	26	27	28	29	30
R										
1	9709	9759	9802	9837	9866	9891	9911	9928	9941	9953
2	8547	8741	8913	9065	9198	9315	9417	9505	9581	9647
3	6385	6731	7055	7358	7639	7899	8137	8355	8553	8732
4	3895	4274	4650	5022	5387	5742	6086	6416	6732	7031
5	1910	2195	2495	2810	3135	3469	3810	4154	4500	4845
6	0748	0905	1079	1272	1484	1713	1958	2220	2495	2784
7	0234	0298	0374	0463	0566	0684	0817	0965	1130	1311
8	0058	0078	0104	0135	0173	0219	0274	0338	0413	0500
9	0011	0016	0023	0031	0042	0056	0073	0094	0121	0152
10	0002	0003	0004	0006	0008	0011	0015	0021	0028	0037
11			0001	0001	0001	0002	0002	0003	0005	0007
12									0001	0001

P	31	32	33	34	35	36	37	38	39	40
R										
1	9962	9969	9975	9980	9984	9988	9990	9992	9994	9995
2	9704	9752	9794	9829	9858	9883	9904	9922	9936	9948
3	8893	9038	9167	9281	9383	9472	9550	9618	9678	9729
4	7314	7580	7829	8060	8273	8469	8649	8813	8961	9095
5	5187	5523	5852	6171	6481	6778	7062	7332	7587	7827
6	3084	3393	3709	4032	4357	4684	5011	5335	5654	5968
7	1509	1722	1951	2194	2452	2722	3003	3295	3595	3902
8	0599	0711	0837	0977	1132	1302	1487	1687	1902	2131
9	0190	0236	0289	0351	0422	0504	0597	0702	0820	0950
10	0048	0062	0079	0099	0124	0154	0190	0232	0281	0338
11	0009	0012	0016	0022	0028	0037	0047	0059	0075	0093
12	0001	0002	0003	0004	0005	0006	0009	0011	0015	0019
13					0001	0001	0001	0002	0002	0003

P	41	42	43	44	45	46	47	48	49	50
R										
1	9996	9997	9998	9998	9999	9999	9999	9999	10000	10000
2	9958	9966	9973	9979	9983	9987	9990	9992	9994	9995
3	9773	9811	9843	9870	9893	9913	9929	9943	9954	9963
4	9215	9322	9417	9502	9576	9641	9697	9746	9788	9824
5	8052	8261	8454	8633	8796	8945	9080	9201	9310	9408
6	6274	6570	6856	7131	7392	7641	7875	8095	8301	8491
7	4214	4530	4847	5164	5478	5789	6095	6394	6684	6964
8	2374	2630	2898	3176	3465	3762	4065	4374	4686	5000
9	1095	1254	1427	1615	1818	2034	2265	2510	2767	3036
10	0404	0479	0565	0661	0769	0890	1024	1171	1333	1509
11	0116	0143	0174	0211	0255	0305	0363	0430	0506	0592
12	0025	0032	0040	0051	0063	0079	0097	0119	0145	0176
13	0004	0005	0007	0009	0011	0014	0018	0023	0029	0037
14			0001	0001	0001	0002	0002	0003	0004	0005

$$n = 16$$

P	01	02	03	04	05	06	07	08	09	10
R										
1	1485	2762	3857	4796	5599	6284	6869	7366	7789	8147
2	0109	0399	0818	1327	1892	2489	3098	3701	4289	4853
3	0005	0037	0113	0242	0429	0673	0969	1311	1694	2108
4		0002	0011	0032	0070	0132	0221	0342	0496	0684
5			0001	0003	0009	0019	0038	0068	0111	0170
6					0001	0002	0005	0010	0019	0033
7							0001	0001	0003	0005
8										0001

P	11	12	13	14	15	16	17	18	19	20
R										
1	8450	8707	8923	9105	9257	9386	9493	9582	9657	9719
2	5386	5885	6347	6773	7161	7513	7830	8115	8368	8593
3	2545	2999	3461	3926	4386	4838	5277	5698	6101	6482
4	0907	1162	1448	1763	2101	2460	2836	3223	3619	4019
5	0248	0348	0471	0618	0791	0988	1211	1458	1727	2018
6	0053	0082	0120	0171	0235	0315	0412	0527	0662	0817
7	0009	0015	0024	0038	0056	0080	0112	0153	0204	0267
8	0001	0002	0004	0007	0011	0016	0024	0036	0051	0070
9			0001	0001	0002	0003	0004	0007	0010	0015
10							0.001	0001	0002	0002

TABLE I (*continued*)

P	21	22	23	24	25	26	27	28	29	30
R										
1	9770	9812	9847	9876	9900	9919	9935	9948	9958	9967
2	8791	8965	9117	9250	9365	9465	9550	9623	9686	9739
3	6839	7173	7483	7768	8029	8267	8482	8677	8851	9006
4	4418	4814	5203	5583	5950	6303	6640	6959	7260	7541
5	2327	2652	2991	3341	3698	4060	4425	4788	5147	5501
6	0992	1188	1405	1641	1897	2169	2458	2761	3077	3402
7	0342	0432	0536	0657	0796	0951	1125	1317	1526	1753
8	0095	0127	0166	0214	0271	0340	0420	0514	0621	0744
9	0021	0030	0041	0056	0075	0098	0127	0163	0206	0257
10	0004	0006	0008	0012	0016	0023	0031	0041	0055	0071
11	0001	0001	0001	0002	0003	0004	0006	0008	0011	0016
12						0001	0001	0001	0002	0003

P	31	32	33	34	35	36	37	38	39	40
R										
1	9974	9979	9984	9987	9990	9992	9994	9995	9996	9997
2	9784	9822	9854	9880	9902	9921	9936	9948	9959	9967
3	9144	9266	9374	9467	9549	9620	9681	9734	9778	9817
4	7804	8047	8270	8475	8661	8830	8982	9119	9241	9349
5	5846	6181	6504	6813	7108	7387	7649	7895	8123	8334
6	3736	4074	4416	4759	5100	5438	5770	6094	6408	6712
7	1997	2257	2531	2819	3119	3428	3746	4070	4398	4728
8	0881	1035	1205	1391	1594	1813	2048	2298	2562	2839
9	0317	0388	0470	0564	0671	0791	0926	1076	1242	1423
10	0092	0117	0148	0185	0229	0280	0341	0411	0491	0583
11	0021	0028	0037	0048	0062	0079	0100	0125	0155	0191
12	0004	0005	0007	0010	0013	0017	0023	0030	0038	0049
13		0001	0001	0001	0002	0003	0004	0005	0007	0009
14								0001	0001	0001

P	41	42	43	44	45	46	47	48	49	50
R										
1	9998	9998	9999	9999	9999	9999	10000	10000	10000	10000
2	9974	9979	9984	9987	9990	9992	9994	9995	9997	9997
3	9849	9876	9899	9918	9934	9947	9958	9966	9973	9979
4	9444	9527	9600	9664	9719	9766	9806	9840	9869	9894
5	8529	8707	8869	9015	9147	9265	9370	9463	9544	9616
6	7003	7280	7543	7792	8024	8241	8441	8626	8795	8949
7	5058	5387	5711	6029	6340	6641	6932	7210	7476	7728
8	3128	3428	3736	4051	4371	4694	5019	5343	5665	5982
9	1619	1832	2060	2302	2559	2829	3111	3405	3707	4018
10	0687	0805	0936	1081	1241	1416	1607	1814	2036	2272
11	0234	0284	0342	0409	0486	0574	0674	0786	0911	1051
12	0062	0078	0098	0121	0149	0183	0222	0268	0322	0384
13	0012	0016	0021	0027	0035	0044	0055	0069	0086	0106
14	0002	0002	0003	0004	0006	0007	0010	0013	0016	0021
15					0001	0001	0001	0001	0002	0003

$$n = 17$$

P	01	02	03	04	05	06	07	08	09	10
R										
1	1571	2907	4042	5004	5819	6507	7088	7577	7988	8332
2	0123	0446	0909	1465	2078	2717	3362	3995	4604	5182
3	0006	0044	0134	0286	0503	0782	1118	1503	1927	2382
4		0003	0014	0040	0088	0164	0273	0419	0603	0826
5			0001	0004	0012	0026	0051	0089	0145	0221
6					0001	0003	0007	0015	0027	0047
7							0001	0002	0004	0008
8										0001

P	11	12	13	14	15	16	17	18	19	20
R										
1	8621	8862	9063	9230	9369	9484	9579	9657	9722	9775
2	5723	6223	6682	7099	7475	7813	8113	8379	8613	8818
3	2858	3345	3836	4324	4802	5266	5711	6133	6532	6904
4	1087	1383	1710	2065	2444	2841	3251	3669	4091	4511
5	0321	0446	0598	0778	0987	1224	1487	1775	2087	2418
6	0075	0114	0166	0234	0319	0423	0548	0695	0864	1057
7	0014	0023	0037	0056	0083	0118	0163	0220	0291	0377
8	0002	0004	0007	0011	0017	0027	0039	0057	0080	0109
9		0001	0001	0002	0003	0005	0008	0012	0018	0026
10						0001	0001	0002	0003	0005
11										0001

TABLE I (continued)

P	21	22	23	24	25	26	27	28	29	30
R										
1	9818	9854	9882	9906	9925	9940	9953	9962	9970	9977
2	8996	9152	9285	9400	9499	9583	9654	9714	9765	9807
3	7249	7567	7859	8123	8363	8578	8771	8942	9093	9226
4	4927	5333	5728	6107	6470	6814	7137	7440	7721	7981
5	2766	3128	3500	3879	4261	4643	5023	5396	5760	6113
6	1273	1510	1770	2049	2347	2661	2989	3329	3677	4032
7	0479	0598	0736	0894	1071	1268	1485	1721	1976	2248
8	0147	0194	0251	0320	0402	0499	0611	0739	0884	1046
9	0037	0051	0070	0094	0124	0161	0206	0261	0326	0403
10	0007	0011	0016	0022	0031	0042	0057	0075	0098	0127
11	0001	0002	0003	0004	0006	0009	0013	0018	0024	0032
12				0001	0001	0002	0002	0003	0005	0007
13									0001	0001

P	31	32	33	34	35	36	37	38	39	40
R										
1	9982	9986	9989	9991	9993	9995	9996	9997	9998	9998
2	9843	9872	9896	9917	9933	9946	9957	9966	9973	9979
3	9343	9444	9532	9608	9673	9728	9775	9815	9849	9877
4	8219	8437	8634	8812	8972	9115	9241	9353	9450	9536
5	6453	6778	7087	7378	7652	7906	8142	8360	8559	8740
6	4390	4749	5105	5458	5803	6139	6465	6778	7077	7361
7	2536	2838	3153	3479	3812	4152	4495	4839	5182	5522
8	1227	1426	1642	1877	2128	2395	2676	2971	3278	3595
9	0492	0595	0712	0845	0994	1159	1341	1541	1757	1989
10	0162	0204	0254	0314	0383	0464	0557	0664	0784	0919
11	0043	0057	0074	0095	0120	0151	0189	0234	0286	0348
12	0009	0013	0017	0023	0030	0040	0051	0066	0084	0106
13	0002	0002	0003	0004	0006	0008	0011	0015	0019	0025
14				0001	0001	0001	0002	0002	0003	0005
15										0001

P	41	42	43	44	45	46	47	48	49	50
R										
1	9999	9999	9999	9999	10000	10000	10000	10000	10000	10000
2	9984	9987	9990	9992	9994	9996	9997	9998	9998	9999
3	9900	9920	9935	9948	9959	9968	9975	9980	9985	9988
4	9610	9674	9729	9776	9816	9849	9877	9901	9920	9936
5	8904	9051	9183	9301	9404	9495	9575	9644	9704	9755
6	7628	7879	8113	8330	8529	8712	8878	9028	9162	9283
7	5856	6182	6499	6805	7098	7377	7641	7890	8122	8338
8	3920	4250	4585	4921	5257	5590	5918	6239	6552	6855
9	2238	2502	2780	3072	3374	3687	4008	4335	4667	5000
10	1070	1236	1419	1618	1834	2066	2314	2577	2855	3145
11	0420	0503	0597	0705	0826	0962	1112	1279	1462	1662
12	0133	0165	0203	0248	0301	0363	0434	0517	0611	0717
13	0033	0042	0054	0069	0086	0108	0134	0165	0202	0245
14	0006	0008	0011	0014	0019	0024	0031	0040	0050	0064
15	0001	0001	0002	0002	0003	0004	0005	0007	0009	0012
16							0001	0001	0001	0001

$$n = 18$$

P	01	02	03	04	05	06	07	08	09	10
R										
1	1655	3049	4220	5204	6028	6717	7292	7771	8169	8499
2	0138	0495	1003	1607	2265	2945	3622	4281	4909	5497
3	0007	0052	0157	0333	0581	0898	1275	1702	2168	2662
4		0004	0018	0050	0109	0201	0333	0506	0723	0982
5			0002	0006	0015	0034	0067	0116	0186	0282
6				0001	0002	0005	0010	0021	0038	0064
7							0001	0003	0006	0012
8									0001	0002

P	11	12	13	14	15	16	17	18	19	20
R										
1	8773	8998	9185	9338	9464	9566	9651	9719	9775	9820
2	6042	6540	6992	7398	7759	8080	8362	8609	8824	9009
3	3173	3690	4206	4713	5203	5673	6119	6538	6927	7287
4	1282	1618	1986	2382	2798	3229	3669	4112	4554	4990
5	0405	0558	0743	0959	1206	1482	1787	2116	2467	2836

TABLE I (continued)

P	11	12	13	14	15	16	17	18	19	20
R										
6	0102	0154	0222	0310	0419	0551	0708	0889	1097	1329
7	0021	0034	0054	0081	0118	0167	0229	0306	0400	0513
8	0003	0006	0011	0017	0027	0041	0060	0086	0120	0163
9		0001	0002	0003	0005	0008	0013	0020	0029	0043
10					0001	0001	0002	0004	0006	0009
11								0001	0001	0002

P	21	22	23	24	25	26	27	28	29	30
R										
1	9856	9886	9909	9928	9944	9956	9965	9973	9979	9984
2	9169	9306	9423	9522	9605	9676	9735	9784	9824	9858
3	7616	7916	8187	8430	8647	8839	9009	9158	9288	9400
4	5414	5825	6218	6591	6943	7272	7578	7860	8119	8354
5	3220	3613	4012	4414	4813	5208	5594	5968	6329	6673
6	1586	1866	2168	2488	2825	3176	3538	3907	4281	4656
7	0645	0799	0974	1171	1390	1630	1891	2171	2469	2783
8	0217	0283	0363	0458	0569	0699	0847	1014	1200	1407
9	0060	0083	0112	0148	0193	0249	0316	0395	0488	0596
10	0014	0020	0028	0039	0054	0073	0097	0127	0164	0210
11	0003	0004	0006	0009	0012	0018	0025	0034	0046	0061
12		0001	0001	0002	0002	0003	0005	0007	0010	0014
13						0001	0001	0001	0002	0003

P	31	32	33	34	35	36	37	38	39	40
R										
1	9987	9990	9993	9994	9996	9997	9998	9998	9999	9999
2	9886	9908	9927	9942	9954	9964	9972	9978	9983	9987
3	9498	9581	9652	9713	9764	9807	9843	9873	9897	9918
4	8568	8759	8931	9083	9217	9335	9439	9528	9606	9672
5	7001	7309	7598	7866	8114	8341	8549	8737	8907	9058
6	5029	5398	5759	6111	6450	6776	7086	7379	7655	7912
7	3111	3450	3797	4151	4509	4867	5224	5576	5921	6257
8	1633	1878	2141	2421	2717	3027	3349	3681	4021	4366
9	0720	0861	1019	1196	1391	1604	1835	2084	2350	2632
10	0264	0329	0405	0494	0597	0714	0847	0997	1163	1347
11	0080	0104	0133	0169	0212	0264	0325	0397	0480	0576
12	0020	0027	0036	0047	0062	0080	0102	0130	0163	0203
13	0004	0005	0008	0011	0014	0019	0026	0034	0044	0058
14	0001	0001	0001	0002	0003	0004	0005	0007	0010	0013
15						0001	0001	0001	0002	0002

P	41	42	43	44	45	46	47	48	49	50
R										
1	9999	9999	10000	10000	10000	10000	10000	10000	10000	10000
2	9990	9992	9994	9996	9997	9998	9998	9999	9999	9999
3	9934	9948	9959	9968	9975	9981	9985	9989	9991	9993
4	9729	9777	9818	9852	9880	9904	9923	9939	9952	9962
5	9193	9313	9418	9510	9589	9658	9717	9767	9810	9846
6	8151	8372	8573	8757	8923	9072	9205	9324	9428	9519
7	6582	6895	7193	7476	7742	7991	8222	8436	8632	8811
8	4713	5062	5408	5750	6085	6412	6728	7032	7322	7597
9	2928	3236	3556	3885	4222	4562	4906	5249	5591	5927
10	1549	1768	2004	2258	2527	2812	3110	3421	3742	4073
11	0686	0811	0951	1107	1280	1470	1677	1902	2144	2403
12	0250	0307	0372	0449	0537	0638	0753	0883	1028	1189
13	0074	0094	0118	0147	0183	0225	0275	0334	0402	0481
14	0017	0022	0029	0038	0049	0063	0079	0100	0125	0154
15	0003	0004	0006	0007	0010	0013	0017	0023	0029	0038
16		0001	0001	0001	0001	0002	0003	0004	0005	0007
17									0001	0001

$$n = 19$$

P	01	02	03	04	05	06	07	08	09	10
R										
1	1738	3188	4394	5396	6226	6914	7481	7949	8334	8649
2	0153	0546	1100	1751	2453	3171	3879	4560	5202	5797
3	0009	0061	0183	0384	0665	1021	1439	1908	2415	2946
4		0005	0022	0061	0132	0243	0398	0602	0853	1150
5			0002	0007	0020	0044	0085	0147	0235	0352
6				0001	0002	0006	0014	0029	0051	0086
7						0001	0002	0004	0009	0017
8								0001	0001	0003

TABLE I (continued)

P / R	11	12	13	14	15	16	17	18	19	20
1	8908	9119	9291	9431	9544	9636	9710	9770	9818	9856
2	6342	6835	7277	7669	8015	8318	8581	8809	9004	9171
3	3488	4032	4568	5089	5587	6059	6500	6910	7287	7631
4	1490	1867	2275	2708	3159	3620	4085	4549	5005	5449
5	0502	0685	0904	1158	1444	1762	2107	2476	2864	3267
6	0135	0202	0290	0401	0537	0700	0891	1110	1357	1631
7	0030	0048	0076	0113	0163	0228	0310	0411	0532	0676
8	0005	0009	0016	0026	0041	0061	0089	0126	0173	0233
9	0001	0002	0003	0005	0008	0014	0021	0032	0047	0067
10				0001	0001	0002	0004	0007	0010	0016
11							0001	0001	0002	0003

P / R	21	22	23	24	25	26	27	28	29	30
1	9887	9911	9930	9946	9958	9967	9975	9981	9985	9989
2	9313	9434	9535	9619	9690	9749	9797	9837	9869	9896
3	7942	8222	8471	8692	8887	9057	9205	9333	9443	9538
4	5877	6285	6671	7032	7369	7680	7965	8224	8458	8668
5	3681	4100	4520	4936	5346	5744	6129	6498	6848	7178
6	1929	2251	2592	2950	3322	3705	4093	4484	4875	5261
7	0843	1034	1248	1487	1749	2032	2336	2657	2995	3345
8	0307	0396	0503	0629	0775	0941	1129	1338	1568	1820
9	0093	0127	0169	0222	0287	0366	0459	0568	0694	0839
10	0023	0034	0047	0066	0089	0119	0156	0202	0258	0326
11	0005	0007	0011	0016	0023	0032	0044	0060	0080	0105
12	0001	0001	0002	0003	0005	0007	0010	0015	0021	0028
13				0001	0001	0001	0002	0003	0004	0006
14									0001	0001

P / R	31	32	33	34	35	36	37	38	39	40
1	9991	9993	9995	9996	9997	9998	9998	9999	9999	9999
2	9917	9935	9949	9960	9969	9976	9981	9986	9989	9992
3	9618	9686	9743	9791	9830	9863	9890	9913	9931	9945
4	8856	9028	9169	9297	9409	9505	9588	9659	9719	9770
5	7486	7773	8037	8280	8500	8699	8878	9038	9179	9304
6	5641	6010	6366	6707	7032	7339	7627	7895	8143	8371
7	3705	4073	4445	4818	5188	5554	5913	6261	6597	6919
8	2091	2381	2688	3010	3344	3690	4043	4401	4762	5122
9	1003	1186	1389	1612	1855	2116	2395	2691	3002	3325
10	0405	0499	0608	0733	0875	1035	1213	1410	1626	1861
11	0137	0176	0223	0280	0347	0426	0518	0625	0747	0885
12	0038	0051	0068	0089	0114	0146	0185	0231	0287	0352
13	0009	0012	0017	0023	0031	0041	0054	0070	0091	0116
14	0002	0002	0003	0005	0007	0009	0013	0017	0023	0031
15			0001	0001	0001	0002	0002	0003	0005	0006
16									0001	0001

P / R	41	42	43	44	45	46	47	48	49	50
1	10000	10000	10000	10000	10000	10000	10000	10000	10000	10000
2	9994	9995	9996	9997	9998	9999	9999	9999	9999	10000
3	9957	9967	9974	9980	9985	9988	9991	9993	9995	9996
4	9813	9849	9878	9903	9923	9939	9952	9963	9971	9978
5	9413	9508	9590	9660	9720	9771	9814	9850	9879	9904
6	8579	8767	8937	9088	9223	9342	9446	9537	9615	9682
7	7226	7515	7787	8039	8273	8488	8684	8862	9022	9165
8	5480	5832	6176	6509	6831	7138	7430	7706	7964	8204
9	3660	4003	4353	4706	5060	5413	5762	6105	6439	6762
10	2114	2385	2672	2974	3290	3617	3954	4299	4648	5000
11	1040	1213	1404	1613	1841	2087	2351	2631	2928	3238
12	0429	0518	0621	0738	0871	1021	1187	1372	1575	1796
13	0146	0183	0227	0280	0342	0415	0500	0597	0709	0835
14	0040	0052	0067	0086	0109	0137	0171	0212	0261	0318
15	0009	0012	0016	0021	0028	0036	0046	0060	0076	0096
16	0001	0002	0003	0004	0005	0007	0010	0013	0017	0022
17				0001	0001	0001	0001	0002	0003	0004

TABLE I (continued)

$$n = 20$$

P	01	02	03	04	05	06	07	08	09	10
R
1	1821	3324	4562	5580	6415	7099	7658	8113	8484	8784
2	0169	0599	1198	1897	2642	3395	4131	4831	5484	6083
3	0010	0071	0210	0439	0755	1150	1610	2121	2666	3231
4		0006	0027	0074	0159	0290	0471	0706	0993	1330
5			0003	0010	0026	0056	0107	0183	0290	0432
6				0001	0003	0009	0019	0038	0068	0113
7						0001	0003	0006	0013	0024
8								0001	0002	0004
9										0001

P	11	12	13	14	15	16	17	18	19	20
R
1	9028	9224	9383	9510	9612	9694	9759	9811	9852	9885
2	6624	7109	7539	7916	8244	8529	8773	8982	9159	9308
3	3802	4369	4920	5450	5951	6420	6854	7252	7614	7939
4	1710	2127	2573	3041	3523	4010	4496	4974	5439	5886
5	0610	0827	1083	1375	1702	2059	2443	2849	3271	3704
6	0175	0260	0370	0507	0673	0870	1098	1356	1643	1958
7	0041	0067	0103	0153	0219	0304	0409	0537	0689	0867
8	0008	0014	0024	0038	0059	0088	0127	0177	0241	0321
9	0001	0002	0005	0008	0013	0021	0033	0049	0071	0100
10			0001	0001	0002	0004	0007	0011	0017	0026
11						0001	0001	0002	0004	0006
12									0001	0001

P	21	22	23	24	25	26	27	28	29	30
R
1	9910	9931	9946	9959	9968	9976	9982	9986	9989	9992
2	9434	9539	9626	9698	9757	9805	9845	9877	9903	9924
3	8230	8488	8716	8915	9087	9237	9365	9474	9567	9645
4	6310	6711	7085	7431	7748	8038	8300	8534	8744	8929
5	4142	4580	5014	5439	5852	6248	6625	6981	7315	7625
6	2297	2657	3035	3427	3828	4235	4643	5048	5447	5836
7	1071	1301	1557	1838	2142	2467	2810	3169	3540	3920
8	0419	0536	0675	0835	1018	1225	1455	1707	1982	2277
9	0138	0186	0246	0320	0409	0515	0640	0784	0948	1133
10	0038	0054	0075	0103	0139	0183	0238	0305	0385	0480
11	0009	0013	0019	0028	0039	0055	0074	0100	0132	0171
12	0002	0003	0004	0006	0009	0014	0019	0027	0038	0051
13			0001	0001	0002	0003	0004	0006	0009	0013
14							0001	0001	0002	0003

P	31	32	33	34	35	36	37	38	39	40
R
1	9994	9996	9997	9998	9998	9999	9999	9999	9999	10000
2	9940	9953	9964	9972	9979	9984	9988	9991	9993	9995
3	9711	9765	9811	9848	9879	9904	9924	9940	9953	9964
4	9092	9235	9358	9465	9556	9634	9700	9755	9802	9840
5	7911	8173	8411	8626	8818	8989	9141	9274	9390	9490
6	6213	6574	6917	7242	7546	7829	8090	8329	8547	8744
7	4305	4693	5079	5460	5834	6197	6547	6882	7200	7500
8	2591	2922	3268	3624	3990	4361	4735	5108	5478	5841
9	1340	1568	1818	2087	2376	2683	3005	3341	3688	4044
10	0591	0719	0866	1032	1218	1424	1650	1897	2163	2447
11	0220	0279	0350	0434	0532	0645	0775	0923	1090	1275
12	0069	0091	0119	0154	0196	0247	0308	0381	0466	0565
13	0018	0025	0034	0045	0060	0079	0102	0132	0167	0210
14	0004	0006	0008	0011	0015	0021	0028	0037	0049	0065
15	0001	0001	0001	0002	0003	0004	0006	0009	0012	0016
16						0001	0001	0002	0002	0003

P	41	42	43	44	45	46	47	48	49	50
R
1	10000	10000	10000	10000	10000	10000	10000	10000	10000	10000
2	9996	9997	9998	9998	9999	9999	9999	10000	10000	10000
3	9972	9979	9984	9988	9991	9993	9995	9996	9997	9998
4	9872	9898	9920	9937	9951	9962	9971	9977	9983	9987
5	9577	9651	9714	9767	9811	9848	9879	9904	9924	9941

TABLE I (continued)

P R	41	42	43	44	45	46	47	48	49	50
6	8921	9078	9217	9340	9447	9539	9619	9687	9745	9793
7	7780	8041	8281	8501	8701	8881	9042	9186	9312	9423
8	6196	6539	6868	7183	7480	7759	8020	8261	8482	8684
9	4406	4771	5136	5499	5857	6207	6546	6873	7186	7483
10	2748	3064	3394	3736	4086	4443	4804	5166	5525	5881
11	1480	1705	1949	2212	2493	2791	3104	3432	3771	4119
12	0679	0810	0958	1123	1308	1511	1734	1977	2238	2517
13	0262	0324	0397	0482	0580	0694	0823	0969	1133	1316
14	0084	0107	0136	0172	0214	0265	0326	0397	0480	0577
15	0022	0029	0038	0050	0064	0083	0105	0133	0166	0207
16	0004	0006	0008	0011	0015	0020	0027	0035	0046	0059
17	0001	0001	0001	0002	0003	0004	0005	0007	0010	0013
18						0001	0001	0001	0001	0002

$$n = 50$$

P R	01	02	03	04	05	06	07	08	09	10
1	3950	6358	7819	8701	9231	9547	9734	9845	9910	9948
2	0894	2642	4447	5995	7206	8100	8735	9173	9468	9662
3	0138	0784	1892	3233	4595	5838	6892	7740	8395	8883
4	0016	0178	0628	1391	2396	3527	4673	5747	6697	7497
5	0001	0032	0168	0490	1036	1794	2710	3710	4723	5688
6		0005	0037	0144	0378	0776	1350	2081	2928	3839
7		0001	0007	0036	0118	0289	0583	1019	1596	2298
8			0001	0008	0032	0094	0220	0438	0768	1221
9				0001	0008	0027	0073	0167	0328	0579
10					0002	0007	0022	0056	0125	0245
11						0002	0006	0017	0043	0094
12							0001	0005	0013	0032
13								0001	0004	0010
14									0001	0003
15										0001

P R	11	12	13	14	15	16	17	18	19	20
1	9971	9983	9991	9995	9997	9998	9999	10000	10000	10000
2	9788	9869	9920	9951	9971	9983	9990	9994	9997	9998
3	9237	9487	9661	9779	9858	9910	9944	9965	9979	9987
4	8146	8655	9042	9330	9540	9688	9792	9863	9912	9943
5	6562	7320	7956	8472	8879	9192	9428	9601	9726	9815
6	4760	5647	6463	7186	7806	8323	8741	9071	9327	9520
7	3091	3935	4789	5616	6387	7081	7686	8199	8624	8966
8	1793	2467	3217	4010	4812	5594	6328	6996	7587	8096
9	0932	1392	1955	2605	3319	4071	4832	5576	6280	6927
10	0435	0708	1074	1537	2089	2718	3403	4122	4849	5563
11	0183	0325	0535	0824	1199	1661	2203	2813	3473	4164
12	0069	0135	0242	0402	0628	0929	1309	1768	2300	2893
13	0024	0051	0100	0179	0301	0475	0714	1022	1405	1861
14	0008	0018	0037	0073	0132	0223	0357	0544	0791	1106
15	0002	0006	0013	0027	0053	0096	0164	0266	0411	0607
16	0001	0002	0004	0009	0019	0038	0070	0120	0197	0308
17			0001	0003	0007	0014	0027	0050	0087	0144
18				0001	0002	0005	0010	0019	0036	0063
19						0001	0003	0007	0013	0025
20							0001	0002	0005	0009
21								0001	0002	0003
22										0001

P R	21	22	23	24	25	26	27	28	29	30
1	10000	10000	10000	10000	10000	10000	10000	10000	10000	10000
2	9999	9999	10000	10000	10000	10000	10000	10000	10000	10000
3	9992	9995	9997	9998	9999	10000	10000	10000	10000	10000
4	9964	9978	9986	9992	9995	9997	9998	9999	9999	10000
5	9877	9919	9948	9967	9979	9987	9992	9995	9997	9998
6	9663	9767	9841	9893	9930	9954	9970	9981	9988	9993
7	9236	9445	9603	9720	9806	9868	9911	9941	9961	9975
8	8523	8874	9156	9377	9547	9676	9772	9842	9892	9927
9	7505	8009	8437	8794	9084	9316	9497	9635	9740	9817
10	6241	6870	7436	7934	8363	8724	9021	9260	9450	9598

TABLE I (*continued*)

P / R	21	22	23	24	25	26	27	28	29	30
11	4864	5552	6210	6822	7378	7871	8299	8663	8965	9211
12	3533	4201	4878	5544	6184	6782	7329	7817	8244	8610
13	2383	2963	3585	4233	4890	5539	6163	6749	7287	7771
14	1490	1942	2456	3023	3630	4261	4901	5534	6145	6721
15	0862	1181	1565	2013	2519	3075	3669	4286	4912	5532
16	0462	0665	0926	1247	1631	2075	2575	3121	3703	4308
17	0229	0347	0508	0718	0983	1306	1689	2130	2623	3161
18	0105	0168	0259	0384	0551	0766	1034	1359	1741	2178
19	0045	0075	0122	0191	0287	0418	0590	0809	1080	1406
20	0018	0031	0054	0088	0139	0212	0314	0449	0626	0848
21	0006	0012	0022	0038	0063	0100	0155	0232	0338	0478
22	0002	0004	0008	0015	0026	0044	0071	0112	0170	0251
23	0001	0001	0003	0006	0010	0018	0031	0050	0080	0123
24			0001	0002	0004	0007	0012	0021	0035	0056
25				0001	0001	0002	0004	0008	0014	0024
26						0001	0002	0003	0005	0009
27								0001	0002	0003
28									0001	0001

P / R	31	32	33	34	35	36	37	38	39	40
1	10000	10000	10000	10000	10000	10000	10000	10000	10000	10000
2	10000	10000	10000	10000	10000	10000	10000	10000	10000	10000
3	10000	10000	10000	10000	10000	10000	10000	10000	10000	10000
4	10000	10000	10000	10000	10000	10000	10000	10000	10000	10000
5	9999	9999	10000	10000	10000	10000	10000	10000	10000	10000
6	9996	9997	9998	9999	9999	10000	10000	10000	10000	10000
7	9984	9990	9994	9996	9998	9999	9999	10000	10000	10000
8	9952	9969	9980	9987	9992	9995	9997	9998	9999	9999
9	9874	9914	9942	9962	9975	9984	9990	9994	9996	9998
10	9710	9794	9856	9901	9933	9955	9971	9981	9988	9992
11	9409	9563	9683	9773	9840	9889	9924	9949	9966	9978
12	8916	9168	9371	9533	9658	9753	9825	9878	9916	9943
13	8197	8564	8873	9130	9339	9505	9635	9736	9811	9867
14	7253	7732	8157	8524	8837	9097	9310	9481	9616	9720
15	6131	6698	7223	7699	8122	8491	8805	9069	9286	9460
16	4922	5530	6120	6679	7199	7672	8094	8462	8779	9045
17	3734	4328	4931	5530	6111	6664	7179	7649	8070	8439
18	2666	3197	3760	4346	4940	5531	6105	6653	7164	7631
19	1786	2220	2703	3227	3784	4362	4949	5533	6101	6644
20	1121	1447	1826	2257	2736	3255	3805	4376	4957	5535
21	0657	0882	1156	1482	1861	2289	2764	3278	3824	4390
22	0360	0503	0685	0912	1187	1513	1890	2317	2788	3299
23	0184	0267	0379	0525	0710	0938	1214	1540	1916	2340
24	0087	0133	0196	0282	0396	0544	0730	0960	1236	1562
25	0039	0061	0094	0141	0207	0295	0411	0560	0748	0978
26	0016	0026	0042	0066	0100	0149	0216	0305	0423	0573
27	0006	0011	0018	0029	0045	0070	0106	0155	0223	0314
28	0002	0004	0007	0012	0019	0031	0048	0074	0110	0160
29	0001	0001	0002	0004	0007	0012	0020	0032	0050	0076
30			0001	0002	0003	0005	0008	0013	0021	0034
31					0001	0002	0003	0005	0008	0014
32						0001	0001	0002	0003	0005
33								0001	0001	0002
34										0001

P / R	41	42	43	44	45	46	47	48	49	50
1	10000	10000	10000	10000	10000	10000	10000	10000	10000	10000
2	10000	10000	10000	10000	10000	10000	10000	10000	10000	10000
3	10000	10000	10000	10000	10000	10000	10000	10000	10000	10000
4	10000	10000	10000	10000	10000	10000	10000	10000	10000	10000
5	10000	10000	10000	10000	10000	10000	10000	10000	10000	10000
6	10000	10000	10000	10000	10000	10000	10000	10000	10000	10000
7	10000	10000	10000	10000	10000	10000	10000	10000	10000	10000
8	10000	10000	10000	10000	10000	10000	10000	10000	10000	10000
9	9999	9999	10000	10000	10000	10000	10000	10000	10000	10000
10	9995	9997	9998	9999	9999	10000	10000	10000	10000	10000
11	9986	9991	9994	9997	9997	9998	9999	9999	9999	10000
12	9962	9975	9984	9990	9994	9996	9998	9999	9999	9998
13	9908	9938	9958	9902	9933	9955	9970	9981	9988	9995
14	9799	9858	9902	9933	9955	9970	9981	9988	9992	9987
15	9599	9707	9789	9851	9896	9929	9952	9968	9980	9987

TABLE I (continued)

P R	41	42	43	44	45	46	47	48	49	50
16	9265	9443	9585	9696	9780	9844	9892	9926	9950	9967
17	8757	9025	9248	9429	9573	9687	9774	9839	9888	9923
18	8051	8421	8740	9010	9235	9418	9565	9680	9769	9836
19	7152	7617	8037	8406	8727	8998	9225	9410	9559	9675
20	6099	6638	7143	7608	8026	8396	8718	8991	9219	9405
21	4965	5539	6099	6635	7138	7602	8020	8391	8713	8987
22	3840	4402	4973	5543	6100	6634	7137	7599	8018	8389
23	2809	3316	3854	4412	4981	5548	6104	6636	7138	7601
24	1936	2359	2826	3331	3866	4422	4989	5554	6109	6641
25	1255	1580	1953	2375	2840	3343	3876	4431	4996	5561
26	0762	0992	1269	1593	1966	2386	2850	3352	3885	4439
27	0432	0584	0772	1003	1279	1603	1975	2395	2858	3359
28	0229	0320	0439	0591	0780	1010	1286	1609	1981	2399
29	0113	0164	0233	0325	0444	0595	0784	1013	1299	1611
30	0052	0078	0115	0166	0235	0327	0446	0596	0784	1013
31	0022	0034	0053	0079	0116	0167	0236	0327	0445	0595
32	0009	0014	0022	0035	0053	0079	0116	0166	0234	0325
33	0003	0005	0009	0014	0022	0035	0053	0078	0114	0164
34	0001	0002	0003	0005	0009	0014	0022	0034	0052	0077
35		0001	0001	0002	0003	0005	0008	0014	0021	0033
36				0001	0001	0002	0003	0005	0008	0013
37						0001	0001	0002	0003	0005
38								0001	0001	0002

$n = 100$

P R	01	02	03	04	05	06	07	08	09	10
1	6340	8674	9524	9831	9941	9979	9993	9998	9999	10000
2	2642	5967	8054	9128	9629	9848	9940	9977	9991	9997
3	0794	3233	5802	7679	8817	9434	9742	9887	9952	9981
4	0184	1410	3528	5705	7422	8570	9256	9633	9827	9922
5	0034	0508	1821	3711	5640	7232	8368	9097	9526	9763
6	0005	0155	0808	2116	3840	5593	7086	8201	8955	9424
7	0001	0041	0312	1064	2340	3936	5557	6968	8060	8828
8		0009	0106	0475	1280	2517	4012	5529	6872	7939
9		0002	0032	0190	0631	1463	2660	4074	5506	6791
10			0009	0068	0282	0775	1620	2780	4125	5487
11			0002	0022	0115	0376	0908	1757	2882	4168
12				0007	0043	0168	0469	1028	1876	2970
13				0002	0015	0069	0224	0559	1138	1982
14					0005	0026	0099	0282	0645	1239
15					0001	0009	0041	0133	0341	0726
16						0003	0016	0058	0169	0399
17						0001	0006	0024	0078	0206
18							0002	0009	0034	0100
19							0001	0003	0014	0046
20								0001	0005	0020
21									0002	0008
22									0001	0003
23										0001

P R	11	12	13	14	15	16	17	18	19	20
1	10000	10000	10000	10000	10000	10000	10000	10000	10000	10000
2	9999	10000	10000	10000	10000	10000	10000	10000	10000	10000
3	9992	9997	9999	10000	10000	10000	10000	10000	10000	10000
4	9966	9985	9994	9998	9999	10000	10000	10000	10000	10000
5	9886	9947	9977	9990	9996	9998	9999	10000	10000	10000
6	9698	9848	9926	9966	9984	9993	9997	9999	10000	10000
7	9328	9633	9808	9903	9953	9978	9990	9996	9998	9999
8	8715	9239	9569	9766	9878	9939	9970	9986	9994	9997
9	7835	8614	9155	9508	9725	9853	9924	9962	9982	9991
10	6722	7743	8523	9078	9449	9684	9826	9908	9953	9977
11	5471	6663	7663	8440	9006	9393	9644	9800	9891	9943
12	4206	5458	6611	7591	8365	8939	9340	9605	9773	9874
13	3046	4239	5446	6566	7527	8297	8876	9289	9567	9747
14	2076	3114	4268	5436	6526	7469	8234	8819	9241	9531
15	1330	2160	3173	4294	5428	6490	7417	8177	8765	9196
16	0802	1414	2236	3227	4317	5420	6458	7370	8125	8715
17	0456	0874	1492	2305	3275	4338	5414	6429	7327	8077
18	0244	0511	0942	1563	2367	3319	4357	5408	6403	7288
19	0123	0282	0564	1006	1628	2424	3359	4374	5403	6379
20	0059	0147	0319	0614	1065	1689	2477	3395	4391	5398

TABLE I (continued)

P / R	11	12	13	14	15	16	17	18	19	20
21	0026	0073	0172	0356	0663	1121	1745	2525	3429	4405
22	0011	0034	0088	0196	0393	0710	1174	1797	2570	3460
23	0005	0015	0042	0103	0221	0428	0754	1223	1846	2611
24	0002	0006	0020	0051	0119	0246	0462	0796	1270	1891
25	0001	0003	0009	0024	0061	0135	0271	0496	0837	1314
26		0001	0004	0011	0030	0071	0151	0295	0528	0875
27			0001	0005	0014	0035	0081	0168	0318	0558
28			0001	0002	0006	0017	0041	0091	0184	0342
29				0001	0003	0008	0020	0048	0102	0200
30					0001	0003	0009	0024	0054	0112
31						0001	0004	0011	0027	0061
32						0001	0002	0005	0013	0031
33							0001	0002	0006	0016
34								0001	0003	0007
35									0001	0003
36										0001
37										0001

P / R	21	22	23	24	25	26	27	28	29	30
1	10000	10000	10000	10000	10000	10000	10000	10000	10000	10000
2	10000	10000	10000	10000	10000	10000	10000	10000	10000	10000
3	10000	10000	10000	10000	10000	10000	10000	10000	10000	10000
4	10000	10000	10000	10000	10000	10000	10000	10000	10000	10000
5	10000	10000	10000	10000	10000	10000	10000	10000	10000	10000
6	10000	10000	10000	10000	10000	10000	10000	10000	10000	10000
7	10000	10000	10000	10000	10000	10000	10000	10000	10000	10000
8	9999	10000	10000	10000	10000	10000	10000	10000	10000	10000
9	9996	9998	9999	10000	10000	10000	10000	10000	10000	10000
10	9989	9995	9998	9999	10000	10000	10000	10000	10000	10000
11	9971	9986	9993	9997	9999	9999	10000	10000	10000	10000
12	9933	9965	9983	9992	9996	9998	9999	10000	10000	10000
13	9857	9922	9959	9979	9990	9995	9998	9999	10000	10000
14	9721	9840	9911	9953	9975	9988	9994	9997	9999	9999
15	9496	9695	9823	9900	9946	9972	9986	9993	9997	9998
16	9153	9462	9671	9806	9889	9939	9967	9983	9992	9996
17	8668	9112	9430	9647	9789	9878	9932	9963	9981	9990
18	8032	8625	9074	9399	9624	9773	9867	9925	9959	9978
19	7252	7991	8585	9038	9370	9601	9757	9856	9918	9955
20	6358	7220	7953	8547	9005	9342	9580	9741	9846	9911
21	5394	6338	7189	7918	8512	8973	9316	9560	9726	9835
22	4419	5391	6320	7162	7886	8479	8943	9291	9540	9712
23	3488	4432	5388	6304	7136	7856	8448	8915	9267	9521
24	2649	3514	4444	5386	6289	7113	7828	8420	8889	9245
25	1933	2684	3539	4455	5383	6276	7091	7802	8393	8864
26	1355	1972	2717	3561	4465	5381	6263	7071	7778	8369
27	0911	1393	2009	2748	3583	4475	5380	6252	7053	7756
28	0588	0945	1429	2043	2776	3602	4484	5378	6242	7036
29	0364	0616	0978	1463	2075	2803	3621	4493	5377	6232
30	0216	0386	0643	1009	1495	2105	2828	3638	4501	5377
31	0123	0232	0406	0669	1038	1526	2134	2851	3654	4509
32	0067	0134	0247	0427	0693	1065	1554	2160	2873	3669
33	0035	0074	0144	0262	0446	0717	1091	1580	2184	2893
34	0018	0039	0081	0154	0276	0465	0739	1116	1605	2207
35	0009	0020	0044	0087	0164	0290	0482	0760	1139	1629
36	0004	0010	0023	0048	0094	0174	0303	0499	0780	1161
37	0002	0005	0011	0025	0052	0101	0183	0316	0515	0799
38	0001	0002	0005	0013	0027	0056	0107	0193	0328	0530
39		0001	0002	0006	0014	0030	0060	0113	0201	0340
40			0001	0003	0007	0015	0032	0064	0119	0210
41				0001	0003	0008	0017	0035	0068	0125
42				0001	0001	0004	0008	0018	0037	0072
43					0001	0002	0004	0009	0020	0040
44						0001	0002	0005	0010	0021
45							0001	0002	0005	0011
46								0001	0002	0005
47									0001	0003
48										0001
49										0001

TABLE I (continued)

P / R	31	32	33	34	35	36	37	38	39	40
1	10000	10000	10000	10000	10000	10000	10000	10000	10000	10000
2	10000	10000	10000	10000	10000	10000	10000	10000	10000	10000
3	10000	10000	10000	10000	10000	10000	10000	10000	10000	10000
4	10000	10000	10000	10000	10000	10000	10000	10000	10000	10000
5	10000	10000	10000	10000	10000	10000	10000	10000	10000	10000
6	10000	10000	10000	10000	10000	10000	10000	10000	10000	10000
7	10000	10000	10000	10000	10000	10000	10000	10000	10000	10000
8	10000	10000	10000	10000	10000	10000	10000	10000	10000	10000
9	10000	10000	10000	10000	10000	10000	10000	10000	10000	10000
10	10000	10000	10000	10000	10000	10000	10000	10000	10000	10000
11	10000	10000	10000	10000	10000	10000	10000	10000	10000	10000
12	10000	10000	10000	10000	10000	10000	10000	10000	10000	10000
13	10000	10000	10000	10000	10000	10000	10000	10000	10000	10000
14	10000	10000	10000	10000	10000	10000	10000	10000	10000	10000
15	9999	10000	10000	10000	10000	10000	10000	10000	10000	10000
16	9998	9999	10000	10000	10000	10000	10000	10000	10000	10000
17	9995	9998	9999	10000	10000	10000	10000	10000	10000	10000
18	9989	9995	9997	9999	9999	10000	10000	10000	10000	10000
19	9976	9988	9994	9997	9999	9999	10000	10000	10000	10000
20	9950	9973	9986	9993	9997	9998	9999	10000	10000	10000
21	9904	9946	9971	9985	9992	9996	9998	9999	10000	10000
22	9825	9898	9942	9968	9983	9991	9996	9998	9999	10000
23	9698	9816	9891	9938	9966	9982	9991	9995	9998	9999
24	9504	9685	9806	9885	9934	9963	9980	9990	9995	9997
25	9224	9487	9672	9797	9879	9930	9961	9979	9989	9994
26	8841	9204	9471	9660	9789	9873	9926	9958	9977	9988
27	8346	8820	9185	9456	9649	9780	9867	9922	9956	9976
28	7736	8325	8800	9168	9442	9638	9773	9862	9919	9954
29	7021	7717	8305	8781	9152	9429	9628	9765	9857	9916
30	6224	7007	7699	8287	8764	9137	9417	9618	9759	9852
31	5376	6216	6994	7684	8270	8748	9123	9405	9610	9752
32	4516	5376	6209	6982	7669	8254	8733	9110	9395	9602
33	3683	4523	5375	6203	6971	7656	8240	8720	9098	9385
34	2912	3696	4530	5375	6197	6961	7643	8227	8708	9087
35	2229	2929	3708	4536	5376	6192	6953	7632	8216	8697
36	1650	2249	2946	3720	4542	5376	6188	6945	7623	8205
37	1181	1671	2268	2961	3731	4547	5377	6184	6938	7614
38	0816	1200	1690	2285	2976	3741	4553	5377	6181	6932
39	0545	0833	1218	1708	2301	2989	3750	4558	5378	6178
40	0351	0558	0849	1235	1724	2316	3001	3759	4562	5379
41	0218	0361	0571	0863	1250	1739	2330	3012	3767	4567
42	0131	0226	0371	0583	0877	1265	1753	2343	3023	3775
43	0075	0136	0233	0380	0594	0889	1278	1766	2355	3033
44	0042	0079	0141	0240	0389	0605	0901	1290	1778	2365
45	0023	0044	0082	0146	0246	0397	0614	0911	1301	1789
46	0012	0024	0046	0085	0150	0252	0405	0623	0921	1311
47	0006	0012	0025	0048	0088	0154	0257	0411	0631	0930
48	0003	0006	0013	0026	0050	0091	0158	0262	0417	0638
49	0001	0003	0007	0014	0027	0052	0094	0162	0267	0423
50	0001	0001	0003	0007	0015	0029	0054	0096	0165	0271
51		0001	0002	0003	0007	0015	0030	0055	0098	0168
52			0001	0002	0004	0008	0016	0030	0056	0100
53				0001	0002	0004	0008	0016	0031	0058
54					0001	0002	0004	0008	0017	0032
55						0001	0002	0004	0009	0017
56							0001	0002	0004	0009
57								0001	0002	0004
58									0001	0002
59										0001

TABLE I (concluded)

P \ R	41	42	43	44	45	46	47	48	49	50
1	10000	10000	10000	10000	10000	10000	10000	10000	10000	10000
2	10000	10000	10000	10000	10000	10000	10000	10000	10000	10000
3	10000	10000	10000	10000	10000	10000	10000	10000	10000	10000
4	10000	10000	10000	10000	10000	10000	10000	10000	10000	10000
5	10000	10000	10000	10000	10000	10000	10000	10000	10000	10000
6	10000	10000	10000	10000	10000	10000	10000	10000	10000	10000
7	10000	10000	10000	10000	10000	10000	10000	10000	10000	10000
8	10000	10000	10000	10000	10000	10000	10000	10000	10000	10000
9	10000	10000	10000	10000	10000	10000	10000	10000	10000	10000
10	10000	10000	10000	10000	10000	10000	10000	10000	10000	10000
11	10000	10000	10000	10000	10000	10000	10000	10000	10000	10000
12	10000	10000	10000	10000	10000	10000	10000	10000	10000	10000
13	10000	10000	10000	10000	10000	10000	10000	10000	10000	10000
14	10000	10000	10000	10000	10000	10000	10000	10000	10000	10000
15	10000	10000	10000	10000	10000	10000	10000	10000	10000	10000
16	10000	10000	10000	10000	10000	10000	10000	10000	10000	10000
17	10000	10000	10000	10000	10000	10000	10000	10000	10000	10000
18	10000	10000	10000	10000	10000	10000	10000	10000	10000	10000
19	10000	10000	10000	10000	10000	10000	10000	10000	10000	10000
20	10000	10000	10000	10000	10000	10000	10000	10000	10000	10000
21	10000	10000	10000	10000	10000	10000	10000	10000	10000	10000
22	10000	10000	10000	10000	10000	10000	10000	10000	10000	10000
23	10000	10000	10000	10000	10000	10000	10000	10000	10000	10000
24	9999	9999	10000	10000	10000	10000	10000	10000	10000	10000
25	9997	9999	9999	10000	10000	10000	10000	10000	10000	10000
26	9994	9997	9999	9999	10000	10000	10000	10000	10000	10000
27	9987	9994	9997	9998	9999	10000	10000	10000	10000	10000
28	9975	9987	9993	9997	9998	9999	10000	10000	10000	10000
29	9952	9974	9986	9993	9996	9998	9999	9999	10000	10000
30	9913	9950	9972	9985	9992	9996	9998	9999	9999	10000
31	9848	9910	9948	9971	9985	9992	9996	9998	9999	10000
32	9746	9844	9907	9947	9970	9984	9992	9996	9998	9999
33	9594	9741	9840	9905	9945	9969	9984	9991	9996	9998
34	9376	9587	9736	9837	9902	9944	9969	9983	9991	9996
35	9078	9368	9581	9732	9834	9900	9942	9968	9983	9991
36	8687	9069	9361	9576	9728	9831	9899	9941	9967	9982
37	8196	8678	9061	9355	9571	9724	9829	9897	9941	9967
38	7606	8188	8670	9054	9349	9567	9721	9827	9896	9940
39	6927	7599	8181	8663	9049	9345	9563	9719	9825	9895
40	6176	6922	7594	8174	8657	9044	9341	9561	9717	9824
41	5380	6174	6919	7589	8169	8653	9040	9338	9558	9716
42	4571	5382	6173	6916	7585	8165	8649	9037	9335	9557
43	3782	4576	5383	6173	6913	7582	8162	8646	9035	9334
44	3041	3788	4580	5385	6172	6913	7580	8160	8645	9033
45	2375	3049	3794	4583	5387	6173	6911	7579	8159	8644
46	1799	2384	3057	3799	4587	5389	6173	6911	7579	8159
47	1320	1807	2391	3063	3804	4590	5391	6174	6912	7579
48	0938	1328	1815	2398	3069	3809	4593	5393	6176	6914
49	0644	0944	1335	1822	2404	3074	3813	4596	5395	6178
50	0428	0650	0950	1341	1827	2409	3078	3816	4599	5398
51	0275	0432	0655	0955	1346	1832	2413	3082	3819	4602
52	0170	0278	0436	0659	0960	1350	1836	2417	3084	3822
53	0102	0172	0280	0439	0662	0963	1353	1838	2419	3086
54	0059	0103	0174	0282	0441	0664	0965	1355	1840	2421
55	0033	0059	0104	0175	0284	0443	0666	0967	1356	1841
56	0017	0033	0060	0105	0176	0285	0444	0667	0967	1356
57	0009	0018	0034	0061	0106	0177	0286	0444	0667	0967
58	0004	0009	0018	0034	0061	0106	0177	0286	0444	0666
59	0002	0005	0009	0018	0034	0061	0106	0177	0285	0443
60	0001	0002	0005	0009	0018	0034	0061	0106	0177	0284
61		0001	0002	0005	0009	0018	0034	0061	0106	0176
62			0001	0002	0005	0009	0018	0034	0061	0105
63				0001	0002	0005	0009	0018	0034	0060
64					0001	0002	0005	0009	0018	0033
65						0001	0002	0005	0009	0018
66							0001	0002	0004	0009
67								0001	0002	0004
68									0001	0002
69										0001

TABLE II
$L_{N^*}(u)$, the Unit Normal Loss Integral

D	.00	.01	.02	.03	.04	.05	.06	.07	.08	.09
.0	.3989	.3940	.3890	.3841	.3793	.3744	.3697	.3649	.3602	.3556
.1	.3509	.3464	.3418	.3373	.3328	.3284	.3240	.3197	.3154	.3111
.2	.3069	.3027	.2986	.2944	.2904	.2863	.2824	.2784	.2745	.2706
.3	.2668	.2630	.2592	.2555	.2518	.2481	.2445	.2409	.2374	.2339
.4	.2304	.2270	.2236	.2203	.2169	.2137	.2104	.2072	.2040	.2009
.5	.1978	.1947	.1917	.1887	.1857	.1828	.1799	.1771	.1742	.1714
.6	.1687	.1659	.1633	.1606	.1580	.1554	.1528	.1503	.1478	.1453
.7	.1429	.1405	.1381	.1358	.1334	.1312	.1289	.1267	.1245	.1223
.8	.1202	.1181	.1160	.1140	.1120	.1100	.1080	.1061	.1042	.1023
.9	.1004	.09860	.09680	.09503	.09328	.09156	.08986	.08819	.08654	.08491
1.0	.08332	.08174	.08019	.07866	.07716	.07568	.07422	.07279	.07138	.06999
1.1	.06862	.06727	.06595	.06465	.06336	.06210	.06086	.05964	.05844	.05726
1.2	.05610	.05496	.05384	.05274	.05165	.05059	.04954	.04851	.04750	.04650
1.3	.04553	.04457	.04363	.04270	.04179	.04090	.04002	.03916	.03831	.03748
1.4	.03667	.03587	.03508	.03431	.03356	.03281	.03208	.03137	.03067	.02998
1.5	.02931	.02865	.02800	.02736	.02674	.02612	.02552	.02494	.02436	.02380
1.6	.02324	.02270	.02217	.02165	.02114	.02064	.02015	.01967	.01920	.01874
1.7	.01829	.01785	.01742	.01699	.01658	.01617	.01578	.01539	.01501	.01464
1.8	.01428	.01392	.01357	.01323	.01290	.01257	.01226	.01195	.01164	.01134
1.9	.01105	.01077	.01049	.01022	$.0^2 9957$	$.0^2 9698$	$.0^2 9445$	$.0^2 9198$	$.0^2 8957$	$.0^2 8721$
2.0	$.0^2 8491$	$.0^2 8266$	$.0^2 8046$	$.0^2 7832$	$.0^2 7623$	$.0^2 7418$	$.0^2 7219$	$.0^2 7024$	$.0^2 6835$	$.0^2 6649$
2.1	$.0^2 6468$	$.0^2 6292$	$.0^2 6120$	$.0^2 5952$	$.0^2 5788$	$.0^2 5628$	$.0^2 5472$	$.0^2 5320$	$.0^2 5172$	$.0^2 5028$
2.2	$.0^2 4887$	$.0^2 4750$	$.0^2 4616$	$.0^2 4486$	$.0^2 4358$	$.0^2 4235$	$.0^2 4114$	$.0^2 3996$	$.0^2 3882$	$.0^2 3770$
2.3	$.0^2 3662$	$.0^2 3556$	$.0^2 3453$	$.0^2 3352$	$.0^2 3255$	$.0^2 3159$	$.0^2 3067$	$.0^2 2977$	$.0^2 2889$	$.0^2 2804$
2.4	$.0^2 2720$	$.0^2 2640$	$.0^2 2561$	$.0^2 2484$	$.0^2 2410$	$.0^2 2337$	$.0^2 2267$	$.0^2 2199$	$.0^2 2132$	$.0^2 2067$

2.5	$.0^2 2004$	$.0^2 1943$	$.0^2 1883$	$.0^2 1826$	$.0^2 1769$	$.0^2 1715$	$.0^2 1662$	$.0^2 1610$	$.0^2 1560$	$.0^2 1511$
2.6	$.0^2 1464$	$.0^2 1418$	$.0^2 1373$	$.0^2 1330$	$.0^2 1288$	$.0^2 1247$	$.0^2 1207$	$.0^2 1169$	$.0^2 1132$	$.0^2 1095$
2.7	$.0^2 1060$	$.0^2 1026$	$.0^3 9928$	$.0^3 9607$	$.0^3 9295$	$.0^3 8992$	$.0^3 8699$	$.0^3 8414$	$.0^3 8138$	$.0^3 7870$
2.8	$.0^3 7611$	$.0^3 7359$	$.0^3 7115$	$.0^3 6879$	$.0^3 6650$	$.0^3 6428$	$.0^3 6213$	$.0^3 6004$	$.0^3 5802$	$.0^3 5606$
2.9	$.0^3 5417$	$.0^3 5233$	$.0^3 5055$	$.0^3 4883$	$.0^3 4716$	$.0^3 4555$	$.0^3 4398$	$.0^3 4247$	$.0^3 4101$	$.0^3 3959$
3.0	$.0^3 3822$	$.0^3 3689$	$.0^3 3560$	$.0^3 3436$	$.0^3 3316$	$.0^3 3199$	$.0^3 3087$	$.0^3 2978$	$.0^3 2873$	$.0^3 2771$
3.1	$.0^3 2673$	$.0^3 2577$	$.0^3 2485$	$.0^3 2396$	$.0^3 2311$	$.0^3 2227$	$.0^3 2147$	$.0^3 2070$	$.0^3 1995$	$.0^3 1922$
3.2	$.0^3 1852$	$.0^3 1785$	$.0^3 1720$	$.0^3 1657$	$.0^3 1596$	$.0^3 1537$	$.0^3 1480$	$.0^3 1426$	$.0^3 1373$	$.0^3 1322$
3.3	$.0^3 1273$	$.0^3 1225$	$.0^3 1179$	$.0^3 1135$	$.0^3 1093$	$.0^3 1051$	$.0^3 1012$	$.0^4 9734$	$.0^4 9365$	$.0^4 9009$
3.4	$.0^4 8666$	$.0^4 8335$	$.0^4 8016$	$.0^4 7709$	$.0^4 7413$	$.0^4 7127$	$.0^4 6852$	$.0^4 6587$	$.0^4 6331$	$.0^4 6085$
3.5	$.0^4 5848$	$.0^4 5620$	$.0^4 5400$	$.0^4 5188$	$.0^4 4984$	$.0^4 4788$	$.0^4 4599$	$.0^4 4417$	$.0^4 4242$	$.0^4 4073$
3.6	$.0^4 3911$	$.0^4 3755$	$.0^4 3605$	$.0^4 3460$	$.0^4 3321$	$.0^4 3188$	$.0^4 3059$	$.0^4 2935$	$.0^4 2816$	$.0^4 2702$
3.7	$.0^4 2592$	$.0^4 2486$	$.0^4 2385$	$.0^4 2287$	$.0^4 2193$	$.0^4 2103$	$.0^4 2016$	$.0^4 1933$	$.0^4 1853$	$.0^4 1776$
3.8	$.0^4 1702$	$.0^4 1632$	$.0^4 1563$	$.0^4 1498$	$.0^4 1435$	$.0^4 1375$	$.0^4 1317$	$.0^4 1262$	$.0^4 1208$	$.0^4 1157$
3.9	$.0^4 1108$	$.0^4 1061$	$.0^4 1016$	$.0^5 9723$	$.0^5 9307$	$.0^5 8908$	$.0^5 8525$	$.0^5 8158$	$.0^5 7806$	$.0^5 7469$
4.0	$.0^5 7145$	$.0^5 6835$	$.0^5 6538$	$.0^5 6253$	$.0^5 5980$	$.0^5 5718$	$.0^5 5468$	$.0^5 5227$	$.0^5 4997$	$.0^5 4777$
4.1	$.0^5 4566$	$.0^5 4364$	$.0^5 4170$	$.0^5 3985$	$.0^5 3807$	$.0^5 3637$	$.0^5 3475$	$.0^5 3319$	$.0^5 3170$	$.0^5 3027$
4.2	$.0^5 2891$	$.0^5 2760$	$.0^5 2635$	$.0^5 2516$	$.0^5 2402$	$.0^5 2292$	$.0^5 2188$	$.0^5 2088$	$.0^5 1992$	$.0^5 1901$
4.3	$.0^5 1814$	$.0^5 1730$	$.0^5 1650$	$.0^5 1574$	$.0^5 1501$	$.0^5 1431$	$.0^5 1365$	$.0^5 1301$	$.0^5 1241$	$.0^5 1183$
4.4	$.0^5 1127$	$.0^5 1074$	$.0^5 1024$	$.0^6 9756$	$.0^6 9296$	$.0^6 8857$	$.0^6 8437$	$.0^6 8037$	$.0^6 7655$	$.0^6 7290$
4.5	$.0^6 6942$	$.0^6 6610$	$.0^6 6294$	$.0^6 5992$	$.0^6 5704$	$.0^6 5429$	$.0^6 5167$	$.0^6 4917$	$.0^6 4679$	$.0^6 4452$
4.6	$.0^6 4236$	$.0^6 4029$	$.0^6 3833$	$.0^6 3645$	$.0^6 3467$	$.0^6 3297$	$.0^6 3135$	$.0^6 2981$	$.0^6 2834$	$.0^6 2694$
4.7	$.0^6 2560$	$.0^6 2433$	$.0^6 2313$	$.0^6 2197$	$.0^6 2088$	$.0^6 1984$	$.0^6 1884$	$.0^6 1790$	$.0^6 1700$	$.0^6 1615$
4.8	$.0^6 1533$	$.0^6 1456$	$.0^6 1382$	$.0^6 1312$	$.0^6 1246$	$.0^6 1182$	$.0^6 1122$	$.0^6 1065$	$.0^6 1011$	$.0^7 9588$
4.9	$.0^7 9096$	$.0^7 8629$	$.0^7 8185$	$.0^7 7763$	$.0^7 7362$	$.0^7 6982$	$.0^7 6620$	$.0^7 6276$	$.0^7 5950$	$.0^7 5640$

Note: $L_{N_*}(-u) = u + L_{N_*}(u)$

Source: Reprinted with the permission of the President and fellows of Harvard College, Cambridge, Massachusetts.

TABLE III
The Normal Probability Density Function

$P(u)$

u	.00	.01	.02	.03	.04	.05	.06	.07	.08	.09
.0	.3989	.3989	.3989	.3988	.3986	.3984	.3982	.3980	.3977	.3973
.1	.3970	.3965	.3961	.3956	.3951	.3945	.3939	.3932	.3925	.3918
.2	.3910	.3902	.3894	.3885	.3876	.3867	.3857	.3847	.3836	.3825
.3	.3814	.3802	.3790	.3778	.3765	.3752	.3739	.3725	.3712	.3697
.4	.3683	.3668	.3653	.3637	.3621	.3605	.3589	.3572	.3555	.3538
.5	.3521	.3503	.3485	.3467	.3448	.3429	.3410	.3391	.3372	.3352
.6	.3332	.3312	.3292	.3271	.3251	.3230	.3209	.3187	.3166	.3144
.7	.3123	.3101	.3079	.3056	.3034	.3011	.2989	.2966	.2943	.2920
.8	.2897	.2874	.2850	.2827	.2803	.2780	.2756	.2732	.2709	.2685
.9	.2661	.2637	.2613	.2589	.2565	.2541	.2516	.2492	.2468	.2444
1.0	.2420	.2396	.2371	.2347	.2323	.2299	.2275	.2251	.2227	.2203
1.1	.2179	.2155	.2131	.2107	.2083	.2059	.2036	.2012	.1989	.1965
1.2	.1942	.1919	.1895	.1872	.1849	.1826	.1804	.1781	.1758	.1736
1.3	.1714	.1691	.1669	.1647	.1626	.1604	.1582	.1561	.1539	.1518
1.4	.1497	.1476	.1456	.1435	.1415	.1394	.1374	.1354	.1334	.1315
1.5	.1295	.1276	.1257	.1238	.1219	.1200	.1182	.1163	.1145	.1127
1.6	.1109	.1092	.1074	.1057	.1040	.1023	.1006	.09893	.09728	.09566
1.7	.09405	.09246	.09089	.08933	.08780	.08628	.08478	.08329	.08183	.08038
1.8	.07895	.07754	.07614	.07477	.07341	.07206	.07074	.06943	.06814	.06687
1.9	.06562	.06438	.06316	.06195	.06077	.05959	.05844	.05730	.05618	.05508
2.0	.05399	.05292	.05186	.05082	.04980	.04879	.04780	.04682	.04586	.04491
2.1	.04398	.04307	.04217	.04128	.04041	.03955	.03871	.03788	.03706	.03626
2.2	.03547	.03470	.03394	.03319	.03246	.03174	.03103	.03034	.02965	.02898
2.3	.02833	.02768	.02705	.02643	.02582	.02522	.02463	.02406	.02349	.02294
2.4	.02239	.02186	.02134	.02083	.02033	.01984	.01936	.01888	.01842	.01797

x									
2.5	.01753	.01709	.01667	.01625	.01585	.01545	.01506	.01468	.01431	.01394
2.6	.01358	.01323	.01289	.01256	.01223	.01191	.01160	.01130	.01100	.01071
2.7	.01042	.01014	$.0^{2}9871$	$.0^{2}9606$	$.0^{2}9347$	$.0^{2}9094$	$.0^{2}8846$	$.0^{2}8605$	$.0^{2}8370$	$.0^{2}8140$
2.8	$.0^{2}7915$	$.0^{2}7697$	$.0^{2}7483$	$.0^{2}7274$	$.0^{2}7071$	$.0^{2}6873$	$.0^{2}6679$	$.0^{2}6491$	$.0^{2}6307$	$.0^{2}6127$
2.9	$.0^{2}5953$	$.0^{2}5782$	$.0^{2}5616$	$.0^{2}5454$	$.0^{2}5296$	$.0^{2}5143$	$.0^{2}4993$	$.0^{2}4847$	$.0^{2}4705$	$.0^{2}4567$
3.0	$.0^{2}4432$	$.0^{2}4301$	$.0^{2}4173$	$.0^{2}4049$	$.0^{2}3928$	$.0^{2}3810$	$.0^{2}3695$	$.0^{2}3584$	$.0^{2}3475$	$.0^{2}3370$
3.1	$.0^{2}3267$	$.0^{2}3167$	$.0^{2}3070$	$.0^{2}2975$	$.0^{2}2884$	$.0^{2}2794$	$.0^{2}2707$	$.0^{2}2623$	$.0^{2}2541$	$.0^{2}2461$
3.2	$.0^{2}2384$	$.0^{2}2309$	$.0^{2}2236$	$.0^{2}2165$	$.0^{2}2096$	$.0^{2}2029$	$.0^{2}1964$	$.0^{2}1901$	$.0^{2}1840$	$.0^{2}1780$
3.3	$.0^{2}1723$	$.0^{2}1667$	$.0^{2}1612$	$.0^{2}1560$	$.0^{2}1508$	$.0^{2}1459$	$.0^{2}1411$	$.0^{2}1364$	$.0^{2}1319$	$.0^{2}1275$
3.4	$.0^{2}1232$	$.0^{2}1191$	$.0^{2}1151$	$.0^{2}1112$	$.0^{2}1075$	$.0^{2}1038$	$.0^{2}1003$	$.0^{3}9689$	$.0^{3}9358$	$.0^{3}9037$
3.5	$.0^{3}8727$	$.0^{3}8426$	$.0^{3}8135$	$.0^{3}7853$	$.0^{3}7581$	$.0^{3}7317$	$.0^{3}7061$	$.0^{3}6814$	$.0^{3}6575$	$.0^{3}6343$
3.6	$.0^{3}6119$	$.0^{3}5902$	$.0^{3}5693$	$.0^{3}5490$	$.0^{3}5294$	$.0^{3}5105$	$.0^{3}4921$	$.0^{3}4744$	$.0^{3}4573$	$.0^{3}4408$
3.7	$.0^{3}4248$	$.0^{3}4093$	$.0^{3}3944$	$.0^{3}3800$	$.0^{3}3661$	$.0^{3}3526$	$.0^{3}3396$	$.0^{3}3271$	$.0^{3}3149$	$.0^{3}3032$
3.8	$.0^{3}2919$	$.0^{3}2810$	$.0^{3}2705$	$.0^{3}2604$	$.0^{3}2506$	$.0^{3}2411$	$.0^{3}2320$	$.0^{3}2232$	$.0^{3}2147$	$.0^{3}2065$
3.9	$.0^{3}1987$	$.0^{3}1910$	$.0^{3}1837$	$.0^{3}1766$	$.0^{3}1698$	$.0^{3}1633$	$.0^{3}1569$	$.0^{3}1508$	$.0^{3}1449$	$.0^{3}1393$
4.0	$.0^{3}1338$	$.0^{3}1286$	$.0^{3}1235$	$.0^{3}1186$	$.0^{3}1140$	$.0^{3}1094$	$.0^{3}1051$	$.0^{3}1009$	$.0^{4}9687$	$.0^{4}9299$
4.1	$.0^{4}8926$	$.0^{4}8567$	$.0^{4}8222$	$.0^{4}7890$	$.0^{4}7570$	$.0^{4}7263$	$.0^{4}6967$	$.0^{4}6683$	$.0^{4}6410$	$.0^{4}6147$
4.2	$.0^{4}5894$	$.0^{4}5652$	$.0^{4}5418$	$.0^{4}5194$	$.0^{4}4979$	$.0^{4}4772$	$.0^{4}4573$	$.0^{4}4382$	$.0^{4}4199$	$.0^{4}4023$
4.3	$.0^{4}3854$	$.0^{4}3691$	$.0^{4}3535$	$.0^{4}3386$	$.0^{4}3242$	$.0^{4}3104$	$.0^{4}2972$	$.0^{4}2845$	$.0^{4}2723$	$.0^{4}2606$
4.4	$.0^{4}2494$	$.0^{4}2387$	$.0^{4}2284$	$.0^{4}2185$	$.0^{4}2090$	$.0^{4}1999$	$.0^{4}1912$	$.0^{4}1829$	$.0^{4}1749$	$.0^{4}1672$
4.5	$.0^{4}1598$	$.0^{4}1528$	$.0^{4}1461$	$.0^{4}1396$	$.0^{4}1334$	$.0^{4}1275$	$.0^{4}1218$	$.0^{4}1164$	$.0^{4}1112$	$.0^{4}1062$
4.6	$.0^{4}1014$	$.0^{5}9684$	$.0^{5}9248$	$.0^{5}8830$	$.0^{5}8430$	$.0^{5}8047$	$.0^{5}7681$	$.0^{5}7331$	$.0^{5}6996$	$.0^{5}6676$
4.7	$.0^{5}6370$	$.0^{5}6077$	$.0^{5}5797$	$.0^{5}5530$	$.0^{5}5274$	$.0^{5}5030$	$.0^{5}4796$	$.0^{5}4573$	$.0^{5}4360$	$.0^{5}4156$
4.8	$.0^{5}3961$	$.0^{5}3775$	$.0^{5}3598$	$.0^{5}3428$	$.0^{5}3267$	$.0^{5}3112$	$.0^{5}2965$	$.0^{5}2824$	$.0^{5}2690$	$.0^{5}2561$
4.9	$.0^{5}2439$	$.0^{5}2322$	$.0^{5}2211$	$.0^{5}2105$	$.0^{5}2003$	$.0^{5}1907$	$.0^{5}1814$	$.0^{5}1727$	$.0^{5}1643$	$.0^{5}1563$

Note: Because of symmetry, $f(-x) = f(x)$.

Thus, $f(-2.83) = f(2.83) = 0.007274$.

Source: Reprinted, with permission, from Anders Hald, *Statistical Tables and Formulas*, John Wiley & Sons, Inc., 1952.

Index

This book has been set in 10 point and 9 point Times Roman, leaded 2 points. Chapter numbers are in 14 point Helvetica and 48 point Baskerville; chapter titles are in 18 point Helvetica. The size of the type page is 26 × 45½ picas.